Eastern Africa Series

TANZANIAN
DEVELOPMENT

Eastern Africa Series

Tanzanian Development

A Comparative Perspective

EDITED BY DAVID POTTS

JC JAMES CURREY

James Currey
is an imprint of Boydell & Brewer Ltd
www.jamescurrey.com

and of

Boydell & Brewer Inc.
668 Mt Hope Avenue, Rochester, NY 14620-2731 (US)
www.boydellandbrewer.com

The publisher has no responsibility for the continued existence or accuracy of URLs
for external or third-party internet websites referred to in this book, and does not
guarantee that any content on such websites is, or will remain, accurate or appropriate

British Library Cataloguing in Publication Data

A catalogue record for this book is available from the British Library

ISBN 978-1-84701-197-8 (James Currey cloth)

This publication is printed on acid-free paper

Typeset in 10 on 12pt Cordale with Gill Sans MT display
by Avocet Typeset, Somerton, Somerset TA11 6RT

Contents

Illustrations

Tables

Figures

Map

Contributors

Nicola Banks is a Lecturer in Global Urbanism and Urban Development at the Global Development Institute, University of Manchester. Her research explores experiences of urban poverty among different groups of urban residents and how layers of disadvantage along social, political and economic lines can impose significant constraints on these groups. This research, funded by the ESRC, explores youth, poverty and inequality among urban youth in Tanzania.

Dan Brockington is the Director of Sheffield Institute of International Development. He was previously Professor of Conservation and Development at the University of Manchester. Dan's research has focused on Tanzania, where he has worked on livelihood change, natural resource governance, microfinance and institutional performance; he has also worked in South Africa, Australia, New Zealand and India. His broader interests include work on global overviews of the social impacts of protected areas, media and conservation, and continental-wide examinations of the work of conservation NGOs in sub-Saharan Africa.

Andrew Coulson was employed in the planning unit of the Ministry of Agriculture in Dar es Salaam from 1967 to 1971, where he worked on capital projects, and took part in the policy reviews that were part of the Second Five-Year Development Plan, 1969–1974. From 1972 to 1976 he taught development economics and agricultural economics at the University of Dar es Salaam and subsequently at the University of Bradford where he wrote *Tanzania: A Political Economy* (1982). A second edition with a new introduction was published in 2013. He has published papers in the *Journal of Peasant Studies* and the *Review of African Political Economy* and in a Festschrift for Kjell Havnevik on small-scale and large-scale agriculture in Tanzania. He is Chair of the Britain Tanzania Society. His most recent book, written with Antony Ellman and Emmmanuel Mbiha, is *Increasing Production from the Land: A Sourcebook on Agriculture for Teachers and Students in East Africa*, Mkuki na Nyota publishers, Dar es Salaam, 2018. Andrew has retired from the University of Birmingham, where he worked from 1984, but continues his link with its International Development Department.

Olivia Howland is a post-doctoral researcher at the University of Sheffield specializing in East Africa. She is currently working on the project 'Long-term Livelihood Change in Tanzania'. Olivia has a background in mixed-methods ethnography, working with marginalized peoples, and uses art as a means of communicating research.

Bahati Ilembo is a Lecturer in Statistics at Mzumbe University in Tanzania. He did his PhD in agricultural economics in 2015 and since then has been attached to a long-term project on the potential and limitations of contract farming in small farming business in the tobacco and sunflower sector.

Hossein Jalilian is Reader in Development Economics at the University of Bradford and specializes in applied quantitative methods. He has extensive experience in South East Asia, particularly Cambodia. He has also visited Tanzania in furtherance of a collaborative programme between the University of Bradford and Mzumbe University.

Julia Jeyacheya is a Senior Lecturer in International Tourism Management at Manchester Metropolitan University. Her research interests include the political economy of tourism development in South East Asia and Southern Africa. Her research has been supported by the World Bank, Commonwealth Secretariat, Department for International Development (DfID) and the Foreign and Commonwealth Office (FCO).

Faustin Kamuzora is a Professor of Economic Development with years of experience in academic and policy implementation. His research interests include sustainable local economic development and development informatics. His career started as a district agricultural development officer for four years before moving to academic work at Mzumbe University for more than twenty years. He served as Deputy Vice Chancellor for eight years and now is back in the central government as a Permanent Secretary responsible for union matters and environment management in the United Republic of Tanzania.

Joseph Kuzilwa is Professor of Economics (International Monetary Economics) at Mzumbe University, Tanzania. He has authored and co-authored a number of books and articles, most recently Kuzilwa, Fold, Henningsen and Nylandsted (eds), *Contract Farming and the Development of Smallholder Agricultural Businesses: Improving Markets and Value Chains in Tanzania* (2017). He is a founding fellow of the Tanzania Academy of Sciences, where he currently serves as honorary Vice President. He also served as Deputy Vice Chancellor, Academic

(2002–7) and subsequently as Vice Chancellor (2007–14) of Mzumbe University.

Peter Lawrence is Emeritus Professor of Development Economics at Keele University. He has researched and published on various aspects of African development. He undertook his doctoral research on Tanzania's sisal plantation industry as a research associate at the University of Dar es Salaam's Economic Research Bureau in the period following the Arusha Declaration, and subsequently lectured in the University's Department of Economics. He is a founding editor of the *Review of African Political Economy* and a current member of its editorial board.

Michael Lofchie is Professor of Political Science at the University of California, Los Angeles. He served as the director of UCLA's James S. Coleman African Studies Center from 1978 to 1989. His research focuses on the politics of economic reform in Africa. He is the author of many books, including *The Political Economy of Tanzania: Decline and Recovery* (2014) and *The Policy Factor: Agricultural Performance in Kenya and Tanzania* (2013).

Vesa-Mati Loiske is a Senior Lecturer at the School of Natural Science, Technology and Environmental Studies, Södertörn University, Stockholm. He has a PhD in Human Geography and has mainly worked on socio-economic aspects of rural development in Tanzania. His main focus has been on reasons for land degradation and on agricultural intensification.

Anna Mdee is Associate Professor of International Development at the University of Leeds, and a Research Associate of The Overseas Development Institute in London. Previously she was a senior lecturer in Bradford Centre for International Development. She is a development anthropologist with over 20 years of experience of rural livelihoods and local governance in Tanzania.

Moses Mnzava is at the Department of Sociology and Anthropology of the University of Dar es Salaam where he teaches social policy and policy analysis, sociological theory, social work and the law, social security systems and social research methods. His primary research interest is in studying social and economic issues of contemporary Tanzanian and African societies. His doctoral research investigated initiatives to integrate the traditional pastoral economy into the market-led economy in Tanzania. Recently he has been co-investigator in a three-year research project supported by the DfID-ESRC Growth Research Programme (DEGRP) to examine long-term livelihood change in Tanzania.

Daniel Mpeta is a Lecturer in the Institute of Rural Development Planning, Dodoma. He holds a PhD from Mzumbe University. His research has specialized in agricultural markets and prices, and sugarcane crops.

Honest Prosper Ngowi is Professor of Economics at Mzumbe University, Dar es Salaam Campus College. He has published and lectured widely on various aspects of economics and business, including foreign direct investment, privatization, public-private partnerships and natural resources management.

Christine Noe is a Senior Lecturer in the Department of Geography at the University of Dar es Salaam. She is a human geographer with research interests in conservation and development politics and their influence on rural livelihoods, land tenure and security dynamics. Her research in Tanzania has recently focused on trans-frontier conservation areas, conservation partnerships and emerging trends in land tenure, ownership dynamics and livelihoods.

David Potts is a Senior Lecturer at the University of Bradford and former Head of Bradford Centre for International Development. He specializes in project analysis and is author of *Project Planning and Analysis for Development* (2002). He worked in Tanzania for six years (1981–7) as an FAO economist and joint head of the Project Preparation Unit of the Project Preparation and Monitoring Bureau in the Ministry of Agriculture and Livestock Development. He has visited Tanzania frequently as a consultant and in relation to various collaborative programmes between the University of Bradford and Mzumbe University. He has also undertaken assignments in a number of other countries, including Ethiopia. His publications on Tanzania include three chapters on aspects of estate agriculture and economic policy and a working paper on *Policy Reform and the Economic Development of Tanzania* (2008). He is a member of the Britain Tanzania Society.

Michael Tribe is a development economist who started his academic career in 1967 lecturing in the Economics Department of Makerere University College when it was part of the University of East Africa. His career continued in the Universities of Glasgow, Strathclyde and Bradford in the UK after he left Makerere in 1971, while he spent two years in the mid-1980s at the University of Cape Coast in Ghana. He has published widely on development economics and development planning.

Brian Van Arkadie has worked, on and off, in East Africa since arriving as a visiting scholar, on leave from Yale, at Makerere University College in Uganda in 1963. He edited Tanzania's Second Five-Year Plan (1969–1974), and has published extensively on Tanzania. From 1987 to 1991 he was visiting professor at the University of Dar es Salaam. He is co-editor (with R.H. Green and D.G. Rwegasira) of *Economic Shocks and National Policy Making: Tanzania in the 1970s* (1980) and (with Samuel Wangwe) of *Overcoming Constraints on Tanzanian Growth: Policy Challenges Facing the Third Phase Government* (2000).

John Weiss is Emeritus Professor of Development Economics at the University of Bradford and an independent economic consultant. He specializes in project analysis and industrialization and industrial policy. He is the author of *Practical Appraisal of Industrial Projects* (1980), co-author (with Steve Curry) of *Project Analysis in Developing Countries* (2000), author of *the Economics of Industrial Development* (2011) and joint editor (with Michael Tribe) of the *Routledge Handbook on Industry and Development* (2016). He has worked on industrial policy in Mozambique and Ethiopia (for the World Bank), in Mexico (for the Government) and in Mongolia (for UNIDO).

Kifle Wondemu is currently an independent consultant working mainly for the African Development Bank. His recent work includes studies on the African cocoa and coffee sectors. He was a Senior Economist for the Government of Ethiopia before completing his PhD at the University of Bradford and working as a lecturer teaching economics and quantitative methods.

Acknowledgements

This book owes its existence to many individuals and institutions.

My interest in Tanzania goes back to my undergraduate dissertation, which was supervised by Brian van Arkadie, the author of Chapter 4. Initially the subject of my dissertation was going to be an analysis of Chilean five-year plans but, during the summer vacation, the Allende regime was overthrown and Brian suggested that I look at Tanzania. Some years later, in the 1980s, I spent six years working as an FAO economist in the Project Preparation and Monitoring Bureau (PPMB) of the Tanzanian Ministry of Agriculture and Livestock Development. Although this period was a very difficult time for Tanzanians, I was fortunate to work with a very good team and I have good memories of their friendship and cooperation, particularly from my former counterparts Johnson Mawalla and Asibwene Mwaipopo. Without them and my other Tanzanian colleagues I could not have had such an interesting and stimulating time. Particular thanks also to Mama Michael, the office cleaner, who consistently refused to speak any English to me and insisted that I try to learn to speak Kiswahili, and the project drivers, who taught me a great deal about the need for patience and how to get a four-wheel drive vehicle out of mud and sand. *Asanteni sana*!

The first Tanzanian I ever met was a staff member from Mzumbe University, the late Epaphrah Mushi, who was studying at the University of East Anglia when I was doing my MA. Later, when I joined Bradford University, a number of Mzumbe staff members came to attend short training courses. They included Joe Kuzilwa, who eventually became Vice Chancellor. Later on I met up with Faustin Kamuzora when he came to Bradford to study for his PhD. My connections with Mzumbe University are part of the reason why I have been delighted to include contributions to this book from a number of Mzumbe University staff members. A number of other chapters also involve collaboration between Tanzanian academics and academics from other European universities, so I am happy to acknowledge the contributions from staff of the University of Dar es Salaam and the

Institute of Rural Development Planning, Dodoma as well as a number of universities in Europe and the United States.

Having spent six years in Tanzania as well as many subsequent shorter visits, mainly on training missions, I have always wanted to make a more substantial contribution to the literature than the few papers I have written over the years. The nucleus of this book is derived from a fortunate combination of mutually reinforcing conference papers plus some additional invited contributions to provide a balance between economic sectors and wider development issues. I was fortunate that all the people I contacted were willing to contribute, and I thank them for their contributions and their patience.

Finally, I would like to thank my wife Sally, for her patience during the process of writing and assembling the material for the book, the anonymous reviewers for their feedback on earlier drafts of the book and the encouragement and constructive advice provided by Jaqueline Mitchell throughout the whole period of development and production of the book. I would also like to thank Nick Bingham and Lynn Taylor for their valuable contributions to the final stages of production and Marie-Pierre Evans for her excellent work in preparation of the index.

David Potts

I

Introduction – Tanzanian Development: A Comparative Perspective

David Potts

Tanzania today is in a much stronger position economically than at any time in the past, yet, as with many African countries, it is evident that this economic improvement is not evenly spread. Many people still struggle to achieve an acceptable standard of living and the rate of population increase remains relatively high, diluting the impact of economic growth on the improvement of living standards. This book examines the development of Tanzania from a range of perspectives and disciplines as well as different issues and sectors. Comparisons are also made with other relevant countries in a number of chapters.

Tanzania has maintained some form of parliamentary democracy continuously since independence, with competitive elections under a single party until 1994 and with a multi-party system subsequently. However, the advent of multi-party democracy has not, so far, resulted in any change of government, and claims of irregularities in the 2015 elections were made by Chadema, the main opposition party. The increasing significance of revenue derived from mineral wealth has also highlighted issues related to corruption. The authoritarian response taken by the government under President Magufuli, ostensibly to tackle corruption issues, has implications for wider issues of democracy and human rights and has been criticized, both by opposition parties and by Amnesty International.

Although largely stable internally, Tanzania has been affected at various times by conflict and instability in some neighbouring states. This has induced immigration from the countries affected by conflicts, including Rwanda, Burundi, the Democratic Republic of the Congo and Mozambique, as well as migration from Malawi mainly for economic reasons. Adverse economic consequences have also been experienced from the Uganda war (1978–9) and political disagreements with Kenya leading to the break-up of the East African Community from 1977 to 2000.

A number of important books have been published on Tanzania over the years. In the 1970s Lionel Cliffe and John Saul published their two volumes on *Socialism in Tanzania* (Cliffe and Saul 1972 and 1973). Their twin volumes covering both politics and the economy were important sources for students of Tanzania in the 1970s, generally sympathetic to the aims of Tanzanian socialism (*ujamaa*). They included an essay by Issa Shivji, and his essays over the years have provided a strong critique of the neo-liberal orthodoxy that has dominated economic policy in Tanzania and elsewhere in the last thirty years (Shivji 2006). Prominent among the issues that critics from the radical left have to contend with is the disappointing economic performance of Tanzania in the latter half of the 1970s compared to the rapid economic growth experienced since the mid-1990s.

Aminzade (2013) provides an historical analysis of the social and political development of Tanzania including the intended 'politics of inclusion' and the 'creation of a pan-ethnic and multiracial identity' (p. 162). He describes the origins of the process of 'bribing corrupt state-socialist bureaucrats' (p. 219) and refers to the importance of maintenance of national unity in changing circumstances. While national unity can be regarded as a major success, the issue of corruption is clearly an ongoing problem.

Two of the contributors to this volume (Andrew Coulson and Michael Lofchie) have written important books on Tanzania (Coulson 2013[1]; Lofchie 2014). Their very different perspectives are represented in Chapters 2 and 3 of this book.

More recently Adam, Collier and Ndulu (eds) (2017) have compiled a substantial volume that focuses on the economic policy challenges for the future of Tanzania. Their perspective is essentially economic and it encompasses a range of important aspects of the Tanzanian economy, including management of natural resources, urbanization, trade, infrastructure and economic policy.

Given the range of general resources available on Tanzania, what justifies this volume? Firstly, it is multidisciplinary. In common with the Cliffe and Saul collection it includes both political science approaches and economics, and it reflects the importance of past history as a guide to future potential.

Secondly, it is not monolithic. It reflects a wide range of different opinions and perspectives. It can be argued that political scientists and economists inhabit parallel universes and do not communicate with each other. In this volume it is assumed that, while there is no absolute truth, a deliberate attempt to include research from different disciplines and perspectives can be a valuable source on a range of issues that are important for Tanzania.

This book seeks to provide a wide-ranging review of the experience of Tanzania. It encompasses different views of the Tanzanian experience as well as comparisons with other developing countries both in Africa and elsewhere. While the book is primarily about Tanzania, it

---

[1] Andrew Coulson's book is an update of a previous book published in 1982.

places present-day Tanzania in an international context. The authors contributing to the book come from a variety of institutions in Tanzania and elsewhere, many of whom have had extensive experience working in Tanzania. They include authors with experience of Tanzania over many years as well as recent researchers with ideas about aspects that have been neglected in the past, such as the position of urban youth and the interpretation of information derived from rural household survey data.

The Development of Tanzania

Tanganyika achieved independence in 1961. It was initially colonized by Germany and subsequently, after the First World War, it was administered by the UK government under a mandate from the League of Nations and subsequently as a United Nations Trust Territory. Tanganyika became the United Republic of Tanzania following union with Zanzibar in 1964. Within the East African region Tanzania is a large country in terms of both area (945,203 km^2) and population, estimated at 55.6 million in 2016 (WDI 2017).

The first President of Tanzania, *Mwalimu*[2] Julius Nyerere, was prominent in the non-aligned movement, and his brand of non-aligned, non-Marxist socialism was influential in the search for an alternative approach to Western capitalism and Soviet-style socialism. Tanzania maintained a principled stand against racism both through active support of liberation movements such as the South African ANC and FRELIMO in Mozambique, and in criticizing the racist policies followed by the Ugandan regime of Idi Amin and, to a lesser extent, Kenya in relation to their Asian minorities. Tanzania has been consistent in its opposition to tribalism of all forms and in its support for religious tolerance. Tanzania has also had a long-standing commitment to universal primary education despite being one of the poorest countries in the world.

However, Tanzania has also experienced problems. The economic policies of Nyerere's *ujamaa*[3] failed to take account of the capacity constraints in managing a socialist economy and the willingness of Western donors to continue to support policies that paid insufficient attention to the role of markets and the private sector in the post-Cold War era. The structural adjustment policies that were forced on the country in the 1980s and 1990s meant the end of many of Nyerere's

---

[2] *Mwalimu* is the kiswahili word for 'teacher', often used to refer to Tanzania's first President, Julius Nyerere.
[3] *Ujamaa* is a kiswahili word that can be translated as 'extended family' or 'brotherhood', and on this basis it was used by President Nyerere to refer to a form of socialism based on African extended family traditions.

policies, but the alternative was often as bad or worse. There was no growth in real incomes in the ten years following structural adjustment (Figure 1.1).

Economic performance in the early years of independence was relatively good, but a combination of nationalism with a socialist orientation and impatience with a perceived lack of investment from the private sector, predominantly owned by foreigners and ethnic minorities, was reflected in an address to the Tanzanian National Assembly on 8 June 1965 in which President Nyerere stated:

> The amount of private investment which has taken place over the past year is, quite frankly a disappointment to us. We have special tax concessions to encourage new investment; we have investment guarantees for bringing capital into the country; and we have many other arrangements designed to encourage private investment of a character which will serve our nation. Yet the level of private investment does not appear to be as great as that provided for in the Plan. (Nyerere 1968: 35)

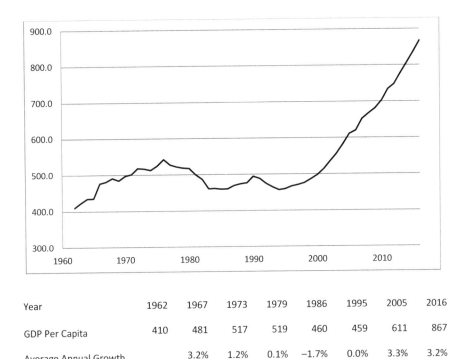

Year		1962	1967	1973	1979	1986	1995	2005	2016
GDP Per Capita		410	481	517	519	460	459	611	867
Average Annual Growth			3.2%	1.2%	0.1%	−1.7%	0.0%	3.3%	3.2%

Sources: 1988–2016: World Development Indicators (2017); 1962–1987: Own estimates derived from World Bank sources

Figure 1.1 GDP Per Capita Tanzania, 1962–2017 ($US constant 2010 prices)

This perception of a private sector that was reluctant to invest contributed to the Arusha Declaration of 1967 and subsequent nationalization of the 'commanding heights' of the economy. Although similar measures were undertaken in a number of other African economies, such as Ghana, Zambia and Uganda, Tanzania took the process further and with a more conscious attempt to construct the policy of *ujamaa*, derived, at least in part, from indigenous traditions of cooperation.

Following the Arusha Declaration economic growth continued at a slightly reduced rate, although still above population growth, but further impatience with the speed of reform led to a second round of nationalizations in 1973 accompanied by a drive for 'villagization'. This was a process by which the largely scattered rural communities were initially encouraged and eventually forced to come together in village settlements, ostensibly to allow the provision of schools and health centres, but also to try to encourage at least some level of cooperative agriculture through village farms.[4] The process was less disruptive in areas that were already relatively densely populated but much more problematic in areas with scattered populations where people were moved considerable distances from the areas where they either cultivated or had planted tree crops, and there was significant disruption to agricultural production and livelihoods. Economic growth slowed down in the period 1973–9, partly as a consequence of oil price rises and some drought-affected years, but also as a result of the increasing incapacity of the state to manage all the activities it had taken over. The growing crisis was hidden to some extent by the relatively benign aid environment experienced during the Cold War, when the non-aligned countries could potentially influence the balance of power between East and West.

In 1979 Tanzania was hit by the second oil crisis and a war with Uganda. These events precipitated a prolonged economic crisis, which also coincided with less sympathetic donor attitudes to the policies of countries, like Tanzania, that tried to follow a socialist path to development. The crisis culminated in an agreement with the International Monetary Fund (IMF) in 1986, involving substantial and ongoing currency devaluation as well as a significant change of policy in relation to the role of the state. While the immediate crisis was in some sense resolved, the Tanzanian economy continued to perform relatively poorly for another nine years, with no real overall growth in per capita income. However, since 1995, overall economic performance has been consistently good, with average economic growth exceeding 6 per cent per annum in real terms since 2000 (Figure 1.1). On the face of it liberalization in Tanzania has eventually been highly successful, but success has been unevenly distributed.

---

[4] See Von Freyhold (1979), Coulson (1982, Ch. 22), Hyden (1980, Ch. 4 and 5) and Ponte (2002, Ch. 3) for more detailed descriptions of the villagization process as well as Chapters 2 and 3 in this book.

Tanzania is not alone in the improvement in its economic performance. A number of other African countries have achieved remarkable economic growth in the last twenty years. Tanzania's growth performance is broadly in line with that of Ghana, Zambia and Uganda but not as rapid as that of Mozambique, Ethiopia and Rwanda, all of which have lower per capita incomes than Tanzania (Figure 1.2). Ethiopia, Zambia, Ghana and Uganda are referred to in Chapters 9, 11 and 12, and the industrial performance of Tanzania in relation to Africa in general is discussed in Chapter 8. The case of another 'socialist reformer', Vietnam, is referred to in Chapters 2, 4 and 9. The experiences of China and Malaysia are also referred to in Chapters 2 and 9.

Economic growth cannot really be seen as development if it does not improve the position of the poorest. Evidence on the extent to which growth has been pro-poor is patchy, partly because the household expenditure surveys on which poverty data are based are intermittent. Evidence for Tanzania suggests that the growth in the last twenty-five years has been accompanied by some increase in the level of inequality, although not by as much as in some other countries. Overall the incomes of the poorest 20 per cent have increased at roughly the same rate as those of the top 20 per cent but the bottom 40 per cent have done

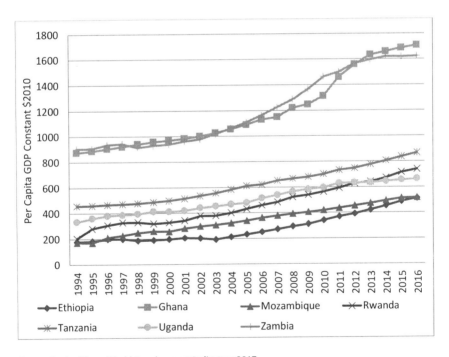

Source: Derived from World Development Indicators 2017

Figure I.2 Economic Growth in Selected African Economies

Table 1.1 Income Growth of Different Groups and Changes in the Kuznets Ratio

Country	Period	GDP	Top 10%	Top 20%	Bottom 40%	Bottom 10%	Kuznets Ratio Start	Kuznets Ratio End
Ethiopia	1995–2010	4.3%	2.0%	2.8%	5.7%	5.7%	3.18	2.02
Ghana	1988–2006	1.9%	2.5%	2.4%	1.2%	−0.4%	2.34	3.21
Mozambique	1996–2008	5.4%	5.5%	5.5%	5.2%	4.4%	3.31	3.50
Rwanda	2000–2010	5.2%	6.1%	5.8%	4.6%	5.6%	3.91	4.33
Tanzania	1991–2011	2.1%	2.8%	2.4%	2.0%	2.8%	2.26	2.48
Uganda	1992–2012	3.8%	3.9%	3.9%	3.6%	3.7%	2.90	3.06
Zambia	1993–2010	2.2%	3.1%	2.7%	3.6%	4.2%	5.62	5.78

Source: Own estimates derived from World Development Indicators 2016

worse. The Kuznets ratio is often used as an indicator of inequality. The experience for the poor in Tanzania has been better than that for most of the other countries with similar growth patterns but not as favourable as for Ethiopia, which has experienced a smaller decline in the relative importance of agriculture than any of the other countries referred to in Figure 1.2. Table 1.1 shows available data for the share of income accruing to different income groups and the Kuznets ratio[5] for the countries appearing in Figure 1.2.

Agriculture remains the most important sector in terms of overall contribution to GDP and employment, although its relative importance is declining. The welfare of the rural majority is therefore still of fundamental importance, and the livelihoods of the vast majority of these people depend mainly on agriculture. The majority of the population are still rural, and the rural population has increased by 273 per cent since independence (WDI 2017). On current trends it will still take another twenty years or so before the majority of Tanzanians live in urban areas.

Origin and Structure of the Book

The idea for this book can be traced to a pre-conference discussion where five of the contributors to the book, with very different views, discussed the state of Tanzania and the paths it took to get there. What transpired was that people with different perspectives can throw light on the possible reasons for the outcomes even if they don't always agree on the causes or on what should have been done that wasn't. The

[5] The Kuznets ratio measures the ratio of the income share of the top 20 per cent to that of the bottom 40 per cent of the population so the higher the value of this ratio the greater the level of inequality.

contributors to the discussion included Andrew Coulson (Chapters 2 and 6), Mike Lofchie (Chapter 3), Brian Van Arkadie (Chapter 4) and the then Vice Chancellor and Deputy Vice Chancellor of Mzumbe University, Joseph Kuzilwa (Chapter 6) and Faustin Kamuzora (Chapter 13).

In Chapter 2 Andrew Coulson reviews the use of the term 'political economy' over time and relates the changes to the debates that took place in Tanzania from the neo-Marxist approaches of the 1970s to the very different political economy that has influenced current policy since the reforms started in the 1980s. In line with the Marxist tradition he analyzes the class interests involved and discusses the implications of recent policy initiatives and more general issues for the development of capitalism in Tanzania, including the issue of corruption that dominated the 2015 election. He points out that Tanzania has no alternative to working with international companies and organizations and must embrace technical change. However, it is also important to pay proper attention to the improvement of public health, maintenance of infrastructure and reduction of corruption, as well as an open society that pays attention to the issue of inequality.

In Chapter 3 Mike Lofchie analyzes the decline of the Tanzanian economy in the 1970s, tracing it to the 'bureaucratic controls over agricultural production' introduced in the 1960s and the willingness of aid donors to continue supporting an 'ailing system' for a long time after its shortcomings were evident. Subsequent changes in donor attitudes, particularly of the Nordic countries, were critical in pressurizing Tanzania into reform. The limitations of the informal sector as a source of supplementary earnings for the elite may have been an important factor in acceptance of the reforms. The subsequent rapid growth of the economy has not been shared evenly and most Tanzanians remain 'desperately poor'. The efforts of the current Magufuli administration to curb corruption are welcomed but come at the expense of 'heavy-handed repression' of opposition groups and the media.

Although the proportion of Tanzania's population living in the rural areas is decreasing, agriculture is still a major source of income for the majority of the population. Chapters 4, 5, 6 and 7 discuss different aspects of the agricultural sector.

In Chapter 4, Brian van Arkadie provides a wide-ranging review of the state of Tanzanian agriculture and its future potential, suggesting that 'slow results over the longer term' are preferable to ill-thought-out attempts at transformation. The chapter includes a comprehensive set of information on the production, since independence, of a wide range of important crops in Tanzania.[6] Brian was involved in the coordination of the second Tanzanian five-year plan (1969–74) and subsequently in proposals for the revival of export crop production in the 1980s. He

[6] Brian was assisted in the collection of data by Kevin Rugaimukamu and Innocencia John.

also draws on his experience of agricultural development in Vietnam to make comparisons in terms of impact on overall growth, exports and poverty reduction.

Chapter 5, by Dan Brockington, Olivia Howland, Vesa-Mati Loiske, Moses Mnzava and Christine Noe, analyzes the methodological challenges of longitudinal surveys and their potential use in understanding the dynamics of rural poverty and differentiation and changes in livelihoods over time. Their study suggests that farmers in the pilot study area have experienced improvements in both prices and productivity. As a result there has been a substantial move out of poverty for a large proportion of households. While this cannot necessarily prove that such changes have taken place more widely, the authors do raise the question as to how estimates of subsistence production are made and whether the apparently slow pace of poverty reduction in the rural areas recorded in available statistics is consistent with findings at the micro level. The study also throws light on movements both into and out of poverty, potentially helping us to understand the factors that cause some farmers to prosper and others to lose their assets.

An important issue for small-scale farmers is the marketing of their crops. For many years crop marketing in Tanzania was dominated by cooperative unions and nationalized marketing parastatals. The situation has changed dramatically now with considerable variation in farmer organizations and increasing importance of large international commercial buyers. In Chapter 6 Joseph Kuzilwa, Bahati Ilembo, Daniel Mpeta and Andrew Coulson report on research work on the marketing of smallholder tobacco and sunflower. Although production of both crops has increased substantially, there are inherent problems in complex grading systems, supply of inputs and the balance of power between the large numbers of small farmers and the small number of buyers.

Agriculture depends on water, and intensification of agriculture often involves increased use of irrigation. Chapter 7 by Anna Mdee compares and contrasts two irrigation schemes in Morogoro Region, one informal farmer-led scheme and a larger donor-supported scheme on a former state farm. While both schemes have led to significant increases in output there are issues relating to the sustainability of both schemes. In one case the main issue is that of water rights while, in the other, the extent of donor support raises questions about financial sustainability.

Chapters 8 and 9 discuss different aspects of industrialization in Tanzania with reference to the experiences of other developing countries. The industrial sector has an important role in providing employment for the increasing proportion of Tanzanians living in the urban areas. In Chapter 8 Peter Lawrence discusses the experience of Tanzanian industrial policy in the context of the wider African experience of industrialization. He notes that Tanzania, in common with other African countries, has not had a clear overall industrial strategy other than simple import substitution, although recent cooperation with

China in the development of iron and steel production may represent a shift in strategy.

In Chapter 9 John Weiss and Hossein Jalilian discuss evidence on the competitiveness of Tanzanian manufacturing, making comparisons with Ethiopia, Zambia, Vietnam and China. They argue that African industrialization has been held back by relatively low productivity in relation to wage costs and that this applies to the specific case of Tanzania. However, firm-level evidence suggests that Tanzania is competitive in some relatively labour-intensive and resource-based industries including shirts, leather goods and wheat milling, and they suggest that such activities can provide the basis for further diversification.

In Chapter 10, Nicola Banks investigates the situation of urban youth in Arusha. Tanzania's urban population is growing very fast but many of the young people coming out of education have limited employment opportunities, leading to high rates of urban unemployment. Work opportunities for young people are 'limited in number, low-paid and insecure' despite increasing urbanization and improvements in education. Not surprisingly, this situation results in adverse effects on happiness and self-esteem. There is a need for both better preparation for employment and greater institutional support for young people entering the labour market.

Tanzania has been a major recipient of aid from a wide range of sources, but the effectiveness of aid in delivering development outcomes has been questioned both generally and in the specific case of Tanzania. In Chapter 11 Michael Tribe analyzes the Tanzanian aid experience and makes comparisons with the cases of Uganda and Ghana. Aid funding has been important for non-recurrent expenditure in all three countries and accounted for about 70 per cent of Tanzanian government expenditure in 2012, much of it in the form of budget support. However, concerns about corruption and the use of aid funds has led the DfID, the UK aid agency, to suspend its aid in the form of budget support to Tanzania.

The exchange rate issue was very sensitive in Tanzania in the first half of the 1980s. Following agreement with the World Bank and the IMF, Tanzania has devalued the Shilling on a regular basis since 1985, partly to take account of the difference between domestic and international inflation rates, and partly in a deliberate attempt to increase competitiveness. Similar but less drastic measures took place in Ethiopia at more or less the same time. In Chapter 12 David Potts and Kifle Wondemu compare the experiences of the two countries since the mid-1980s. Both countries have experienced rapid economic growth as well as export growth, but Tanzania has a more diversified export base that may be due in part to deliberate currency undervaluation.

Tourism is an increasingly important source of foreign exchange for Tanzania in general and Zanzibar in particular. In Chapter 13 Faustin

Kamuzora and Julia Jeyacheya review the contribution of the tourism industry to Tanzanian development. Among the important issues they raise is the need to strengthen the economic linkages to the communities in the areas that receive tourists and reduce the leakages of revenue from imported goods and services. There is also a need for greater Tanzanian ownership of tourist enterprises and more diversity in tourist destinations as well as better training of the tourism workforce.

Chapter 14 by Prosper Ngowi and David Potts investigates the specific case of the gold service levy paid to Geita District Council and the benefits derived for the local community, but it also reviews some of the issues surrounding the wider returns to Tanzania from its mineral wealth. This is a controversial issue since the two bills passed by parliament in 2017 allow the Government to cancel and renegotiate existing contracts for both mining and energy companies if the terms are deemed unfavourable. There is no doubt that Geita District gains revenue from mining, but whether the compensation for the depletion of resources and environmental damage is adequate and how much of the revenue should be retained locally rather than by central government are both contentious issues.

The issues of inequality and the apparent relative stagnation of rural incomes are important. To what extent can the mineral wealth of the country be used to address the infrastructure and marketing constraints faced by a population that is still predominantly rural? Can the democratic process be used to restrain the Tanzanian elite and ensure a fairer distribution of the benefits of development? Recent concerns about the legitimacy of Tanzanian election results raise questions about the extent to which the political elite are willing to accept government change by the ballot box. Such questions cannot be answered by this book, but it is hoped that it will enhance knowledge, stimulate debate and provide a valuable resource to inform that debate.

2

The Political Economy of Tanzania 1967–2017: Reimagining the State

Andrew Coulson

This chapter uses the concept of political economy to structure a brief economic history of Tanzania before reviewing Tanzania's current plans and strategies. A short final section examines some of the challenges that face the present leadership.

Political Economy

The classical economists, notably Adam Smith, David Ricardo and Thomas Malthus, wrote about how wealth was created, and how profit was distributed between classes – landlords, owners of finance, and workers. This they called *political economy*.

Karl Marx, in *Das Kapital Volume 1*, turned this into a determinist theory of development. Societies would proceed, from a state of primitive existence, to feudalism, which would give way to capitalism, which would then pave the way for a socialist revolution in which the working class would take over the state. A capitalist economy would grow when manufacturing entrepreneurs, part of the urban elite or bourgeoisie, invest and create new capacity to create goods. Crises of capitalism would occur when the demand or purchasing power for these goods was not sufficient to buy what could be produced. In his later years, however, Marx recognized that the stages were not predetermined, that some feudal, and some 'Asiatic', societies would be stable and might innovate and develop, and hence that each society should be studied on its own terms. A path to socialism was far from inevitable (Shanin 1983; Ramirez 2011; Coulson 2014).

However, Marxists in the mainstream tradition stayed with the earlier Marx. Lenin, in *The Development of Capitalism in Russia* (1899) and *Imperialism: The Highest Stage of Capitalism* (1917), took determinist theory as given. In the 1950s this approach was applied to third world development in what became known as *dependency theory* (e.g. Baran 1957; Prebisch 1963; Amin 1977). Colonies were exploited by the capitalist classes of their ruling countries for their raw materials: minerals and agricultural products; and after independence, this exploitation continued through the activities of large multinational companies. The only way to respond to this imperialism (and the neo-colonial imperialism that succeeded it) was for socialist political parties to take over the state, create surpluses, and invest them in factories. Neo-Keynesian economists also argued that these countries had to industrialize, and that, in the short term, the only means to accumulate the surpluses for this was to increase their exports of primary raw materials (Nurkse 1953; Lewis 1955; Rostow 1960).

Hindess and Hirst (1975), among others, attempted to specify ideal types for 'pre-capitalist modes of production' and the transition from feudalism to capitalism. There was a reaction against this by scholars who pointed out that classes do not inevitably act in their class interests and that this kind of sociology takes the history and agency out of political economy. Leaders have choices, and how they make them influences what happens in their countries (Hussain & Tribe 1981: 148–9). Coulson (1982, 2013) used political economy in this way to provide a framework for a historical approach to events as they unfolded in Tanzania.

In 1981 Robert Bates published a study of marketing boards in Africa, showing how they operated to transfer resources from the agricultural sector to the state. This led to research on institutions in African countries and reinforced the emphasis of the Washington consensus in favour of market-based policies in the 1990s. The language of political economy began to be used by economists and political scientists who recognized that political power and resulting policies and strategies impact on economic growth and they reacted against the narrow empiricism that characterized much of economics and development economics. This is how Wikipedia summarises this approach:

> Today, political economy, where it is not used as a synonym for economics, may refer to very different things, including Marxian analysis, applied public-choice approaches emanating from the Chicago school and the Virginia school, or simply the advice given by economists to the government or public on general economic policy or on specific proposals. A rapidly growing mainstream literature from the 1970s has expanded beyond the model of economic policy in which planners maximize utility of a representative individual toward examining how political forces affect the choice of economic policies, especially as to distributional conflicts and political institutions.
> (Wikipedia, 'political economy' [accessed 17 May 2014], at http://en.wikipedia.org/wiki/Political_economy)

However, when used in this way, the language of political economy often ignores the manner in which surpluses (or surplus value in Marxist language) are transferred from one economy to another. This may happen through direct exploitation – transfer of profits out of the country or through marketing arrangements that under-reward (or exploit) primary producers, such as the marketing boards studied by

Bates. It can also occur through transfer pricing in which a company pays high prices for what it imports but receives low prices for what it produces. If the international dimension is ignored, the scope of political economy reduces to a discussion of individual economies, a form of nationalism. It also avoids discussion of how classes within an economic system hold power, the discretion they have, and how one class may exploit another. These ideas underlie the argument in this chapter.

The Political Economy of the Tanzanian State

In 1970, Issa Shivji published his essay 'Tanzania: The Silent Class Struggle', as a special issue of the student magazine *Cheche*.[1] His 1976 book, *Class Struggles in Tanzania*, developed these arguments. Independence meant that the class enemy – the ruling classes and owners of large companies in the West – now colluded with a 'bureaucratic bourgeoisie' inside Tanzania. Power had passed to a small educated elite after independence, who were recruited into political leadership, the civil service or other parts of public administration. It was this group that signed contracts and had some discretion in what transpired, even if, overwhelmingly, the underlying power was held outside the country.

In 1961, when Tanzania gained independence, it remained dependent on foreign experts. The number of graduates was tiny, and there were only a handful of Tanzanian graduate engineers. Most of the factories or workshops, and all but the smallest trading activities, were in the hands of an Asian minority. Investments in infrastructure had been neglected by the British. As late as in the 1950s all-weather roads had not been constructed between the towns already connected by railways. Thus the only roads from Dar es Salaam to Mwanza that were reliable in the rainy seasons were either via Mbeya and Tabora, or via Nairobi. Kenya was a more attractive location for private investors. There was African leadership and initiative in the cooperative movement, but this was young and weak – cooperatives in the cotton-growing areas around Mwanza had been permitted for less than ten years before Independence.

The political economy, and the strategies, before and after Independence in 1961 (1964 for Zanzibar), were therefore not materially different from those that could be found elsewhere in Africa. However, agricultural production and exports grew, based largely on small-scale agriculture and cooperative marketing ('the improvement approach'). The First Five Year

[1] This was reproduced by Zenit Publishers, Lund, Sweden, with commentaries by Tamza Szentes, Walter Rodney and John Saul, 1970. The four papers were then reprinted in Lionel Cliffe and John Saul (eds), *Socialism in Tanzania Volume 2* (East African Publishing House 1973), pp 303–358. For the background and flavour of the period, see Hirji (ed.) (2010).

Plan, for 1964–9, also promoted the 'transformation approach' (large-scale agriculture and irrigation), and especially 'settlement schemes' similar to those in Kenya, though most were on virgin land rather than former settler farms, where individuals would have their own farms but work together cooperatively. However, by 1966, it was clear that the settlement schemes would not be viable and that the country was most unlikely to catch up with Kenya in its industrialization.

It was in that context that President Julius Nyerere developed his thinking on African Socialism. The 1967 Arusha Declaration had two balancing components – 'leadership conditions', designed to prevent an elite becoming distanced from the rest of the population; and use of state power to take over the large-scale means of production. Nationalization of the banks and major industries was followed by that of other financial institutions, most of the sisal estates, all imports, including consumer goods, and most purchasing of crops, including food crops such as maize. A second 1967 policy statement 'Education for Self-Reliance', proposed a reorientation of education to make it directly relevant to development challenges.[2] A third policy statement, 'Socialism and Rural Development', was a commitment to *'ujamaa'* (socialist) villages. These were to be voluntary cooperatives of farmers but, starting in 1969 and becoming a national policy in 1973, 'villagization', that is, living in villages, was imposed by force. Cooperative farming, such as it was, largely ceased. Nationalization of the major industries was followed by a rapid rise in the number of factories, almost all sponsored by the state. However, these were open to exploitation, for example by companies more interested in the profits from the sales of machinery than in what could be earned from sales of the resulting products. Even when they were profitable, most of these industries required tariffs to be imposed on imports of the products they made, which led to higher prices for customers and pressures on wage rates.

The forced villagizations had an adverse impact on agriculture in the parts of the country where they were implemented.[3] State control

[2] One of the paradoxes was that the commitment to self-reliance made the country attractive to aid donors. Financial assistance to Tanzania rapidly increased, especially from the Nordic countries and the World Bank. Sebastian Edwards titled his book *Toxic Aid* (2014), on the basis that the donors were uncritical of what was happening at this period, and should have reduced their aid or at the very least threatened to do so.

[3] This was not the whole country, because the people living in the coffee-growing highland areas were deemed already to be in villages, and much of the cotton-growing area South of Lake Victoria was already densely settled, as were cities such as Dar es Salaam. Thus Edwards's claim that the numbers of people living in villages was 9 million by 1975 and 13 million – nearly the whole population – by 1977 is an overestimate; people living in the coffee- and most of the cotton-producing areas did not move, nor in the cities (Edwards 2014: 88); Lofchie's figure of 1.6 million by the end of 1974 is nearer the mark (Lofchie 2014: 81).

of the import trade led to shortages of many essential items. By 1979 the IMF had made it clear to Tanzania that there was a structural imbalance in the balance of payments, and recommended retrenchment in the public finances, and devaluation. Nyerere refused. He was supported internally by the academic-turned Minister of Finance, Kighoma Malima, and externally by a number of academics including Ajit Singh of the University of Cambridge and Reg Green, a former adviser to the Treasury.[4] Informally in 1982 and more formally in 1984–5, under the auspices of the IMF, a group of economists, including Gerry Helleiner, Knud Eric Svendsen, Tony Killick and the Tanzanians Benno Ndulu and Ibrahim Lipumba tried to broker a deal. Significant devaluations ensued, but not enough to deal with the rampant inflation and the rising disparity between the official foreign exchange rate and the unofficial rate. In 1985 Nyerere stood down as President and was succeeded by Ali Hassan Mwinyi.

Mwinyi quickly came to terms with the IMF. The Tanzanian shilling was devalued significantly, followed by further depreciation.[5] The marketing of some crops and the import of consumer goods were opened to the private sector. Much of Tanzania's accumulated national debt was written off, and a number of foreign donors again started lending to Tanzania. The cuts in government spending were such that many of the achievements of the Nyerere period, notably near-comprehensive primary education, a health point in almost every village, and large-scale drinking water supplies, were threatened.

As Debbie Bryceson put it at the 2017 REPOA Research Workshop, structural adjustment pushed Tanzania back 25 years. The position of all but the highest paid became very difficult. Wages and salaries did not rise in line with the rapidly rising prices. Families could barely survive on government (or university) salaries. Michael Lofchie, in the next chapter of this book, shows how, to survive those years, a family needed additional sources of income, from small businesses, essentially extending into the informal sector – keeping chickens, owning a *daladala* (small bus), or purchasing foreign exchange at official rates and using it to import goods that could be sold at much higher black market prices. Others moved from the public sector and set up businesses, consultancies or NGOs.

President Benjamin Mkapa was elected in 1995 in the first multi-party general election following a decision, made in 1992, to allow other parties to compete with Chama Cha Mapinduzi (CCM). Under Mkapa many state enterprises were privatized. Factories closed. Salaries rose. But most living in the rural areas, or employed in the informal sectors in the urban areas, were little better off (Atkinson & Lugo 2010). The population grew to 55 million by 2017, with Dar es Salaam exceeding

---

4 This paragraph draws on Edwards (2014: 96ff.).
5 The exchange rate issue in Tanzania is discussed in more detail in Chapter 12.

5 million – Tanzania was becoming an urban economy – but with overall population growing at just less than 3 per cent annually, the numbers in the rural areas also continued to increase. The state was no longer willing to support many of the industries that had been created, and, even after the devaluations, many could not compete. A more measured process might have enabled more of them to adapt and survive.

However, from around 2000 until the present, Tanzania has recorded significant growth in its GDP – at close to 7 per cent annually in real terms (Adam, Collier & Ndulu 2017). The game parks of Northern Tanzania and the beaches of Zanzibar became attractive to long-haul tourists – especially when there was instability in neighbouring Kenya – and tourism became the single biggest source of foreign exchange.

The world price of gold rose to unprecedented levels in the crisis years at the end of the decade, and five large mines opened in an area around Lake Victoria, in a strange synergy with semi-official artisanal mining in which Tanzanians took their lives in their hands by digging in tunnels and mines – thereby showing where there was gold – and large companies followed and dug much deeper (Bryceson & Jønsson 2013); Tanzania became for a time the third largest producer of gold in Africa (after South Africa and Ghana).[6]

Natural gas had been discovered on Songo Songo island near Kilwa some years earlier; now it started to be exploited, and more gas was discovered in the far south of the country. When prospecting took place offshore, huge reserves were found, and it appeared as if Tanzania would become a major supplier of gas on world markets, even though this gas would be expensive to bring ashore. World prices of gas and oil subsequently halved, and there is less optimism now about when or whether this may happen in a world determined to reduce uses of carbon fuels to combat global warming.

Mobile phones spread to all but the smallest centres of population, and settlements on main roads were linked to the internet by fibre optic cables. The road network was improved by new tarmac and bridges (e.g. over the Rufiji South of Dar es Salaam, creating an all-weather land link to the south for the first time, over the Ruvu river near Bagamoyo, and at the far end of Dar es Salaam harbour). There were building booms in urban centres, especially in Dar es Salaam, including hotels, supermarkets, and high-rise offices and apartments. The boom in construction was partly financed by overseas investors attracted by the stability of the country relative to many other African countries, but also by money invested from the Middle East and elsewhere, often with few questions asked about its origins.

There was a revival in manufacturing. Some of the firms that had survived were able to export to nearby countries. Ambitious plans were prepared for duty-free industrial areas, new or revitalized ports, and new

---

[6] Some of the issues related to gold mining are discussed in Chapter 14.

forms of public transport (notably the advanced bus-based rapid transit system for Dar es Salaam, where the construction involved extensive demolition and road widening). Agriculture became a qualified success, increasing, according to the official figures, at a little under 4 per cent per annum, above the rate of population growth, and the country became close to self-sufficient in maize and significantly increased its production of rice. Only a little of this prosperity trickled down to less well-off Tanzanians, and more in some parts of the country (especially where agriculture prospered, as in the Southern Highlands) than in parts where it struggled (e.g. the Kilimanjaro and Kagera regions).

John Magufuli was elected to be Tanzania's fifth president in October 2015. He was the candidate of the ruling party, CCM, chosen after one of the front-runners, Edward Lowassa, who several years earlier had resigned from the cabinet because of his associations with one of the corruption scandals, defected to the main Opposition party, CHADEMA, and became their candidate. Magufuli campaigned as the candidate who would end corruption and, as soon as he was elected, he declared war on waste, inefficiency and corruption, especially in the civil service. Foreign travel by ministers and civil servants was reined in. Extra payments for attendance at conferences were removed. Over 19,000 'ghost workers' were removed from government payrolls. The processes of clearing goods through the ports were speeded up, rates of tax collection increased, teachers with forged certificates lost their jobs, and special courts were created to deal with corruption. Many top managers lost their jobs when their performance was perceived as ineffective. Magufuli also introduced some pro-poor policies, including the abolition of school fees.

All these measures were popular. But there was an authoritarian and at times defensive side. The President could criticize unacceptable behaviour, but he made it harder for the Opposition to do so, or the press. Political rallies by Opposition parties were banned. Laws were introduced requiring only official data to be quoted. There was of course only so much that one person could do. Certain areas of public administration, such as the poor performance of the port, were given repeated attention; others were left largely unchecked. And information continued to flow through social media and blogs. The whole of Africa was watching to see how far this attack on corruption and waste would go.

Strategies, Plans and the Ruling Class

The key economic strategy statement of the 1960s was the 1969–74 Second Five-Year Plan, drafted in 1968 by a team coordinated by Brian Van Arkadie, under the direction of Cleopa Msuya, who was then Principal Secretary at the Ministry of Economic Development and Planning, and later Minister of Finance.[7] Volume 1, an in-depth analysis of policies, based on the detailed studies of about fifty working parties, was based on an assumption that it was possible for the country to grow at 6.5 per cent per annum. The target growth rate for marketed agriculture was 7.3 per cent per annum. Volume 2 set out proposals for specific investments. These included investments in infrastructure, especially improvements in roads, hydroelectricity and water supplies (the agreement by the Chinese to build the TAZARA railway from Dar es Salaam to Zambia came a year later and was not part of the Plan). It referred to a list of 380 industrial projects – mostly import substitution or processing of agricultural products such as cotton – but there was little discussion of how these might be coordinated, or funded. Most were never implemented.

At face value the Plan set out to implement the policies of the Arusha Declaration. But some of the commitments were skin-deep. Thus Brian van Arkadie has described how the word '*ujamaa*' (socialist) was added at almost every place where the word 'village' appeared in the draft. There were strong commitments to rural water supply projects, health and education. In terms of political economy, the Plan reinforced the centralizing role of the state, as the deliverer of projects, and so consolidated the power of the bureaucratic bourgeoisie. The industrial projects were of obvious attraction to potential board members or executives. They were also attractive to the donors and investors who would expect to be their partners.

In 1971 the Tanzanian economist Justinian Rweyemamu was awarded a doctorate for his PhD at Harvard, published two years later as *Underdevelopment and Industrialization in Tanzania; a study of perverse capitalist industrial development* (Rweyemamu 1973). This was an attack on the uncritical adoption of the import substitution strategies of the First and Second Five-Year Plans, proposing instead a 'basic industries strategy' in which industrialization would proceed through the deliberate creation of factories producing intermediate goods – steel, chemicals, cement, plastics and textiles, as well as electricity generation and machines to make machines. In 1974 the Caribbean economist C.Y. Thomas then at the University of Dar es Salaam formalized this. He defined basic industries as those which, in a developed economy, have forward linkages to a wide range of other sectors. A country that possessed these, could, he argued, manufacture almost any consumer good. This was how the Soviet Union had industrialized in the 1930s,

---

[7] The Three-Year Plan for 1961–4 was written by the colonial civil servant Sir Earnest Vasey before Independence. The First Five-Year Plan (1964–9) was heavily influenced by the World Bank and expatriate civil servants and consultants. The 1969–74 Plan was the first that Tanzanians could properly call their own.

and small countries in Africa and the Caribbean should follow a similar strategy (Thomas 1974). Whether and how it would work in a country as backward and open as Tanzania was another matter. In 1978 this thinking was incorporated in a Third Five-Year Plan, but it quickly became clear that the rapid rises in the world price of oil meant that the wherewithal to invest in factories, most of which would not be profitable for several years, was not there. Meanwhile another group of left-inclined academics was looking at the Tiger economies of Asia, especially South Korea and Taiwan, and arguing for an industrialization in which the state did not necessarily own the factories, but steered them to make key investments (Kay 1975; Warren 1980; Foster-Carter 1985; Sender & Smith 1986).

There were no five-year plans in the years of structural adjustment. However, by the start of the new millennium, it was clear to both donors and to the Tanzanian elite that strategic visions were needed. Numerous plans or strategies for sectors were published, most with donor support and influence. The *Tanzania Development Vision 2025*, launched in 1999, aimed to transform the country in 25 years, i.e. by 2025, 'from a low productivity agricultural economy to a semi-industrialized one, led by modernized and highly productive agricultural activities which are effectively integrated and buttressed by supportive industrial and service activities in the rural and urban areas'. Its aim, still frequently quoted in speeches and official documents, was for the country to become 'a middle income economy by 2025'. *MKUKUTA*, the National Strategy for Growth and Reduction of Poverty, prepared in 2005 and revised in 2010, set out policies to combat poverty, demonstrating how Tanzania was responding to the targets of the UN's Millennium Development Goals, thereby making it acceptable for donors to write off much of the country's foreign currency debt. The emphasis was on social policies, especially health, education and domestic water supplies, rather than economic policies, agriculture or manufacturing.

A five-year 'Sustainable Industrial Development Policy' had been published in 1996. Its purpose was to consolidate the position of recently privatized businesses and to reassure private sector investors. A second phase (2001–2005) was mainly a programme to establish export-processing zones. A third was to be about establishing plants to process Tanzania's minerals, especially coal and iron (Mussa 2014).

An *Agriculture Sector Development Strategy* was prepared in 2001. Funding proposals for the period 2006–2013 were agreed in the *Agriculture Sector Development Programme* (ASDP 2013a). This was prepared jointly with the World Bank, USAID, British Aid and other donors, who agreed to contribute funds to a 'basket', which would pay for some revenue costs as well as capital costs.[8]

---

[8] Basket funding meant that the consortium agreed on the projects, and agreed to fund a high proportion of their costs, and to monitor their implementation.

In 2005, when the ASDP was in its final stages of preparation, and in the run-up to the 2005 election at which President Jakaya Kikwete was elected, the Government made commitments to irrigation that led to almost 80 per cent of the money in the ASDP being allocated for irrigation (Therkildsen 2011: 14–21; ASDP 2013; Coulson 2015). Much of this was to rehabilitate irrigation schemes from earlier years, without much examination of the economic and/or social reasons which had caused them to fail. Most of the remaining 20 per cent was to be allocated to policies to support small farmers, especially through extension workers, now paid through District Councils. However, a policy that only money that had reached the Treasury could be allocated, agreed earlier to control deficits in government budgets, meant that much of this did not materialize. This affected all parts of the spending by local governments, including that on agriculture. A further ASDP was prepared in 2013 but not officially launched, again proposing large sums for irrigation (URT 2013).

Meanwhile 2009 saw a commitment to *Kilimo Kwanza* ('Agriculture First'). At that time there were shortages of maize and rice on world markets, and private sector investors from around the world were looking for opportunities to grow these crops and also 'biofuels' that could be converted into fuels to replace petrol or diesel. *Kilimo Kwanza* was the first public policy document since the early years of Independence to favour large-scale private agriculture. It can be seen as a reaction, or correction, to some aspects of the ASDP. It was prepared, not in the ministries responsible for agriculture, but by two organizations that included representatives of large farmers – the Tanzania National Business Council and the Agricultural Council of Tanzania – who asked a group of academics from Sokoine University of Agriculture to write a first draft. It comprised broad-brush policies, set out in ten 'pillars' (URT 2009b). Pillar 5 strengthened the power of the state to allocate land for large scale agriculture. Pillar 2 committed the country to substantially increased spending on agriculture, and especially on irrigation, so meeting the Maputo Declaration target that 10 per cent of the Government budget be spent on agriculture, and among other measures, to create a Tanzania Agricultural Development Bank.

A year later similar thinking influenced SAGCOT, the Southern Agricultural Growth Corridor of Tanzania, launched in Dar es Salaam in 2010 and then at the World Economic Forum in Davos, Switzerland, with the aim of attracting private investment. It covers more than a quarter of Tanzania's land area – from Dar es Salaam and Kilwa on the coast

---

The ASDP basket for agricultural support was funded by the World Bank, African Development Bank, IFAD, the European Union, and Japan. Other donors, including DfID, dropped out during the negotiations. One of the problems in the implementation was that the Government of Tanzania found it hard to meet its obligations, especially the large components of recurrent funding delegated to the district councils.

across to Lakes Tanganyika, Rukwa and Nyasa, including almost the whole catchments of the Rufiji, Wami, Ruvu and Malagarasi rivers – not a 'corridor' in the normal use of the word. The proposals were prepared by two small British companies, AgDevCo and Prorustica, with support from the Norwegian fertilizer producer Yara International and a range of powerful international organizations and donors, who were also involved with proposals for large-scale agricultural investments along the Zambezi River in Mozambique and Zambia. Its website describes it as 'an inclusive, multi-stakeholder partnership to rapidly develop the region's agricultural potential'. But when it came to implementation it turned out that biofuels could not easily be profitable in Tanzania, and it was not easy to find large areas of virgin land that could be allocated to large-scale foreign investors. So SAGCOT did not live up to its initial expectations, and it was not until about five years later that it started to make progress, this time giving more emphasis to small 'outgrower' farmers.

A *Five-Year Development Plan 2011/2012–2015/2016* was published in 2011 (URT 2011).[9] It was written in the Planning Commission, with assistance from two UK government-supported agencies, the International Growth Centre and the Overseas Development Institute. Its subtitle was 'unleashing Tanzania's latent growth potential', and it included chapters on both social policies and directly productive sectors, and costs for a large number of investment projects. The main source of finance would be direct investment from the private sector. The public sector would be confined largely to social projects and infrastructure.

South-to-South Exchanges

By the end of the 2000s, many Tanzanians began to realize that, while an open economy and the ready availability of consumer goods was desirable, completely unfettered markets had not served the country well. This was especially the case with manufacturing, where liberalization had forced many factories to close, including in sectors such as textiles where some local producers should have been able to compete with imported products. It was also the case in agriculture, where the private sector had not coped well with the marketing of products grown by small farmers such as cashewnuts or cotton. They looked to the Tiger economies of South East Asia for models of how to get the best of both worlds.[10]

[9] In reality this was the fourth Five-Year Plan. The choice of title suggests a reluctance to make comparisons with earlier plans.
[10] The point was made at the Annual Research Workshops of the organization REPOA in 2012 by speakers from Vietnam and China, in 2013 by a keynote speaker from Malaysia, and in 2014 by speakers from Japan.

The first comparisons were with Vietnam, which had survived a long and unpleasant war, followed by a period of socialism, and then, in the mid-1980s, structural adjustment. Tanzania and Vietnam had similar GDP per capita in 1986, but thereafter growth in Vietnam had been much faster (Van Arkadie & Mallon 2003; Van Arkadie & Dinh 2004; Dinh et al. 2012; Gray 2012; Dinh 2013; Kilama 2013). Many factories were privatized but the state had kept control of key aspects of the economy. The Vietnamese Professor Do Duc Dinh, who spoke in Dar es Salaam at the 2012 REPOA Research Workshop, compared the paper mills in Tanzania and Vietnam: they were two projects of similar size, both built with support from the Government of Finland. The Tanzanian project was sold to a South African investor for $1; the Vietnamese mill was retained in Government ownership, and became one of their most profitable companies (Dinh 2012; 2013). In contrast, the Tanzanian leadership did not succeed in preserving key factories and sectors. Having failed in their stand against the IMF and devaluation, they now followed its advice rather uncritically.

Links were also maintained with China – which had successfully built the TAZARA railway to Zambia in the 1970s. Now their contracting firms increasingly won building contracts in international competition, and there was talk that they would transfer a large part of their manufacturing technology to Africa, building perhaps 700 factories, many of which would be in Tanzania.

President Kikwete visited Malaysia in 2011, and was impressed with their 'delivery lab' approach to planning, in which stakeholders from both the public and private sectors worked together to create action plans for their sectors. The Malaysians agreed to send key experts from PERMANDU, their Performance Management and Delivery Unit, to explore how such an approach might work in Tanzania (Tan 2013). In October 2012 six 'focus areas' were agreed by the Cabinet: Agriculture, Education, Energy, Transportation, Water and Resource Mobilization (but surprisingly not manufacturing). Between February and April 2013 the six 'labs' worked long hours at the White Sands Hotel outside Dar es Salaam. Their proposals, branded as *Big Results Now*, were then agreed by the Cabinet (BRN 2013a; 2013b; 2013c). The total cost was estimated at over $10bn over three years. However, for the first year, less than half of this was available from the government budget or other sources; it was hoped that the balance would come from the private sector (BRN 2013a). The key targets, to be achieved in just two years, are shown in Figure 2.1.

Such an approach is plausible in sectors such as transportation, where projects can be identified (such as reconditioning the Central Line railway, or improving the capacity of the ports) or energy (a series of power generating projects). It is less clear that it can lead to radically improved pass rates in education. Getting a water supply to 15 million people involves detailed work in very many different

Implementation Status

- National Key Results Areas (NKRA)

Big Results by 2015

Agriculture	<ul><li>25 commercial farming deals for paddy and sugarcane</li><li>78 collective rice irrigation and marketing schemes</li><li>275 collective warehouse-based marketing schemes</li></ul>
Education	<ul><li>Pass rate of 80% for primary and secondary school students</li><li>Improve students' mastering of 3R in Standard I and II by implementing skills assessment and training teachers</li></ul>
Energy	<ul><li>Increase generation capacity from 1.010 to 2.260 MW</li><li>Access to electricity to 5 mil more Tanzanians</li><li>Eliminate EPP reliance</li></ul>
Transportation	<ul><li>Passage of 5 mil tons per year through the Central Corridor</li><li>Increase port throughput by 6 mil tons, rail by 2.8 mil tons</li><li>Reduce road travel time from 3.5 to 2.5 days</li></ul>
Water	<ul><li>Sustaining water supply to 15.2 mil people</li><li>Restoring water supply to 5.3 mil people</li><li>Extending water supply to 7 mil new users</li></ul>
Resource mobilisation	<ul><li>Increase tax revenue by TSh. 3 trillion</li><li>Implementation of PPP projects valued at Tsh. 6 trillion</li></ul>

Figure 2.1 Big Results Now

places and cannot be planned in a few weeks at a workshop in Dar es Salaam.

The plans for agriculture were extremely ambitious (BRN 2013b). Twenty-five commercial farms for rice and sugar cane, in total over 350,000 hectares, were planned, with almost the same area to be farmed by smaller-scale 'outgrowers' supplying their crops to one of the commercial farms, all to be under development in three years. To achieve this there would be fast-track routes for the private sector to gain access to the necessary land, and a dedicated unit to attract outside investors. A 'land task force' would visit the areas affected, to work with the existing small-scale farmers on 'pre-engagement training' and conduct soil surveys, environmental assessments and land use plans (including demarcating the sites and erecting beacons). Rice yields on the 78 collective rice irrigation and marketing schemes were expected to double. The 275 warehouse-based marketing schemes were designed to assist farmers in the Southern Highlands, Rukwa, Mpanda and Songea.

What followed was a harsh reality check on the dangers of planning from the top. Sites were identified for a few large farms, but nowhere near the number or sizes targeted. Warehouse Receipt Schemes did not win the trust of farmers. There were problems with the management of large-scale irrigation projects. The plans to improve the efficiency of the port of Dar es Salaam were more successful (Ndulu & Mwase 2017: 39), and there was some success in rehabilitating rural drinking water supplies. But the plans did not deal quickly with the problems of electricity supply (Policy Forum 2015), or in education. *Big Results Now* was abandoned after President Magufuli's election in 2015.

It epitomized top-down planning. Plans were drawn up by committees of technical experts and investors or potential investors with interests in the specialist areas. Only a fraction of the money needed was identified. Many of the targets were unrealistic – as with those for irrigated agriculture, or improvements in education. Villagers or local residents were involved, if at all, in a cursory manner – as the objects of a process not the subjects. As far as ambitions for large-scale agriculture are concerned, nothing on this scale had been seen since the Groundnuts Scheme of the 1950s – and what was proposed risked repeating many of the mistakes made at that time.

The new Second Five-Year Development Plan 2015/16–2020/21

The five-year plan for the period 2011–2016 was low key. Its successor, from 2015, had a higher profile. It set out to bring together the social strategies of MKUKUTA and the economic strategies of the sectoral plans, through industrialization. Production of the plan was coordinated by Dirk Willem te Velde of the Overseas Development Institute in London, working with researchers there, in the Planning Commission and in the influential research organization and consultancy REPOA in Dar es Salaam (ODI 2016).

A *Human Development Report*, funded by UNDP and published in 2015, had set out to show what was needed to produce 'economic transformation for human development'. It also related investments in human development and poverty alleviation to directly productive investment, though without specifying detailed projects (URT 2015a). One of its working papers (Wuyts & Gray 2017) suggested that many of the problems in the Tanzanian economy lay in the failure of industrialization to produce goods at affordable prices for the mass of the population, especially in the rural areas, and argued for a close integration of economic and social policies to ensure that the mass of the people benefited.

The strategy of the Plan was different. Following the approach of the Center for International Development at Harvard University and its Director Ricardo Hausmann, it cautioned the government to avoid attempts to 'pick winners' and instead to concentrate on creating conditions that would attract private sector investment, without asking too many questions about what they would invest in. In his presentation at the 2017 REPOA Annual Research Workshop, Hausmann's colleague Lant Pritchett showed that one of the main differences between developed and less developed countries was the number of products they exported, and from that he concluded that, to be successful, Tanzania needed to export a wider range of products. The governments should not attempt to identify these in advance. He also argued for a strategy that could be compared to that of a starfish. This does not have a central brain, only tentacles with sensors, and when a tentacle finds food it pulls the others in that direction.

This was noticeably less proactive than the approach proposed at the previous year's REPOA Workshop by the Chinese-American Professor of Economics at the University of Beijing, Justin Lin, previously Chief Economist at the World Bank. His argument was that many countries in Africa now have wage rates lower than those in South East Asia. They should therefore examine their cost structures and identify sectors where they can undercut producers in Asia; then they should provide the infrastructure to attract clusters of investors in those sectors, mainly oriented to exporting globally. Wages would be low but the companies would be profitable, and there could be many of them. The resulting industrialization should be sustainable (Lin 2012; 2016). Whether the ruling classes in countries like Tanzania were ready to commit to such large low-paid labour forces was another matter.

All these plans and strategies have in common that they support the emerging Tanzanian middle class and business class. They also serve the interests of large multinational companies and associated financial institutions, not least the World Bank. They do not present proposals to reduce inequality, and insofar as they propose solutions based on large-scale agriculture rather than small-scale and large modern factories rather than the informal sector, they offer little to the majority of the people.

Corruption

Corruption had been a feature of the Cooperative Unions as early as 1966. From there it spread to the newly created parastatal bodies, and then, in the hard years of the 1980s and 1990s, it emerged at a low level, where police and civil servants introduced charges and penalties for anything that would earn them some money. But it also became overt at high levels, involving senior politicians and administrators. Multi-party democracy meant that political parties needed funds to pay staff and fight elections, and this made them open to corrupt proposals. The Government connived in this. Thanks to Wikileaks, and to court cases inside and outside Tanzania, the details of many corrupt deals are in the public domain (see for example Kelsall 2013: 58–61; Policy Forum 2015: 1–11).

The ability to influence governments affected taxation. The World Bank economist Barak Hoffman, writing in 2013, identified the five wealthiest Tanzanians at that time as Said Salim Bakhresa (of the Bakhresa Group and Azam Industries); Gulam Dewji of the METL Group;

Rostam Aziz of Tanzania International Container Terminal Services (TICTS), Vodafone and other companies; Reginald Mengi of IPP Media and Coca-Cola (the last 'a license to print money'); and Ali Mufuruki of Infotech. Only one of these (TICTS) was one of the top corporate tax payers in Tanzania: 'Airtel, with 28% of the mobile market is the eighth largest taxpayer, while Vodafone, which has 43% of the market, is not on the list at all. ... Aziz owns close to one fifth of Vodacom Tanzania' (Hoffman 2013: 15).[11]

Corruption is not always completely dysfunctional. It may, as Lofchie argues, have beneficial consequences if it enables entrepreneurs to break free of bureaucratic regulation and red tape, and get a problem sorted out quickly. To have a monopoly of a market for an initial period in which to get established without having to face the full blast of international competition from the start is similar to a tax, but paid to an individual instead of to a Government (Khan e.g. 2000; Chang 2008: 160–81; Lofchie 2014: 179–80). But it is also debilitating, and creates an atmosphere of resentment and disillusion. Corrupt practices that lead to successful investments may be a necessary evil. Corrupt practices that enable individuals to move money outside an economy with no economic return in that economy are a disaster.

Class Dynamics in Contemporary Tanzania[12]

The term 'bureaucratic bourgeoisie' still provides the closest specification of the ruling class. It controls the government, the military, parastatal bodies, and the agencies of law and order. It includes leading politicians, many of whom have technocratic backgrounds as economists, engineers or scientists.

Large parts of business are externally owned, including most of the former state-owned companies that were privatized, and new investments in mobile phones, mining, banking, international-standard hotels, supermarket chains, and other parts of the economy. The larger companies all have means and contacts for liaising with the top decision-makers.

The number of powerful Tanzanian business leaders is growing, including those already referred to in areas of near monopoly, such as beer and soft drinks, the milling of imported wheat and its conversion

[11] Aziz and Dewji both come from long-established business families. In 2013 both were reported to be dollar billionaires, the first from Tanzania. Both also became MPs. By the time Aziz was forced to resign in 2011 he had enabled all his constituents to have access to water, electricity and a dispensary (Wikipedia, *Rostam Aziz* and *Gulam Dewji*, quoting *Forbes Magazine*, downloaded 15 May 2017).

[12] For an article that makes a strong case for the use of class analysis in studies of development, see Campling, Miyamura, Pattenden and Selwyn (2016).

into bread and biscuits, mobile phone networks, and media, especially TV. Others run transport companies, hotels, building contractors, large farms, and consultancies. Some of the Asian families who ran smaller businesses before independence are still doing so, most making products for local consumption.

This local business class includes executives who worked for state-owned industries and stayed in business when these were privatized as well as politicians and civil servants who have retired and gone into business, for example in farming. Some control large amounts of assets, however acquired, but the richest Tanzanians are probably, as noted earlier, of Asian extraction, from families that were already involved in business. Some of their businesses are highly diversified, for example the Bakhresa Group sells a wide range of food products, while the METL Group includes textile factories, oil milling, soaps, detergents and large-scale farms, as well as an insurance company.[13]

The bureaucratic bourgeoisie govern in close alliance both with this emerging business class and with donors and their organizations. Many of them depend on large international companies. Their interests are in exploiting Tanzania's raw materials, including agricultural products produced on large farms, and in developing industries, primarily to substitute for imports, especially to meet the demands of the expanding middle classes.

Below this is a class of petty bourgeoisie, owning smaller businesses, but aspiring to grow them into larger ones, in transport, construction, hotels, and many other activities. This in turn overlaps with the owners of the more successful businesses in the informal sector who employ others, in construction, trading, wood or metal-working workshops, hotels and restaurants, and many other activities. Competition ensures that most of these make only small profits, but a few are very successful. To these may be added the majority of teachers, health workers, extension officers and other middle-level civil servants, professionals such as accountants and lawyers, and the middle managers in many parts of the private sector.

The numbers of formal sector jobs created have not kept up with the growth of cities, especially Dar es Salaam. So the great majority are in informal employment. The working class, in regular jobs with employment rights, is still small.

For at least a generation a majority of Tanzanians will live in rural areas and depend mainly on agriculture for survival and their needs for cash. Their numbers are increasing, despite migration to the cities. Any transition from small-scale to large-scale farming will employ less labour, so small-scale agriculture will be needed to grow food and find

---

[13] Its website explains that the '$1.5 billion revenue from our group of companies constitutes a little over 3.5% of the GDP of Tanzania and employs 5% of the formal employment sector. By 2018 we expect to hit revenues of $5 billion.'

incomes for very large numbers of people. In recent years the productivity of small-scale agriculture has increased, as have agricultural surpluses, and this may continue, but only if the bureaucratic bourgeoisie recognize its potential and importance, and the need for small farmers to adopt strategies that minimize their risks. Much of the hard work is done by women, but they are not necessarily involved in the decision-making about cash crops, and are at risk of losing their land and livelihood if anything goes wrong (Da Corta & Magongo 2011). They will not gain much from large-scale farming (Koopman & Faye 2012).

The greatest constraints on increased production from small-scale farmers lie in marketing – if farmers are not paid, or not paid on time, or not paid fairly or, if they have no way of preventing their crops from deteriorating when stored, they will choose crops that can be sold in small quantities on local markets, or look for other means of earning the cash they need. Thus the emphasis on warehouses and storage makes good sense, as well as small-scale irrigation, provided that these are run without corruption and without all the benefits arising for larger farmers. There is potential in the south and south-west to expand the 'green revolution' based on hybrid maize and fertilizer (Rasmussen 1986), and to increase production of other foods such as potatoes, sweet potatoes, onions, tomatoes and cassava.

In many parts of the country the investments that would most help small-scale agriculture are in feeder roads and better market information systems. It would be possible to write a political manifesto for the rural areas of Tanzania, just as the 'peasant parties' did in Central Europe between the two World Wars and won large numbers of votes (Mitrany 1951). But so far there is little indication in Tanzania that small farmers can organize themselves as a political force, and contest elections, or that 'worker–peasant alliances' can be formed in which the workers produce the agricultural implements, inputs and consumer items needed to improve productivity in the rural areas, while the farmers produce the food to feed both urban and rural areas. The politics of Tanzania remains urban, and, in the last resort, elitist and clientalistic.

Last but not least there is the proletariat – in the rural areas those with no land or insufficient land to survive without other income, who depend on casual *kibarua* work, often on a daily basis; and in the urban areas those who queue up for work as casual labourers. If the population continues to increase, and urbanization continues, the size of this proletariat will increase, and so will the challenges both for them and for the country.

The Future

Any forecast for the future in this time of great uncertainty throughout the world, risks looking foolish. But the analysis above brings out some of the requirements for Tanzania to grow and for the majority of its citizens to prosper. So this chapter concludes with ten prescriptions that may assist the ruling class as it endeavours to expand the forces of production.

1. For the next generation at least, there is no realistic alternative other than to work with monopoly capitalists – companies, donors, international organizations, firms of consultants. But this must not be uncritical. There will be occasions, perhaps many, when the advice they give is inappropriate; then those who have commissioned it must have the confidence to reject it or to seek out different advice. South–South relationships may turn out to be easier to negotiate and more relevant to the current situation.
2. Tanzania needs to be at the forefront of technical changes and interpretations, not reacting to conventional wisdom. Good examples of the need to think ahead come from climate change, where it appears that renewable forms of energy, from solar, wind, hydro and other sources are likely to increasingly displace the burning of hydrocarbons. This may not be the best time to become a major exporter of natural gas, and it may not happen anyway.
3. Tanzania also needs to think imaginatively about public health. Tobacco has long been recognized as a killer, and if the country does not reduce its consumption it will, as its population ages, end up with an epidemic of lung cancer. Sugar is the next target for campaigners because it destroys teeth and leads to heart diseases; many Western countries are considering taxes on sugary bottled drinks. Health is also badly affected by poor air quality, from polluting factories, but especially from diesel-powered lorries and cars. Diesel vehicles are undoubtedly causing respiratory conditions and death in Dar es Salaam, and it is time to explore how these vehicles can be phased out of urban areas.
4. Tanzania needs a culture of conservation and maintenance, to make the most of what it has. Planned maintenance of roads, water supply systems, irrigation infrastructure, and hydroelectric schemes, implies a culture of ownership and responsibility. Revenue budgets need to be carefully allocated, and funded, not just new capital spending.
5. There is a need to be ruthless with inefficiency, waste and corruption. These are some of the main planks of President Magufuli's administration, but they need to be embedded in systems such as strong regulatory bodies, audits, inspections, efficient and non-corrupt police and courts. Maybe the problems are so widespread that

Tanzania needs a Truth and Reconciliation Commission in which those who admit crimes are spared severe sentences, provided they come clean and explain who else was involved, and return money illegally acquired.

6. The leadership must be willing to let go, wherever it can. It needs an effective and self-supporting and profitable banking system. It also needs cooperative organizations, as far as possible self-policing. It needs to trust markets where they work effectively. It needs to encourage local innovation and to accept the resulting local centres of power.

7. It needs to be patient. Creating skills and training workforces takes time. So does research and development, especially agricultural research. Tanzania can learn much from Vietnam about how to create a climate of innovation and the right institutions.

8. It needs realistic targets. If targets are over-ambitious they become depressing for all involved when they are not achieved, and there is likely to be a lot of waste when facilities are built earlier than they are needed. It is much better to have modest targets, and then to celebrate when they are achieved.

9. Western capitalism has many crises and has not solved its fundamental contradictions. There is a need for strong states, but also for more equality. More equal societies are happier, and more innovative. That means new forms of taxation – perhaps on transactions, land values, property above a certain value, and products that have a cost to society, e.g. those that create poor environmental conditions, or bad health.

10. An open society. Tanzania needs its critical friends, to identify corruption, inefficiency and waste. This includes a critical but responsible press and media, civil society organizations at national and local levels, and a self-confident academia involved internationally but able to speak out and contribute on local issues.

Together these prescriptions give an indication of the kinds of strategies and self-confidence that the bureaucratic bourgeoisie will need if it is to make Tanzania a middle-income country. Whether it can rise to this kind of challenge remains a very open question.

3

Reflections on the Tanzanian Trajectory: Decline and Recovery

Michael F. Lofchie

The U-shaped arc of Tanzania's post-independence economic trajectory is broadly familiar. It divides into two periods of unequal length. After a brief period of growth immediately following independence, Tanzania entered an era of economic decline that lasted for about twenty years, from the mid-1960s through the mid-1980s. This was followed by economic reforms that have led to three decades of economic expansion, from the mid-1980s to the present. Several questions suggest themselves: What caused the economic decline? Why did it persist for so long? Why did Tanzania change its policies in the mid-1980s? And, what has the change meant for ordinary Tanzanians?

Introduction

Academic discussions of Tanzania frequently begin – and often end – with consideration of the influence of founder-president Julius Nyerere. His humanistic socialism portrayed a self-reliant society that would devote its resources to improving economic conditions for the poorest Tanzanians. Nyerere's philosophical idealism provides ongoing subject-matter for nostalgic discussions in scholarly conferences and required reading in university classes on African politics. It also provides a counter-culture of social justice against which some Tanzanians judge the current administration. Some narrators abet this imagery by portraying the Tanzanian story as one of Nyerere's personal idealism brought low by a fatal combination of forces including self-interested political opponents, the class interests of those who might lose out under socialism, and the corrosive force of individual acquisitiveness (Mwakikagile 2009).

Not all agree. Coulson (2013) directs attention to the dissonance between Nyerere's vision and the dismal reality of an economy whose failings placed its most valued components, universal access to primary education and basic health services, at risk. Tanzania's decline is well documented. The World Bank's classic study of Africa's economic crisis,

Accelerated Development in Sub-Saharan Africa: An Agenda for Action (World Bank 1981), known as the *Berg Report,* singled out Tanzania alongside Ghana as one of Africa's leading examples of poor economic performance. The Berg Report (p. 26) emphasized the loss of foreign exchange earnings caused by a decline in agricultural exports:

> During the last 15 years, the volume of exports in Tanzania has declined dramatically. In 1980, the total exports of the country's major commodities (cotton, coffee, cloves, sisal, cashew nuts, tobacco and tea, which account for two-thirds of the nation's export earnings) were 28 percent lower than in 1966 and 34 percent lower than in 1973.

Potts (2008: 16) presents an even bleaker picture, showing that by the mid-1980s, the volume index of per capita export crop production had fallen to one-third or less of the 1965–6 level.

The foreign exchange scarcity caused by falling export volumes fed on itself and spread to other sectors. Without adequate foreign exchange, agricultural inputs became scarce. Without inputs, production dropped further, causing an additional decline in hard currency earnings. This spread difficulty throughout the economy, imposing adverse conditions on manufacturing and public services. For want of inputs, Tanzania's public services operated intermittently at best and sometimes not at all. Electricity was subject to frequent disruption and water supply was erratic, especially in the working-class areas of Dar es Salaam. Garbage collection was irregular owing to the poor condition of vehicles, resulting in threats to public health. Failing transportation services imposed especially painful difficulties: Dar es Salaam is a sprawling city and Tanzanian workers sometimes had to walk for hours each way from their homes to their places of employment. Sometimes the core operations of the government seemed threatened: Tanzanian schools lacked instructional materials; Tanzanian hospitals and clinics lacked medications and bandages; police cars lacked fuel and spare parts; government offices lacked functioning equipment.

Tanzania reached an economic low point in the mid-1970s, only about a decade or so after independence. Inappropriate policies had brought about a decline in the food-producing sector as well as the export sector documented by the Bank. In 1974/5, Tanzania experienced poor grain harvests and was able to avert rural starvation only by importing massive amounts of food grains, which were only partly financed by the donor community. Farmers from the most affected regions began to migrate to Dar es Salaam, accentuating the city's existing problems of poverty and unemployment. Signs of political discontent began to emerge among smallholder farmers, precisely the segment of the population that Nyerere's philosophy had claimed to favour. The party's ten-house cell system, initially explained as the institutional building block of village-level democracy, became a vehicle for monitoring villagers' behaviour. The reversal of fortune was breath-taking. During the 1960s, Tanzania was the only independent country in sub-Saharan Africa that enjoyed a greater rate of increase in food production than the rate of population increase (World Bank 1999: 156), making it possible for food exports to complement traditional exports as a source of foreign exchange buoyancy.

The crisis imposed a psychic toll as well. Tanzanians suffered the indignity of unremitting poverty, the insecurity of not knowing how long the decline would continue, how bad conditions might become, and the demoralization of knowing that high-ranking members of the political elite, through corruption and special privileges, were able to avoid the hardships ordinary citizens suffered on a daily basis. A country with an ethos of self-reliance had become embarrassingly dependent on the generosity of its donors. In private conversations, some Tanzanians began to question whether the struggle for independence had been worth it.

Why Did Tanzania Decline?

What caused all this? The Bank's approach focused on the crop marketing system, especially the continent-wide tendency to employ government-operated monopoly marketing mechanisms for export crops. The Berg Report showed that the suppression of producer prices, implemented through the crop marketing boards, led to decreasing volumes of marketed production. The Bank's inventory of dysfunctionalities included outright price suppression, price suppression through currency overvaluation, excessive taxes on exports, burdensome operating charges and the demoralization of export-oriented farmers caused by the corrupt practices of the officials who regulated their activities.

Single-channel marketing monopolies had a long history in sub-Saharan Africa. Colonial governments had used the boards principally as a means of stabilizing producer prices. After independence, governments changed the way they used the marketing board system. Under independent African regimes, smallholder welfare had become a lower priority, secondary to imposing taxes that would finance an expansion of public services and the bureaucracies necessary to operate them. Tanzania offered a striking example. Export-oriented farmers seemed to be a relatively prosperous segment of the society, and it seemed natural for a socialist government to tax these farmers to improve the well-being of poorer Tanzanians.

Since the adverse effects of this policy became visible early on, what remained was to provide a political explanation for why the government persisted with these policies. Robert Bates (1981), building on the foundational work of Michael Lipton (1977), chose an interest group approach familiarly known as urban bias. In his view, Africa's urban populations, though vastly outnumbered by their rural counterparts, had a shared economic interest in adding to urban well-being by imposing taxes on rural producers. They enjoyed a disproportionate political strength afforded by the superior organizational attributes of urban interest groups, their proximity to the seat of power, and a pattern of personal and familial ties that linked the highest-ranking members of the urban political elite. Urban dwellers could exercise influence through an array of well-organized civil society groups including trade unions, professional associations, and business lobbies. Smallholder farmers did not enjoy those advantages: collective action difficulties were commonplace. Farmer cooperatives were hampered by the distances between individual members and between farm communities and the capital city. They were also prone to principal/agent difficulties.

The urban bias approach found a certain amount of empirical support in research by Barkan (1983), who made special note of the Tanzanian Government's 1976 decision to dissolve the agricultural marketing cooperatives (p. 7). Since these had provided an important vehicle for the expression of farmers' economic interests, their disappearance tilted the already declining rural–urban terms of trade against rural producers. Barkan's research supported the Lipton–Bates–Berg thesis that post-independence agricultural policies transferred wealth from agricultural producers to urban dwellers. Leading studies of agricultural policy in Tanzania adopted this perspective (e.g. Temu 1999; Ponte 2002) for good reasons. Tanzania stands practically alone among African countries in having extended the marketing board model from traditional exports to the food crop sector. In February, 1968, the Tanzanian parliament passed legislation (URT 1968a) creating the National Milling Corporation (NMC), a single-channel monopoly mandated to carry out the same set of functions for the food crop sector – the procurement, processing, and marketing of major commodities – as the export marketing boards.

The government's assumption that this system would work in the food sector made no sense. The single-channel model has some economic plausibility as applied to export crops. These crops typically exit the country through a single port where a bottleneck effect makes it simple and efficient to affix duties and surcharges. The revenue gain is large relative to the cost of imposing the tax. The marketing of food crops differs entirely. Food staples are marketed in millions of discrete transactions to millions of individual consumers in locations spread across the country. The consumers for one farmer's maize crop could as easily be the teachers in the village school or members of the professional elite in Dar es Salaam.

The NMC was an economic disaster. Almost overnight, the NMC began to deprive countless thousands of independent transporters, millers, and vendors of staple grains of their economic livelihood. In their place, it substituted a labyrinthine bureaucracy that began with the creation of grain procurement centres in local villages, then added the construction of innumerable grain-processing and storage centres in regional towns, and, at the apex, included the massive storage and distribution warehouses in Dar es Salaam that were the epicentre of the system.

The NMC quickly became a major example of the way government policy degraded agricultural performance. Once the decision to create a national grain bureaucracy had been made, it seemed as if there was no one in authority with responsibility for cost containment. Village-level grain procurement centres that operated mostly during the few weeks of the harvest period were staffed on a year-round basis. Storage and processing facilities that were required principally during the harvest season were constructed on the basis of peak need. The same was true of the NMC's fleet of trucks, which were acquired on the basis of anticipated transportation need: there were transportation bottle-necks during the harvest period while trucks, storage warehouses, and processing facilities remained idle for most of the year (Reichert 1980). The NMC seemed unable to calibrate its pricing policies at a level that would incentivize adequate production for national needs, thereby contributing to the acute food scarcities of the mid-1970s (Green, 1980: 24–6). The bureaucratic costs of the NMC system were enormous. As the NMC bureaucracy expanded, it seemed as if even mid-range NMC employees were entitled to NMC housing, an NMC car, and NMC per diem allowances. Rather than providing much-needed revenue for the government, the NMC incurred losses that had to be subsidized by the Tanzanian treasury.

The legislation that gave the NMC its monopoly status made it illegal for Tanzanian farmers to transport or market grain on their own. As a result, the NMC system gave rise to a vast secondary enforcement bureaucracy. One of the most common experiences in the lives of rural Tanzanians was to be halted at police roadblocks on the pretext of a search for contraband grains. These roadblocks became notorious for the bribery opportunities they conferred on local police officials. Indeed, corruption soon came to pervade the entire NMC bureaucracy. Some NMC officials began to use their positions to engage in informal grain trade. Rural correspondents reported that NMC officials some-times used their NMC cars to transport the purloined grain. Coulson's dissonance between Nyerere's vision and the on-the-ground reality could not have been greater: Villagers listening to Nyerere's speeches about rural self-reliance on Radio Tanzania were subjugated to a mono-lithic bureaucracy that extracted bribes to travel from one village to the next.

The failings in the country's agricultural marketing systems gave credibility to external reformers' insistence on the need to liberalize agricultural marketing. Since reforms in this sector have helped to stimulate an agricultural recovery, there is much to be said for this viewpoint. The emphasis on agricultural marketing, however, has a major shortcoming: it mistakes the instrument of an economic policy for the broad policy framework, rather like blaming the Internal Revenue Service for the tax system it implements.

Suppression of the agricultural sector was not an end in itself, nor was it narrowly intended to finance enhanced public services. The purpose of agricultural policy in Tanzania and in countless other newly independent countries in sub-Saharan Africa and, indeed, throughout the developing world was to finance an industrial revolution. The influence of economic ideas provides a better explanation for Tanzania's choice of development strategy. The governing elite of post-independence Tanzania was in thrall to two distinct economic philosophies. The first was the socialism of President Nyerere whose ideas were stated in plainly understandable language and took the form of widely published monographs and speeches. His ideas provided the ideology for the governing party and the justification for its claim to political power. The second was a sizable body of scholarly literature that has come to be aggregated under the broad rubric of development economics. This school of economic thought enjoyed a high degree of academic prestige and policy influence during the decades following the Second World War, a period that included the first decade or so of Tanzanian independence (Rostow 1990).

Although the development economists differed widely among themselves, they shared common presuppositions that contrasted markedly with Nyerere's outlook. The most important was their belief in the need for industrial development. Whereas Nyerere addressed himself principally to the rural sector (Nyerere 1967), the development economists believed that a society's economic well-being would only improve if there was a major expansion of the industrial sector. The leading development economists generally doubted the economic value of investment in agriculture and emphasized the importance of transferring economic resources to industry as the basis for economic growth. Inherent in this viewpoint was a belief that the agricultural sector should best be treated as a source of revenues that would help the government to take a prominent role in financing new industries. In Tanzania, as in numerous other developing countries, this set of ideas guided the decisions of those who actually formulated and implemented the country's fiscal, monetary, trade, and agricultural policies.

There were important political differences between Nyerere's vision and the development economics understanding of what would be required to accomplish industrial growth. Whereas Nyerere seemed to feel that development should occur in a democratic manner, the development economists were mute on the democracy question, insisting instead on the need for effective, long-term central planning (Ndulu 2008). Their emphasis on a centrally planned economy accounts for another of Tanzania's contradictions, that between Nyerere's proclamation of democratic principles and the government's tendency to suppress political opposition. Leading Tanzanian economists shared the development economists' belief that agriculture could provide labour and capital for the new industries (Malima 1971). This dissonance explains another of the contradictions of the Nyerere era; the inconsistency between Nyerere's emphasis on agricultural self-sufficiency and the government's tendency to treat agriculture in ways that degraded its performance.

The development economists derived their influence from several sources. The first was their status as some of the most renowned members of the economics profession: W. Arthur Lewis and Gunnar Myrdal were Nobel Prize winners; Barbara Ward was honoured by the British monarch as Baroness Jackson of Lodsworth; Albert Hirschman became one of the most famous economists of the post-war era while teaching at Yale University. An entire generation of influential African economists came under the influence of their approach.[1] Perhaps more importantly, development economics informed the thinking and the lending practices of large-scale funding organizations such as the World Bank and numerous bi-lateral development agencies.

The development economists' policy prescription for economic growth consisted basically of an updated version of the old infant industry model. Development would begin by identifying a group of industries whose products could substitute easily for imported ones. The next step would be to capitalize these industries, a process that would require a mixture of foreign and domestic investment. Foreign donors would provide the funds for the improvements in infrastructure necessary to create an industrial base; private investors, attracted by the prospect of producing for a protected market, would provide a share of the investment capital for the new firms along with the Tanzanian Government, which would assume a position of co-ownership. Responsibility for generating the local tax revenues necessary to implement this model rested with the marketing board system.

Launching an industrial revolution would require detailed central planning. A host of questions cried out for systematic attention: which industries to protect; the form, level, and timing of protection, and how to mix foreign public, foreign private, and domestic (government) investment in optimal proportions. Even planning was an acquired skill. Tanganyika's first multi-year development plan (1961–4) was not really an economic plan at all: it was essentially a shopping list of infrastructure projects for which the government hoped to attract donor support. Tanzania's most comprehensive effort at multi-year planning was its first five-year plan (URTZ 1964). Aside from a bland opening quotation from the TANU creed ('I Believe in Human Brotherhood and the Unity

---

[1] Dr Malima was perhaps the most famous Tanzanian among these economists. He received economics graduate training at the MA level at Yale under Albert Hirschman and completed his PhD at Princeton, with W. Arthur Lewis.

of Africa'), its two lengthy volumes contain no reference to Nyerere's social vision. It does, however, reflect an uncritical confidence that a systematic reallocation of internal economic resources, accompanied by generous in-flows of foreign funds, would enable Tanzania to industrialize.

This confidence was short-lived, especially as it pertained to foreign participation in the Tanzanian growth process. Within two years, the government had reappraised the economic assumptions underlying the plan:

> Experience with development finance at mid-point of the Plan, however, shows a completely different picture. During the first half of the plan, external sources contributed only ... 40.9 percent of the total expenditure, the balance of 59.1 percent came from internal sources. While difficulties and delays in aid negotiations and withdrawal of some aid for political reasons resulted in lower foreign aid commitments than anticipated, the actual use of aid has been still lower than that committed. (URT 1967)

The planners' disappointment was palpable (URT 1969). Tanzania's first economic shock was the realization that foreign development funds, either private investment or public aid, would not be forthcoming in amounts even close to those estimated by the planners.

The shortfall in foreign financing had mixed causes. The multi-lateral and bi-lateral donors were sceptical of Tanzania's technical capacity to manage a wide range of development projects spread across remote regions of the country. Foreign private investors had begun to discover that it was more profitable, as well as risk-free, to sell Tanzania the capital goods, raw materials, and other inputs needed for the new industries rather than to co-invest with an insecure government whose leader was becoming known for his socialist leanings. The process of selling industrial inputs, rather than co-investing with an ideologically untrustworthy government, also lent itself to the over-invoicing of industrial inputs, an exploitive device that was later given much emphasis by dependency theorists (Kaplinsky 1980).

The Mid-Term Appraisal was a slender volume (39pp) with an out-sized impact on Tanzanian economic history. Its discovery of investor scepticism meant that Tanzania's first five-year plan had become largely irrelevant before its first two years had elapsed. This brought about a reversal in the government's core assumption about how Tanzania could finance economic development. Henceforth, Tanzania would need to go it alone, generating the funds for industrial development from domestic sources. That meant agriculture. The Appraisal study launched the sequence of decisions that caused the agricultural decline. The first was the steady increase in taxes on the agricultural sector including implicit taxes such as currency overvaluation. The second was the decision to extend the monopoly marketing system from the export sector to food staples. The government's decision to pursue agricultural collectivization may also fall into this category as it intensified the bureaucratic controls over agricultural production. By the late 1960s, the agricultural sector was suffering from a host of government-imposed ills that included lowered producer prices that induced production shortfalls, the growth of the informal sector, and heightened dependence on foreign aid.

The failure of Tanzania's development model is painfully familiar. A series of World Bank studies[2] present a picture of an economy that had been dragged down by a failing sector that pulled much down in its wake. By the early 1980s, in the aftermath of the Uganda war, the Tanzanian economy was at the point of collapse. Many factories were in a derelict state; shuttered, surrounded by protective fencing, and staffed only by security details to prevent looting of whatever valuable items remained. Others were barely operational. Despite a vast inflow of government and donor subsidies, most were able to operate at only a small fraction of their installed capacity, producing goods of poor quality for a high price.

Why Did the Crisis Go On for So Long?

By the time Mwinyi's reforms began in the summer of 1986, Tanzania's economic crisis had gone on for more than a decade, an era Potts (2008: 7) has aptly described as one of lost opportunity. Twelve years had elapsed since the famine conditions of 1974/5. The Tanzania–Uganda War, which went on for about five months from late 1978 to early 1979, had worsened economic conditions. The need to mobilize and provision nearly 100,000 soldiers and then conduct military operations in a war zone more than 1,000 miles away from the country's principal ports and transportation centres, seemed to absorb what little remained of the country's hard currency. The government's ability to invest in the operation of its cherished social services or in the maintenance of its economic infrastructure fell dramatically. The 1978–9 war with Uganda devastated the civil economy. It was estimated to cost about $500 million, nearly doubling defence expenditures as a percentage of GDP (Klugman et al., 1999: 72). Its most damaging effects were in precisely those areas of the country that were most vital agriculturally, the north-central and north-western regions. When the war ended, thousands of demobilized soldiers found themselves re-entering an economy in which both agricultural and industrial production fell short of national needs. The urban crime rate spiralled upwards.

---

[2] See for example World Bank (2001) Ch. 1: 1–8, World Bank (2002) Ch. 1 and World Bank (2002) Ch. 2.

For the hundreds of thousands of Tanzanians whom *ujamaa* had dispossessed from their traditional farms to the barely operational collective villages in the early 1970s, the crisis had gone on even longer. For the thousands of Tanzanians who had lost their businesses and their livelihoods owing to the creation of the NMC in the late 1960s, and for the countless food-producing farmers who suffered from its many predations, the drift towards impoverishment had gone on for nearly twenty years. The massive effort to create large-scale industries during the 1960s and 1970s had also taken a toll on a proto-industrial sector, marginalizing the countless small-scale privately held firms that were already in place and producing the very same set of goods including soft drinks, alcoholic beverages, tobacco products, shoes, and wearing apparel. Few Tanzanians were unaffected by the country's decline.

The economic conditions that prevailed in Tanzania throughout the 1970s and into the 1980s resulted in acute shortages of essential goods in official markets (Sharpley 1985: 80; Ndulu 1987). The scarcity of essential goods resulted in price inflation, which made it more and more difficult for Tanzanians to acquire basic necessities. The government's attempt to control prices through a system of state-operated stores and a National Price Commission only made matters worse by creating a painful discrepancy between official markets where goods were unavailable at posted prices and the informal marketplace where goods were available but at inflation-adjusted prices that reflected scarcity and risk. For a host of goods, ranging from necessities such as food items and wearing apparel to luxury items such as beer and cigarettes, Tanzanians who could afford to do so had long since turned to the country's informal markets where there was an abundant supply of items that seemed to have disappeared from official markets. The informal markets fuelled the spread of corruption. Few Tanzanians could afford informal market prices at their existing wage levels; public sector workers began to demand side payments for their services. Vast numbers of Tanzanians were poorly fed, poorly clothed and lacked basic medical care.

How could the policies that produced these results have remained in place for so long? There are two answers. The first focuses on the economic interests of the country's governing elite; the second, on the role of foreign aid in enabling harmful economic policies.

Elite Interests

An economic decline does not affect all strata of the population equally, and members of the political establishment were well positioned to immunize themselves from its effects. This is Jonathan Barker's 'paradox of development', which asks why members of a political elite would voluntarily reform a set of economic policies from which they personally derive economic benefits (Barker 1971). Tanzania's political elite enjoyed numerous privileges under the existing system. Higher-ranking political leaders and administrators, for example, had government housing and government-provided automobiles. They had special access to medical care, sometimes overseas, for themselves and family members, and privileged access to imported goods that were unavailable to other Tanzanians. In addition to official salaries, many had generous per diem allowances for domestic or international travel. There were numerous informal ways to acquire wealth. Many profiteered from the conditions of scarcity by devising ways to extract bribes. Even lower-level officials could often do so: postal clerks, traffic police, and, after the nationalization of housing in 1967, building inspectors could almost always expect – and extort – some sort of bribe from the citizens who needed their services.

For those at the very top of the political establishment, the benefits were even greater. A high-ranking political position provided the influence necessary to award a government contract to one's associates or political allies, the opportunity to secure a government position for close relatives or influential supporters, or the basis for wedging one's way into lucrative business arrangements. Overvaluation of the Tanzania shilling provided a world of opportunity to gain wealth; those officials who could obtain hard currency at the official exchange rate, and there were many, could engage in profitable currency transactions in the informal currency markets. A government position offered the additional advantage of protection from prosecution. Many government officials used the income from rent-seeking and the immunity of high office to lever their way into covert business partnerships with the venturesome entrepreneurs who were developing Tanzania's wildly spreading informal markets. The great paradox of early Tanzanian development was that many members of the political and administrative elite, whose official responsibilities had to do with the construction of a socialist society, were profiting from their covert investments in informal sector enterprises.

The lucrative returns from informal sector business activities created an economic stake in the conditions of scarcity that prevailed in official markets. The greater the scarcity in the shrinking formal sector marketplace, the higher the prices and, therefore, the greater the returns on investments in informal markets. Political leaders who were officially bound by the TANU code of conduct, which specified that no leader or government official have secondary sources of income, were accruing wealth from their private ventures in informal markets. The more entrepreneurial the government official, the greater were the rewards. The net result was that well-connected Tanzanians lived well, often very well, while most Tanzanians did not. This explains why an influential portion of the Tanzanian elite was reluctant to support economic reform.

The economic reforms that began in the mid-1980s changed things dramatically. Since government officials were no longer constrained by a leadership code that discouraged secondary incomes, they felt less pressure to conceal their wealth. The difference between today's Tanzania and Nyerere's Tanzania may not lie in the extent of the wealth gap between the affluent and the poor, but, rather, in the propensity of the elite to engage in conspicuous forms of ownership and consumption. Almost any Dar es Salaam taxi driver can provide a guided tour of the luxurious homes in the coastal neighbourhoods north of the city centre.[3] Many are owned by members of the political oligarchy. This has had an all-too predictable effect on social morale.

Perhaps the most frequently asked question about contemporary Tanzania is whether the liberal economic reforms have worsened socio-economic inequality. Because an increasing proportion of economic activity in pre-reform Tanzania was in the informal sector and, therefore, 'off the books', this question is impossible to answer. Since much of the income of Tanzanian leaders and officials earned during the pre-reform period was undocumented and unrecorded, there is little empirical evidence on the basis of which to determine whether the income gap between the political oligarchy and ordinary citizens has worsened in the last two and a half decades. The prudent answer is that members of the Tanzanian elite enjoyed an affluent lifestyle during the pre-reform decades even as ordinary Tanzanians were suffering greatly; they continue to enjoy a set of privileges that sets their lives apart from the vast majority of their fellow citizens.

Foreign Aid

The second answer to the question as to how Tanzania could have continued for so long with a policy framework that was imposing hardships on the majority of Tanzanians emphasizes the role of foreign aid. Moyo (2009) has argued that donor financial support has enabled predatory governments to continue their inappropriate economic policies. Tanzania fits her theory. Donor support enabled Tanzanian leaders to ignore repeated, urgent, and publicly stated appeals for reform of the policies that were doing such great damage to the nation's economy. In 1979, Minister of Finance Edwin Mtei called for modest adjustments in the country's radically overvalued exchange rate. Nyerere dismissed him and replaced him with Dr Malima, who was known for his staunch defence of the state-based industrial strategy.[4] During fiscal year 1981/82, the Ministry of Planning and Economic Affairs called for modest policy changes to boost agricultural production (URT 1981). Its

---

[3] *The Guardian* (Dar es Salaam), 'The Secret behind Dar's Posh Homes', 5 December 2010.
[4] This episode is dramatically recorded in Mtei's compelling autobiography (Mtei 2009).

recommendations were ignored. The following year, it published a more urgent and comprehensive set of recommendations (URT 1982a). These proposals were also ignored. The same year, the Ministry of Agriculture produced its own report detailing the shortcomings of the country's agricultural policy framework (URT 1982b). Its recommendations were also stymied by anti-reform elements at the very top of the political hierarchy.

Foreign aid was a vital factor in enabling the system to continue (Edwards 2014). Aid provided an important part of the funding for such educational and medical services as the country could provide; it was essential in enabling Tanzania to provide even minimal levels of infrastructure maintenance, including road repair and construction, and the provision of water and electricity. Large amounts of direct budgetary assistance meant that it was possible for the Tanzanian government to pay civil servants and soldiers, and to maintain the routine operations of government on a day-to-day basis. There were several reasons for the donors' willingness to provide financial support to an ailing system. One was the ongoing influence of the development economics paradigm, which held that a combination of industrial protectionism and centrally planned allocation of resources to selected industries could nurture industrialization. Although there were several early challenges to this viewpoint as early as the 1960s (Berg 1964), it remained highly influential among those who formulated and implemented Tanzania's development policies. For much of sub-Saharan Africa, including Tanzania, this paradigm continued to dominate policy approaches until the publication of the Berg Report in 1981. Even more time elapsed before Berg's analysis trickled down to the bi-lateral donor missions.[5]

Donor practices could also be faulted: much donor assistance was provided on a project-by-project basis that does not lend itself to holistic policy analysis. Donors also prefer to provide aid on a multi-year basis so that recipient countries could plan ahead, and there is a legitimate concern about the disruptive effect of cancelling long-term commitments. Individual donor countries also had their own reasons for a willingness to continue to provide assistance. The UK and the United States tended to view Tanzania in Cold War terms, as a moderate country that, despite its socialist ideology, did not align itself with the Soviet bloc in international affairs. Among the Nordic countries and the Netherlands, there was sympathy for the Tanzanian social model articulated by Nyerere.

---

[5] There were some notable individual exceptions. For Africa as a whole, see Berg (1964) and for Tanzania, see Ellis (2003). The Ellis research had been circulating in Tanzania as a conference paper for several years before its publication in *World Development*.

Why Did All This Change?

Just as the willingness of the Nordic countries and the Netherlands to fund the Tanzanian experiment helped to prolong it, a turnabout in the Nordics countries' position was instrumental in bringing about greater receptivity towards economic reform. The Tanzanian Government had always been able to depend upon the Nordic countries for financial support that was not tied to the stringent conditions set by the International Monetary Fund (IMF). The Norwegian economist Kjell Havnevik (1993) records the pivotal moment when this changed:

> In November, 1984, during a joint high level Nordic/Tanzania government sponsored symposium, the head of SIDA (Swedish International Development Agency) in his introductory closed the door to this option saying that 'a basic assumption on the Nordic side at the outset of these deliberations, hence our working hypothesis, is that resources from our countries would serve to supplement, and not be a substitute for, those emanating from an agreement with the Fund'.

The Nordic countries' change of position was another major shock event: the Tanzanian Government could no longer depend upon donor support for its existing economic framework. It took nearly two years and a change of president for the Nordics' change of heart to have a full effect on government policy. But by 1984, the die was cast: foreign aid could no longer be taken for granted despite the shortcomings of domestic policy.

Exactly why the Nordic countries changed their position is uncertain. Conventional wisdom calls attention to a change towards the political centre on the part of Scandinavian electorates, which had begun to doubt the wisdom of taxpayer-funded aid expenditures that seemed to be producing so few results. Academic observers, such as Coulson (1982) and Fortmann (1980), had begun to call attention to the gap between Nyerere's depiction of a bucolic and socially egalitarian countryside and the reality of an overweening, exploitative, and politically repressive bureaucracy. By 1984, it had become impossible even for the most sympathetic observers to ignore the political shortcomings, economic failings, and depth of rural resistance to the Nyerere model.

Tanzania's tipping moment was the six-month period between mid-1984 and the Nordic announcement. It seems evident, in retrospect, that the Nordic countries had made their intentions known to Tanzania in advance of the more open statement at the joint November symposium. In early June, 1984, the Minister of Finance, Cleopa Msuya, had delivered a budget address that announced major changes in economic policy (*Tanzanian Affairs* 1984). These included a significant currency devaluation, improvements in producer prices for agricultural commodities, a shift in responsibility for agricultural marketing away from the crop authorities and back to cooperative unions, and a set of measures to lower deficits and restore market determination of agricultural prices.

The annual budget address is a major event in Tanzania; it is widely reported in the Tanzanian press and closely studied by aid missions as a statement of the government's intentions. Most Tanzanians assume that any major announcements in the budget address must have received the prior approval of the president. By late 1984, President Nyerere, who almost certainly had been informed in advance of the change in the Nordic countries' position, had indicated his willingness to step down from the presidency to allow the election of a reform-minded president in the next election, scheduled for late 1985. Within months of Ali Hassan Mwinyi's inauguration, the Tanzanian Government had concluded a successful agreement with the IMF.

The unification of the donor community could not have brought about a change in Tanzanian policies without a corresponding shift in the policy preferences of the Tanzanian oligarchy. Several factors induced the change. The conspicuous and prolonged failure of the existing system made it untenable to cling to the view that the state-managed economy could work. Economic decline had finally eroded the legitimizing value of Nyerere's philosophy. Although Nyerere remained personally popular, few Tanzanians remained persuaded by his economic views. This had given political space and heightened credibility to a younger generation of Tanzanian economists such as Benno Ndulu and Samuel Wangwe who believed that market forces should have a greater role in determining the society's allocation of economic resources. Through the force of their scholarly research and the persuasiveness of their consulting work within the Tanzanian Government, they helped to bring about an official atmosphere more receptive to market-driven approaches.

A second cause of policy change was the increasingly vocal expression of frustration by major social groups. Owing to the government's tendency to over-tax and over-regulate agriculture, farmers had never been supporters of the *ujamaa* system. Industrial workers, whose support had been lukewarm during the early years, when it appeared that the factory system might work, were suffering from high unemployment, inflated consumer prices, delayed wages, unpaid pensions, and the jeopardy of jobs that depended on government subsidies. Despite pandemic corruption, the lower tiers of the Tanzanian civil service pyramid included numerous workers whose positions did not afford bribe-seeking opportunities: they suffered along with other Tanzanians from spiralling prices, goods scarcities, and deteriorating public services.

The driving factor, however, was a metamorphosis in the relationship of the political elite to the economy. Until the 1980s, Tanzania's state elite had benefited from a binary economic system in which the shortcomings of the state-led sector made for greater profits on covert and not so covert investments in the informal sector. Even in a lax and corrupt system, there was an upper limit to this method of acquiring wealth. Tanzania's major industrial enterprises were still under a form state ownership that afforded protection from private competition, both from domestic firms and from multinational corporations. So long as that system was in place, the entrepreneurs in the informal sector, no matter their level of business acumen, could not expect to make the transition to ownership of large-scale enterprises. It was one thing to have investments in small kiosk-scale businesses selling food items, wearing apparel, cigarettes, or alcoholic beverages. It would require a different economic system for those individuals to own a major industrial enterprise such as a brewery, cigarette factory, or clothing plant. The presence of the state industries prevented small-scale informal sector entrepreneurs from upgrading their investments to include large-scale enterprises.

The state sector had undergone a gradual but fundamental trans-formation in its politico-economic effect. In the early decades of the Nyerere Government, the failings of the state sector created opportuni-ties for profitable side-investments in informal sector enterprises that could deliver the goods and services unavailable from state enterprises. By the mid-1980s, however, that was no longer so. Entrepreneurs who had thrived in the informal sector – and many were members of the political oligarchy – realized that there were greater profits to be made by privatizing the state economy and taking over the failed firms. Those who could take over failed state firms at bargain basement prices stood to gain a huge financial windfall. The Tanzanian Government had already done much of the investment necessary to construct the factory buildings and set in place the basics of their infrastructural requirements. If Tanzania transformed its economic system, so that private investors could assume ownership of those firms, they would be able to take advantage of investments that had already taken place at taxpayer expense. This was a powerful incentive to proceed with economic reforms.

The state industries were in a decrepit condition but they retained a considerable economic value as physical structures with access to physical infrastructure and utilities. All that remained in many cases was to take possession of the physical plant and modernize its produc-tive machinery. The possibility of earning large profits by doing so transformed the dominant economic interest of the political oligarchy. It now lay in the direction of privatizing the economy. Well before the era of economic reform Tanzania's political oligarchy had already become a politico-economic oligarchy. But its economic activities were constrained by the entrenched state system of production. Reform would make it possible for the political oligarchy to engage openly and expand further the range of economic activities in which they were already informally involved.

Viewed in retrospect, the far-reaching policy changes of the mid-1980s may appear as the inevitable outcome of the changing dynamics of Tanzania's political elite and the hardening position of the donor community. This would be misleading because it overlooks the intense conflicts over economic policy that were taking place among Tanzanians (Aminzade 2013). At every level of Tanzanian society, there was a clash of ideas between Tanzanians who, out of genuine commitment, economic self-interest, or a mix of the two, were committed to the Nyerere ideal of a socially egalitarian society, and those who favoured the neo-liberal reforms advocated by the World Bank and International Monetary Fund. Those who were involved in this conflict did not in any way feel that the outcome was inevitable. The idea of inevitability overlooks the crushing feelings of defeat and foreboding among Tanzanians who felt their leaders were entrusting their country's fate to a set of economic ideas about which they had the gravest doubts on both scientific and moral grounds.

Economic Recovery: A Tale of Two Tanzanias?

Over three decades of economic reforms have taken place since the mid-1980s, and these have brought about an impressive turnaround in economic performance. The current economic growth rate, estimated at around 7 per cent per year (Economist Intelligence Unit 2017), does not reveal the full magnitude of Tanzania's economic parabola. Some observers suggested that if Tanzania's GDP during the 1970s were calculated on the basis of parallel market exchange rates, GDP growth during the post-independence era may have been sharply negative (Kaufman & O'Connell 1999). If their estimate is correct, the Tanzanian growth turnaround has been huge, and may amount to as much as 10 per cent per year, more than 5 per cent per capita. The one undisputed fact about Tanzania's post-independence economic trajectory is that the change in the country's policy framework has brought about a dramatic reversal in its GDP figures.

Tanzania's economic recovery has a number of tangible manifestations including booming growth in real estate and retail trade. The real estate boom has changed the appearance of Dar es Salaam. Those who enjoyed the opportunity to visit, reside, work, or study in Tanzania during the 1960s might not recognize it today. The predominantly low-lying architecture of the post-colonial era has given way to high-rise commercial buildings that provide expensive office space for multinational firms that provide banking, law, accounting, information technology, and other services. The real estate boom also includes massive growth in residential construction, often consisting of luxury housing in expensive neighbourhoods. The expansion in retail trade is no less visible. The shopping malls that have sprung up in various parts of Dar es Salaam feature the global brands of luxury items affordable only by affluent consumers.

Economic growth has transformed the city of Dar es Salaam, which has grown from a somewhat slow-paced, post-colonial capital city to a teeming metropolitan centre. Always a city that seemed to spread in all directions, Dar es Salaam now extends for additional miles north towards Bagamoyo, west towards Morogoro, and even south across the harbour entrance. The same process of expansion has affected other major urban centres as well. Arusha is now encircled by its own complex of small towns and villages. Dar es Salaam has always been an impressively multicultural city with a population that constituted a rich admixture of the country's numerous ethnic groupings. It has now become even more multicultural with communities of permanent or semi-permanent residents composed of NGO representatives, investors, the employees of global corporations, traders, and skilled professionals from a host of countries around the world.

All of these trends and the massive traffic congestion in and around Dar es Salaam attest to the rising prosperity of some Tanzanians. The African Development Bank (2011: Table 4) estimated Tanzania's upper middle class to be about 1.3 per cent of the total population, almost 700,000 persons. It consists of the professional, managerial, technical, and clerical workers who have found lucrative employment opportunities in the growth sectors of the economy. Most live in Dar es Salaam and a few other major urban centres. One of the surest signs of Tanzania's economic recovery is return migration. Many members of the expanding middle class are Tanzanian professional people and business entrepreneurs who have returned home after a period of economic exile in other countries.

The challenging question is how to interpret the quantitative and visual indicators of economic recovery. It is difficult to concur with the World Bank's optimistic judgment that Tanzania's policy reforms have led to a substantial reduction in the percentage of rural Tanzanians living in poverty (Ferreira 1996). Much evidence contradicts the Bank's suggestion that economic growth is providing spillover benefits for poorer Tanzanians, especially in the rural areas where a variety of factors suggest a contrary trend. First-hand observers point, for example, to population increase, which has decreased land availability per capita. The inventory of contrary indicators also includes soil depletion, land concessions (LRRRI 2008), and land grabbing (HAKHI-ARDHI 2011), as well as adverse weather conditions. Lack of clarity and insecurity of land tenure have given rise to fear that the government may seize lands for transfer to large-scale investors (Boudreaux 2012).

In some rural areas, there is a declining cycle of income. The need to survive has compelled some smallholders, especially those who cannot afford purchased inputs such as fertilizers, to deplete the soil, resulting in less production from one year to the next. Population pressure has also caused more and more rural dwellers to move into areas that were always economically marginal. There has been some tendency to interpret rural poverty as the result of climate change, especially the increasing frequency of drought conditions. Although climate change has been a significant factor, population growth has compelled increasing numbers of rural dwellers to seek their livelihood in regions where soil fertility and rainfall patterns were never propitious. The increase, magnitude, and depth of rural poverty create a basis for scepticism about the World Bank's claim that the percentage of rural Tanzanians living in poverty has declined.

Doubts about poverty reduction are further abetted by growing evidence of rural social stress including clashes between pastoral and agricultural communities, sporadic violence against albinos and individuals suspected of witchcraft, and the emergence of vigilante justice against individuals suspected of theft. There is a worrisome discrepancy between macro-level economic data that indicates rising per capita income with micro-level household budget surveys that indicate income stagnation or decline among poorer Tanzanians in both rural and urban areas (Danielson 2001: 6–10; Demombynes & Hoogeveen 2004). It is vital to recall that even the most dramatic increases in the rate of increase in GDP and, hence, in GDP per capita are not a proxy for poverty alleviation or the remediation of inequality. The impressive figures on Tanzania's economic turnaround contain scant evidence that the economic boom has improved the lives of the vast majority of Tanzanians, whose lives have barely been touched by the new economic conditions: they continue to be desperately poor.

Tanzania has no immunity from socio-economic trends that have affected other developing countries, namely, the global tendency towards a binary separation between the small percentage of the population that benefits from economic growth and the larger percentage of the population that does not (Piketty 2014). Thirty years of market-based economic reforms have shaped Tanzania's social structure in ways that resemble other market-based economic systems; these include the tendency towards a sharply unequal distribution of wealth and the marked decline in opportunities for mobility between different social strata. Contrary to Nyerere's vision of a society in which Tanzanians would share the country's good or bad economic conditions as members of a unified society, Tanzania is evolving into two separate societies. The first is rich, powerful and able to avail itself of the amenities available to the globally affluent. The second is poor and lacking in the opportunities necessary to alter that status. In Tanzania as elsewhere, poverty has taken on the appearance of permanence.

The Tanzanian economic elite consists principally of members of the politico-economic oligarchy that has governed the country since independence, together with their family members, close relatives, and business associates. The Tanzanian 1 per cent has always enjoyed a material lifestyle that differentiates it from the majority of the Tanzanian people. During the pre-reform era, the country's socialist ethos and a leadership code that forbade second incomes, however porous owing to malfeasance, acted as a deterrent on the conspicuous display of wealth. The highest-ranking members of the country's political and administrative elite learned to be circumspect about their display of personal wealth or find ways to store it overseas. Politico-economic inequality was not invisible, but it did not appear to reach proportions that scandalized the country's egalitarian principles.

All this has now changed. The transition to a market-based economy has introduced permissiveness for socio-economic inequality, epitomized in President Mwinyi's doctrine of *'ruksa'*, a term that means permission but was widely construed as licence to engage in private sector profiteering. Under *ruksa*, the Tanzanian 1 per cent can now engage in a conspicuous accumulation of wealth without fear of official sanction. Although the Tanzanian oligarchy does not flaunt the gluttonous forms of consumption that characterized the North African countries that experienced the Arab Spring, it openly enjoys a material lifestyle comparable to that of wealthy Europeans or North Americans. The members of this class are also in a strong position to pass on their good fortune to their children. They can provide all of the amenities of superior educational opportunity, including a better study environment, access to private schools, personal tutoring, adequate funding for education in American and European universities, and informal connections to the educational authorities who provide overseas fellowship opportunities. The wealthiest and most powerful Tanzanians are their social friends. This creates a dinner-table atmosphere that envisions an unlimited horizon of opportunity. The members of the Tanzanian elite take it for granted that their children will enjoy higher education and that, once they complete their university degrees, they will have successful careers in government, business, or the professions.

None of this is available to poorer Tanzanians, a stratum of the population that includes small farmers, unskilled and semi-skilled workers, and Tanzanians at the very bottom of the social hierarchy such as household and custodial workers. For those at the bottom of the social scale, access to education, where available, is of limited duration. It does not constitute the beginning of an educational pathway that will lead to opportunities for higher education and the improved income that may afford. Whereas middle-class Tanzanians have enjoyed a modest amount of social mobility and aspire to more, poorer Tanzanians, both in the countryside and in the urban areas, do not enjoy a socio-economic environment that makes social mobility seem even remotely feasible.

The Magufuli Era

The Nyerere model may well have been an economic failure but it left behind some important social accomplishments. Tanzanians point with pride to the enduring legacy of Nyerere's determination to create a political culture that discourages appeals to ethnicity, race, or religion. Although some opposition parties have sought to build a base of support on religious or racial appeals, they have had only the most limited success with the mainland Tanzania electorate. In addition, Nyerere's commitment to a free and open educational system with generous bursaries at the university level provided a vital source of upward social mobility for poorer Tanzanians. Especially in the early years, the TANU/CCM system made it possible for Tanzanians from a variety of socio-economic backgrounds to attain economic success.[6] Many of the members of today's professional and entrepreneurial elites received their start in life from the educational system that Nyerere set in place. In that respect, at least, Tanzania was an open society. Although they may have been few in number, the social opportunities they enjoyed, which did not depend upon ethnic identity, political connections, or family ties, lent an element of credence and legitimacy to the system even as its economic shortcomings became painfully apparent.

The portentous feature of Tanzanian society today is that so many younger Tanzanians have begun to lose faith in the system, and are becoming convinced that the most valued elements of the Nyerere legacy have begun to disappear. The members of Tanzania's younger generation do not have personal memories of the economic hardships of the Nyerere era, and among many there is a nostalgia for the socialist ethos that created a sense of shared national purpose. Many Tanzanians have come to believe that the wealth of the dominant oligarchy is not the product of an open society that rewards educational achievement, professional skill, or entrepreneurial success. Instead, there is a widespread belief that the pathway to status, wealth, and power in today's Tanzania is through political connections, which alone can provide the portals of opportunity for personal enrichment. Increasing numbers of Tanzanians had begun to question the idea that multi-party democracy would ensure a fairer distribution of wealth, social opportunity, and political access before John Magufuli was elected president in autumn 2015. His actions have abetted this tendency.

Tanzanians describe the Magufuli administration as a mixture of positive and negative features, pointing to a set of seemingly contradictory tendencies. Since winning the 2015 election, Magufuli has initiated policy measures that exhibit three salient themes. First, he has undertaken a widely publicized anti-corruption effort that may – or may not – have had real-world effects in abating this problem. The

---

[6] The author is indebted to Professor Joseph Lugalla for this observation.

second is a tendency towards heavy-handed repression of opposition groups, political leaders, journalists, and media outlets the government perceives as critical of its policies. The third is a form of economic nationalism that treats multinational corporations, especially those in the extractive sector, as adversarial actors whose economic activities are potentially inimical to improvements in national well-being.

Anti-Corruption Efforts

Since assuming office, Magufuli has taken a number of steps to reduce or eliminate Tanzania's notorious corruption problem. Given that ordinary Tanzanians attach a high priority to this goal, Magufuli's efforts, which are widely reported in the Tanzanian media, have generally won public acclaim. He has eliminated large numbers of ghost workers, discharged a number of low and mid-range governmental officials as well as a few at the highest level (including a prominent cabinet minister in the energy sector), and sought to reform the most corruption-prone agencies such as the Ministry of Transportation, the Tanzania Port Authority, and Tanzania Revenue Authority. To demonstrate the government's commitment to treat taxpayer monies with utmost fiscal prudence, he has also shifted government funds from show projects such as holiday celebrations to social purposes such as health care. He has also dismissed the long-time Director General of Tanzania's Prevention and Combatting of Corruption Bureau (PCCB), Dr Edward Hoseah, on the grounds that this agency was too slow in addressing the problem. It remains unclear whether these actions have been effective or whether they are little more than political theatre in a society where citizen outrage had begun to focus on this issue more than any other governmental shortcoming.

Sustaining the anti-corruption effort, even as political theatre, however, may prove challenging. Previous administrations have launched anti-corruption initiatives only to have these founder because corruption has become so deeply embedded in the country's economic and political processes. In Tanzania, as in many other countries, corruption performs social functions that many Tanzanians value, even as they oppose it in principle. Hoseah (2018: 33) documents the many challenges of dealing with this problem and shows that rural villagers in Tanzania expect public officials from their village to bring gifts when they return for a visit. When they do so, they are acclaimed as heroes; when they do not, this is a cause of shame. For middle-level and low-paid civil servants and government workers, corruption provides an essential income supplement as living costs continue to outstrip meagre salaries. For wealthy business supporters of the CCM, some of whom also hold high party positions, corruption assures lucrative, risk-free government contracts. And for the highest rank of party leaders, it provides an essential basis of political cohesion in an era when the shared ideology of the Nyerere era can no longer do so. Tightening electoral competition in post-socialist Tanzania has made the CCM apparatus more dependent than ever on the popular support afforded by political patronage. These pressures place an outer limit on Magufuli's ability to eliminate this phenomenon.

Whether or not the government's anti-corruption campaign has been effective or is a form of political theatre with diminishing popular returns, there is no doubt of its popularity. Some Tanzanians report with genuine approval that real changes have taken place, and that it is now possible for ordinary individuals to enter a government office, find the key staff members present at their desks, and conduct business without the need for a side payment to assure service.

Political Repression

Tanzanians speak less favourably about the Magufuli administration's tendency to deal oppressively with opposition organizations, dissenting viewpoints, and vulnerable social groups such as Tanzania's LGBTI community. Amnesty International (2018) presents a dismal picture: 'The government continued its crackdown against LGBTI people, closing down health centres and threatening to deregister organizations that provided services and support to them.' The government has threatened to deport any foreign national working in the area of LGBTI rights.

Since assuming office, Magufuli's government has also shown a willingness to abridge the hard-won political freedoms that were restored to Tanzanians with the return to a multi-party system in the 1990s. It has imposed extended bans on popular newspapers, and ordered the closures of a number of radio and television stations, disrupted opposition gatherings and rallies, and engaged in the physical harassment of journalists attempting to report on these events. Human Rights Watch (2017) calls attention to the government's far-reaching effort to quell dissent:

> Critical journalists, politicians, human rights defenders, civil society activists and senior United Nations officials have faced various threats, intimidation and arbitrary detention by government authorities... Authorities arbitrarily arrested or otherwise threatened and harassed rights activists and numerous prominent members of opposition parties who were critical of the government or the president.

The Tanzania Legal and Human Rights Centre (2017) has corroborated a pervasive pattern of threats, harassment, and intimidation of journalists and opposition groups, sometimes by the top ranks of government officials including district and regional commissioners. The attempted assassination of an opposition leader in September 2017 has added to fears that the government is prepared to engage in violent and lawless behaviour to assure its grip on political power.

Magufuli's bullying behaviour towards the opposition and his efforts to silence public criticism place him in common category with populist authoritarians elsewhere. These leaders exhibit a set of common characteristics including impatience with the give and take of the democratic process, an indifference towards citizen rights if these are perceived to stand in the way of their goals, a willingness to use physical intimidation to silence opposition leaders and groups, lack of tolerance for criticism in the media, and an inclination towards the expansion and arbitrary use of executive authority. Populist governments, especially those whose power rests on a corrupt oligarchy, rarely distribute power or wealth, and the Magufuli administration is unlikely to be an exception. Magufuli's behaviour has become an instructive example of the ease with which a determined leader can subvert laws and institutions designed to protect individual rights and freedoms.

Magufuli's anti-democratic tendencies have given rise to deep concern about Tanzania's political future. Tanzanians are mindful that until the multi-party reforms of the 1990s, their country had a single-party regime with an institutional framework that accorded the president vast discretion to act arbitrarily against individuals and groups of which he disapproved. Nyerere had justified that approach based on the view that a classless society did not require political opposition. That justification is no longer available, and few Tanzanians are anxious to return to a single-party autocracy. For the overwhelming majority of Tanzanians, the purpose of restoring their country's democratic institutions was to make political involvement available to those whose political preferences could not be satisfied within the CCM monopoly. That aspiration has become less tenable during the Magufuli era.

Economic Nationalism

The third theme in Magufuli's set of policy initiatives is his effort to stir nationalist resentments against foreign elements that have an important presence in Tanzania's economic life, especially multinational extractive corporations. This approach has a long tradition in developing countries where dependency theory, which treats multinational corporations as a basic cause of national poverty, has had a strong intellectual hold. Tanzania was among these. Despite thirty years of liberal economic policies, a residue of this viewpoint has persisted to this day. Among both political leaders and ordinary citizens there is a willingness to believe that extractive companies have taken advantage of Tanzania's institutional vulnerabilities to craft production-sharing agreements (PSAs) that transfer the country's natural wealth to overseas investors.

The merits of this belief – and ways to ensure that the financial benefits of commodity wealth accrue fairly to the citizens of the host country – demand the most serious consideration. Within Tanzania and many other developing countries in Africa, this conversation is complicated by long-standing suspicion of the West and the large global corporations that play such an important role in its economic life. There are no easy answers. The economics of the relationship between developing countries and the global companies that export their primary commodities is among the most complex and controversial topics in the field of development studies. It would require a separate treatise, far beyond the scope of this chapter, even to describe the voluminous economic literature on this subject. Even if the economic issues could be resolved clearly, which they cannot, Tanzanians would still harbour questions about how best to derive the greatest benefit from their natural resources for both the present and future generations.

Magufuli has been able to take political advantage of this concern. In spring 2017, the Tanzanian National Assembly, acting at the President's behest, passed a series of laws governing the country's economic relationship with multinational extractive corporations. The most of important of these was a law entitled The Natural Wealth and Resources Contracts (Review and Re-Negotiation of Unconscionable Terms) Act, 2017.[7]

The purpose of this law, as its title implies, was to enable the Government of Tanzania to renegotiate the terms of any production-sharing agreement with the multinational corporations that were developing and exporting its natural resources. As the term 'unconscionable' suggests, this legislation springs from Magufuli's deep suspicion, shared by many in the Tanzanian National Assembly, that international corporations take unfair advantage of Tanzania's natural resources.

The question that addresses itself to any concerned observer of Tanzania is whether the Magufuli administration is seeking, in its own way, to cope with economic issues of bewildering difficulty and needs to curb questionable behaviour on the part of large extractive companies, or whether it is seeking political advantage by playing upon long-standing popular suspicion of Western business interests. There is a solid basis for both points of view. Several large extractive companies, including Acacia Mining, a large gold company, have been able to evade substantial tax liabilities by systematically under-reporting their volumes of production and exports. Their success in corrupting

---

[7] The Natural Wealth and Resources Contracts (Review and Re-Negotiation of Unconscionable Terms) Act, 2017. The other two important laws were The Natural Wealth and Resources (Permanent Sovereignty) Act 2017 and The Written Laws (Miscellaneous Amendment Act 2017.

local officials played a role in enabling this. At the same time, a certain amount of scepticism is warranted. Anti-global ideas have always enjoyed a certain level of popularity among Tanzanian political leaders for the simple reason that these ideas tend to assign blame for the country's economic difficulties to external actors rather than to a poor choice and poor implementation of economic policies.

Magufuli's anti-corruption measures and his determination to improve the financial arrangements whereby Tanzanian commodities are sold on world markets share a common stated purpose, that is, to bring about an improvement in the Tanzanian Government's revenue position so that it can better afford the social services Tanzania so urgently needs. That goal is unexceptionable, but there is a vital missing ingredient. It has to do with what the Magufuli administration has thus far left unexplained: how it plans to use its improved revenues to address the nation's drift towards widening socio-economic inequality and why it has chosen to approach this objective in such an authoritarian manner.

4

Agricultural Development in Tanzania

Brian van Arkadie*

Introduction

A World Bank report from several years ago (World Bank 2012) stated that, despite Tanzania's reasonable growth performance in recent years, the benefits of growth had flowed insufficiently to rural households. That report painted a dismal picture of agricultural performance, the conventional interpretation of the record. In turn, the view that agriculture has been quite stagnant spurs a search for new approaches to 'transforming' agriculture (e.g. through the Southern Agricultural Growth Corridor of Tanzania (SAGCOT)).

This chapter accepts that:

- Since the early 1970s, export crop production has generally performed poorly. The performance of so-called 'cash' crops has been one source of the pessimistic view of agricultural performance.
- The gap between rural and urban incomes has widened. However, this is a virtually universal characteristic of economic growth at early stages of development. From the point of view of poverty reduction the rural–urban income gap is less important than the actual growth in rural incomes. In a dynamic economy fast growth is likely to be associated with both a widening urban-rural gap and growing rural incomes.
- Some rural areas have stagnated or even regressed. This is true of Kagera, which, at independence, was one of the most prosperous parts of Tanzania.

* I would like to thank Kevin Rugaimukamu and Innocencia John for their help as research assistants, particularly in preparing tables and figures. I have also greatly benefited from attending two seminars, in Bradford and Copenhagen, where Andrew Coulson presented a paper on long-term trends in Tanzanian agriculture, which appears in a Festschrift volume for Kjell Havnevik (ed. Stahl), published by the Nordic African Studies Centre, Uppsala (2015). Broadly, Andrew's conclusions are consistent with the views I have presented in this chapter.

- The rate of growth of rural household incomes has fallen short of what is desirable and possibly achievable.

Nevertheless, there have been profound changes and significant progress in many aspects of the rural economy, with a realistic economic response to evolving market opportunities, notably through the expansion of food crop supply to urban areas, and significant progress in living conditions.[1]

If this perception is correct, it is misleading to characterize the rural economy and smallholders as inherently 'backward' and unresponsive to potential opportunities. The view sometimes expressed that there is a need for a fundamental change in the 'mind-set' of small farmers and promotion of large-scale farming may also be misleading.

The failure of so many agricultural interventions and projects by government and donors cannot be ascribed to an inherent resistance of small farmers to change. It is not small farmers who have failed to identify and exploit potential development opportunities, but rather the 'experts' who have designed and implemented flawed rural programmes.

This, in turn, leads to another question, which this chapter raises, although a definitive answer is not established. As many of those involved in project and policy design were technically knowledgeable, why did donor and government interventions in agriculture not achieve greater success?

Part of the explanation lies in politically motivated choices that led to negative results.[2] Also, institutional weaknesses limited performance, both at the national level and among donors. As donor and government interventions seem to have been persistently less effective in agriculture than in other subsectors (e.g. roads and education), it is likely that there was a mismatch between chosen modalities for intervention and the specific characteristics of small-scale agriculture.

The dismal record of agricultural exports from the early 1970s until the mid-1980s was not evidence of the inherent lack of responsiveness of the agricultural sector to economic opportunities. Actually, in the 1960s a number of export crops achieved rates of growth on a par with more recent achievements in South East Asia, now held up as a model. Peasant farmers were quite eager to take up new crops that

---

[1] This study is largely based on long-term aggregate data, backed up by personal observations of markets in Dar es Salaam over five decades. Ponte (2002) and his follow-up report on research in progress, 'Long Term Livelihood Changes in Tanzania', provide more micro evidence of changes at the village level (http://blog.cbs.dk/dbp/2017/03/30/long-term-livelihood-changes-in-tanzania-personal-reflections-from-revisiting-villages-after-20-years/), as does Chapter 5 of this book.

[2] See Chapters 2 and 3 for differing perspectives on some of the policy failures experienced in Tanzania.

Table 4.1 Growth Rates of Main Export Crops, 1960/62–1967

Annual percentage compound growth rates

Commodity	Marketed Quantities	Value
Sisal	+0.9	−4.7
Lint cotton	+12.6	+11.9
Clean coffee	+12.1	+14.5
Cashew nuts	+11.7	+17.4
Sugar	+14.0	+13.7
Tea	+9.3	+7.0
Tobacco	+23.2	+17.9
Pyrethrum	+25.4	+27.6

Source: Background to the Budget 1968–69

could increase the value of household incomes. This is illustrated in Table 4.1.

What put a stop to the earlier buoyant growth in agricultural exports? A series of government interventions and donor initiatives at best had no positive impact, and at worst were so dysfunctional as to undermine agricultural export performance in the 1970s. The extended macro-economic crisis from the mid-1970s to the mid-1980s also provided a very poor economic environment for the performance of all sectors, particularly export agriculture.

Given the lively growth performance of the 1960s, the question must arise as to why the government did not leave the existing production and distribution system alone. An obvious influence on policy was impatience. Tanzania had to 'run to catch up' (*Mwalimu*'s phrase[3]), and the pace of spontaneous rural growth was seen to be insufficient.

Possibly it was a natural enough perception to believe that more intervention in the rural sector would accelerate growth in a period in which the government took on a much more activist role in economic affairs. This view was implicitly shared by aid agencies, who were persuaded, on the basis of little concrete evidence, that agricultural development schemes must be useful because of the importance of agriculture. In part, this incorporated the perception of the educated 'modern' elite, that backwardness was exemplified by the 'traditional' ways of the peasantry. It is not very far from such a view to believe that the ignorant peasants should be cajoled or pushed into changing their ways. This attitude was carried to an extreme when confronting pastoral nomadism.

[3] *Mwalimu* is the kiswahili word for 'teacher' often used to refer to Tanzania's first President, Julius Nyerere.

Indeed, this belief in the efficacy and capability of government in sponsoring agricultural change remains pervasive; almost all agricultural studies conclude with policy advice that suggests additional government intervention.

One ongoing issue, therefore, is the persistent tendency of those in authority, both national and donor, to misunderstand and misinterpret rural development. The fact that the national elite at independence were only one generation away from the peasantry (either farmers' children, or the children of teachers, chiefs and minor officials, themselves from peasant families) did not engender understanding. Education was about learning modern ways and getting away from the peasant life; having struggled for knowledge, it had to imply a superiority of know-how: it is probably easier for an expatriate intellectual emerging from an urban culture to be enthusiastic about the knowledge of rural folk than those who have struggled to escape from the rural existence.

Historical Role of Agriculture

In settler and plantation economies, development of the smallholder economy was repressed by policies that aimed to ensure the continuing supply of cheap labour to the 'modern', expatriate-dominated agricultural sector. By contrast, in colonial economies without an expatriate enclave, the rural economy was expected to generate export crops (so-called 'cash crops'), which played a key role in generating foreign exchange and fiscal revenue. Tanganyika fell between the two classic colonial models, with a roughly even balance between exports from expatriate controlled farms and plantations and African smallholders.[4]

The emphasis placed on 'cash' (i.e. export) crops was partly because of the obvious need to generate foreign exchange to fund imports and provide revenue for the colonial state, but it also reflected the reality of a very limited cash domestic food market at that time.

Agricultural research and such interventions as were undertaken to support rural development largely aimed to maximize the growth of export crops, and success or failure in agricultural performance tended to be measured by the growth of export crops, a tendency that was deep-seated enough to persist until the present day. The surprisingly persistent vocabulary emerged in which agricultural output was perceived as being divided between 'food crops' and 'cash crops'.

Until the 1970s, the perception of the critical economic role of export agriculture was plausible, as crop exports were the predominant source of foreign exchange, which in turn constrained the rate of capital formation. The overall pace of economic growth was closely linked to

[4] A valuable source on smallholder farming in Tanzania shortly after independence is Ruthenberg (1968).

the rate of growth of export revenues. At independence, export crops were also the leading source of farmers' cash incomes.

The emphasis on the primacy of export crops persisted after independence, and has sometimes resulted in perverse bureaucratic interventions – for example, measures to prevent farmers from shifting from export crop production to the presumably less desirable production of food crops.

Historically, encouragement of the marketing of export crops was combined with a tendency to discourage trade in food crops. In the colonial period this was based on the notion that local autarky was likely to reduce the risk of famine. Recurring efforts to curb cross-border trade in food crops seemed to imply that it was less desirable to sell beans to Kenya than to export coffee to European markets.

A corollary of the emphasis on export crops was that whereas national statistics on export crop production were quite detailed and comprehensive, data on food crop production were at best highly sketchy. Along with the lack of detail regarding non-export agricultural production, there was little systematic data on the nature and evolution of the non-agricultural rural economy.

Technical Change and Innovation

The process of innovation in Tanzanian smallholder agriculture has come mainly through the introduction of new crops and new varieties. This was most obviously the case with the colonial promotion of export crops, initially coffee, cotton and sisal, and in the 1950s and 1960s cashewnuts, tobacco and smallholder tea.

However, although the colonial period involved an acceleration of change through new crop introductions, there had been a process of change over the centuries, evidenced by the fact that such non-indigenous staples as bananas and maize were already established before the arrival of the European colonialists.

In the period from roughly 1970, the process of change has been largely driven through the introduction of new food crops, the rapid rise in the production of what had been minor food crops and the introduction of new varieties and seeds for existing food crops. The spread of rice production, the rapid growth in citrus production, the commercial exploitation of other fruits, the introduction of new vegetables and of new varieties (e.g. of tomatoes) have all been part of a continuing process of agricultural change.

Frequently in discussion in Tanzania, slow agricultural progress is attributed to the lack of mechanization and the continuing dependence on the hand hoe. However, the essence of the Green Revolution in Asia was the introduction of improved seed varieties and fertilizer. In Asia mechanization was more a result of the success of the Green Revolution than a cause. In many areas of Tanzania, labour is still relatively abundant so labour saving innovation is not necessarily the first priority for achieving progress.[5]

Performance of Export Crops

The diversity of export crops depended on varying local conditions and the historical stimulus of international markets. At the end of the colonial period, export crops were dominated by sisal (in the drier areas on the coastal and central areas), coffee and cotton. In the 1960s diversity increased, with the rapid expansion of tea, cashewnuts and tobacco.

The initial decline in export growth in the 1970s had a number of causes. Government interventions in the marketing system were an important negative influence. The *ujamaa* villagization programme probably also had a negative impact, particularly on cashewnuts. Also, at independence about half of the cash crop exports were controlled by non-African farmers, particularly the then largest export, sisal. The nationalization of the sisal industry in 1967, following the collapse of the world market in 1965, was succeeded by the decline of what had been Tanzania's largest export crop. When a number of coffee and mixed farms were also taken over in the early 1970s, the non-African-owned sector seemed to have had its day. If one considers the performance of African export agriculture over the long term the performance is somewhat better than suggested by the overall data.

By the end of the 1970s, the deep macroeconomic crisis had a further negative impact. Poor incentives for export crops acted as a spur for farmers to look elsewhere for cash income. That opportunity came from rapidly expanding demand for food products.

Since the improvement in the macroeconomic environment and the reform of the foreign exchange regime, from the late 1980s onwards there has been a recovery in export agriculture, but the vigorous growth performance of the 1960s has not been repeated. With smallholder cash incomes now being derived from domestic food crop sales more than from export crops, this is hardly surprising. The following sections briefly review what has happened to the main export crops.

Coffee

Since the decline of sisal, coffee has been Tanzania's leading agricultural export (Figures 4.1 and 4.2). However, it produces less than 1 per cent of world output, so Tanzania is a price taker in international markets. Before 1990 the Coffee Marketing Board and the cooperative unions

---

[5] For a comparison of agricultural performance in Tanzania and Vietnam, see van Arkadie and Do Duc Dinh (2004).

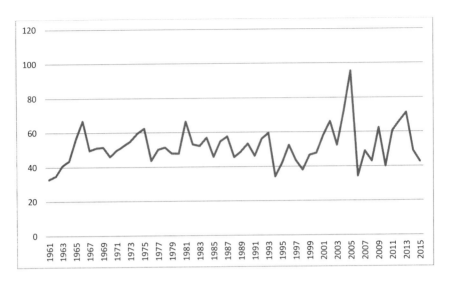

Source: FAOSTAT

Figure 4.1 Coffee Production in '000 tonnes (1961–2015)

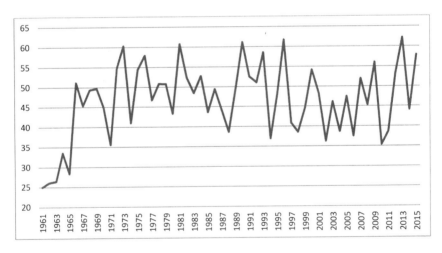

Source: FAOSTAT

Figure 4.2 Coffee Exports in '000 tonnes (1961–2015)

operated as a single-channel coffee marketing system (including input provision, transportation and processing). In the 1970s, for a period, the cooperatives were closed down and the crop marketing authorities handled the trade, but from 1981 onwards efforts were made to revive the cooperatives.

Reforms introduced in 1990 affected inputs, price announcements and dollar export earnings retention. More comprehensive reforms began in 1994/95, allowing private traders to purchase coffee directly from growers and to process it in their own factories for the first time in more than thirty years. With the dismantling of the single-channel marketing monopoly and successive devaluations of the Tanzanian shilling, in the late 1980s coffee production expanded somewhat. However, although supply has shown a response to real prices, the response has been limited, partly because of declining use of fertilizers (there is an absence of a stable system for providing inputs on credit) and a long-term reduction in planted area. One cause of the reduction in acreage was the substitution of coffee for food crop production. Reports that district authorities in Kilimanjaro took steps to ban the uprooting of coffee trees suggests that it may have been significant.

Cotton

Cotton is Tanzania's second export crop, contributing around a quarter of total agricultural exports, and around 400,000 ha are dedicated to cotton growing (Figures 4.3 and 4.4). It provides income and employment to about half a million households.

Before the introduction of single channel marketing, cotton was traded and processed by a mixture of cooperatives and private traders. In the 1960s private traders were displaced, and with the abolition of the cooperatives in 1973, there was a period when purchasing and processing was concentrated in the hands of the crop authority. After 1982 there was a restoration of cooperative marketing, with most cotton marketing and trade being handled by cooperative unions and the Tanzanian Cotton Board. Further reform began slowly in 1990,

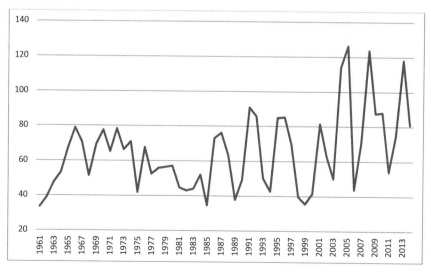

Source: FAOSTAT

Figure 4.3 Cotton Lint Production in '000 tonnes (1961–2014)

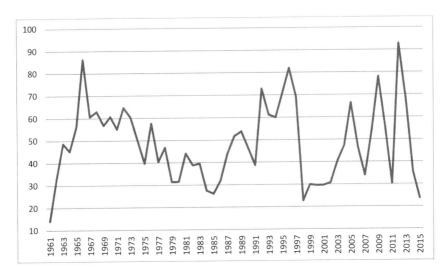

Source: FAOSTAT

Figure 4.4 Cotton Exports in '000 tonnes (1961–2015)

with the biggest step coming in 1994 when the government eliminated the monopoly held by the board and unions, and allowed competition in marketing and ginning. However, the new structure did not perform very well, particularly in relation to maintenance of the quality of Tanzanian cotton. The reforms increased the producers' share of export prices, but official statistics show no evidence of an immediate supply response. Producer prices of cotton have been erratic, with peaks in 1986, 1992 and 1996. Cotton production has also followed a similarly volatile pattern, with a one- or two-year lag.

Cotton is an annual crop, competing with food crops. In wide areas of the Lake Victoria cotton zone, cotton competes with rice as a source of cash income, which is one reason why cotton production fluctuates significantly, although with a slight upward trend since the mid 1980s. However, exports remain at the levels achieved in the mid-1960s, partly because some cotton is used for local textile production.

Cashewnuts

Cashewnut production has had a volatile history, with production peaking at more than 140,000 tonnes in the early 1970s, falling below 20,000 tonnes in the late 1980s, and more recently again being one of the success stories of agricultural exporting (Figure 4.5).

The decline in the early 1970s had a number of causes. With the end of the Mozambique war, cashews no longer flowed northwards across the border (i.e. part of the record crop had not been produced in Tanzania). There were also disease problems. Villagization had a negative impact as it was implemented particularly vigorously in some cashew-growing

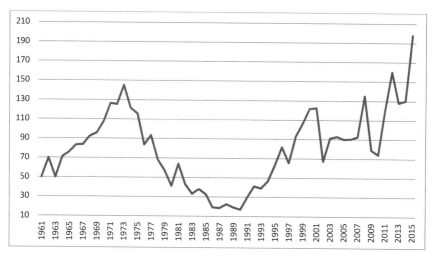

Source: FAOSTAT

Figure 4.5 Cashewnut Production in '000 tonnes (1961–2015)

areas, and the shift to nuclear villages made it more difficult to tend the trees, originally planted around the homesteads. However, subsequent performance suggests that the dominant negative factors were poor marketing and price incentives.

From the mid-1980s, exchange rate reforms and trade liberalization, which increased competition among buyers, resulted in sharp increases of real producer prices between the mid-1980s and the mid-1990s, with a delayed response (normal for a tree crop), with output recovering to over 100,000 tonnes by 1998. Cashews are produced in areas that are not favourable for surplus food production, and with favourable prices and competitive marketing arrangements there may be future expansion.

Tobacco

Tobacco is produced by more than 70,000 smallholders and offers employment opportunities in the three processing factories in Morogoro and Ruvuma regions (Figure 4.6). Tobacco is grown in areas with low rainfall and sandy soils, and is an appropriate smallholder crop owing to its intensive requirements of labour and crop-specific skills.

Tobacco production has increased significantly in recent years, partly associated with marketing and credit activities. These activities are discussed in Chapter 6.

Tea

Tea is the fifth largest export crop after cashews, coffee, cotton, and tobacco, with more than three-quarters of the output being exported (Figure 4.7). Tea is also the most popular non-alcoholic beverage in Tanzania, even in coffee-growing areas. Although tea is economically

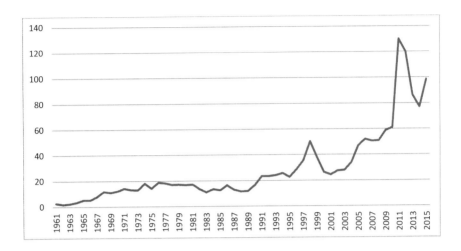

Source: FAOSTAT

Figure 4.6 Tobacco Production in '000 tonnes (1961–2015)

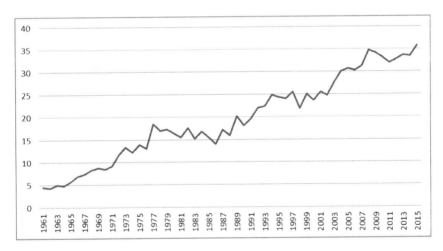

Source: FAOSTAT

Figure 4.7 Tea Production in '000 tonnes (1961–2015)

important for Tanzania, it markets less than 1 per cent of estimated world tea production.

Before independence, large estates dominated but, from the early 1960s, smallholder production was encouraged, and by 1985 small-holder out-growers accounted for almost 30 per cent of output. However, late payments to farmers by the Tea Board, the collapse of the research system, and inadequate investment in tea factories, roads and trans-port equipment contributed to stagnation in production for a decade, from the late 1970s.

The government tried to revive the sector in the mid- to late 1980s by privatizing and rehabilitating two tea estates, one of which had been nationalized in the 1970s; restructuring the Tea Board; privatizing the six state tea factories; and revamping public research on tea. These policy initiatives have had some success. The industry, however, complains that it is held back by a complex and onerous tax system.

Sisal production

Sisal was introduced by the German colonialists, using henequen plants acquired from Florida.[6] It was initially grown mainly for the production of marine twine.[7]

In the early 1960s, Tanzania was the world's leading sisal fibre exporter, exporting more than 200,000 tonnes of fibre annually (Figure 4.8). Sisal was the leading foreign exchange earner, and the First Five-Plan (1964–9) contained targets for further expansion (to 270,000 tonnes). However, in the first year of the First Plan, the world hard fibre market changed dramatically with the introduction of synthetic polypropylene twines in competition with sisal for naval and related twines.

The sisal industry consisted of large-scale plantations, non-African-owned and managed, but using labour-intensive cultivation tech-

Source: FAOSTAT

Figure 4.8 Sisal Production in '000 tonnes (1961–2015)

---

[6] Henequen was produced in the Yucatan peninsula of Mexico and was known as sisal fibre in Europe because it was exported through the Yucatan port of Sisal.

[7] At the beginning of the twentieth century, one important strategic use was the provision of naval twine for the German navy.

niques. The work was unpleasant and low-paid, and workers were drawn from the least developed parts of Tanganyika, and neighbouring countries.

Since the industry was the largest privately owned industry, playing a leading role in the colonial economy, it was not surprising that, following the Arusha Declaration, the major part of the industry was nationalized. The legislation was passed with little debate in late 1967. However, given the market crisis the industry was facing and the prospect of declining markets, from an economic viewpoint the nationalization was a mistake, taking over a declining asset with a poor future.

The industry went into severe and continuing decline, with even the remaining private sector shrinking rapidly. Brazil expanded production to displace Tanzania as the largest producer. Sisal is grown in the poor region of the north-east of Brazil, largely on small and medium-sized farms, and the industry received state support given the lack of alternative options in the poverty-stricken region.

Despite frequent optimistic plans to revive the industry and hopes based on the presumed natural comparative advantage of Tanzania in producing the crop, there has been no revival, and the likelihood is that Tanzania will continue with an industry producing 10 to 20 per cent of the production levels in the heady days of the last sisal boom in the early 1960s.

Cross-Border Trade

Public policy has tended to discourage or even prevent cross-border trade in agricultural products for fiscal reasons, particularly for traditional export crops. As a result, reliable data on its extent and composition are scarce.

As the food trade has developed to feed the fast-growing urban areas of Tanzania, not surprisingly, some of this trade has spilled over as exports to neighbouring countries. Anecdotal evidence suggests significant exports of beans to Kenya, matoke[8] to Uganda (where it is claimed it reappears in London markets as Ugandan matoke) and rice and citrus, particularly supplying oranges to the Nairobi market. Such trade is likely to grow, since some of the border regions of Tanzania are nearer to external markets than the main urban markets of Tanzania. Such trade enhances rural household incomes and the development of an efficient regional food supply system and contributes to foreign exchange earnings.

---

[8] Matoke is a variety of cooking banana grown extensively in north-west Tanzania and Uganda.

Food Crops

With the limited degree of urbanization at independence, agricultural cash income necessarily came largely from export crops, as there was only a small domestic market. The identification of 'export crops' with 'cash crops', and food production with subsistence, was roughly correct (although even at independence, there was a larger local trade in food than available data suggested). However, with rapid urbanization, farmers face the choice of producing food for the domestic market, or producing export crops.

Over the past fifty years Tanzanian agriculture has been remarkably successful in providing food not only to the expanding rural population but also to the rapidly growing urban areas. This is not to say that there have not been problems of food security and nutrition, including a national crisis in food supply in 1973–6, but household challenges have resulted more from issues of household entitlement and incomes, and from localized climatic conditions than from overall food supply scarcity.

The population of Tanzania more than quadrupled from 12.4 million in 1967 to 53.5 million in 2015, with an annual average growth rate of 3.1 per cent. In the 2012 Census, Dar es Salaam was found to have a population of 4.3 million, nearly 9 per cent of the total. If peri-urban settlements are included, the total would be significantly larger. It is likely that recent growth rates in both the national and urban populations will continue over the medium term. There is little sign yet of demographic transition. The urban population in Tanzania was estimated at 16.9 million in 2015, growing from 528,508 in 1960 (WDI 2016). It is likely that a majority of the population will be living in the urban areas in twenty years' time.

Household Budget data indicate the growing importance of the food crop trade as a crucial link between the rural and urban economies. Data from the Household Budget Surveys indicate that, by 1991/92, the sale of food crops already far outweighed the sale of so-called cash crops as a source of household cash income in the rural areas, and that, by 2007, food crop sales were more than three times as important as 'cash' crop sales (Table 4.2). That being so, the persistence of the use of the food crop/cash crop classification in descriptions of Tanzanian agriculture, in official and other sources, is rather peculiar.

The most recent sample census of agriculture (2007/08) indicated that for 61.6 per cent of the estimated 5.839 million rural households, the main source of cash income was sale of food crops. Less than 10 per cent of households reported so-called 'cash' crops as the main source of cash income.

According to the 2007 Household Budget Survey, more than half of Dar es Salaam household incomes (50.8 per cent) went on cash purchases for food, although this declined from 53.1 per cent in 2000

Table 4.2 Distribution of Main Sources of Household Cash Income

	Dar es Salaam			Other urban areas			Rural areas			Mainland Tanzania		
	91/92	00/01	07	91/92	00/01	07	91/92	00/01	07	91/92	00/01	07
Sales of food crops	1.7	2.8	4.3	20.7	13.8	17.6	48.5	48.9	50.4	41.4	40.6	39.4
Sales of cash crops	1.2	0.6	2.3	8.3	7.4	6.3	25.6	20.5	15.3	21.6	17.2	12.2
Sales of charcoal, timber/poles and firewood	n/a	n/a	2.8	n/a	n/a	2.8	n/a	n/a	3.1	n/a	n/a	3.0
Sales of other non-timber products	n/a	n/a	1.2	n/a	n/a	1.4	n/a	n/a	1.3	n/a	n/a	1.3
Business income	26.8	31.1	27.7	26.8	30.3	23.9	6.1	8.1	7.4	10.4	13.0	12.7
Wages or salaries in cash	62.7	40.7	52.7	31.1	23.9	32.7	5.8	3.8	8.9	13.1	9.3	18.0
Other casual cash earning	2.9	15.2	3.6	4.9	12.0	3.9	1.9	4.2	1.5	2.4	6.1	2.2
Cash remittances	1.0	4.8	3.0	2.1	5.4	4.8	1.0	3.0	2.5	1.1	3.5	3.0
Fishing	0.7	0.6	0.4	2.0	0.8	1.8	1.9	2.2	2.6	1.9	1.9	2.2
Selling of local brew	n/a	n/a	0.7	n/a	n/a	3.0	n/a	n/a	2.4	n/a	n/a	2.4
Other	3.0	3.9	0.1	3.7	5.3	0.5	3.9	3.6	0.2	3.8	3.9	0.3
Total	100.0	100.0	100.0	100.0	100.0	100.0	100.0	100.0	100.0	100.0	100.0	100.0

Source: Tanzania National Bureau of Statistics: Tanzania National Household Budget Surveys 1991/2 and 2001/2

(the usual expectation being that as incomes per capita rise the proportion spent on food will decline).

Crop Production

The diversity of agricultural conditions has resulted in a diversity of traditional food staples. In some areas (e.g. Kagera, Kilimanjaro and Mbeya) various varieties of bananas provided the main source for food and alcohol. In other areas, maize had become the basic staple, displacing such grains as sorghum and millet. Over recent decades, rice has begun to compete as a food staple. Sweet potatoes, and to a lesser extent, Irish (round) potatoes play a supplementary role but, with urbanization, Irish potatoes are becoming a more significant food staple.

Food staples include maize, sorghum, millet, rice, wheat, pulses (mainly beans), cassava, potatoe, and various types of bananas. In terms of cash sales, maize and rice are the most important, although some other marketed staples are under-reported[9]). The crop most sold by farmers is maize, although many small farmers continue to grow maize mainly as a subsistence crop. A larger proportion of farmers who cultivate paddy sell their output.

On the mainland, of 14.517 million hectares of potentially 'usable' land, over 70 per cent was utilized, with the average household cultivating 2 hectares. Annual crops were the dominant use, accounting for 73 per cent of land used (8.756 million hectares). From the 2007/08 Agricultural Census, the main planted annual crops were:

	'000 hectares
Maize	4,087
Paddy	907
Beans	50
Cotton	575
Sorghum	569

The picture of land pressure was quite varied, with 66 per cent of households using all available land, 37 per cent of households responding that they had sufficient land, while 63 per cent responding that they did not. The most important roots crops were cassava and sweet potatoes, followed by Irish potatoes.

The worst crisis in food supply since independence came in the early 1970s (1973–6), a period that witnessed a decline in farm production,

[9] Some descriptions of Tanzanian agriculture suggest that bananas are mainly subsistence crops; a cursory observation of Dar es Salaam markets indicates that this is quite false – the banana trade is evidently sizeable even if under-reported.

including that of food crops, mainly due to drought in 1973–4 and massive displacement of rural people relocated to *ujamaa* villages in some areas (Isinika et al. 2003).

After 1975, a new set of factors came into play to influence the food situation in the country. Subsidized input supply and pan-territorial pricing had positive impacts, while poor marketing arrangements and weak price incentives for export crops led to a switch from export crops to food crops. This involved both an increase in the area under food crops and intensification of production. A study by Meertens et al. (1995) in Usukumaland provided evidence of crop intensification up to 1991. Other documented examples of intensification of food production include application of high fertilizer rates for maize production in the Southern Highlands under the World Bank-sponsored Maize project from the 1970s. The adoption of high-yielding hybrid maize and improved varieties of Irish potatoes, also in the Southern highlands and intensive rice cultivation in Shinyanga region, were among other examples of more intensive crop production (Meertens et al. 1995; World Bank 2000).

Maize

It has been estimated that maize provides as much as three-fifths of dietary calories and more than half of utilizable protein to the Tanzanian population, so the maize supply is essential for national food security, and periods of food shortages are typically associated with shortage of maize (Figure 4.9). Annual volatility of production relates

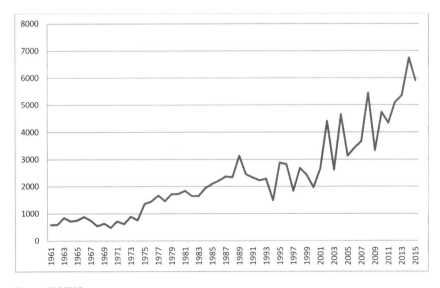

Source: FAOSTAT

Figure 4.9 Maize Production in '000 tonnes (1961–2015)

to weather conditions. Over the longer term, the trend in maize production has kept up with population growth, although there have been periods (e.g. the early 1970s and the 1990s), when production growth failed to match population growth.

Paddy

Over the longer term, one of the quiet success stories of Tanzanian agriculture has been the expansion of paddy production, with output increasing substantially over the past five decades. Increases have mainly resulted from an expansion in total land planted rather than increases in yield. In the Lake cotton-growing areas, rice competes as a source of cash income with cotton, with rice supply affected by the cotton prices and vice versa (Figure 4.10).

Production has increased in response to the fast-growing domestic market – rice has high income elasticity and is a convenient cereal for use by the urban household. Rice is mainly produced for the domestic market, although there has been some exporting in recent years. For those farmers able to grow paddy, it is a productive and profitable crop even if, by international standards, yields per hectare are low.

Rice is now an important cash crop and a significant source of employment, and income for many farming households. According to the Agricultural census of 2007/08, more than 19 per cent of agricultural households grew rice (an increase of a fifth since the 2002/03 census). Rice production covered approximately 907,000 hectares, representing

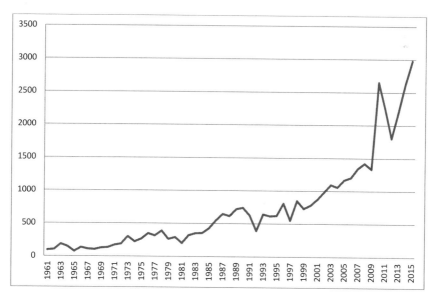

Source: FAOSTAT

Figure 4.10 Paddy Production in '000 tonnes (1961–2015)

18 per cent of cultivated land. Virtually all rice (99 per cent) is grown by smallholder farmers using palatable traditional seed varieties. Rice productivity is lower than in most neighbouring countries. Rice is grown within three main ecosystems: rain-fed lowlands (about two-thirds of acreage); rain-fed uplands (20 per cent); and irrigated rice cultivation (12 per cent). The most important regions in terms of production and area are Shinyanga, Morogoro, Mwanza and Mbeya.

Most irrigated plots are part of small, village-level schemes, although some are part of large-scale schemes that were formerly state-managed farms (Minot 2010).

Sorghum/Millet

Sorghum and millet continue to play a significant role as a food source and as inputs for local brewing (Figure 4.11). However, production has not grown as much as maize and paddy, as the cash market has not grown in the same way. The decline in relative importance of these traditional grains has food security implications since these grains are more drought-resistant than maize.

The central regions of Tanzania stretching from Dodoma to Mwanza account for three-quarters of the annual sorghum harvest. Smaller quantities are harvested in Mtwara region. Almost all of Tanzania's pearl millet is grown in the dry central regions. While both crops are drought-tolerant, pearl millet can withstand periods of heat stress better than sorghum. Pearl millet production is concentrated in the drought-prone areas of Dodoma, Singida and Shinyanga.

Sorghum and pearl millet are grown almost entirely by small-scale farmers on small plots of land, typically 1.5 to 3 hectares (Minde & Mbiha 1993). Most of these farmers also plant maize. If early-season rains are favourable, a larger area may be planted to maize. If early-season rains are poor, relatively more land may be planted to sorghum or pearl millet.

Few farmers have invested in improving the management of their sorghum or millet crops. Where fertilizer is available, it is more likely to be used on maize or another cash crop. However, despite limited investments in improved crop management, Tanzania's average sorghum and pearl millet yields are among the highest in southern Africa, reflecting the relatively long growing season and favourable soils found in the sorghum and pearl millet production zones Nonetheless, grain yields could be improved through the adoption of improved inputs. The extension efforts of the NGO Sasakawa Global 2000 suggested that small-scale farmers can readily achieve sorghum yields above 2 tonnes/ ha through the use of better seed and small quantities of chemical fertilizer, but adoption rates for these inputs sharply declined once Global 2000 stopped providing them to farmers. Rural markets generally do not stock improved seed and fertilizer. Production of these crops is indicated in Figure 4.11.

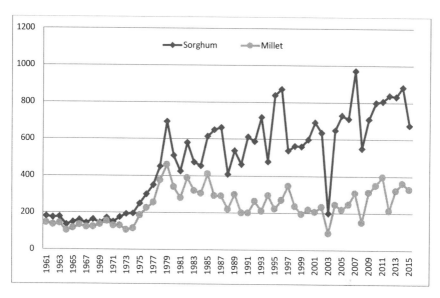

Source: FAOSTAT

Figure 4.11 Sorghum and Millet Production in '000 tonnes (1961–2015)

The limited commercial market for these crops encourages farmers to maintain a low level of technology and production. Yet the development of a commercial market is discouraged by the lack of a consistent marketable surplus.

The urban population of Tanzania has become increasingly committed to the consumption of bread made from white flour, which is highly import dependent. This bread is not very nutritious, and, to a palate familiar with the range of breads available internationally, not very palatable. A successful Dar es Salaam bakery reported that efforts to introduce wholewheat or multi-grain bread are not met with a positive consumer response. Could promotional campaigns emphasizing the dietary merits of traditional grains in bread and in breakfast cereals change this? Could the large-scale millers be persuaded to experiment with mixed-grain flour?

A second neglected area is the production of traditional brews. An important part of the household income, diet (and indeed pleasure) of rural Tanzanians comes from the production and consumption of locally produced alcoholic beverages. It can be argued that the extraordinary diversity of local brews is a rich part of Tanzania's cultural traditions, but little is done to support and promote such activity, with the likelihood that it will be steadily displaced by large-scale commercial brewing. Official puritanism might explain why little effort has been put into improving the quality of local alcohol production, or recording the extraordinary diversity of alcoholic beverages. More could be done to record the diversity of local

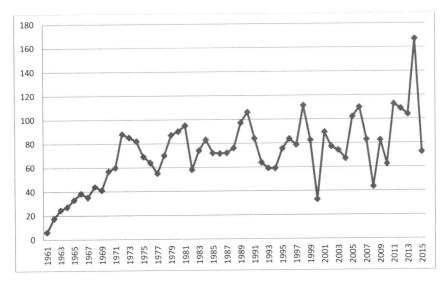

Source: FAOSTAT

Figure 4.12 Wheat Production in '000 tonnes (1961–2015)

brewing, improve hygiene and promote the use of local brews, using locally grown ingredients and providing household incomes to small-scale producers.

Wheat
Wheat production typically accounts for less than one-fifth of total domestic consumption (Figure 4.12). It is the fourth most important staple in the diet of Tanzanians, accounting for almost 30 per cent of total agricultural imports with an average import bill of over US$150 million per year. Over 90 per cent of wheat produced in Tanzania comes from Arusha, Iringa, Mbeya, Kilimanjaro and Manyara regions. Kilimanjaro, Arusha and Manyara are located in the northern part of the country and the rest are located in the Southern Highlands. While wheat production in the Southern Highlands is predominantly small-scale, production in the north is mainly on large-scale farms. Efforts to boost wheat production through the Canadian mechanized wheat project proved to be economically unviable. Perhaps if the same resources had been committed to expanding small and medium-sized production the results would have been more positive.

Other Food Crops
Leliveld et al. (2013) have reinforced the view presented in this chapter that, in recent years, there has been considerable growth in food crop production, particularly of minor crops. Their study identified sweet potatoes, groundnuts, bananas, sesame, cowpeas, pigeon peas,

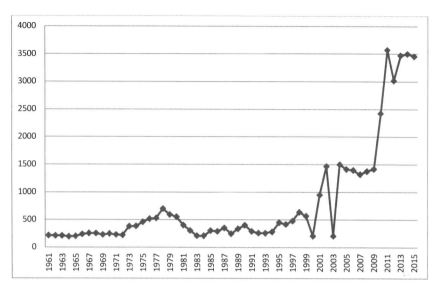

Source: FAOSTAT

Figure 4.13 Sweet Potato Production in '000 tonnes (1961–2015)

sunflower and pulses as being particularly successful food crops over the decade 2000–10. The recent experience of a substantial increase in sunflower production is discussed in Chapter 6.

Sweet potatoes
Sweet potatoes are grown throughout Tanzania (Lake Zone, Western Zone, Southern Highlands Zone, Eastern Zone and Northern Zone) (Figure 4.13). It is a hardy crop with broad adaptability to climate and soils, hence it offers a sustainable food supply when other crops fail. The relative importance of sweet potatoes has increased significantly in recent years owing to problems faced by other crops (e.g. cassava mosaic and brown streak, and banana bacterial wilt, sigatoka, nematodes and weevils). Production has increased substantially, but yields are low owing to the lack of high-quality planting material of improved varieties and to disease problems. A major limiting factor for increased sweet potato production is the shortage of clean planting materials of superior varieties (McKnight Foundation 2006).

Bananas
Cooking bananas are grown in somewhat cooler, wetter areas. Kagera, Kilimanjaro and Mbeya are the most prominent producers of bananas. These areas are the main source of cooking bananas marketed in Dar es Salaam. Casual observation suggests it is a significant trade, although there is no statistical evidence of its size.

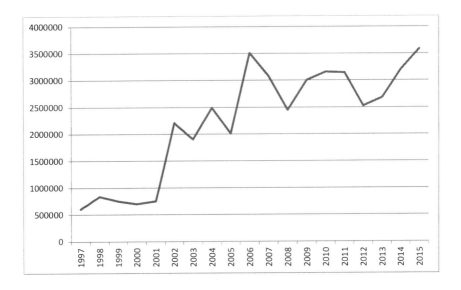

Source: FAOSTAT

Figure 4.14 Banana Production in '000 tonnes (1997–2015)

In the areas where bananas are grown, they are a leading staple used in varying forms: cooking bananas (matoke and ndizi), as fruits and for beer brewing (e.g. lubize in Kagera and mbege in Kiliman-jaro) (Figure 4.14). They are also a source of actual and potential cash income, delivering to urban markets and in cross-border trade (notably to Uganda).

Banana cultivation has not received sufficient attention from the agricultural services, given its actual and potential significance. This is becoming an important issue, as the crop is increasingly susceptible to disease and pests (e.g. the spread of nematodes). Production statistics for earlier years are probably not very reliable, but recent production trends show a slight increase with significant fluctuations.

Cassava
Cassava is particularly produced for home consumption or marketed locally, although it enjoys a lively market in Dar es Salaam during Ramadan (Figure 4.15). Historically it was seen very much as a famine crop, and the colonial authorities promoted it in that role. Cassava production increased substantially until the late 1980s but fell subsequently and now fluctuates with no obvious trend.

Pulses
Pulses are grown throughout Tanzania, often intercropped with maize (Figure 4.16). Production has followed an upward trend with considerable fluctuations. Pulses are highly commercialized and make a significant contribution to exports as well as to the nutrition of the population.

Source: FAOSTAT

Figure 4.15 Cassava Production in '000 tonnes (1961–2015)

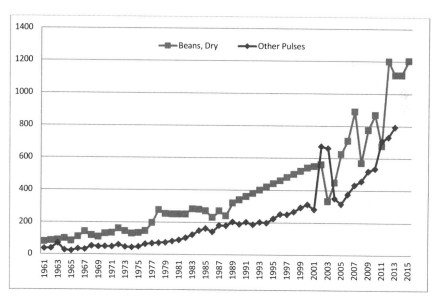

Source: FAOSTAT

Figure 4.16 Dry Beans and Pulse Production in '000 tonnes (1961–2015)

Vegetables and fruit

Personal observation of Dar es Salaam markets over five decades indicates the growth in the quantity and variety of fruit and vegetables supplied to a rapidly growing market. This aspect of agricultural growth is incompletely recorded in available data. It is surprising to remember, when in the two citrus seasons Dar es Salaam is swamped with oranges, that in the late 1960s they were virtually absent from the Dar market.

Tomatoes are the largest recorded commercial vegetable crop covered by the Census. The combined area planted with tomatoes in the Mainland and Zanzibar was 26,612 hectares. In the Mainland 17,228 hectares. were planted in the long rains and 8,163 hectares. in the short rains. Tomatoes contributed the highest percentage of marketed quantity (321,128 tonnes) to the recorded harvested quantity of fruits and vegetables (URT 2012).

Most vegetables are planted in the long rains, except water melons, which are grown more in the short rainy season. Marketed vegetables include tomatoes, onions, leeks, shallots, chives, sweet peppers, cabbages, Chinese cabbages, lettuce, cauliflower, peas, carrots, cucumber, water melon, string-less beans, peas, mushrooms, eggplants, African eggplants, okra, collards/mustards, green leafy vegetables such as amaranths, nightshades, pumpkin leaves, sweet potato leaves, cassava leaves, and some wild varieties such as wild mushrooms and milk weed. Pineapples, passion fruits, citrus fruits, mangoes, peaches, pears and desert bananas are important marketed fruits.

Production of most horticultural crops is by small-scale farmers. Some high-value exportable crops such as cut flowers and some vegetables such as green beans, peas, courgettes, baby corn, chillies, baby carrots and baby leeks are produced by large-scale farmers. For the future, small-scale production is likely to be critical for the supply of domestic markets, and the spread of new crops, improved seeds and new varieties is therefore of great importance.

Livestock

Livestock products are another area where Tanzania is largely self-sufficient. The urban market for livestock products has grown rapidly, and with rising urban incomes can be expected to grow faster than urban populations, as the demand for meat tends to be income-elastic.

From the 2007/08 Agricultural Census, about 2.3 million households kept livestock. In the surveyed households, there were 21.281 million cattle, 15.154 million goats, 5.716 million sheep and 1.584 million pigs. Most livestock (99 per cent) was kept by smallholders. Of the 1.699 million cattle-keeping households, 72 per cent kept between 1 and 10 head of cattle. The average numbers of cattle, goats and sheep per household were 13, 9 and 9 respectively while, on average, 12 chickens were kept.

The heaviest concentration of livestock production was in the Northern regions, mainly Shinyanga and Arusha, with a total of 4.2 million and 2.5 million livestock units respectively. The two regions were followed by Tabora, Mwanza, Manyara, Mara and Singida, with about 2.0 million units each.

The cattle population is mainly made up of indigenous breeds (96.2 per cent). Improved beef and dairy breeds only contributed 0.9 per cent and 2.9 per cent respectively in the Mainland. When compared to the 2002/03 Agricultural Census, the population of cattle increased from 16,999,793 to 21,280,875 in 2007/08, an average annual growth rate of about 4 per cent over the five-year period. The number of goats increased from 10,628,401 to 15,085,150, a 30 per cent increase during the period 1995–2008, with an annual growth rate of 5 per cent between 2003 and 2008. Over the 1995–2008 period, there has been a large increase in the number of sheep, from about 3.4 million to 5.7 million head, growth coming particularly between 2003 and 2008, with a big increase in the number of households raising sheep, from 496,000 in 2002/03 to 639,000 in 2007/08.

In the Mainland, there were about 42.6 million chickens of which 96 per cent were local birds. The number of households engaged in more sophisticated production was still relatively small. Larger-scale poultry production is concentrated around Dar es Salaam.

Despite the general trend of increasing livestock numbers, diseases (especially Tick Borne Diseases (TBD)) have remained a widespread problem. TBD diseases were reported by 37.4 per cent of the livestock-keeping households. Control methods were spraying (29 per cent), dipping (10 per cent) and smearing (9 per cent). However, there were still a significant number of households (61 per cent) that did not use any of the control methods. Foot and Mouth Disease (FMD) was reported by 253,000 livestock-keeping households. Helminths and Trypanosomosis were other common problems.

Newcastle Disease (NCD) is a devastating poultry disease, but only 22 per cent of the households regularly vaccinated their chicks against the disease, while 26 per cent used local herbs and 52 per cent did not take any measures.

Other livestock included stingless bees, which accounted for 76 per cent of the farmed bee population. Honey was produced by 129,000 households, representing 2 per cent of the households involved in crop production. The leading regions in honey production include Tabora, which produced 3,862,000 litres, followed by Mbeya, which produced 3,395,000 litres, and Rukwa, which produced 2,311,000 litres. Beekeeping households produced in the range of 300–420 litres of honey per household.

The availability of livestock services and infrastructure varied between types of services and regions. Services are more accessible in urban and peri-urban areas. Regions such as Shinyanga and Mwanza, which had large populations of livestock, had less access to livestock services than regions such as Dar es Salaam with relatively fewer livestock. Access to livestock services is more available in regions like Kilimanjaro and Mbeya where farming is more intensive and infrastructure more developed.

Smallholder producers have done remarkably well in expanding production to supply growing urban demand, without particularly effective support services. For the future, to continue to supply the expanding market there will be a need for improved livestock husbandry and disease control, requiring improved support services.

Improvements in the Quality of Rural Life

Given the low levels of rural income and the large and increasing gap between rural and urban incomes, it is easy to conclude that the quality of rural life must have stagnated. This conclusion might easily be arrived at on observing the conditions of rural life for the first time. However, there has been significant if slow improvement. This is evident in the data for improved roofing and other aspects of housing construction, improvements in sanitation, the better provision of social services (e.g. the great increase in literacy), improvements in clothing (e.g. wearing of shoes) and increasing access to the radio.

One area of speculation concerns the possible impact of current innovations on rural life. The extraordinary expansion in the use of mobile phones has demonstrated how a modern technical innovation can transform an aspect of rural living over a short period. The use of mobile phones for the transfer of funds is transforming financial connections between urban areas and the countryside. The introduction and rapid spread of the *bodaboda* (motorcycle for hire) has greatly increased the accessibility of villages not served with improved roads, both for human carriage and for the transport of goods. Solar energy, although still not very widespread, may hold out a prospect for the extension of electricity in those areas too remote or too sparsely populated to be serviced by the grid in the foreseeable future.

The contrast between fast growth in urban incomes and much slower growth in rural incomes is an almost universal characteristic of development. Agricultural growth and the expansion of rural incomes is more or less limited by biological constraints, and the income of rural labour is limited by its excess supply. At this stage of Tanzania's development the best that can aspired to is steady growth in per capita rural incomes of one to two per cent per annum, and in periods of rapid urban growth this is likely to result in an increasing gap between urban and rural incomes. Nevertheless, over a generation this can result in a substantial improvement in rural welfare. Starting from a low base, modest improvements can result in a significant change in the quality of rural life.

The emphasis offered in this section on the positive changes in the quality of life in rural areas is not meant to imply that the conditions of rural living are satisfactory. Poverty is still widespread, and indices on infant mortality, malnutrition and endemic diseases indicate that life is often precarious and very difficult. However, it is important to note the positive developments providing indications of the potential for further improvement, particularly through the link with urban development provided by the trade in food. This has resulted in increases in rural household cash incomes, which in turn has spurred growth in rural services. For the future, if this pattern of growth persists there seems a reasonable prospect for a steady improvement in rural welfare.

The increase in the cash income from agricultural production will be somewhat greater than might be suggested by the growth in agricultural output, which is measured in physical terms. As household members move to the city, those remaining monetize what had previously been household subsistence.

Over the longer term, as the rural urban population shift continues, it can be expected that the supply of rural labour will tighten and rural wage rates will rise. However, such a virtuous path is not inevitable. A significant part of past growth has come about by bringing more land into production rather than through increases in land productivity. Such growth at the extensive margin makes reasonable economic sense while new land is available, but this will become less possible with time – at the margin, new land being brought into production is likely to be of declining potential fertility. The growth process will only be sustainable if land productivity increases, either by increasing yields of existing crops or by shifting to higher-value crops.

Efforts to Achieve Rural 'Transformation'

One recurring aspect of official attitudes in agriculture in Tanzania has been frustration with the slow progress perceived to be characteristic of smallholder farming, even to the point of viewing it as essentially stagnant and of low potential. The reaction to such frustration has been to seek out ways to transform agriculture at a leap. This was true of five interventions:

- the colonial Groundnuts scheme,
- the commitment to the so-called 'Transformation Approach' (endorsed by the first World Bank country report and an important feature of the First Five-Year Plan),
- the Ujamaa initiative,
- the Canadian wheat programme, and now
- SAGCOT.

In the late colonial period, the Groundnuts Scheme was an extraordinary flop, but it is no longer studied or even much known about. This is a pity as its forgotten history contains signal lessons of how not to do agricultural development.

The scheme was proposed as a solution to the problem of supplying food oils for the British population in light of the extreme scarcity of foreign exchange. Officials of the United Africa Company, a subsidiary of Unilever, suggested to the UK government that the problem could be resolved by cultivating groundnuts in the British colonies. The government authorized £25 million to cultivate 150,000 acres over six years. By the time of the abandonment of the project in 1951, £49 million had been spent. At current prices, the cost of the project was much more than £1 billion. Most of the scheme's operations were located in southern Tanganyika.

After great difficulties, the first nuts were planted, but when the rainy season arrived, flash floods swept away the workshops and stores and, during the subsequent dry season, the clay soils baked into a hard surface impeding harvesting. The original target of 150,000 acres was gradually reduced to 50,000 acres and, after two years, only 2,000 tonnes of groundnuts were harvested. Later efforts to grow sunflowers failed because of a heavy drought. The project was cancelled in January 1951.

There were many reasons for failure. The belief that mechanized agriculture would be straightforward proved incorrect. The inexperience of the drivers and the harshness of the conditions resulted in the wreckage of many of the tractors. By the end of the summer of 1947, two-thirds of the imported tractors were out of use.

There was an implicit arrogance regarding African farmers. One simple question that was not addressed was why the land chosen was uncultivated. Evidently African farmers knew something the scheme planners didn't. Such arrogance also led to the failure to consider the alternative of promoting smallholder production of groundnuts and oil-seeds. In the 1950s and 1960s Tanganyika's smallholders demonstrated extraordinary responses to market opportunities – if the huge sums used had been spent to encourage small farmers, using simple labour-intensive technologies that were known to work, it is reasonable to speculate that much more would have been achieved.

Towards the end of the colonial period, the idea of providing a short cut to more rapid development resulted in the so-called 'Transformation Approach' that was to be contrasted with the slow-moving 'Improvement Approach' to accelerating agricultural growth. This was designed by the colonial authorities, endorsed by the World Bank (1961) in their first report on *The Economic Development of Tanganyika*, and was incorporated into the First Five-Year Plan, with the commitment to develop 70 settlement schemes and the creation of a special ministry dedicated to this approach. That approach was mostly unsuccessful and was drastically scaled down in 1965/66.

The belief in the need to 'transform' smallholder agriculture was one of a number of strands in the thinking that led to the Ujamaa village programme. The large-scale Canadian wheat project was another instance of an effort to by-pass smallholder agriculture through a large-scale mechanization programme, which turned out to be economically non-viable.

The thinking guiding the current Southern Corridor Programme and some recent donor (G7) initiatives also seems to be influenced by the idea that there is a superior, large-scale alternative to ensuring future food supply. There is one critical point to be made here.

Even if large-scale mechanized food production was successful, it would not make much contribution to food security. The problem of food security in Tanzania is not a matter of overall food supply but of household entitlements, and therefore of household incomes. The families facing food insecurity are those with low incomes. If national food supply were enhanced by large-scale production displacing the small-scale producer, this would cut off one plausible avenue to rural poverty reduction and would reduce rural food security.

This is not to say that large-scale production cannot play a positive role in stimulating smallholder production. There has been symbiotic development through outgrowing, for example in tobacco, pyrethrum, tea and sugar. Where larger-scale operators can run efficient processing facilities and provide a market for smallholder output, models can develop to the mutual benefit of both.

The Future of Agriculture

Underlying agricultural capacity
Tanzania has always seemed to be a relatively sparsely populated country, even today after generations of rapid population growth. It is therefore not difficult to believe that there must be a store of unexploited arable land, leading to some claims that as little as 11 per cent of potential arable land is currently farmed. Such statements can easily lead to visions of rapidly expanding agriculture acreages, possibly through large-scale mechanized development.

However, in reality there is wide variability in agricultural potential and the hospitality of the environment, as is evidenced by the diversity of rural population density in Tanzania. The economic potential of arable land depends not only on fertility but on many other factors. Availability of water is a critical constraint in many areas (including those central areas of Tanzania that achieve substantial food surpluses in years of good rainfall, but which may only be one year in three or four). Access is important; the potential of south-west Tanzania was only slowly exploited because of its remoteness from national markets. Remoteness is not only a matter of access to major transport systems, but also local access though all-weather feeder roads. In the short term, exploitation of land is also limited by inhospitable living conditions (e.g. malarial mosquitoes, or trypanosomiasis-bearing tsetse).

The last agricultural census indicated that a majority of rural households would like more farm land, and over the medium term, readily cultivable land will become scarcer, so improvement of land productivity will become more important (e.g. through improved irrigation, use of purchased inputs, improved seeds and more valuable crops). A big question therefore is whether government can do better to help enhance agricultural productivity than the somewhat dismal record of the past.

The government apparatus
In the British colonial period, Tanganyika was ruled by a modest bureaucratic apparatus. Steps to begin to develop a local cadre to take over came very late, and in the years following Independence, the weak bureaucracy was buffeted as a result of self-induced instability. During the implementation of the Arusha Declaration, top civil servants were called on to staff the greatly expanded parastatal sector. Continuing changes in the government structure, with 'decentralization', followed by the abolition of district government, the shift of agricultural marketing to the cooperatives, only to be followed by their abolition and then revival, and the challenges of implementing Ujamaa all took their toll. The demands placed on government by the demise of the East African Community in the mid-1970s placed added burdens on the system.

A system that was already weak was hit by the negative economic conditions from 1973 onwards, leading to an erosion of incentives. By the early 1980s, the civil servant's joke that 'the government pretends to pay us, and we pretend to work' had a ring of truth. When 'structural adjustment' was implemented from 1985 onwards, too little attention was given to the steps needed to enhance government capability – and indeed some aspects of the fiscal package further eroded civil service capacity (e.g. strict controls over recruitment of new staff).

The general debility of government was reflected in the erosion of field capacity in the agricultural sector. Budget limitations prevented field staff contacting their potential clients and left gaps in the staff. Moreover, frequent reorganizations of both the extension and research services eroded already weakened capabilities.

After Arusha there was also a good deal of emphasis on political direction of development activities. That this was not always effective was spelt out in eloquent comment by the late Phil Raikes (1986):

> leaders whose knowledge about agriculture, economics, or the constraints of peasant farming were minimal, felt free, indeed obliged, to issue directives, to show their commitment. A significant proportion

of ... extension advice was already of dubious value ... further simplifi-
cation. ... increased the proportion which was irrelevant or technically
incorrect. ... Apart from the considerable waste of time and/or energy
involved in either complying with or evading directives, they appear
to have contributed significantly to a decline in morale: a feeling that
whatever one does to try to organize one's life sensibly, some clown in
an office will come along and mess it up.

Suggestions that government or donor should do this or that useful
thing must be tempered by a realistic assessment of the potential effectiveness of the organizational apparatus. The weaknesses of government are possibly most obvious, but, in relation to rural development,
donors have hardly done better. Their poor performance is hardly
surprising given their dependence on short-term 'expert' missions
for project design, their unwillingness to make the stable long-term
commitment necessary to develop agricultural research, their slowness
to recognize and respond to failures, their lack of institutional memory
and their susceptibility to fashions embodied in novel vocabulary.

Grassroots contact between the government agricultural service and
smallholders is intended to be through the extension service, and in the
last few years the government has made efforts to boost effectiveness
by recruiting more extension workers. Census data suggest that now
a significant majority of small farmers have some access to the extension service. However, the extension service in Tanzania does not have
a good record of productivity. Three key weaknesses have tended to
undermine effectiveness.

A fundamental issue with the agricultural service is a deep-seated
tradition that its primary function is, at worst, to direct the farmer and
in general pass down information from the top. This approach should
change, with the first task of the service being seen as monitoring the
needs of the farming community and passing up information regarding
farmers' needs and the constraints they face.

A second issue relates to accessibility. There is no point in employing
extension staff if the means are not available for them to visit their
clients, and in the past, budgetary constraints have limited staff movement. With the improvement of local transport infrastructure it should
be possible for extension staff to move through the countryside on
motorbikes. It will only make sense to expand staffing in pace with the
availability of funds to provide transport support, for example by the
widespread provision of motorbikes and fuel.

The third issue relates to effective extension 'messages'. Offering
conventional advice on field practice (e.g. spacing; early planting)
is rarely productive – farmers have heard it before and if such advice
is ignored it is because it is often irrelevant. Extension is likely to be
productive if it responds to the real needs of farmers and provides knowledge of new seeds and crops and highly specific help with handling crop
pests, etc. For such productive advice to be available, extension has to

be the final link in a two-way chain, backed up by effective research and input supply.

In recent years the government has made efforts to rebuild the extension service, but it needs to go much further in thinking through how it can aid the development of smallholder farming, rather than chasing illusions of 'transforming' agriculture and making big breakthroughs through large-scale mechanized agriculture.

Agricultural investment

In exploring options for future government intervention, the possible role of public investment needs to be clarified. The most important on-farm investments are made by farm households, and are very incompletely recorded in official data. The key public investment role is to provide the conditions to encourage on-farm investment, most notably those that make it profitable to produce more output. Moreover, the most important government investments for agriculture do not fall under the budgets of the agricultural ministries – particularly investments in all-weather roads, to provide ready market access. To assess public expenditure commitment to agriculture by the size of the budgets of the agricultural ministries is simply naïve.

Marketing

The history of agricultural marketing in Tanzania has demonstrated that the institutional structure is at least as important as price policy in determining incentives. Large-scale, monopolistic state trading did not work well for farmers in Tanzania. Monopolistic state marketing had a poor record in handling payments and managing crop storage and sales. Arguably, the move to single-channel agricultural marketing was the worst economic mistake made by the government of President Nyerere. Repetitive and misguided government interventions to control, restrict and even eliminate the 'middle man' reflected a failure to understand the traders' positive contribution.

Given the evident importance of agricultural trading as the link between farmer and market it is surprising that traders do not receive more positive recognition. However, it is much easier to cast the trader as villain than hero. This is not unique to Tanzania – the trader, labelled as a parasite, is an easy target for populist politics. If the trader is seen as exploitative and parasitic, it is not surprising that policy-makers sought a short cut to improving the lot of the farmer by eliminating the private trader. In the initial post-colonial period, suspicion of traders also had an ethnic motivation – most private traders were of Asian origin.

Restraints on rural trade had roots in the colonial period. Colonial ordinances restricting intra-district food trade were enacted before the Second World War, as local self-sufficiency was seen as countering the risk of famine. Export marketing boards were initiated by the colonial authorities in the 1940s. The justification offered was the need to stabilize prices. However, the export marketing boards, by accumulating sterling balances during periods of commodity boom, were also a useful mechanism for UK balance of payments management, given British balance of payments problems at that time.

During the colonial period, cooperative trading had developed, but was mainly effective for standardized products with long shelf-lives – particularly for cotton and coffee. Initially, in the case of the KNCU in the 1920s, the colonial authorities opposed such development but, after the Second World War, British colonial policy supported cooperative development. The cooperatives had not only been successful in processing and trading, but also took on development tasks, such as supporting access to higher education.

The government, after Independence, supported the extension of the cooperative model throughout the country, enforcing the displacement of local traders by the cooperatives, resulting in the virtual disappearance of the local Asian traders who had been the mainstay of the local trading system. The previous mix of small traders, cooperatives and private wholesalers was replaced by a single-channel marketing system, with a chain running from the primary cooperative, through the cooperative union to a marketing board (later a crop authority), with monopoly at each stage.

The effort to extend the cooperatives beyond the thriving voluntary institutions created a quite inefficient system. Already, by 1966, weaknesses in the cooperatives had occasioned a Presidential commission of inquiry (URT 1967). There was an oscillation between the promotion of marketing cooperatives and constraining them, to the point of abolition (1973–82), with the amalgamation of local marketing functions, the previous activities of the Marketing Boards, and some of the extension responsibilities of the Ministry of Agriculture under Crop Authorities.

The inefficiency of these large monopolies became a prime cause of the deterioration in agricultural incentives. Management at various levels was not subject to the discipline of competition, or to stiff sanctions from above or democratic control from below. By the end of the 1970s the system had become very costly and quite ineffective – most infamously in delaying payment for produce supplied for long periods. In addition an over-valued exchange rate in effect taxed export agriculture heavily by the end of the 1970s. Even when exchange rates were adjusted, initially the benefit to farmers was limited, given the inefficiency of the marketing system.

When faced with the need to reform, *Mwalimu* had little faith in the potential efficacy of private trade. When it was proposed to abolish the NMC monopoly on food trade, the President honestly felt that it would lead to a collapse in the food trade and to food riots. However, when trade was liberalized, the response of local traders was impressive, and very quickly a network of traders emerged that effectively supplied food to Dar es Salaam. Given the apparent effectiveness of food trading networks, the most important future agricultural policy need is to promote such trading and to avoid interventions that disrupt or discourage traders (e.g. 'rent-seeking' police controls harassing transporters).

What is to be done?

Recognition of the primacy of food production

One simple, but clear conclusion arising from the discussion above is the need to recognize the prime importance of small-scale commercial food production to the rural economy. The anachronistic distinction between 'food' and 'cash crop' production should be dropped from official vocabulary and statistical descriptions. The performance of agriculture should be increasingly judged by its success in feeding the population, and priorities for research and the development of infrastructure adjusted in light of this recognition.

Future role of public interventions

Given the rather poor record of public (government and donor) interventions in agriculture it would not be difficult to come to a 'free market' conclusion that a laissez-faire approach might be better than misguided government interventions and failed donor investments. However, the successful mix of government and market initiatives has facilitated 'Green Revolutions' elsewhere, for example in many Asian countries including Vietnam.

This suggests that the key future role from public support is through effective applied research providing the basis for a flow of knowledge that farmers need but cannot supply for themselves. Only with effective research support will the resources spent on extension become productive.

There can be no question that Tanzania has some good agricultural researchers and also has access to the research of CGIAR (Consultative Group for International Agricultural Research) organizations, some of which have branches in Tanzania. However, activity is fragmented. Reviews of the agricultural research effort in Tanzania indicate a number of weaknesses:

1. The resources devoted to agricultural research (e.g. as a percentage of agricultural GDP) are on the low end of international practice.
2. The sector has suffered from institutional instability – for a long period research was a parastatal activity, it was then reincorporated into the Ministry of Agriculture and has now once again been hived off under autonomous bodies.
3. Finance has been unstable – for a long period research was

over-dependent on donor finance, which was volatile and did not provide the comprehensive, predictable and long-term support needed for operation of an effective national research programme.

4. For a decade, measures to control public expenditure resulted in a block on recruitment to the agricultural research service. In recent years, as staff recruitment actively resumed, the long gap in recruitment resulted in a scarcity of top (PhD) level staff, who had drifted off to international jobs and university posts. Efforts have been made to fill the gaps by bringing retirees back into service.

Agricultural research is a lengthy process, requiring efforts over a number of years. For example, plant breeding requires commitment over many years for the development of improved varieties. The gaps resulting from the chequered history of the research programmes left Tanzanian farmers either without access to improved seeds or dependent on imports, for example from Kenya. The 'Green Revolution' in Asia involved the development and promotion of new seeds. The weaknesses in this regard of the Tanzanian system can be seen as a crucial factor in holding back agricultural progress.

From the early 1970s until 1990 the government was responsible for national seed production and distribution, through the Tanzania Seed Company Ltd (TANSEED), established in 1973 to produce certified seed and to provide seed extension, dissemination and advisory services. However, TANSEED was beset with problems of insufficient transport and funding, lack of humidity-controlled warehouses, and inadequate seed-drying equipment, resulting in seeds with low germination rates, but at prices much greater than unimproved seed.

Government liberalized the seed industry in 1990. After liberalization, a number of foreign and domestic private seed companies entered the seed sector to produce, distribute and market improved seed, which concentrated on hybrid and composite maize seed, leaving a gap in the availability of improved seeds for other food crops. There have, of course, been a number of initiatives by international NGOs to support innovation in agriculture, and some of these have been successful, but such piecemeal and fragmented efforts are no substitute for a comprehensive national programme. This is clearly an area in which new efforts need to be made by government.

The contrast with Vietnam is instructive. Both countries have done well, but the Vietnamese performance has been ahead of Tanzania, in overall growth, in export expansion and in poverty alleviation. The World Bank (2012) has identified the agricultural performance of Vietnam as a key factor in its exemplary record of poverty alleviation. Vietnam maintained an effective apparatus of agricultural research and, in implementing economic reforms, achieved an effective blend of state and private institutions.

'Slow results' over the longer term

Understandable desire for 'transformation' and rapid growth has led government to seek quick fixes (e.g. the so-called 'Big Results Now' programme). Yet the real success story of Tanzanian agriculture has been in the steady growth over the long term of small-scale agriculture, with expansions in food supply and a largely unrecorded process of innovation through the introduction of new crops and new varieties.

It is through support and promotion of this process, rather than large-scale, mechanized projects, that future rural development is most likely to occur. Public support will be needed, particularly in those areas in which small farmers and local traders/processors cannot themselves invest, such as local and national transport infrastructure and agricultural research that can support the process of innovation that is already happening spontaneously.

For such a government role to be effective, the first need is an enhanced effort to record and understand what is happening on the ground in the rural economy.

5

Assets and Poverty Dynamics: The Methodological Challenges of Constructing Longitudinal Surveys in Tanzania

Dan Brockington, Olivia Howland, Vesa-Mati Loiske, Moses Mnzava and Christine Noe

Introduction

This chapter reports on a particularly Tanzanian research project into the consequences of economic growth for rural poverty. The project explores the poverty dynamics apparent in changing asset portfolios of rural families in Tanzania from the late 1980s onwards (and mainly the 1990s and 2000s). At the time of writing we are half way through data collection for this project. This chapter focuses on the methodological challenges that we have found.

The project is particularly Tanzanian in three important ways. First, it addresses a specifically Tanzanian aspect of debates about poverty dynamics and economic growth and the data deficiencies surrounding both. Second, it is a risky project but is most likely to succeed in a place like Tanzania. The risks arise from its deceptively simple method. We revisit families who were surveyed by researchers in the 1990s, we reinterview them paying particular attention to changing asset bundles, and we explore the reasons behind any changes in prosperity and poverty that we find. However, locating the surveys requires the strong research networks that Tanzania affords, as described in this chapter. The final reason why this is a particularly Tanzanian project is that undertaking this work entails getting to grips with problems of asset ownership and family dynamics that are the bread and butter of rural research in Tanzania.

Our argument is that assets matter when exploring the long-term dynamics of poverty, prosperity and livelihood. By assets we mean, *inter alia*, land, livestock, houses, household goods and farming implements. Some recent analyses also include education as an asset, blurring the boundaries between social capital and assets (Young 2012). Assets matter because local definitions of what it means to be rich or poor hinge on the bundles of assets to which families have access, and their effective use (see the descriptions in Table 5.1). They capture aspects of poverty and wealth that matter to rural communities. Many measures of poverty, such as poverty lines, which are derived from measures of weekly expenditure, and debates about poverty dynamics around those lines, overlook assets. They may miss important aspects in rural life for that reason. We also argue, however, that measuring change in assets is hard, and we explore the reasons for that in this chapter. The central dilemma our project faces is that assets are not owned by individuals and so have to be explored in larger social units. These units are, however, unstable and this poses a challenge for longitudinal work.

Our contribution to the collection therefore is twofold. First, we shed light on the nature and constitution of economic change in Tanzania over the last few decades, and the methods and concepts that need to be employed in order to understand them. We add to the existing methods that can be used by those interested in studying rural differentiation and class formation. Second, we provide a focus on some of the smaller-scale village-level dynamics as a complement to the larger national-scale concerns of some of the other contributions. Taken together these contributions suggest new possible ways of thinking about class dynamics in rural locations.

We first introduce the study, its origins and potential contributions to debates about poverty dynamics and economic growth. Second, we describe the locations and original studies we are revisiting. Finally, we examine some of the methodological difficulties.

The Economy, the Rural Poor and their Assets in Tanzania

The origins of this project lie in one of those moments of field research that jump out at you because they are so surprising. Dan Brockington was undertaking sabbatical research on the slopes of Mt Hanang in Manyara region in 2012–13. There he read Vesa-Matti Loiske's PhD thesis 'The Village that Vanished', which was written in the early 1990s and described the village of Gitting, also on the slopes of Hanang and just a short bike ride away from his own work. Reading Loiske's thesis twenty years after its research had been undertaken was astonishing. Loiske had undertaken a participatory wealth ranking of the village and, in his thesis, described levels of poverty and destitution which were just unrecognizable. Nearly 60 per cent of Gitting was described as poor or destitute according to local categories (Table 5.1). Meanwhile Brockington's own survey conducted just twenty years later in Gitting's neighbour, Meascron, found low levels of destitution and relatively slight incidences of poverty. People were poor in all sorts of ways, but they were not nearly as poor as Loiske had found. What could possibly explain the difference?

Loiske's original wealth profile of Gitting was robust. He had used a participatory wealth ranking obtained from a large number of

Table 5.1 Wealth Stratification Systems for Tanzania

Wealth Group Characteristics in Gitting	*Distribution in early 1990s (%)*	*Distribution in 2013 (%)*
Immensely Rich Knows no barriers, has cars, lorries etc.	1	<1
Very Rich Many cattle and much land; owns a tractor but not a lorry. Has businesses and land in towns	1	1
Rich Employs many *vibarua*; has many cattle. Has businesses	3	2
Above Average farmer Some cattle; farms their own land and uses *vibarua* work occasionally	17	59
Average farmer A few cattle, farms their own land without using *vibarua* work	19	26
Poor Rents land out to others; depends on casual *vibarua* work for daily needs; few if any livestock	27	9
Extremely poor Unable to get work easily; hard to rent their land out to others; suffering from alcoholism and/or illness	32	2

Note: Reference to *vibarua* work refers to casual labour

observers (18) separately and then amalgamated the findings. These rankings were then backed up with interviews in people's homes. One possible explanation for the change over time was that the poorer households, which had lived in this area and in Gitting in particular, had left. We suspected at first that they had been forced to leave and head for urban areas. Another possibility, which we thought unlikely at the time, was that people had got richer. The poverty Loiske had found in the early 1990s may have ceased because the rural economy had flourished.

At the time of Brockington's sabbatical Loiske was, fortunately, also visiting Tanzania on study tours with his students, and he and Brockington were able to correspond and meet in the nearby town of Babati. Loiske provided a list of the original families he visited, and during the rest of his sabbatical Brockington went back to Gitting and revisited as many families as he could, reaching 77 of 84 families that were identified.

That work (which we have written up elsewhere) piloted the present project, showing that in the first instance such a study was possible

(Brockington et al. 2016). The levels of attrition were low. Many families were still present, they remembered the earlier research and they were able to talk about the changes their families had experienced in the intervening years. This provided the basis for the research project whose achievements thus far we detail below. It proved to be an accurate predictor of how relatively straightforward it can be to undertake these longitudinal studies.

But the success of the method also showed, to our considerable surprise, that many families were much wealthier than before. This was the case both for the sample that Loiske had visited and for the village as a whole. We explore the precise patterns and possible reasons for this elsewhere. Suffice to say that our first hypothesis, that the poor had left the village, was comprehensively refuted. The challenge we faced was how to explain why, how and in what ways people had become richer as well as how the meaning of wealth had changed over time (cf. Mushongah & Scoones 2012).

The reasons appear to be a mixture of the structural and personal. The structural reasons are that, independent of any transport improvements, there have been good returns to cash crops that allow people to prosper from relatively small farms in ways they could not before. This reflected changing class relations at the village level. Previously larger wealthier farmers, who controlled the few tractors, were able to rent land on excessively favourable terms. Now there are more tractors, as well as ox-ploughs, and the power of the wealthy families has diminished. The personal reasons reflect a decline in levels of alcoholism, due to both individual resolve, and to children (sometimes wives and children) taking control of the family farm and preventing alcoholic fathers and husbands renting the land out to feed their habit. There were also cases of declining wealth as richer families aged and invested in their children's education and careers.

But underpinning this increase in prosperity is a deeper point. Wealth, as measured in ways that mattered to the rural poor, was about assets, about relatively large, temporally 'lumpy', investments in land, houses, livestock and technology. It was about the education of children and dependants. It was not well measured by indices of expenditure and consumption as is traditionally the case. If people were poor it was because they could not work their land, or did not have access to livestock and businesses. If they were rich it was reflected in their houses, their vehicles, their large farms.

In this respect these findings are consistent both with more recent wealth rankings in Tanzania as well as larger comparative work on how the poor experience poverty (Higgins & da Corta 2013). For example, as Meizen-Dick and colleagues report, the 'Voices of the Poor' study undertaken by the World Bank found that assets were particularly important for the poor's own understanding of their poverty (Meizen-Dick et al. 2011). Carter and Barrett show that assets are an important aspect of poverty dynamics (Carter & Barrett 2006). Similarly Carter and Lybbert found that families' behaviour with respect to their assets and cash varies according to their wealth, particularly during times of hardship (Carter & Lybbert 2012). They observed that rich families will dispose of assets in order to smooth changes in consumption during droughts in West Africa, whereas the poor will conserve assets and reduce consumption. This also matches Alex de Waal's findings in his research on famine in Sudan (De Waal 1989). The bad famines, the 'famines that kill', were those that forced families to dispose of their assets, which otherwise they suffered to conserve.

Assets, then, matter to the rural poor. Poorer families will restrict consumption in order to build up assets to such a point that they have enough to form a barrier against hard times. We have repeatedly heard from the families we talked to across our resurveys about how they are wealthier now, as measured by local indicators that are replete with assets. But these informants also told us that getting that wealth meant that they had to scrimp, save and suffer. They were more secure as a result, but getting that secure had not been a pleasant or an easy process.[1]

The importance of assets in the definitions of rural poverty in Tanzania that we were discovering also suggested a contribution to larger academic debates about the nature and consequences of economic growth. One debate pitted, roughly speaking, the policy 'right' and the academic 'left' and concerned the nature and benefits of economic growth in the country. The other, which flew in the face of both right and left, argued that both arguments were stymied by the poor quality of the development data being used.

With respect to the first debate, a number of observers celebrated the growth of Tanzania's economy and noted that its rising GDP signified the success of a number of policy measures recommended by the World Bank, IMF and other external bodies. This is thought to be a good thing, although those heralding these changes also note that the economic growth did not seem to touch the agricultural sector (Radelet 2010; Chuhan-Pole & Angwafo 2011).

On the other hand, a series of critics claim that the celebrated levels of economic growth were not having any impact on rural poverty (Mashindano et al. 2013). The common complaint, based on household budget surveys for 2001 and 2007, is that while the economy is growing, rural poverty is not decreasing. Indeed in absolute terms there are over 1 million more poor people in Tanzania (Mueller 2011). Since then, new data on poverty lines from household budget surveys, using new

---

[1] Parenthetically, it is interesting what a nonsense this makes of earlier debates about class formation and accumulation in rural Africa. Earlier dichotomies of subsistence peasants and capitalist farmers attributed to the latter a compulsion to accumulate, but no such pressures on the former (Mueller 2011: 25). This ignores the importance of accumulating assets as a means of coping with risk and insuring against disease and disaster.

methods, have found that poverty does show a decrease (World Bank 2015a). These recent data suggest that national wealth does seem to be better shared, if principally in the urban areas. But the point remains that, for many years, the benefits of growth in GDP were not enjoyed by many poor people, particularly the rural poor. Wealth still needs to be shared more effectively in rural areas.

Our contribution to this debate concerns the sort of poverty that these protagonists are disputing. For this issue hinges on poverty lines that are calculated from household budget survey data that do not measure investment in assets (URT 2007b: 47). Poverty data are based on diaries of expenditure on everyday needs. They are methodologically unsuited to capturing the rare events of asset acquisition (or loss). Indeed, some asset investments are explicitly and deliberately excluded from household budget surveys. They miss therefore the forms of expenditure that the poor scrimp and save in order to afford. If rural families are getting richer in terms of assets, then one would expect that change to be missed by changes in poverty lines. Measures based on daily consumption would not count the things that the poor are prioritizing.

A statement from a participant at a recent focus group makes this point really well. The speaker observed that investment in assets is an important part of rural life, and indeed stems from the nature of rural incomes, which come in sudden bursts after harvests.[2]

> We get money seasonally. This means for all of us here that there are those who have earned three million shillings, or two million shillings, but if right now you were to ask one of us here to lend you a small amount of money he would tell you I haven't even a cent [laughter]. Some people when they get money after the harvest they buy a TV, or solar panels, or all manner of things and they have a good life. But at this time, although he's got his television, if he's struck by some problem and needs 50,000 shillings he'll have to wait 5 months. So we say although our soil is good, it is not a resource for all days of the year. In July if you ask someone for 500,000 shillings they will give it to you, or if you want to borrow a million shillings she will give it, but go to them in November and ask to borrow 200,000 to deal with a problem and they will tell you I have nothing, I have bought a TV, I've bought a plot, I've bought bricks.[3]

The static poverty lines in rural Tanzania that the critics just cited have been lambasting could be concealing investment in assets by the rural poor.

Lest we are misinterpreted, we are not arguing that static poverty lines are a sign of increasing wealth. We are simply arguing that measures such as poverty lines will be insensitive to some growth in asset

[2] The speaker was from south-east Tanzania, in Lindi Region, in an area which has benefited from the recent boom in sesame seed prices.
[3] Kilwa Focus Group, 22 February 2017.

wealth. Just as poverty is multi-dimensional, so too are the dynamics of increasing prosperity. A variety of measures will be needed to capture these dynamics over and above those of poverty lines.

A consequence of this fact is that becoming richer by local measures of wealth will not necessarily result in improved self-assessments. Improvements in prosperity that are only visible in asset bundles, and not in daily measures of consumption, are only a limited gain. Improvements in well-being and prosperity, as measured in assets, will have limited relevance to all sorts of other aspects and dimensions of poverty. This would explain why many families in our surveys who had, on paper, improved their well-being, did not feel that they were better off. Their everyday levels of consumption show little change.

With respect to the second debate, our contribution will be to provide some relatively robust data about rural change. Morten Jerven has argued, in *Poor Numbers*, that the GDP data used to analyze change in numerous African economies, including Tanzania's, are simply too poorly constructed to be worth interpreting (Jerven 2013a). Statistical offices have been starved of funds and support and are poorly equipped to measure difficult things like the informal economy, which dominates life in Tanzania.

The corollary of this argument is that we cannot be sure that growth in the agricultural sector has been as bad as has been reported, simply because it will have been measured poorly. This would make the disagreement between the policy right and the academic left that we have just examined somewhat irrelevant – for there would be little empirical basis for any agreement or disagreement. The value of these restudies is that it provides a better evidential base by which to examine change in rural areas.

The need for better data is especially clear in Tanzania because the normal means of tracking poverty dynamics, which are best done through panel surveys, are almost entirely lacking in the country. They are notably lacking for the period of the late 1980s and early 1990s. For this period we only have three studies. There is the Kagera Health and Demographic Study (hereafter the Kagera study), which spans 1994 and 2004 (De Weerdt 2010; Beegle et al. 2011); the AFRINT study, which covers ten villages from 2002 to 2016 (Djurfeldt et al. 2011); and the Living Standards Measurement Survey (LSMS) data from 2008 to the present, a sample of 3,000 families.[4] Panel data are thin.

We need therefore more longitudinal studies, like that we had undertaken in Gitting, in order to explore some of the possibilities that our pilot study had suggested. The purpose of the '*Mabadaliko*' project that

[4] http://econ.worldbank.org/WBSITE/EXTERNAL/EXTDEC/
EXTRESEARCH/EXTLSMS/0,,contentMDK:
23635561~pagePK:64168445~piPK:64168309~theSitePK:3358997,00.html, accessed 21 December 2016.

we launched in 2015 was to repeat the work that we had undertaken in Gitting in as many villages as possible around the country.[5] This replicated a method that had been undertaken in India and Indonesia, with longitudinal work undertaken by researchers in different villages compared over time (Epstein et al. 1998; Rigg and Vandergeest 2012; Himanshu et al. 2016). It has not, to our knowledge, been attempted in Tanzania on this scale. To do so, however, we had to identify other villages surveyed at the right period whose changes would shed light on the period in question. We also had to address a number of method-ological issues that arise when exploring change as measured through assets. The following sections outline how these were tackled.

Compiling Surveys to Revisit

The first challenge we faced was to build up a suitable list of sites that could be revisited. We had two essential criteria: the researcher had to have visited their study sites between 1985 and 2005, and they had to have a list of the families that they had interviewed in their first survey. The lower limit was put at 1985 because after that problems of recall and domestic unit integrity (on which more below) make the method problematic; 2005 was the upper limit because after that there are panel data in the form of the LSMS, which make the value of these longitudinal reconstructions questionable. The list of family names is compulsory because our method hinges upon revisiting the actual families visited in the original survey in order that we can see how asset ownership changes over time.

   We were able to construct a list of 16 different researchers who have worked in 13 regions, 26 districts and in over 70 villages (see Map 5.1, Tables 5.2 and 5.3). This is fewer than we expected to find. We had thought that there would be many more researchers and that we would be able to compile a suitable list and sample the villages and choose only the best original studies to revisit. This has not been the case. There was no comprehensive list of researchers upon which to draw. COSTECH records (which provide research permission to overseas researchers) and the East Africana library (holding theses written by Tanzanians) proved less forthcoming than we had hoped. We relied on our own networks and connections and our own readings to identify the surveys we used. Fortunately, the network of researchers in Tanzania is strong, and it was possible to find out about possible studies using snowballing and word of mouth enquiries. The list of researchers, and the publication details of their original surveys, are presented in Table 5.2.

---

[5] http://livelihoodchangeta.wixsite.com/tanzania/project-summary, accessed 21 December 2016.

Table 5.2 Study Sites Sorted by Region and District

Region	District	Number of Villages	Researcher
Arusha	Meru	8	Larson
	Ngorongoro	9	McCabe
Dodoma	Chemba	2	Ostberg
Iringa	Iringa Rural	2	Birch-Thomsen, Anderson-Djurfeldt
	Kilolo	4	Birch-Thomsen, Anderson-Djurfeldt
	Mufindi	3	Daley, Anderson-Djurfeldt
Katavi	Mpimbwe	1	Borgerhoff-Mulder
Kilimanjaro	Same	1	Brockington
	Moshi	2	Mdee
Manyara	Hanang	2	Loiske
	Mbulu	1	Snyder
Mbeya	Mbeya Rural	6	Sokoni
Morogoro	Kilombero	5	Anderson-Djurfeldt
	Kilosa	2	Ellis and Mdoe
	Morogoro Rural	3	Ellis and Mdoe
	Mvomero	6	Ellis and Mdoe, Ponte
Njombe	Makete	1	Hansen
	Njombe Rural	1	Hansen
	Njombe	1	Hansen
Rukwa	Kalambo	2	Birch-Thomsen
	Sumbawanga Rural	2	Brockington
Ruvuma	Madaba	1	Ponte
	Namtumbo	1	Ponte
	Songea Rural	1	Ponte
Shinyanga	Kishapu	1	Kingma
Tanga	Lushoto	1	Brockington

Table 5.3 Surveys Sorted by Main Contact

Researchers	Region	District	Number of Villages	Date of Survey(s)	Sources
Agnes Anderson-Djurfeldt	Iringa	Iringa Rural	1	2002, 2008, 2016	(Djurfeldt et al. 2011)
		Kilolo	2		
		Mufindi	2		
	Morogoro	Kilombero	5		
Anna Mdee	Kilimanjaro	Moshi	2	1996, 2005	(Cleaver & Toner 2006)
Torben Birch-Thomsen	Iringa	Iringa Rural	1	1997	(Birch-Thomsen et al. 2001)
		Kilolo	1		
	Rukwa	Kalambo	2	1993, 2010	(Birch-Thomsen & Fog 1996, Grogan et al. 2013)
Monique Borgerhoff-Mulder	Katavi	Mpimbwe	1	1995–2010	(Borgerhoff-Mulder 2009, Borgerhoff-Mulder & Beheim 2011)
Dan Brockington	Kilimanjaro	Same	1	1995–6	(Brockington 2002)
	Tanga	Lushoto	1		
	Rukwa	Sumbawanga Rural	2	1999–2000	(Brockington 2001, Brockington 2008)
Elizabeth Daley	Iringa	Mufindi	1	1999–2000	(Daley 2004)
Frank Ellis & Ntengua Mdoe	Morogoro	Kilosa	2	2001	(Ellis & Mdoe 2003)
		Morogoro Rural	3		
		Mvomero	3		
	Iringa	Kilolo	1		
Esbern Hansen	Njombe	Makete	1	1983–1985	
		Njombe	1	1983–1985	
		Njombe Rural	1	1983–1985	
Koos Kingma	Shinyanga	Kishapu	1	1989, 1999, 2010	
Vesa-Matti Loiske	Manyara	Hanang	2	1991–4	(Loiske 1995)
Terrence McCabe	Arusha	Ngorongoro	9		
Willie Ostberg	Dodoma	Chemba	2	1991–3	(Ostberg 1995, Östberg & Slegers 2010)

Researchers	Region	District	Number of Villages	Date of Survey(s)	Sources
	Morogoro	Mvomero	3		
Stefano Ponte		Madaba	1	1995–6	(Ponte 2002)
	Ruvuma	Namtumbo	1		
		Songea Rural	1		
Rolf Larsson	Arusha	Meru	8	1994/8	(Larsson 2001)
Katherine Snyder	Manyara	Mbulu	1	1989–94	(Snyder 2005)
Cosmas Sokoni	Mbeya	Mbeya Rural	6	1998	(Sokoni 2001)

We do not think that we have identified all possible surveys. And we have certainly not identified a nationally representative sample. Geographically the central eastern regions of Morogoro and Iringa are over-represented. Indeed, it is depressing to see so many researchers basically following the tarred roads south to Mbeya and north to Arusha. Just four of the surveys are in remoter locations: Snyder in Mbulu; Loiske in Gitting; Brockington and Borgerhoff-Mulder, each in Rukwa. Others were in remoter locations (Ponte in Songea, Hansen in Njombe), which are now more accessible. Only one is from the west of the country (Kingma). None are available in the far west or south-east. To some extent this problem is offset by the fact that the Kagera survey, which contains thousands of families, represents the north-west rather well. But the point remains that there are decades of researcher bias visible in the distribution of villages we are considering revisits to. The eastern half, and especially the south-eastern half, of the country is well represented. The west is less so.

Another disappointing aspect is that too few of the researchers who are listed here are Tanzanians. It seems that here we were confronting different cultures of research practice that made recovering the records we required to undertake the surveys unusually problematic. Western-based researchers rarely throw away their PhD or post-doc data. They are kept in boxes and attics awaiting possible reuse. The collector's ethos and spirit is rather deeply engrained. Tanzanian researchers were more likely to have suffered lost data, sometimes inadvertently, on other occasions because it did not seem particularly important to keep it at the time. There was at least one heart-breaking story of questionnaires disposed of when they had been safely stored (because the room they were stored in was reallocated to another use) or of data lost with stolen computers and failed back-ups.

We have, however, identified enough villages to make the study worthwhile. Moreover behind the bald statistics of the numbers are

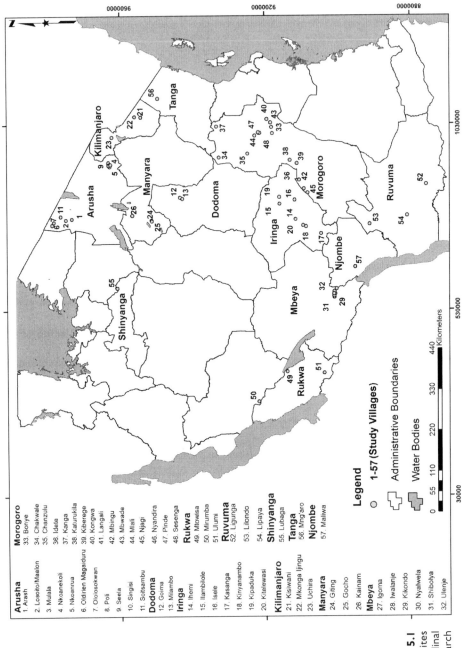

Legend

○ 1-57 (Study Villages)

☐ Administrative Boundaries

▨ Water Bodies

0	55	110	220	330	440
Kilometers

Map 5.1
Potential Study Sites
for Longitudinal
Research

Arusha
1. Arash
2. Losoito/Maalon
3. Mulala
4. Nkoanekoli
5. Nkoannua
6. Oldireri Magaiduru
7. Ololosokwan
8. Poli
9. Seela
10. Singisi
11. Soitsambu

Dodoma
12. Goima
13. Milambo

Iringa
14. Ihemi
15. Ilambilole
16. Isele
17. Kasanga
18. Kinyanambo
19. Kipaduka
20. Kitelewasi

Kilimanjaro
21. Kisiwani
22. Mkonga Ijingu
23. Uchira

Manyara
24. Giting
25. Gocho
26. Kainam

Mbeya
27. Igoma
28. Iwalanje
29. Kikondo
30. Nyalweia
31. Shibolya
32. Ulenje

Morogoro
33. Bonye
34. Chakwale
35. Chanzulu
36. Idete
37. Kanga
38. Katurukila
39. Kiberege
40. Kongwa
41. Langali
42. Mbingu
43. Mbwade
44. Mlali
45. Njagi

Rukwa
46. Nyandira
47. Pinde
48. Sesenga

Rukwa
49. Mtowisa
50. Mirumba
51. Ulumi

Ruvuma
52. Ligunga

Shinyanga
53. Lilondo
54. Lipaya
55. Lubaga

Tanga
56. Mng'aro

Njombe
57. Maliwa

some useful gems. We are fortunate in that in one case, two of the researchers have, coincidentally, worked in the same villages. Both Ponte's work and that of Ellis and Mdoe took them to Mlali, in Mvomero District in Morogoro. This allows us to make stronger comparisons over time because we have two separate surveys from three different time periods in each village.

There are also a number of remarkable studies and surveys the details of which need to be celebrated. Monique Borgerhoff-Mulder had visited her community in Pimbwe every two years since 1995 and rigorously surveyed the entire community each time. The quality of those data will provide a sounding board for the others. Similarly Agnes Anderson-Djurfeldt's work (also known as the AFRINT project aforementioned) already takes the form of a panel data-set that has been surveyed three times (2002, 2008 and 2016). Our contribution here is merely to add some qualitative work and oral history. Again the depth of quantitative data available here will make these data a useful sounding board against which to test other findings.

But the single visit studies are remarkable too. Hansen's resurvey entails revisiting families with whom he worked in the mid-1980s when there were very high levels of poverty and deprivation. He had already begun revisiting these families before we contacted him. Our project merely merged his work with a larger collection. Katherine Snyder's survey, conducted in 1994, came at the end of five years of research work when she had already built up an excellent understanding of local relations and life in Mbulu. Brockington's work in Rukwa entailed a survey of over 400 households from one village, Mtowisa B (and nearly as many from its immediate neighbour, Mtowisa A). Koos Kingma joins the project having visited the same families and women in Shinyanga in the late 1980s, the late 1990s and finally the late 2000s. Anna Mdee is reporting from families in a village that she has been visiting since the mid-1990s, as researcher and also an in-law.

Finally, there is the case of Rolf Larsson's survey from Meru, whose work is being followed up posthumously by Christine Noe. This story is just hard to tell and is best expressed in the words of Christine's blog:

> The research reported here is unusual for a couple of reasons. First, the original work was undertaken by the late Rolf Larson in the mid-1990s. I am, in some ways, following in his footsteps, and how I have come to do so is a moving and difficult story. Rolf was killed in a road accident in Tanzania in 2004, on his way to revisit Meru and the sites of his original research. He had kept his data in meticulous order, however, and a chance encounter with his former colleagues has meant that I have been able to access it and use it. I am [we are] very grateful to Rolf and Göran Djurfeldt for making this possible.

The second is that, in other ways, Rolf was walking where I had trod when he did his research. Unlike most researchers in this livelihood change project, the work in Meru is a return to my homeland, the place I was born and grew up. I studied at Makumira primary and secondary school, in Poli-Ndatu village where I was born, for thirteen years. Poli-Ndatu is among the nine villages that Rolf Larson studied in 1994/1998. Part of my excitement with this project is that I am so well placed to contribute to the interpretation of change in Meru due to my personal experience, the local network, language fluency and connection to the landscape.[6]

Larson's work involved a survey of over 600 families. His notes were kept in meticulous order because he intended to revisit the site. There is no better person to do so than Christine Noe. While her schooling (at the time of Larson's first survey) was in one of the villages where he worked, her home village was not included. This means that, when she returns, she is not visiting neighbours (who might resent the prying of someone they see not as a researcher but a neighbour) but that she, and her family, are known in the area.

The Challenge of Studying Change through Domestic Units

Studying changes in rural prosperity through assets makes sense because assets matter to the poor's own definitions of poverty. But that does not make them necessarily easy to monitor. They are important, but they are not easily observed because of that importance.

First, there is the problem of the unit of analysis. Assets are rarely owned by individuals. They may, nominally, be disposed of by individual family heads (usually men in Tanzanian contexts). But it is more accurate to see ownership of these assets as vested in those individuals. The assets are held on behalf of other family members, of wives and children. Disposal of them requires negotiation. This does not mean that power over them is shared equally. That is patently not true. In most Tanzanian societies men enjoy considerably more freedoms in this respect than their wives, sisters, mothers and daughters. But it is also misleading to believe that family heads enjoy complete freedom to dispose of assets as they wish. It is precisely when men sell livestock or land, or children do not receive the support they require for their education, that conflict can arise. The norms and expectations of the proper use and treatment of collectively owned assets become disputed.

[6] http://livelihoodchangeta.wixsite.com/tanzania/single-post/2016/06/20/ Coffee-BreakPotentials-and-Pitfalls-for-Meru-Farmers-Prosperity, accessed 15 December 2016.

We can illustrate with one example from pastoral households. In the polygamous Maa-speaking communities where Brockington conducted his PhD fieldwork the modus operandi was for households (Maa: *enkang*) to sell cattle in order to buy grain and then eat that staple with milk. Men would sell cattle to meet these and other material needs. However, although men owned the cattle, their herd was divided into stock they alone controlled, and stock that had been allotted to their wives' households (Maa: *aji*), and by their wives, to their children. Herds are allotted to spouses on marriage, and according to luck and circumstances can prosper, or fail completely. But, and this is key, the fortunes of one wife's herd were completely different from those of another wife. It was quite possible, and indeed happened to families in this site, for one wife, and her children, to have a thriving herd, while her co-wife, and her children, had lost their animals completely. When it came to selling stock to meet the *enkang*'s needs the normal practice was for each wife to take it in turns to provide an animal for sale. But which animal (whose) was to be chosen? And, if an *aji* had no stock, how could it or others make up for the deficiency? These questions were the subject of intense negotiations that were just part of the fabric of daily life in these societies (Brockington 2001).

Assets, therefore, have to be explored through the lens of the family, domestic unit or household (and we will use the term 'domestic unit' from here on). But there are a number of obvious problems with this state of affairs. In the first instance, a domestic unit does not stay stable over time. It will grow, change and vary according to the lifecycle of its members (Goody 1958; Stenning 1958). Domestic units can be expected to accrue assets in the earlier stages of their existence as they seek to provide for children and as their members are strong and vigorous. Likewise they will lose them as they age. This has been thoroughly described in earlier anthropological accounts of the process.

This means that, for this method to work, we need to compare domestic units that are at similar stages of their lifecycle. We cannot compare domestic units composed of middle aged adults now with domestic units in the 1990s whose members were old and declining (or vice versa). If we did we might conclude that fortunes had improved (or declined if older families are being compared to younger ones), when in fact we are simply comparing the incommensurable.

One of the limitations of this research is that the network that we have compiled does not always have sample sizes that are large enough to make enough valid comparisons. For example, in most of the original surveys around 30 domestic units were sampled in a village in the mid-1990s. When we return for the resurvey loss due to attrition means that some 25 are available for interview. It is rare that within these 25 we will have enough domestic units of different age categories to make statistically representative comparisons within one village. We have instead to amalgamate samples across villages.

However, in one of the study sites, Mtowisa in Rukwa, we do have a large initial sample. This serves to illustrate the importance of controlling for age of the domestic unit. At Mtowisa, as we describe elsewhere, there has been a significant improvement in the asset base of many families. Moreover we are more than normally confident that the difference is real because the initial 'sample' of families in a survey taken in 2000 was over 400. This is large enough to make meaningful comparisons by age of the family head possible. In the 2000 survey the youngest family head surveyed was around 19, which means that, when we revisited these households in 2016, none of the resurveyed family heads were younger than 35. The comparisons we make are therefore restricted to family heads who were over 35 in *both* surveys. The reasons for this are that younger families tend to be smaller, farm less and own fewer assets (as shown in Table 5.4). If the younger families of 2000 were included in comparisons with the (older) families of the 2016 survey they would distort the results. Their inclusion would have the effect of lowering apparent average asset ownership in 2000 and making the improvement in 2016 more marked. There has been an improvement, but we risk exaggerating it if we do not control for the age of the family.

A second aspect of change and instability is that the membership of domestic units may not be sufficiently constant to be used to explore long-term change. They change and morph over time such that it no longer makes sense to think of longitudinal comparisons because the thing being compared, the family, is so completely different. One universal aspect of this dynamic is the fact that, as children grow up, marry and leave the family, tracking the fortunes of domestic units requires tracking the fortunes of not just the original family, but also the others that have partitioned from them. We call these 'secondary' domestic units in this survey. They are one of the single most significant methodological challenges this project faces.

Table 5.4 Comparison of Selected Domestic Unit Attributes by Age of Family Head in Mtowisa in 2000

Assets and Attributes	Under 35	Over 35
Plough	11%	17%
Shoats	35%	20%
Family size (ae)	2.7	4.4
Land farmed (acres)	2.4	2.6
Number of families	185	215

The main difficulty is finding and tracking these secondary units. In Gitting we found that such units were often invisible in the village registers. Children of living parents might often live in their own houses on their parents' compounds, or on land excised from the family farm. They were not counted, for the purpose of the village registry, as constituting their own family. This meant that, when conducting the village wealth profiles, the profiles could appear excessively wealthy because the poorer, younger, newly formed families were excluded. On the other hand, sometimes families have left the area and are simply not easily contactable. We might be able to phone them up, but establishing who we are, why we are phoning them and how prosperous they are in terms of assets is not easy.

In other social circumstances there is so much change in domestic unit composition that the very notion of comparing change over time through the lens of a domestic unit becomes untenable. Mathew Lockwood's work in the Rufiji delta in the mid-1980s offers a rather telling cautionary tale in this respect. He described levels of instability in domestic unit composition that would have made comparisons across two years impossible, let alone 15 or 20 years:

> The following is the history of the household in which I lived between December 1985 and September 1986. Before I moved in, the household consisted of a man in his forties, A, his wife, son from a previous marriage, aged about 15, and a daughter aged about 5. In December his wife left him and went to live with relatives in Zanzibar. The daughter went to stay with her grandmother in the village. At this point I moved in. January: a cousin of A's arrives, with her teenage daughter. They start preparing to farm rice in the valley. February: A's son argues with his father and leaves for relatives in Mkongo. A's daughter comes back to the house. April: The visiting cousin moves to a *dungu* (small hut in the fields used when cultivation work is heavy) in the rice fields. Her daughter, together with A's daughter, lives half there and half in the village. A's son returns for a short time and then leaves again. Late May/June: A's cousin and her daughter harvest rice and return to the village. They then go off to a village on the road to Dar es Salaam to visit her husband. Throughout this period, A would go to Dar es Salaam for a few days every month, where he acted as a rent collector for someone. The cousin's husband would also come at weekends from the other village, where he was a teacher. (Lockwood 1998: 143 fn 1)

The final problem with using domestic units, and aggregations of experience, to monitor long term change is that they can conceal precisely the dynamics that are interesting and important to observe when exploring long-term change. Terms like 'household', 'family' or 'domestic unit' aggregate and obscure precisely the experiences and relationships whose dynamics and contestations are important to observe. The work of Goody and Guyer emphasizes that gender and generational dynamics risk being obscured by a focus on domestic units (Goody 1958; Guyer 1981).

Similarly, the need for flexibility and variety in the conceptualization of the domestic unit is well established. Units that come together for the purposes of consumption may be different from those that exist for (again diverse) production tasks. The better-designed surveys now allow for people to be members of several domestic units (Randall et al. 2011). Randall and Coast suggest that a basic typology of domestic units should begin by distinguishing between 'open' and 'closed' units, according to the extent of their focus on particular family units, or broader relations (Randall & Coast 2015). The degree of openness (closedness) can be a deliberate element of livelihood strategies and ways of coping with poverty, or seeking prosperity (and will vary according to external environmental criteria). Or they could be more accidental (but equally important for livelihood outcomes and well-being).

The challenge for a study built on looking at asset change through the lens of the domestic unit is clear. If we merely take change to the domestic unit as a whole we risk misunderstanding the very nature of the processes of production that have created these changing asset bases. Exploring how change is gendered within domestic units, how the intergenerational dynamics vary within the same, is a fundamental aspect of the research process.

We tackle these aspects through the qualitative oral histories that we conduct, through focus group work (in which we separate men and women) and through participant observation. We examine how changed cropping practices and labouring practices have different implications for men and women, the youth and the elderly. One of the techniques is to take histories of assets themselves to understand how they were acquired, and how they were lost. Another is to look at the disputes that arise over the control of new revenue streams that result from changing assets and the changing importance of different assets.

For example, in Gitting, one of the reasons why people have become wealthier is because children and wives have been able to wrest control over family farms away from alcohol dependent men. It was possible for men who controlled farms to rent the land out yearly to wealthy farmers. Sale was difficult, as it required high levels of family agreement, but rental was less problematic, and the income from renting land out was sufficient to keep an alcoholic supplied (supplemented with occasional daily labour). This has meant that the struggle to win control over the family farm and prevent fathers or brothers (and sometimes mothers) from renting it to feed a drink habit frequently featured in our research. Domestic unit trajectories only become intelligible in the context of intra-domestic unit dynamics.

Conversely, in Meru, where society is highly patriarchal, but also highly Christian, alcohol dependency is less apparent. However. there are clear contests between men and women over the control of different cash crops, particularly as the importance of coffee has declined and the importance of bananas has increased. Coffee was (and is) a man's crop; bananas were women's. But the demise of coffee has seen cash-strapped men take an increasing interest in women's bananas. As we have documented elsewhere (Howland & Noe, forthcoming), women contest these moves, with varying success. Indeed in some respect the prosperity of the domestic unit can hinge on the extent to which men are prepared to let women earn an income from their banana sales. The point, however, is that once again the dynamics within domestic units is vital to understanding the fate of the domestic unit.

Conclusion

We believe that surveys of assets, and local measures of wealth, can provide new insights into changing fortunes of rural communities. Researchers of different persuasions have thus far concentrated on measures of wealth and poverty which allow international comparison (poverty lines based on consumption), but which are not necessarily representative of the changes that matter to many rural people in Tanzania. Understanding changing assets bundles, and the changing domestic units that provide access to those bundles, will help us to understand important aspects of social and economic life in rural Tanzanian villages.

It is worth adding, this is enjoyable work. Undertaking this research has, thus far, been one of the most enjoyable and pleasant experiences in our research careers. It is always enjoyable to ask senior researchers if they want to return to the field sites where they did their PhDs, and to see their faces light up. A nascent, but enthusiastic network is emerging from this project.

However, we must also draw attention to the limitations of this approach. The methodological challenges are significant. Our work, as with all longitudinal studies, is a survey of the survivors who have been able to remain. This will not, of necessity, produce a sample that is biased to the wealthy (it might be the case that only the poor remain in villages). However, it is difficult using our methods to pick up new immigrant families, or newly formed families. As with any longitudinal work, or indeed any new data source, we have to be attentive to the inevitable blind spots the data create. We are enthusiastic about this study because it can usefully complement other work. We are sanguine about its prospects of being used on its own, without triangulation from other sources.

If used appropriately, with the right caveats and in conjunction with other sources, the method can be insightful. It can tell us more about rural differentiation. If, as Greco contends (2015: 226), the idea of a homogenous Tanzania rural population is still far too prevalent, then understanding how rural communities differ in terms of the asset bundles they command will be important. More than that, given that many researchers already understand the importance of differentiated rural communities, their depictions of that difference will be richer. Descriptions of class difference, for example, tend to concentrate on land holdings and labouring work as the principal marker of difference (see, for example, Mueller 2011). Both matter a great deal. But our work suggests that there are other markers of class, other assets that constitute means of production around which differentiation can occur. As Oya has shown elsewhere (Oya 2007), the stories of individual capitalists' trajectories of accumulation depend upon mobilizing all sorts of assets and capitals in livelihood strategies.

Gitting is not just a story about there being new forms of prosperity (and more of it generally), in rural Tanzania than previously recognized. It is also a story of dynamics, of wealthy farmers being dominant in the 1990s, but losing some of their control over the means of production as poorer families gained access to ploughs, or stopped their land from being rented out. Following this story of asset change helps us to understand how assets are transferred across generations to new configurations of the domestic unit. This is essential to understanding the reproduction of advantage and disadvantage.

Another way of putting this point is that this sort of asset accumulation, and disinvestment, is a useful means of understanding class dynamics in rural areas. Assets provide the basis for local understandings of what wealth, privilege and poverty look like. They also, by definition, constitute some of the means of production. Assets differentiate rural classes in the eyes of those rural classes. Yet currently attention to rural assets is somewhat restricted, focusing primarily on land, rather than other aspects. Understanding the dynamics of rural differentiation under intensifying capitalism – the agrarian question, if you will – requires a better understanding of assets.

If these data are able to make that contribution, then it would be a pleasing endorsement of this sort of research. Getting better data on what economic growth is doing to rural people is important, particularly if what is being measured does not accord well with forms of prosperity that matter in rural areas. But the more important thing is not so much the bald levels of wealth of poverty, but how these changes feed into local forms and processes of differentiation and class and gender dynamics.

Acknowledgement

This research is supported by the ESRC and DfID through the Growth Research Programme (DEGRP; grant ref: ES/L012413/2), and that support is gratefully acknowledged.

6

Contract Farming in Tanzania: Experiences from Tobacco and Sunflower*

Joseph Kuzilwa, Bahati Ilembo, Daniel Mpeta and Andrew Coulson

Contract farming, where farmers sign contracts that commit them to growing specific crops or products and selling them to specific purchasers, is an important part of agriculture in developed countries. They are found in some situations in developing countries, when 'outgrowers' contract to supply an estate or company, which runs a processing operation such as a tea or sugar factory, or when exporters are committed to supply high-value crops for export, such as cut flowers or spices. Their relative importance is likely to continue to increase.

Farmers also sign contracts when they accept inputs on credit. The contracts specify that they will sell their crops to a cooperative or trading organization that has arranged credit, which will deduct the costs of the inputs supplied from the money paid to the farmers for their crops.

This chapter investigates some of the issues that have arisen when contract farming has been attempted in Tanzania. It draws on data from two research studies, which sampled farmers who were growing flue-cured tobacco, where contracts have been institutionalized for more than fifty years, and sunflower where contracts were introduced but did not survive as a significant component of the marketing system. From these studies and desk research, the chapter draws conclusions about what is needed to sustain and further develop contract farming in Tanzania.

Background

Eaton and Shepherd start their widely quoted briefing note by pointing out that contracts are not new and cover many situations. Thus any system of share-cropping, in which a landlord is entitled to a share of

* We gratefully acknowledge the Danish Fellowship Centre for supporting the research upon which this chapter is based, through the Tanzania–Denmark Pilot Research Programme.

the harvest, implies a contract. T. J. Byres shows that the Greeks had systems of share-cropping more than 2,500 years ago (Byres 1983; 3). Some of the most exploitative share-cropping was in the Southern states of the USA in the last half of the nineteenth century. More recently, in Africa, farmers, recruited in the 1950s to the Gezira irrigation scheme on the Nile in the Sudan, signed contracts that required them to grow cotton and sell it to the scheme. The World Bank-funded schemes to support farmers growing a number of crops in Tanzania in the 1970s and 1980s included credit supported by contracts. Contracts are also fundamental to agri-business, when processing companies contract with large farms, but also when large farms or marketing agents contract with smaller outgrowers (Watts 1994: 26–8; Eaton & Shepherd 2001: 1–2). Thus firms producing canned or frozen vegetables require farmers to sign contracts that commit them to delivering specific quantities of a product at specific times with very clear quality requirements, especially for size and colour. The prices may not be high but the farmers get a guaranteed market – they are trading risk for a reliable income.

Contracts between purchasers of crops and farmers are, at least superficially, unequal. A processor, or marketing agent, has the power. The farmers are comparatively weak and divided. The purchaser knows that, if it is not possible to agree a contract with one farmer, there will be others. Hence the theoretical case for farmers' cooperatives, or farmer groups, in which farmers work together to get the best deal for the group as a whole, or in some cases own processing facilities such as ginneries or mills. The practice may of course be different, as when cooperatives are corrupt or inefficient.

In the last 30 years or so, two revolutions have brought contract farming to the fore. The first is the fast food revolution, led by McDonald's and Kentucky Fried Chicken. They sell burgers and chicken, cooked and ready to eat, in industrial quantities. The second, even more fundamental, revolution comes from the supermarket chains, which have developed and promoted the concept of the 'ready meal' prepared in a factory and then frozen or chilled, requiring only heating at home in a microwave, electric or gas oven before serving. These changes raise many questions about a good diet, and have led to obesity as well as some loss of the skills of cooking. But their cheapness and simplicity are undeniable. The supermarkets also persuaded consumers that they can expect to purchase strawberries, apples or tomatoes, and other fruits and vegetables (and also cut flowers) at any time in the year, sourcing them from different parts of the world. Thus in the UK in 2014 the four largest supermarket chains sold over 60 per cent of the food and non-alcoholic drinks. When smaller supermarket chains and sales on the internet are added the figure rises to 87 per cent, leaving only 13 per cent sold through small shops and markets. Purchases by consumers of vegetables, fruits, flour and fresh meat from markets and small shops are all declining (DEFRA 2016: 13 and 19).

The requirements for this kind of marketing of agricultural products – high standards of quality, certification to permit produce to cross international borders, refrigerated and other specialized storage, and advanced logistics to track and order supplies – depend on precise quality standards, timings, and quantities. The farmers know that if they do not meet the quality standards, or supply sufficient quantities, they will lose their market. The contracts involved may be very detailed, or more informal, 'gentlemen's agreements' that are more flexible for both parties. Sourcing of agricultural products for supermarkets in the developed countries is increasingly from a small group of countries including Mexico, Chile, Spain, the Netherlands and Morocco. There are some supplies from sub-Saharan African countries such as Kenya, Ghana and Côte d'Ivoire.

Auctions and commodity exchanges still exist, dealing with cotton, coffee, and non-perishable products such as cereals and oilseeds, or auctions of cut flowers in Amsterdam, but, even with these, production may be based on contracts (for example, contracts to grow the flowers; or the contract of the brewer SAB Miller with Mountainside Farms, a large farm in Tanzania, to purchase barley).

One of the downsides of these developments is wastage at every stage – in the fields if a crop has been grown in excess of a contract, in the logistics train if there are delays or technical failures, at the factory if the quantities contracted for turn out to be more than is needed and in supermarkets when products pass their sell-by dates.

Types of Contract Farming

Eaton and Shepherd (2001) describe how contracts may be specified. In some contracts, the only requirement is to sell to the contractor. At the other extreme, a contract may specify the variety to be grown, inputs and cultivation practices to be used, the times of planting and harvesting, the quality of the product and, if land is leased to the farmers, precisely how it must be used. Prices may be agreed in advance, sometimes in complex formulae, and often relating to market prices at the time of sale. Thus a contract may specify some or all of the following:

1. The duration of the contract – is it for just one season, or longer?
2. The way in which the price is to be calculated:
   - Prices fixed at the beginning of each season?
   - Flexible prices based on world or local market prices?
   - Prices on national or international spot-markets?
   - Consignment prices, when the price that will be paid to the farmer is not known until the raw or processed product has been sold? or
   - Split pricing, when the farmer receives an agreed base price together with a final price when the sponsor has sold the product?
3. Quality standards required by the buyer.

4. A quota: a maximum quantity that the farmer will supply.
5. Cultivation practices required by the sponsor.
6. The arrangements for delivery of the crop.
7. Procedures for paying farmers and reclaiming credit advances.
8. Arrangements covering insurance.

(Eaton & Shepherd 2001: 58–9)

So there are many varieties of contracts; but none are straightforward and all are subject to abuse. Like all long-term contracts, they depend on trust. When all is well, there should not be problems. But if some parts of the contract are not delivered, or if grievances on one side or the other are not dealt with, contracts can go sour. If trust is abused by either side it may be very hard to re-establish. The prices paid are particularly contentious. The farmers are in a position of weakness in relation to the contractors, except that they have the ultimate sanctions of sabotaging the contract by side-selling or by withdrawing completely. Thus contracts are commendable in principle. But in practice they depend on stable and reliable purchasers and processors, and farmers who value the stability of the contracts and who, in return, accept the conditions involved. If either party abuses the contract it can fail.

The purchaser may also grow the crop. In these cases the farmers are *outgrowers*. The purchasers may be processors, for example, companies that operate gins in the cotton-growing areas of Tanzania or mills that crush sunflower seeds to produce oil. Or they may be local traders linked with processors who use the contracts as a way of ensuring that they are able to purchase minimum quantities of the crop. They may be major international or national traders in the commodity, as with the four companies that purchase the flue-cured tobacco grown in Tanzania. Or they may be farmers' groups or cooperatives, who themselves sign contracts to supply purchasers or processors of the crop. This has the advantage that there is an organization to negotiate with the purchaser and to help farmers later if there are disputes. They can also help to ensure that loans are repaid as agreed.

As Minot (2007) points out, there are other stakeholders – farmers excluded from the contract may look at those included with envy, or they may make the most of their freedom to plan their farms as they wish. NGOs or cooperatives may have vested interests in the provision of credit and new technology, and wish to see contracts continue in order to sell specific products or seeds. Governments and local governments may see contracts as an easy way of collecting cesses or taxes.

Advantages and Disadvantages of Contract Farming

Eaton and Shepherd (2001) and da Silva (2005) both explore the possible advantages and disadvantages of contracts, for contractors and for farmers, showing that there are risks for both. Agri-business firms use contracts to ensure that quality standards are met, and that produce is supplied as and when it is needed. The underlying advantage of using outgrowers is a reduction in labour costs when compared with production on an estate or plantation, and less expenditure on management. The contracts enable buyers to ensure that economies of scale in terms of production processes and supplies of inputs are achieved, and that inputs are available and used. Yields on small farms may be as high as or higher than those on large farms. The use of small farmers may be the only way in which large companies can access the required areas of land.

The advantages for farmers are reliable and predictable incomes and a guaranteed market for their produce. Contracts also give them access to credit, and they can benefit from extension advice provided by the contractor and, in some situations, services such as ploughing or spraying.

But there are also possible disadvantages. For example, a farmer may lose the possibility of selling the crop for a higher price elsewhere. There may be situations where the contractor does not collect the crop as agreed, or is slow to pay for it, perhaps because, at that time, it finds that it can source the crop more cheaply on its central farm. The farmer may not want to be compelled to grow a minimum amount of the crop because of possible disruption to the growth of food crops for own use or local sales. Farmers may not want to accept the risks involved if the crop should fail. They may not trust the pricing regime and feel that they are being cheated, especially if prices are falling in the long term. They may not trust the quality requirements specified by the contractor and how these relate to the prices they are paid. Or they may not have confidence in the quality of the inputs being supplied, such as animal feeds or fertilizers, and they cannot source them elsewhere. They may not want to move so far in the direction of monoculture, with its increased risks and costs of controlling diseases and maintaining the fertility of the soil (as forcibly pointed out by Dawson et al. 2016 in their critique of contract farming of maize in Rwanda). Small farmers with contracts may feel that larger farmers are being favoured at their expense.

Many of the possible disadvantages for a contractor relate to these points. Thus a farmer under contract may sell the crop for a higher price elsewhere, hence not supplying the quantities agreed, and not paying back the credit ('side-selling'). The contract may prove inflexible, for example, if there are good harvests elsewhere, the contractor may not be allowed to purchase the crop more cheaply elsewhere. The costs of supervision and enforcement, and of logistics and supply, may be high. The security of supply in the long term is uncertain.

The literature suggests that contracts are likely to be more successful in some circumstances than others; for example, if a crop is perishable, or quality declines if it is not sold quickly (as with tobacco, tea, sugar or flowers), or if it is expensive to transport long distances without processing, as with meat and dairy products, and many fruits and vegetables. Side-selling is hard in these situations.

The next section summarizes how contract farming has developed in Tanzania. This is then illustrated by case studies of contracts for two contrasting crops – detailed and specific for the tobacco crop, almost minimal in the case of sunflower.

Contrasting Contracts in Tanzania

Contract farming in Tanzania was implicit in the arrangements for giving credit to small farmers that were pioneered in the 1960s and supported by large World Bank projects in the 1970s and 1980s. It suffered a setback when the cooperative societies and unions were abolished in 1976. With liberalization, especially after 2000, it was clear that it had a part to play (Matchmaker Associates 2006). This was recognized in the Agriculture Sector Development Programme, which covered the years 2006–13, and in the policy statement *Kilimo Kwanza* (Agriculture First) (TNBC 2009), which was a joint effort of the private sector and the Government of Tanzania. Pillar 7 of *Kilimo Kwanza* emphasized the need for establishing institutional arrangements to increase agricultural production, with particular importance attached to contract farming. It proposed specific laws to guide farmers involved in contract farming, as in India. Several international NGOs became involved in promoting contract farming, including the Tanzania Gatsby Foundation for cotton, the Rural Livelihood Development Programme working on cotton, sunflower and rice, the Netherlands government agency SNV on sunflower and sesame, and Technoserve on organic coffee in the Moshi area.

The first contracts with small farmers were those for tobacco in the 1950s, discussed below. There was also rapid expansion of coffee and cotton produced by small farmers, under what soon became 'single-channel marketing' in which producers had to sell their crops to primary cooperative societies, which purchased the crops at 'pan-territorial prices' (i.e. the same for the whole country). The crops were subsequently sold to cooperative unions, who owned basic processing facilities (coffee pulperies and cotton ginneries), and sold the processed products to marketing boards, who sold them to government purchasers in the UK or (usually for better prices) at international auctions. This system was not particularly fair to the farmers – the Lint and Seed Marketing Board, like other marketing boards in colonial and post-colonial Africa, made significant profits many of which were not ploughed back into the crop (Bates 1981). But it gave the farmers certainty, and made side-selling almost impossible. It was therefore a basis for credit, for the insecticidal sprays used to get good-quality cotton, and sometimes also for fertilizers, supplied at first by the National Development Credit Agency and later by its successor the Tanzania Rural Development Bank. Rather than dealing with each small farmer separately, the banks or agencies providing the credit signed contracts with cooperative primary societies. If an individual farmer defaulted on a loan, the rest of the farmers in that society were still responsible for repaying it.

This system, like many of the arrangements for the marketing of crops, collapsed in the 1980s, when the marketing boards (by then the Tanzania Cotton Authority and the Coffee Authority of Tanzania) lost their powers to purchase and sell cotton lint and coffee (Ponte 2002). Many small firms established ginneries and signed contracts to supply cotton to international buyers, but found it hard to deliver the promised quantities or qualities. So they would buy from any farmer. In this situation it was not possible to control side-selling, as a way of avoiding the payment of taxes and cesses, and the repayment of loans. 'Marching boys' (Kabissa 2014: 234–6) came with lorries in the night and purchased cotton for a higher price than the local ginnery. This in turn led to a collapse in the quality, as farmers added sand, soil, even water, to their cotton, and failed to remove sticks or stained bolls. Since then, the pricing system does not give any extra payment for good-quality cotton, farmers have no incentive to undertake the extra work that this involves. It also makes it almost impossible to enforce any kind of contract for credit, as the Tanzania Gatsby Trust and British Aid found from around 2012 when they made a major effort to re-establish contract farming and credit for cotton growing (Coulson 2016).

In the 1970s and early 1980s the World Bank financed projects to provide credit for most of Tanzania's major crops. The finance was channelled to crop authorities through the Tanzania Rural Development Bank and then to cooperative unions and primary societies. These too failed in the mid-1980s, with the abolition of cooperative societies and lack of resources to pay farmers for growing crops such as cashewnuts or, at times, maize.

Sugar was largely grown on irrigated estates, but two sugar companies, at Kilombero and Mtibwa, both near Morogoro, had limited irrigation and signed contracts with outgrowers – small farmers who grew sugar cane and sold it to the sugar company. Mmari (2015: 58–63) reported a dramatic increase in the production of sugarcane by outgrowers, from 7,148 hectares in 1998 to 22,216 hectares in 2006, and 25,371 hectares by 2013. But in the later period almost all of this increase was at Kilombero. At Mtibwa outgrowers provided 49 per cent of the cane in 2009, but only 19 per cent in 2013. Mmari attributes this to the decline in the effectiveness of the growers' association that negotiated with the company, along with the company's own financial difficulties. In a later study, Herrmann (2017) showed that outgrowers at Kilombero were somewhat better off than other farmers in the area, and more so if they had access to more land.

Like sugar cane, tea is perishable and it deteriorates if not processed quickly. Up to Independence in 1961, tea production was almost entirely from estates. But some of the estates developed outgrower schemes. They agreed to purchase tea from small farms near their estates, and worked with the extension service to give the farmers the necessary skills. In the mid-1970s the first tea factory purely to process small farmer-grown tea was opened, at Mponde in the West Usambara mountains, followed by a second near Bukoba, west of Lake Victoria. The factories contracted to collect the tea on certain days in the week, to ensure that farmers were paid appropriately, and to supply fertilizers. In 1985–6 small farmers contributed more than 28 per cent of the tea grown. But after that, in the chaos surrounding structural adjustment and liberalization, tea was not collected, farmers were not paid, and by 1989 small farmers were contributing only 5 per cent of the production (Tea Detective n.d.).

A detailed review of contract farming in Tanzania was commissioned by the Ministry of Agriculture, Food and Cooperatives. The resulting report (Matchmaker Associates 2006) reported on contract farming for organic coffee, sugar cane, tea, tobacco, pyrethrum, sisal, chickpeas and milk, and on programmes then being developed for cashewnuts, fruits, paprika and other crops, and on marketing arrangements for many other crops where contracts are implicit but not in writing. The researchers obtained copies of 13 contracts for different crops. Their study remains the most detailed report on the opportunities for contract farming in Tanzania, with frank assessments of the challenges and often the disappointments for those involved.

More recently, contracts with small-scale farmers were promoted to grow sunflower, for example, to supply three mills in the Dodoma area, underwritten by the Rural Livelihood Development Company, an NGO supported by the Swiss Government. From the point of view of the farmers the main motivation was to get access to hybrid seeds. The contracts, examined in more detail below, were very informal.

Kilimo Kwanza, the plans for SAGCOT (the Southern Agricultural Growth Corridor of Tanzania, launched in 2010), and for Big Results Now (2012) all included explicit commitments to outgrowers, and hence contract farming. Initially the emphasis was on large-scale farms, but outgrowing was also developed, for example, around Mngeta Farm (Kilombero Plantations Limited) in the Kilombero Valley (Nakano et al. 2014). After about 2015 SAGCOT developed its work with outgrowers rapidly, and these are now a main focus of its programmes to increase production of rice, sugar and other crops.

In order to explore these issues, and the prerequisites for successful contracts with small farmers, the rest of this chapter is a study of two contrasting situations of contract farming. The first is the pioneer of contracts with smallholder farmers in Tanzania, who have been growing flue-cured tobacco in the Urambo area, Tabora Region, since the 1960s. Tobacco has become one of Tanzania's most successful agricultural export crops. The contracts and marketing system have continued broadly unchanged since they were established, but are now under increasing pressure.

The second study is of sunflower growing in Kongwa District, near Dodoma. This is much more recent and, as the crop can be easily transported and does not quickly deteriorate, it is almost impossible to prevent side-selling. A follow-up on these farming contracts, in May 2017, indicated that there are no longer active contract arrangements in sunflower production. Contract farming depended on input provision, particularly of improved seeds. Lack of sufficient capital, coupled with side-selling when harvests are ready, has gravely accelerated the demise of this contract farming.

Tobacco Farming in Urambo

The contracts to grow flue-cured tobacco at Urambo, on land cleared between 1947 and 1950 as part of the Groundnuts Scheme, pioneered the processes of contract farming in Tanzania. Following a successful pilot project in 1951, European settlers were invited to come and grow tobacco. There were around 40 farms, each growing 5–15 hectares of tobacco and similar areas of groundnuts and maize (Boesen & Mohele 1979: 25–40). Each farm had two or three tractors and employed up to 500 seasonal labourers. By 1960 they were growing a total of about 500 hectares of tobacco.

The Tanganyika Agricultural Corporation, which had taken over the land of the Groundnuts Scheme, wanted to encourage African farmers. It permitted them to grow small areas of tobacco and, from 1958, after a design was developed for a small curing barn, to cure it. Up to that time this process was alleged to be too complicated for small farmers.

Tobacco succeeded for a surprising reason: the poverty of the soil and its poor ability to retain nutrients. High-quality tobacco requires exactly the right nutrients, and this is achieved on poor soils by adding chemical fertilizers at the correct times. To harvest a high-quality crop, each leaf must be cut at precisely the right time, in the correct manner. The curing takes six days. Farmers are given thermometers, which show the correct temperature for each of the days. Only if these are adhered to will high grades of tobacco be achieved. Between 1958 and 1962 farmers who wanted to grow the crop had to join a 'school' attached to a larger farm for a year, and after that they had to have a recommendation to the effect that they knew how to grow tobacco; many had worked as labourers on other tobacco farms. By 1964 all the European settlers had left the area.

In 1967 the state created a parastatal body to market the crop, the Tobacco Authority of Tanzania (TAT). Boesen and Mohele show how the area was adversely affected by the compulsory 'villagization' of the early 1970s, during which many barns and homes were destroyed. They also pointed out that the forest was being cut down to provide the firewood for the curing process, at a speed that could not continue indefinitely. The crop survived, even though many farmers had to move. There was a demand, from British American Tobacco's factory in Dar es Salaam, and for export, and the African farmers had shown that they could compete with anyone.

Those growing the crop had to be members of a primary cooperative society, and to sell their crop through the society, which would also supply them with seeds and fertilizers. The period after 1990 saw the subsector liberalized. The Tanzania Tobacco Board was created in 2001, with functions mainly aimed at ensuring the growing and marketing of a quality crop, similar to those of the TAT in the 1960s. From 2009 the primary cooperative societies have contracted with private companies to supply the fertilizers and other inputs.

The marketing of flue-cured tobacco was handled by three international merchants: Alliance One and the Tanzania Leaf Tobacco Company Limited, both with headquarters in the USA, and Premium Tobacco International, which manufactures cigarettes in Ireland (and purchases tobacco in the Chunya and Mpanda areas, not in Tabora and Urambo). These operated together as the Association of Tanzania Tobacco Traders, or 'A-Triple-T'. This association came into existence because of the problem of side-selling and to ensure the orderly conduct of the contracted farmers. It also provided logistical and extension services, and coordinated and supervised market procedures. In 2015 a fourth buyer, Japanese Tobacco International, joined the existing three, and A-Triple-T ceased to exist. Independent farmers were now registered and allowed to produce tobacco.

From 2002, tobacco production increased steadily, mostly flue-cured. Figure 6.1 shows a sharp increase from 60,700 metric tonnes in 2010 to 126,600 metric tonnes in 2012, mainly owing to an increased price in the world market, which persuaded farmers to produce more tobacco (URT 2013d: 121). By 2014 tobacco earned more foreign exchange than any other traditional agricultural product, and had become Tanzania's most successful agricultural product grown specifically for export (Bank of Tanzania 2016).

The Contract Arrangements for Tobacco in Urambo

The legal framework for tobacco production involves three contracts, summarized in Figure 6.2. The first is the *contract between a grower and primary cooperative society* (1st C). This is just one page written in Kiswa-

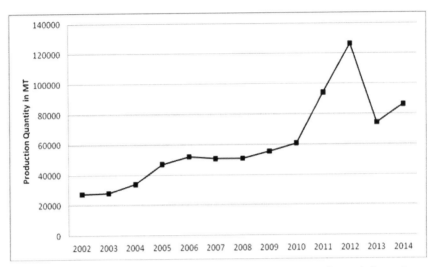

Source: Ministry of Agriculture Food and Cooperatives and Bank of Tanzania Quarterly Economic Bulletin, December 2015, Table 1.13

Figure 6.1 Tobacco Production in Metric Tonnes (2002–2014)

hili, a language all farmers can understand. In this simple contract, an individual tobacco grower must be a member of both a farmer-group and a primary cooperative society. The farmer is committed to taking all inputs during a particular tobacco production period and selling the entire crop for the season to the primary cooperative society. The inputs are supplied by the primary cooperative society. The farmers in the group commit themselves collectively to repaying the credit.

The second contract is between the Primary Cooperative Society, the Western Tobacco Cooperative Union and the Tobacco Processing Company (2^{nd}C). In this contract, the farmers, as producers of green leaf tobacco, are represented by the primary cooperative society, which contracts with the buyers. The cooperative agrees to produce and sell an agreed quantity of tobacco using crop husbandry techniques specified by the Tanzania Tobacco Act, which provides for regulations, improvement and development of the industry. The TPC commits, through a commercial bank (NMB), to provide all inputs estimated and required during the production period. As overseer of primary cooperative societies, the Western Tobacco Cooperative Union (WETCU) also signs the contract.

Before the production calendar starts, each Cooperative Society, through its members, decides which company to sell their tobacco to. The contracts they sign are the same and in principle, once contracts are signed, the prices are determined for each grade, and there is no further competition between the companies for that season. The companies compete with each other not through the details of the contract but through packages not included in the contract such as engagement in social responsibility programmes.

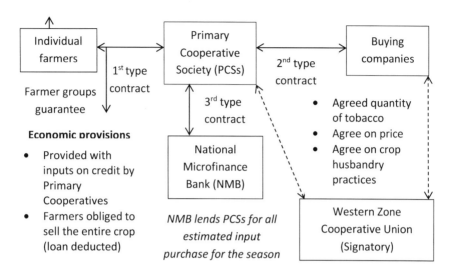

Source: Research Field Visits, 2015

Figure 6.2 Tobacco Contract Arrangements

The third and final contract is the Facility Agreement between the banks and the primary cooperatives (3rdC). This enables a primary cooperative society to borrow from the commercial bank for purposes of purchasing inputs. The inputs purchased include fertilizers (NPK, CAN and Urea), packing materials, agrochemicals and some cash to help the farmers cover the costs of harvesting, grading and marketing.

In this arrangement, the individual smallholder tobacco growers are not directly in contact with the suppliers of the inputs. By signing contracts with the primary cooperative society, the farmers surrender to the society the mandate to negotiate terms with the suppliers. The Tobacco Act and its regulations, and the contract between farmers and primary cooperative societies, prevent farmers not in the contract from growing tobacco.

While registration is a requirement to grow and sell tobacco in the region, use of input credit provided through the contract arrangements is not mandatory. To explore this, a survey of 300 randomly selected tobacco-growing farmers in the Urambo area was carried out in 2012 (Ilembo 2015: 97–8, 105–8). Of these, 245 were users of credit and 54 were not. Non-adopters of credit had on average slightly larger farms than adopters, and grew slightly larger areas of tobacco. They also used more fertilizer – approximately 180 kg per acre compared to 140.2 kg by credit adopters.

Non-credit adopters achieved slightly higher yields compared to those who depended on credit. This difference is not significant, espe-cially considering that the data is for one season only, and it is not clear what caused it. Non-adopters are relatively few in number, mainly

Table 6.1 Production Situation for Credit and Non-Credit Users (mean values)

	Credit input users (246)	Non-credit input users (54)
Farm size (acres)	6.0	7.2
Area of tobacco harvested (acres)	2.2	2.7
Yield (kg per acre)	604	619
Price per kg (TSh)	2519	2489
Fertilizer use (kgs per acre)	140.2	179.5

Source: Ilembo (2015: Table 4.3)

better-off farmers who can obtain inputs, including fertilizer, in other ways, including their own financing. On the other hand, credit input adopters sell their produce at prices that are substantially higher than the prices achieved by non-adopters, probably because, for credit adopters, the buyers employ leaf technicians who have the opportunity to monitor the entire process of tobacco production.

Farming Sunflower Seeds in Dodoma

Kongwa was the main centre of the Groundnuts Scheme, and large areas of land were cleared. There were many mistakes, such as the use of unsuitable machinery and failure to remove the roots from the soil before using tractors. But the main problem was the shortage and unreliability of the rainfall (Coulson 2013: 78–82).

For this reason it was decided that the cleared land should become a cattle ranch. It passed to the Tanganyika Agricultural Corporation and then to the National Agricultural and Food Corporation. But NAFCO failed in 1996 and most of its farms became derelict.

Sunflower had a long history in an area not far away. It was grown by Greek farmers on land near Dakawa close to the Wami river. It was drought-resistant and offered an alternative to maize. It was not, however, a major crop, perhaps because cotton seed-oil and coconut oil offered cheaper alternatives for cooking oil.

However, in recent years, hybrid seeds have become available that are relatively resistant to drought, quick-growing and high-yielding. To get best results they require fertilizer and insecticide. It is on that basis that crop agriculture, in particular the growing of maize and sunflower, has succeeded in the Kongwa area. Contract farming was introduced as a way of ensuring that farmers get access to the new seeds and to fertilizers and sprays.

Unlike tobacco, sunflower is a crop which can either be consumed locally and/or sold on a commercial basis. Demand for sunflower oil,

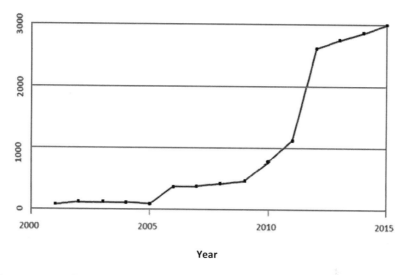

Source: URT 2013 (Economic Survey 2012) and Annual Budget Speeches (URT 2014 & 2015)

Figure 6.3 Sunflower Production in '000 tonnes (2001–2015)

which is cholesterol-free, is increasing and its potential for becoming a major agricultural commodity for export is therefore rising. The total amount produced has increased steadily over time, from an average of 80,000 tonnes per year in 2000/01 to about 2,625,000 tonnes per year by 2015/16 (Ilembo 2015). In 2011 total vegetable oil consumption in Tanzania was estimated at 300,000 tonnes, of which 40 per cent or more came from sunflower seeds. Increase in sunflower production seems to have been accelerated by the introduction of relatively inexpensive oil expellers and filtering machines from China, in addition to extension work provided by government offices, and NGOs such as the Rural Livelihood Development Company (RLDC 2008; 2010).

Sunflower Production and Marketing Contracts

Sunflower production contracts in Kongwa district began in the 2008/09 crop season, as an initiative of two private companies based in Dodoma town (RIG Investment Company, and Uncle Milo Company Sunflower Oil Ltd) and the Rural Livelihood Development Company, an NGO supported by the Swiss Government agency (Helvetas 2016), the Netherlands government agency SNV (2012), and the private sector (JICA 2014). These helped to design contract farming arrangements and organized mobilization seminars in different villages. The framework of the contract is summarized in Figure 6.4.

The contract guaranteed the farmers market outlets for their sunflower produce, and support in terms of inputs and farm implements

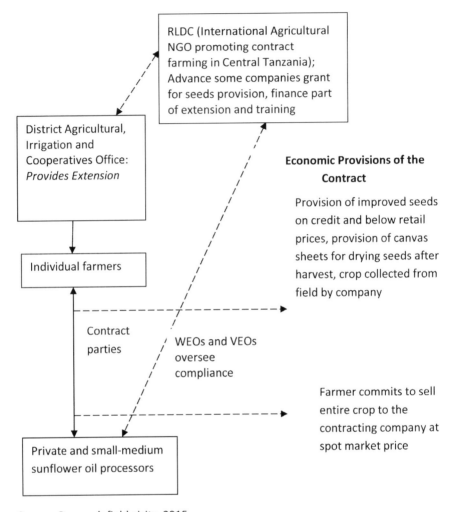

Source: Research field visits, 2015

Figure 6.4 Sunflower Contract Arrangements

such as ploughs, and canvas sheets to ensure that the produce is kept clean enough for quality drying and storage until further processing takes place. It also promised them that they would obtain high-yielding hybrid seeds, particularly the improved variety, *Record*, produced by Mount Meru Seeds in Arusha.

The contractors also promised to establish a sunflower marketing centre in each village, to facilitate the formation of farmer groups, to buy all sunflower produced at the going market price, to facilitate and finance farmers' demonstration plots in the selected villages, to extend appropriate knowledge through seminars on proper sunflower agronomics and contract farming arrangements, and to provide cash on credit to assist farmers with the costs of farm preparation (tilling and obtaining the needed quantity of farm manure, usually cow dung). Farmers, in return, agreed to produce more sunflower and sell to the firms at least 50 per cent of the total sunflower produced on their farms in a season.

A study was conducted in 2012 of eight villages in four administrative wards. A multi-staged stratified sample of 205 contract farmers and 195 non-contract farmers was randomly selected from these villages, a total of 400 smallholder farmers. Table 6.2 indicates that the contracted farmers were growing slightly larger areas of sunflower than the non-contract farmers – a mean of 3.7 acres compared with a mean of 3.3 acres. This suggests that the contracts did not prompt farmers to acquire larger farms or release more land for sunflower from their family land holdings. On the other hand, the contract farmers achieved higher yields and on average 30 per cent more production.

From Table 6.3 it can be seen that, despite the contracts, only 46.3 per cent of the contracted farmers managed to access all the improved seed they needed. They therefore had to use both the improved and local seed varieties, which can be purchased in local markets or saved from their own previous harvest. This suggests that there was a shortage of improved seeds. When farmers were asked why they had joined the contract, 80 per cent of them mentioned the need for better-yielding seed as a major economic motivation. Use of hybrid seed, such as the *Record* varieties of sunflower, requires new seed stock each year. Most of the farmers understand this, and were very disappointed when they could not obtain the quantities of the new seeds they wanted.

Of the farmers in the sample 87.75 per cent signed contracts on an individual basis. Only a few reported belonging to a farmers' group (12.25 per cent). Farmers were initially organized in groups of 70 members. However, over time, most of these producer groups collapsed and the few remaining groups are very weak.

During focus group discussions farmers raised the issue of poor credit services as a pressing problem. It was revealed that no contractor

Table 6.2 Sunflower Production: Contracted and Non-Contracted Farmers

Relevant Variables in Mean Values	*Non-Contract-Farmers*	*Contract Farmers*	*Difference*	*t-Test of difference*
Acreage	3.3	3.7	−0.4	−1.44*
Share of sunflower land	.47	.49	−0.02	−1.06
Yield per acre (kgs)	103.9	121.5	−17.7	−2.17**
Mean output (kgs)	325.1	422.2	−97.1	−2.41**

***, ** and * represent significance at 1%, 5% and 10% levels respectively
Source: Mpeta (2015: 41)

Table 6.3 Inputs and Farm Implements Used for Sunflower Production

| | Contract Farmers | | Non-Contract Farmers | |
	Frequency	Percent	Frequency	Percent
Type of seed used				
Improved seed variety	95	46.34	17	8.72
Local seed variety			177	90.77
Both (improved & local)	110	53.66	1	0.51
Total	205	100	195	100
Cultivation method				
Hand hoe	30	14.63	31	15.90
Ox-plough	162	79.02	154	78.97
Tractor	13	6.34	10	5.13
Total	205	100.00	195	100.00

Source: Mpeta (2014)

had provided cash credits as agreed. Four per cent of the sample had accessed credit services outside the contractual arrangements, mainly through informal savings and credit schemes run by the villagers themselves on a self-help basis, but the loan sizes amounted to no more than a few thousand shillings.

The lack of credit hindered farmers from hiring tractors or ox-ploughs, hiring labour, especially during the labour-intensive activity of weeding, or supplementing their supplies of seed. The majority of farmers in the sample used ox-ploughs to prepare the land (Table 6.3). Without capital to hire more ox-ploughs or tractors, many of these farmers would not be able to start and finish preparing their land before the first rains, which are critical in a climatic area with little and unreliable rainfall. Late planting hinders proper maturity of the crop, and yields are low.

Contract Challenges

Table 6.4 highlights the differences and similarities in the institutional set up and outcomes of the two contract arrangements. Tobacco is a perishable crop, at least at the farm level, where great skill is required to get good quality. Most of the crop is exported, and the quality makes a huge difference to the price. Sunflower seed has a long shelf life, but the quality is depressed if the crop is wet, or contaminated; the prices paid to farmers do not necessarily reflect the quality of the crop.

Table 6.4 Comparison of Tobacco and Sunflower Institutional Set-Ups

Crop Characteristics	Crop	
	Tobacco	*Sunflower*
Perishability at farm level	Perishable	Non-perishable
Use	Export 95%, 5% locally consumed	Food and sale of seeds and oil locally
Experience of contracts	Before independence	Relatively new in Kongwa and Singida (2007)
Market nature for biological supply	Non-competitive: dominance of four giant buying companies; little possibility of side-selling	Competitive: many small/medium processing companies: side-selling possible
Formation	Must join contract farming to receive input credit; can, however, also grow tobacco as an independent farmer	Voluntary (can grow sunflower without joining contract farming)
Formality	Rigid written formal. Defined by Tanzania Tobacco Industry Act, 2001 Three written contracts; the contract involving the growers and the cooperative is relatively simple (one page); the between buyer and cooperative is 22 pages	Relatively simple and informal
Seed and agro inputs	Seeds offered for free but agro inputs all on credit; buyers commit to offer extension services	Initially seeds provided free through a support given to processors by the international NGO RLDC. Currently, with the closure of RLDC, seeds are obtained on credit and agro inputs for cash
Institutional governance	The contract is mandatory for one to receive input credit through the primary cooperative. Farmer must be registered. The contract specifies the market, and the provision of credit, and how the crop must be grown. Premium prices are paid for high quality but farmers are confused by many quality standards	Not mandatory The contract specifies that the trader will purchase the crop, and provide improved seeds on credit; and access to other services like tractors. There is no provision for premium prices for higher-quality crop
	Strong primary cooperatives	No formal farmers' organization
	Contract provided in the Act and Regulations; but compliance and enforcement seen as challenge due to lopsided power relations	Based mainly on trust. No mechanism for dispute settlement

Crop Characteristics	Crop	
	Tobacco	*Sunflower*
Outcomes	Credit adopters access inputs they would otherwise not be able to obtain; credit adoption also contributes to efficiency levels	Contract Farmers attain higher productivity (and therefore higher income) mainly due to use of improved seeds

Whereas the business model in the case of sunflower is direct farmer–buyer/processor contracting, in the case of tobacco it is farmer–farmer group–primary cooperative society/ intermediary–buyer/processor contracting. The nature of the market is also distinctly different, with tobacco having just four large buyers and prices for each grade predetermined for the season, whereas sunflower can be stored and later transported almost anywhere and prices are not agreed in advance.

Another big difference is levels of formality. The tobacco contract is guided by an act of parliament and very formal, while the arrangements for sunflower are more informal.

With both of these crops, a proportion of the farmers chose not to sign the contracts. The reasons for this are not certain, but it is likely that many who did not sign did not want to be bound by the conditions of the contract, which required them to undertake specific activities, in the case of tobacco in very specific ways. They preferred to run their own farms, as they wished. The sections that follow consider some of the main challenges that must be confronted if contract farming is to succeed.

Disputes about Price

Neither of these contracts addresses the issue of price risks. If prices are fixed in advance, or if there are 'indicative prices' that are the best estimates at the start of the buying season, and if prices then rise subsequently, there are strong incentives for farmers to sell outside the contract. If they fall, the buyer will try to pay a lower price and the farmers will feel cheated.

If prices are not fixed in advance and if there are many local outlets, which is the case with sunflower produce, and the spot price rises, then, given the fact that raw sunflower does not require immediate processing before selling (as it is not a perishable commodity), some farmers will breach their contract obligations and side-sell to buyers who offer a better price.

Disputes about Grading – The Need for Premium Prices for Quality Produce

The contract agreements for sunflower do not specify how quality will be reflected in the prices that will be paid when the crop is sold. There are no grades and standards that must be followed during the procurement process. This means that there is no extra reward for farmers who produce good-quality crops. There is no additional gain in terms of price when they sell good-quality produce.

Tobacco, in contrast, has many grades, 64 in the 2011/12 season and 72 in 2012/13. Grading is done at the farm level, the marketing level and at the factory level.

At the farm, each individual farmer has to grade tobacco leaves and bale them before taking them to the Cooperative Society marketing point. Some farmers hire a specialist to assist in this, at a cost of between Tsh. 50 to Tsh. 100 to grade a bundle of 15–20 leaves. The quality of the leaf depends on the way it is cultivated, including the amount of rain and when it falls, appropriate use of fertilizer, the size of each leaf and any blemishes, how it is harvested and finally on how it is cured, a complicated process in which temperature and humidity have to be adjusted and monitored over a six-day period. If the temperature falls too much, water condenses and quality is lost. Each grade has its own price, but it is hard for farmers to obtain the highest grades. Farmers are confused by the number of grades, and often think that their tobacco should get a higher grade and a higher price. They would prefer fewer grades with higher prices for each grade.

Grading at market level is done when the tobacco bales are ready for sale. This time the whole bale is graded. This is where a buyer and a seller meet. Price is not an issue at this point because, once a grade is agreed, the price for that grade is predetermined. But it is common to find disagreements over grades; when this happens, a farmer bargains with a blender and, if that fails, the matter is forwarded to one of the farmers' representatives who are always available during marketing. Although this system allows for negotiation on grades between farmers and traders, and rewards high-quality production, ultimately, farmers have no option other than to agree on the blender's decision, as was put by one of the farmers during the interview:

> ... in disagreement of grades, the Cooperative Society board member has always been there and at least would help. The problem is with the blender (buyer) who is more powerful as he is the buyer's representative. The issue here is, whatever agreement on grade is made, a farmer would ultimately agree as he has no alternative market for the crop.

The tobacco leaves that arrive at the processing factories (which for both Alliance One and Tanzania Leaf Tobacco Company are in Morogoro) are regraded to meet the requirements of the customers before they are processed. The factory-level grading is even more complex and includes about 120 grades that relate to the needs of individual products and factories. The merchants allege that, if tobacco is significantly misclassified, the chance of losing future business is very high, but from the farmers' point of view this makes the whole process even more mysterious and unfair.

Failures to Supply Inputs as Agreed

There are many problems getting the right inputs to where they are needed and distributing them on time.

For sunflower producers the contractors have not been able to supply sufficient quantities of improved seed.

For tobacco, the inputs were originally supplied by the buying companies. But in 2009 they ceased playing this role, and the Cooperative Societies took over. Some farmers were not happy:

> ... with the companies distributing the inputs, they could monitor the Societies accurately and diligently, something which is not done at the moment. Tobacco production strictly follows a calendar and one has to follow it, so if inputs are delayed then that would affect farmers in terms of production, and this has put farmers into so many unrecovered debts.

However, the case of the sunflower farmers shows that private traders also can let the farmers down. The larger tobacco farmers, who can pay in cash, would like to order inputs directly from the suppliers. They believe that this would reduce the challenges they have been facing with the current system, which range from delayed inputs to mismatch between what was ordered and what is received. The current system is associated with malpractices and hidden overhead costs, which reduce what is paid to the farmers. The following quotation is from an interviewee who spoke on behalf of the Cooperative Society:

> ... the shift from companies ordering inputs to the present system is even worse! It is normal to pay for unused inputs and you may find that the Cooperative Society has deducted money even for inputs not delivered. For example, for the 2012/2013 season, the Cooperative Society ordered a total of 5,031 bags of NPK 10:18:24 fertilizer, but received only 4700, while at the bank the record shows 6,186 bags! You can see this discrepancy. We also ordered 1,400 bags of CAN fertilizer but we received 750 bags (each bag weighs 50 kg). This trend causes the Cooperative Society to use internal sources of income to repay bank debts unnecessarily which threatens the sustainability of the Cooperative Societies.

Thus for both sunflower and tobacco, those who supply the inputs are not fulfilling the terms of the contract. If this continues, resentment will increase, and eventually the contracts will collapse.

Farmer Organization and Commitment to Contract Agreements

A contract can fail owing to bad practices by either party. In the case of sunflower, some of the contracting firms are small private enterprises. They are capital-constrained and may find themselves unable to meet the expectations and obligations specified in the contracts, or to obtain the quantities of seeds and other inputs they have contracted to supply to farmers. If farmers feel that the contractors are not doing what they agreed to do, they may side-sell their produce to different buyers even though they had signed a contract promising to sell their produce to the firm that gave them the inputs. Against this background, contract buyers, in some cases, have deliberately chosen not to supply inputs to some farmers as a way to minimize their losses.

On the other hand, enquiries as to why farmers do not honour the contracts and do side selling revealed that farmers have little feeling that they own, and are equal partners in the contracts. The explanation for this appears to be rooted in the way the contracts are formulated. Village meetings held shortly before the farming season commences appear to be the only times when farmers are involved in negotiation of terms of contracts. Farmers are not sufficiently involved. Firms dominate the process. A farmer is just asked to accept or reject the terms and conditions of contracts prescribed. In general, farmers are not involved in the important stage of contract design. This is expressed by the fact that none of the sunflower farmers, when asked during the survey, could produce a written copy of the contract he/she signed. The only written contract document left with a farmer is a sheet on which they sign to acknowledge receipt of inputs supplied, such as seed or canvas sheets.

Similar issues arise with tobacco. The power lies with the purchasers and those who decide the grades of individual leaves and bales, and farmers often feel disappointed and cheated.

Thus for both crops there is a significant imbalance in the contract between farmers and contracting firms. This imbalance could also arise from farmers' own obvious weaknesses – in the case of sunflower because most of them are not organized in strong producer groups.

Conclusions

Tobacco and sunflower are at the extremes of contract farming in Tanzania. For growing tobacco, the contracts are very strong; for sunflower, they are extremely weak. But many of the challenges are similar. Both crops are highly successful in national terms, with quantities produced rising fast. But if farmers lose trust in the marketing arrangements, they will, if they can, sell their crops outside the contracts. In the extreme case they will not grow the crops. In the case of tobacco, the rigid arrangements have made side-selling difficult, but the farmers do not understand the grading systems and often feel cheated in the prices they get.

Contracts are an essential part of any form of marketing that involves credit. But all contracts depend on trust, and trust can easily be lost. Once trust is lost it is hard to rebuild it. In the case of agricultural contracts, if companies do not deliver the inputs or services they have contracted to supply at the agreed times and with appropriate quality, some farmers may resort to side-selling. If they get away with this, then other farmers will do the same, and the contractor who supplied the credit will not be able to continue. There has to be some remedy, or penalty, if either side of a contract does not carry out what they agreed.

In the case of sunflower many farmers signed contracts in order to be sure of getting access to hybrid seeds. However, many farmers did not get the seed they were promised, and some resorted to side-selling, and there are now few farmer groups. If this continues or expands, it will drive the companies that supply inputs and the banks that support them out of the market.

For tobacco growing small farmers have to be members of farmer groups, which are grouped into primary cooperative societies. They sign a written contract, and get paid according to the grades of tobacco they produce. Inputs are bulk purchased by the cooperatives, and they recover their money when the tobacco is sold. The crop is purchased by just four companies in the whole country, but these have built up international contacts, and learnt how to act locally, and under this arrangement production has expanded.

But the survey results show that this is not working well. Many farmers do not understand or trust the grading system, which is complicated and open to abuse by some of those involved. They feel cheated over prices, and the cooperatives have not always delivered the inputs as and when needed.

The system puts power into the hands of the purchasers. They agree the prices, and grade the crops, and it is very difficult for farmers, and even for the Tanzanian government, to know if these prices are fair. This is made more difficult with companies based in the USA or Japan, who are among the few companies in the world that have the trust of the big cigarette manufacturers, and the necessary personal contacts to make forward contracts, that is to agree to supply the tobacco before they have purchased it. The example of cotton, where many ginning companies are now on lists of companies that cannot be relied on to deliver contracts, shows the dangers.

There is therefore pressure to simplify the grading system, to encourage more companies to enter the market and purchase the crop, and to allow farmers to have credit to purchase inputs from suppliers directly, rather than through the cooperatives. Any of these changes runs a risk of destroying the system that has been built up successfully over 60 years. If more companies enter the market to purchase the crop, some may take part in side-selling, and thereby help farmers to avoid paying back their credit, as has happened with cotton in the Lake area. The grading system could no doubt be simplified, but if it is allowed to fall into disrepute, Tanzania will lose its reputation in international markets as a reliable supplier of carefully graded tobacco.

Any government intervention must be very careful with both these crops. For the sunflower crop, the companies who multiply the hybrid seed could give priority to farmer groups. If farmers are not able to organize themselves in farmer groups, it may be possible for them to be supplied with fertilizers and improved seeds through Warehouse Receipt Schemes. For the tobacco crop, the grievances of the farmers must be addressed, but it is also necessary for the relevant authorities to make sure that the farmers understand how the system works. They need to work with the cooperatives to expose any farmer who is found to be involved in side-selling to avoid repaying a loan. It would be very disappointing if either of these crops, both success stories, lost their markets because of failures to understand and enforce good contracts.

Some of the literature on contract farming argues that private firms are generally more trustful and effective than public agencies in delivering the services provided in the contracts (e.g. Umali-Deininger 1997; Bellemare 2010). But the cases of the sunflower farmers and the cotton farmers in the areas around Lake Victoria show that private traders can also let the farmers down.

Farmers need more information about prices. In the case of sunflower they should be given higher prices for clean, dry seed. With tobacco, the mechanism of setting indicative prices is transparent, through a forum that combines key stakeholders in the tobacco industry, but the purchasers are able to influence the prices they would pay more than they would in a more competitive market (Gereffi 1994). The cooperatives need access to independent information about world prices, information about what farmers are paid in nearby countries such as Zimbabwe and Mozambique, and to work with agents in these countries to maximize the prices paid to the farmers.

Taking a broad view, contracts in agriculture are not going to go away, but they can easily go wrong. In future years, more production will be directly commissioned by processing companies in Tanzania or overseas, and supermarkets will wish to purchase fruits and vegetables from reliable sources. But those who are negotiating contracts need to be fair to both sides, for if farmers feel they are being exploited and their grievances are not addressed, they may walk away.

7

'We Just Sell Water – That is All We Do': Two Cases of Small-scale Irrigation in Tanzania*

Anna Mdee

Introduction

The quest for agricultural transformation has been a concern in both colonial Tanganyika and post-colonial Tanzania. In a country with a population that relies on agricultural livelihoods the reduction of poverty must necessarily hinge on such transformation. Irrigation is seen as a vital component of improving agricultural productivity, and has been given renewed attention under recent agricultural initiatives. While small-scale indigenous irrigation has a long history, large donor-funded irrigation schemes have not been very successful. and transformation of agriculture through irrigation remains a potential rather than a reality.

To explore the issue further, this chapter examines the dynamics of irrigation by small-scale farmers in two sites in Tanzania: one is an informal irrigation farmer-led scheme on the Uluguru Mountains; and the other a formalized and donor-supported rehabilitation of a former state rice farm under the cooperative ownership of small-scale farmers. These two cases reveal some critical shortcomings in current institutional arrangements for managing allocations of water in Tanzania, and suggest that, without addressing these, the latent potential of irrigation to transform Tanzanian agriculture will remain latent.

Irrigation and Agricultural Policy in Tanzania

Despite the emergence and development of industries, mining, tourism and services, agriculture continues to be significant for Tanzanian

* This chapter is part of a three-country study, funded by the DFID-ESRC Growth Research Programme (DEGRP), covering Malawi, Tanzania and Bangladesh. The project, 'Innovations to promote growth among small-scale irrigators: An ethnographic and knowledge-exchange approach' (ES/J009414/1), is led by the University of Sussex, with partners at Bunda College of Agriculture, Malawi; Mzumbe University, Tanzania; and Jahangirnagar University, Bangladesh.

development owing to the number of poor people it employs and the strong consumption linkages it has with other sectors (Aman 2005; Coulson 2012; Jenkins 2012). The exact proportion contributed by agriculture to Tanzanian GDP is not universally agreed but ranges from estimates of 25 per cent (UNDP 2012) to around 45 per cent of total GDP (AgWater 2010), and 30 per cent of export earnings (AgWater 2010) to 85 per cent of export earnings (UNDP 2012a).[1] Agriculture continues to provide a significant proportion of the livelihoods of 80 per cent of the population (AgWater 2010; UNDP 2012a; Coulson 2012, 2013). Therefore, support for agricultural development is important for both the nation's overall economic prosperity and for poverty reduction efforts (URT 2005).

Poor transport infrastructure, a lack of appropriate institutional frameworks, unfavourable market conditions, poor technology adoption, restrictive taxation and tariff regimes, and continued reliance on rain-fed agriculture constrain productivity in the agricultural sector (Aman 2005; AgWater 2010; Jenkins 2012). Aman (2005) argues that, despite the abundant water in rivers and lakes, there is little utilization of irrigated agriculture, and this acts as a major constraint to sustainable increases in crop production. Official estimates suggest that only 300,000 of a potential 5.1 million hectares are under irrigation (Keraita et al. 2010). The 2009 National Irrigation Policy confirmed this figure and recognized increased irrigated agriculture as a key component of enhanced agricultural productivity and growth (URT 2009a).

Agricultural transformation and the quest to modernize peasant agriculture have a long history in Tanzania (Coulson 2013). After an active period of donor support for agricultural development in the 1960s and 1970s, the period of structural adjustment saw a decline in donor and state support for agriculture. However, since around 2007, concern for rising food prices, increasing populations, and a renewed quest for structural economic transformation have driven a renewed focus on agriculture (Poku & Mdee 2011).

This chapter does not intend to reprise these narratives in detail, but it should be highlighted that current government initiatives, such as Kilimo Kwanza (Agriculture First), and the donor-funded Southern Agricultural Growth Corridor (SAGCOT), attempt to address the dual aims of enhancing the livelihoods of the poor and increasing commercial opportunities for production (Coulson 2012; Jenkins 2012). The policy environment for agriculture in Tanzania is increasingly contested, and some argue that small-scale farmers are unlikely to see significant tangible benefits from current agricultural support policies and activities[2]

---

[1] These variations arise partly as a result of definitions of the various sectors, partly owing to the valuation of subsistence output and partly to the reference period. In general the relative importance of agriculture has declined over time.
[2] Chapters 2, 4 and 6 of this book also discuss this issue.

(Cooksey 2013; Coulson 2013). It is unclear how the interests of commercial investors and small farmers can be served concurrently. With the reawakening of donor interest in agriculture, Tanzanian ownership of agricultural policy is weakened and reduced to chasing a plethora of competing and incompatible policies and projects.

Irrigation is conceived as a panacea for African agriculture. It is a central component of the push for a second green revolution (Woodhouse et al. 2016). However, the means by which irrigation can be managed efficiently and sustainably is a critical challenge. Mutabazi and colleagues (2013) in their research in Central Tanzania note the importance of investment in increasing the productivity of irrigated land for commercialization of small farmers. However, there is little clarity as to the likely source of this investment and there is considerable competition for existing water sources (Mdee 2017).

Institutional Arrangements for Irrigation among Small-Scale Farmers

The Tanzanian Irrigation Policy emphasizes the use of formal irrigation 'schemes' as the primary mechanism for scaling up irrigated agriculture (URT 2009a). However, the sustainability of existing and future irrigation schemes continues to be problematic for most of the initiatives that the government has attempted to create through the Agricultural Sector Development Plan. Such problems can be explained partly by the continued government efforts to push for rehabilitation of existing schemes and construction of new schemes, while paying insufficient attention to the day-to-day operation and maintenance activities that are critical for their long-term survival (Abernethy 1994; URT 2009a). Such shortcomings and failings are not unique to Tanzania but are found as a challenge in irrigation worldwide (Mwakalila & Noe 2004; Wiggins 2013). 'Traditional'[3] irrigation practices are characterized as inefficient and undesirable in the 2009 Irrigation Policy. The policy therefore aims to formalize and 'improve' such 'traditional' irrigation practices. While a bureaucratic system of water and irrigation management exists in policy and legislation, in practice a complex mix of formal bureaucratic, and more informal and socially embedded relationships exist in complex and multi-layered configurations (Van Eeden et al. 2016; Woodhouse et al. 2016).

The capacity of irrigation management arrangements to manage water resources fairly, effectively and sustainably is much debated in the literature on irrigation in Tanzania (ESRF 1997; Maganga 2003;

[3] By this we mean practices that are rooted in social and political arrangements that often have a long history. However, we recognize that what is 'traditional' is itself subject to contestation and claim-making.

Mdemu et al. 2004; Igbadum et al. 2006; Rajabu & Mahoo 2008). Furthermore, there is insufficient research in Tanzania on the economics of competing uses of water (Mdee 2017). For example, Kadigi et al. (2008) compare water use for hydropower with water use for irrigation. Their conclusion is that water for agriculture has greater pro-poor benefits but water for energy has greater macroeconomic impacts. There is an urgent need to address these trade-offs, but the Tanzanian institutional landscape chronically lacks the capacity to do so.

Therefore, we need to be aware of a Tanzanian policy context that favours private and donor-funded investment in large schemes and formalizing traditional irrigation practice when considering the part irrigated agriculture can play in improving small-scale agricultural livelihoods.

The following parts of this chapter explore two ethnographies of small-scale irrigation in Tanzania in order to explore the landscape of irrigation practice:[4] Choma in the Uluguru Mountains and Dakawa Rice Farm in Mvomero District. Data were derived from a survey of 100 farmers in each location, combined with in-depth interviewing, focused group discussion and observation. The period of data collection spanned June 2013–January 2014. The comparison of these ostensibly very different cases reveals some interesting insights into the challenges of extending irrigation to small-scale farmers in Tanzania.

Informal and 'Traditional': The Case of Choma

Choma was selected as an example of productive small-scale irrigation, using new technology (hosepipes), but organized informally through 'traditional' relationships. At the same time, this small-scale system is threatened by a broader context of water scarcity downstream, as well as an official discourse that characterizes this irrigation as illegal and environmentally destructive.

Choma is situated in the Uluguru Mountains above the city of Morogoro, and lies in one of the catchment zones for the Morogoro Municipality domestic water supply. The Uluguru Mountains are a significant catchment area for the city of Dar es Salaam, and hence the water supply is politically and economically significant. Technical concerns in relation to the capture of water by farmers for irrigation, and the potentially harmful contamination of the water by human and livestock wastes, have led to an ongoing debate concerning the future of settlement in the mountains.

[4] This work was supported by the DfID-ESRC Growth Research Programme (DEGRP) [grant no. ES/J009415/1: Innovations to promote growth among small-scale irrigators].

The settlements of Choma are within the Uluguru Nature Reserve but on the slopes below the reserve. Given the steep terrain, the climatic conditions on the mountain can be highly variable.

There are no accurate population data available for the area known as Choma as the census data are collected at a level of local government above Choma, the Kata (ward) level. Local estimates suggest that the population of Choma is around 600 households. Our survey shows an average of 4 people per household (2 adults and 2 children), which is slightly lower than the census data for the area. The 2012 National Census records a population of 4,893 for the Mlimani area into which our study area falls, with an average family size of 4.3 (URT 2013b). It is striking that 97 per cent of those in our survey reported that they had always lived in their current location. This is confirmed by further interviews and literature (URT 2007c), which report that the Uluguru population are predominantly Muslim and from the WaLuguru ethnic group.

Staff from local NGOs and academics from Sokoine University of Agriculture suggest that there is a strong and uniform pattern of matrilineal inheritance, with the movement of men to the wife's household on marriage. However, the actual practice and patterning of inheritance is perhaps more complicated than this. While some farmers said land was inherited from their mothers, most said that they inherited from their parents without differentiating gender. Some women said they were given land by their husbands, who had themselves inherited it from their parents. The commercial purchase of land in the Choma area always requires approval and consent from the wider WaLuguru clan, and claims over plots can be multiple and contested.

The survey also indicates that farmers control an average of 2.5 acres each, comprising of 1.4 acres of dry land and 1.1 acres of irrigated land. Some 97 per cent of this land is customary freehold and is inherited, although interviewees stated that the informal purchase of small plots is becoming common. The vast majority of land in Tanzania falls under the 1999 Villages Land Act where allocation of land is managed and regulated by the Village Government. Individual land titles are issued under this system and recorded by the village. Land is leasehold and must be used productively or it can be reclaimed for reallocation by the Village Government. In the case of Choma, a more customary freehold system regulated by the WaLuguru remains dominant. There is very little officially titled freehold land in the Ulugurus. However, urban development is increasing rapidly on the lower slopes. According to local retired farmers and local government officials, this type of development is unregistered and illegal.

People living in the Choma area are predominantly farmers. According to our survey 66 per cent only do farming, 15 per cent have other business activities as well as agriculture, 16 per cent practise livestock keeping and 3 per cent have some formal employment. Of those surveyed 93 per cent had primary schooling only, 4 per cent had secondary education and 3 per cent had no education. This education profile is similar to the country as a whole, where in the latest UNDP Human Development Report, the adult population has a mean number of years of schooling of 5.3 (UNDP 2012a).

Support to agriculture and formal registration of land is provided through local government, and a range of NGOs also offer agricultural extension services and support to farmer groups. Morogoro Urban Water and Sewage Authority (MORUWASA) is working on water catchment tanks and improved inflows on the slopes below Choma using the same river as used by the Choma farmers. They also have money from the Millennium Challenge Account for this and for work on the Mindu dam. The Wami-Ruvu River Basin Office has responsibility for the water management as a whole, and for the formal registration of Water Users' Associations (WUAs). At the current time, there is no formally registered Water Users' Association in Choma.

Irrigation and Livelihoods

Irrigation in the Ulugurus has a long history. Where possible, given considerations of topography, most irrigation was practised through a furrow system, first recorded in the nineteenth century and banned around 2004 in the Choma area by local government (Mdee 2014). Farmers in Choma report that when furrows were banned by the local government, they moved to using gravity-fed hosepipes, which tapped into the mountain rivers and streams

Irrigation as currently practised is informal and determined by access to land and capital to purchase hosepipes and sprinklers to tap the water sources. Most farmers spoke of the individual needing to buy and maintain the hosepipes. Sometimes this might be done as a joint activity between neighbours, but the arrangement continues to be highly informal. Hosepipes have extended the area of land that can be irrigated, but there are still technical and topographical limitations.

According to the farmers, the reason that local government restricted the use of the old furrow irrigation system was that this system was very wasteful in terms of water use. The farmers themselves found that the use of hosepipes not only increases efficiency of water use but also decreases their labour requirements in digging and maintaining furrows:

> Before starting pipeline irrigation, with the furrows we would lose most of the water before it got to the farm. They also used a lot of energy to construct them. Using the furrows was the hardest life and this led people to learn a different thing. (Farmer interview (male), August 2013)

Irrigated fields lie alongside the steep river valleys, and on the terraced slopes around Choma. Irrigation is limited by the proximity to water sources and the technical feasibility of hosepipe connection. Farmers report that at certain times of the year, the levels of the streams decline, depending on the extent of the short rains:

> Sometimes there are small disputes arising, especially in December to February, because in these months the levels of the river are dropping, then the one who is up is getting a lot compared to the one who is down and the one who is up may refuse to cut off their pipeline, then we take the dispute to our street (village) chairperson. (Farmer interview (female), September 2013)

There are no formal institutional bureaucratic arrangements for water-sharing, but there is evidence of informal institutions deeply embedded in the socio-cultural life of the people of Choma. Individuals purchase hosepipes but might use them in cooperative arrangements with their friends and families. However, farmers do not reflect on this as being distinctively something of the WaLuguru; rather they express it as cooperation between friends and family who have lived in the same locations for generations:

> The one who is responsible for the pipeline is the person themself. It is their own property. Sharing is important because today you may help somebody and tomorrow you may be helped because nobody knows tomorrow. It is true though that some would like to access water but they fail because they don't have money to buy the pipeline. (Farmer Interview (female), September 2013)

Irrigation practice is embedded and contextualised by longstanding social relationships. People do not articulate these as rules but as their way of being 'together' as friends and family. At the same time, water access is constrained by land ownership (through inheritance or through purchase) and technological limitations. New technology has been adopted into these relationships, but local government intervention has been actively resisted. Most interviewees emphasize fairness and sharing in relation to water use that draws on their social connections:

> I believe in these people that I am sharing the water with since most of them are my relatives and in our tribe we have the system of helping one another. (Farmer interview (male), August 2013)

There is no formal system for determining water availability. Within the cooperative arrangements of neighbours, if it is perceived that water levels to the hosepipes have dropped, they will discuss and agree among themselves on a rota to share the water that is available. If water levels drop very low, then they may irrigate at night to improve efficiency.

Irrigation is central to farmers' livelihoods. Without it they would be dependent on rain-fed agriculture and probably could not sustain themselves in their current location. In our farmer survey, 97 per cent of farmers were irrigating, and 97 per cent of those are using the small streams and rivers flowing down the mountainside. Only 1 per cent reported using a borehole and 2 per cent natural wetlands. On the irrigated land, there is a high diversity of vegetable crops produced, including carrots, celery, onions, lettuce, Chinese cabbages, cabbages, leeks, coriander and others. Fruit crops include tomatoes, peppers, strawberries, raspberries and other berries. Passionfruit, papaya and bananas are also grown on family plots. The vegetable crops have a good market in Morogoro. Farmers often sell direct to expatriates and wealthier local families living in the Forest area of Morogoro. Fruit sellers from the mountains also sell their produce at the door of the local supermarkets in Morogoro.

Strawberry production is unusual in Tanzania and has good markets in Dar es Salaam and Arusha. A small tub of strawberries can be sold on the street for Tsh. 3,000 or to tourists for Tsh. 5,000. At the farm gate, the farmer may receive Tsh. 1,500 per bowl. Production is continuous all year round, depending on the capacity of the plants and farmers keep no written records. Estimates of gross income made from one acre of strawberries varied from Tsh. 800,000 to 2 million. Interviewees report that buyers for strawberries also come direct to their farms.

On the dry land (often steep terraced slopes), farmers predominantly grow a more usual mix of maize and beans once per year according to the rainy season.

Agricultural livelihoods are clearly dependent on water. However, most farmers state that there is always sufficient water. There is seasonality to the flow of water but the cooperative arrangements between farmers are adapted to cope with this. There is much more of an issue with water availability on the rain-fed land where farmers talk about their production as being more risky. Improvements such as contouring and inputs of manure can be helpful, but inputting capital to such land is still risky, as opposed to focusing on the more guaranteed production from the irrigated land.

As described above, there are no formal structures for irrigation management in Choma. However, officials within local government argue that they are needed. This is part of a wider concern with the possible effects of irrigation on downstream water supply, and possibly with the very fact of lack of regulation. Thus, according to interviews with Local Government Extension Workers, Ward Secretaries and Staff of MORUWASA and WRRBO, irrigation in Choma is illegal as farmers have not been organized into groups and issued with water permits. The WRRBO would prefer that the Choma farmers should be organized into Water Users' Associations so that they could be managed and educated more effectively:

> At the moment there seems to be no formal arrangement to manage water access. However, they are in the process of coming up with one.

> This will help to manage water usage, how much that can be used and formal rules that can be applied. (MORUWASA Officer, October 2013)

Another informant from an NGO argues that:

> The population is growing and even their kids are going into the same business. So with the climate change issues and the amount of rain, even with hosepipes then they can't take enough water to meet their family needs. The approach that Wami-Ruvu (WRRBO) is taking is to tell them to pay their bills. They are supposed to establish a water users' association but the people are resisting to pay – they say 'what have you done for us?' (WCST Officer, September 2013)

Our interviews reveal that there seems to be some confusion over which formal institutions are managing the water on the mountain. The actual responsibility for water rights sits with the WRRBO, but local government officials indicate that they think that it rests with MORUWASA. There is a desire to extend the registration of WUAs to the Choma area, but this has not yet been implemented.

As described above, within itself the informal system of purchasing hosepipes appears to be working well, while water use is unregulated by external intervention. Farmers report high levels of cooperation, and there is little evidence of water shortage or conflict among farmers. The challenge lies not with the internal arrangements for water-sharing but rather in the more extensive question of upstream and downstream water use. Local government officials perceive that Choma farmers are in conflict with the urban supply to Morogoro, both in terms of quantity and quality of water. As one told us:

> People are living very close to the intake and they are diverting the water – they are taking more than 50 per cent. In 1999 there were only about 500 people living there and then the government built schools, a hospital and brought electricity. This has encouraged people to come and build. (MORUWASA Official, October 2013)

However, other perspectives tell a different story, suggesting that the small-scale hosepipe irrigation is insignificant with regard to the Morogoro water supply. An alternative explanation is that the real problem is the larger-scale construction of dwellings for wealthier residents on the mountains. For example, we were told that:

> There are many illegal constructions in the mountains and we need to preserve the water sources, but also even big institutions like the Universities and Army bases have not been regulated for their water use. We have not been able to do this as yet. (WRRBO Official, November 2013)

It was this argument over water usage on the mountain that led to an attempt in 2006/7 to evict farmers from Choma (and other areas) and to relocate them:

In 2006/7 there was a huge conflict between the government and the residents from Choma and surrounding areas as the government tried to remove them without consultation. This caused a huge row which ended with the residents going to the President to resist this move. Two years later (2009) they were told that they can stay under certain conditions that they should look after the environment and work with the NGOs. (SUA Academic interview, November 2013)

Farmers themselves do not mention any concern for domestic water supplies to Morogoro other than referring to government criticisms of the furrow system as wasteful. Some suggest that the farmers were targeted for removal from the mountain as they have little voice in local politics and therefore they were easy to blame for the problems of domestic water supply in Morogoro.

The current government position is that, if they cannot force the farmers off the mountains, then they need to be taught to farm in an environmentally sustainable way. This work is seen to be the remit of NGOs, rather than of government agricultural extension officers. At a higher institutional level there appear to be several themes to discussions on the challenges of the informal irrigation arrangements in the Ulugurus, but as yet no implementation or concrete action plan proposed to formalize the irrigation. According to interviewed officials, WRRBO wants to formalize arrangements and make farmers pay for water, but currently it has neither the staff capacity nor the financial resources to do so. Others suggest that ultimately the farmers will have to be moved. Reporting on a discussion from the task force established within the Morogoro Municipality Council to review the issue of water use on the mountain we were told that:

> We talked about the options and we think that there are around 10,000 households that would need to be moved from the mountain and the costs of compensation are just too high. They did a survey about this but it was disrupted by political things. (WCST Staff Member, September 2013)

There are also indications of the significance of the wider political nature of the scheme to move the farmers from the Ulugurus, which connects to a wider landscape of hydro-politics:

> The Mayor of Morogoro told me about the pressure that was put on him to move the people from the mountain. The problem is that the Ulugurus are vulnerable as they provide the water for Dar. The parliamentarians are getting pressure from the big industries such as Coca-Cola and Tanzanian Breweries to increase the water supply, but they are also the ones who should be paying to conserve the environment in the catchments. (SUA Academic, October 2013)

The challenge for the informal nature of water use by the Choma farmers is that they have little visibility and representation as a group while they are informal. They have no official voice within the institutions that manage water. The farmers themselves currently appear to resist formalization for fear that they will be made to pay for the water they use:

> There are no government policies about using water for irrigation and we don't want them because they will disturb us. We need freedom in irrigation. (Farmer (male), October 2013)

The farmers almost universally have an attitude of 'what has the government ever done for us':

> perhaps if they had brought infrastructure here then we might pay something. (Farmer (male), September 2013)

National regulations on the formation of water users' associations and on the issue of formal water user rights have not been implemented in Choma, and Morogoro Municipality simply labels their water use as 'illegal':

> They have created their own way of irrigation that the government does not approve of. The use of hosepipes is against the law and so they do this illegally. The rule is that they are not allowed to farm within 60 metres of the water sources, however none of the residents comply with this. (Local Government Ward Officer, August 2013)

Discussion and Conclusions

If more formal mechanisms for water access were to be imposed through the formalization of water access and creation of WUAs, this could have potentially negative implications for the vulnerability of the Choma farmers as it would constrain their current water use. The impact of introducing a formal set of rules might also disrupt the relatively conflict-free informal water-sharing arrangements. However, formalization could give the Choma farmers a more legitimate voice within the municipality in order to represent their interests.

The farmers themselves use their own production levels as the main indicator for the success and efficiency of their irrigation. There is no other formal monitoring of water levels or water use with regard to irrigation. Although local government officials speak of the desirability of monitoring water availability, they are not sure how to go about it. Similarly, the key informant interviews with WRRBO suggest that ideally they should measure and regulate water use as against the permits issued, but the resources and capacity are lacking to do this. JICA/MoW (2013) confirms this observation in noting a concern that water rights are being sold, but no monitoring of water use is conducted.

This concern was further confirmed by an informal remark from a WRRBO employee:

'We just sell water, that is all we do.'

Formal and Commercialized Irrigation: The Case of Dakawa

Dakawa is situated about 40 km from the city of Morogoro on the road to Dodoma. It is in the Wami-Ruvu River Basin, close to the Wami River, and is the site of one of the largest irrigated rice schemes in Tanzania. Dakawa Rice Farm is a former state rice farm constructed with the assistance of North Korea during the 1980s, but now cooperatively managed by a Water Users' Association of small-scale rice farmers. The case was selected as it is an example of Tanzania's current approach to developing irrigated agricultural production. It relates well to the implementation of Kilimo Kwanza ('Agriculture First') and to the Southern Agricultural Growth Corridor (SAGCOT) initiatives of the Tanzanian Government.

Dakawa Rice Farm appears to have been the site of repeated aid interventions and is currently the focus of USAID and Chinese projects. The farm has a chequered political history, but is currently a 'pin-up' example of how irrigated rice can benefit small-scale farmers in terms of improving their productivity and increasing their incomes. As we will explore below, Dakawa highlights a number of themes that are significant for understanding the politics of small-scale irrigation.

First, there is an underlying issue of the viability of irrigated rice production in the rice farm, given the high costs of pumping water from the Wami River and the low level of the river. In addition, the idea of 'smallness' is a contested theme within different people's understanding of how the scheme works, and this in turn has important links with fairness, trust and transparency in the formal management of the scheme. Lastly, the high level of aid intervention suggests a complex politics of rice production and agricultural intervention in Dakawa, with implications for how donors support such initiatives.

Dakawa: The Settlement and the Scheme

The settlement of Dakawa is relatively new, with an agricultural population centred on the irrigated 2,000-hectare[5] rice farm. Our survey indicates that 77 per cent had not lived in the area for all of their lives, with the most common period of settlement being in the 2000s. Interviewees confirm that the population fluctuates massively in relation to the labour demands of paddy production, and that many of the ethnic groups of Tanzania can be found there. There are significant numbers of Maasai pastoralists in the area, and tensions over access to land and damage to crops are common.

[5] Official documents and donors tend to state farm size in hectares. Farmers within the Dakawa Rice Scheme measure their plots in acres. 1 hectare = 2.47 acres.

Dakawa is said to be a Ward (kata) in the Tanzanian Local Government System but does not appear as such in the 2012 Census Report (URT 2013a). Local government changes seem to have caused confusion, and ward officials could not explain why Dakawa was not listed as a ward in the recent census. They thought perhaps it had been put into the Mvomero ward, which is listed as having a population of 37,321. Dakawa village only has a fraction of this population, but the village office does not have accurate or current population data.

Survey results and observations in Dakawa indicate that livelihoods are predominantly agricultural. Some 51 per cent of our respondents rely only on agriculture. The other 49 per cent combine agriculture with other activities: 35 per cent of all respondents operate a small business (such as shops and bars), 9 per cent are livestock keepers and 5 per cent also have formal paid employment. The predominant crop is irrigated rice paddy, with 78 per cent of survey households doing this. On dry land, 47 per cent of farmers produce maize and 16 per cent rice, with small numbers also producing tomatoes, leafy vegetables and other crops.

Farmers in the Dakawa area tend to have a combination of land within the irrigated scheme and outside of it. Land outside of the scheme is used for rain-fed agriculture. Our survey calculated the average total land holding as 5.76 acres, with 3.5 acres average of irrigated land and 2.2 acres of dry land. Land within the rice farm is accessed by membership of the rice farm cooperative society, which we describe in further detail below.

The Dakawa Rice Farm is operated by Ushirika wa Wakulima Wadogo Wadogo Dakawa (translated as Society of Small Farmers in Dakawa), and known by the acronym UWAWAKUDA. To access land within the scheme an individual must obtain membership of UWAWAKUDA. UWAWAKUDA is working with USAID on a project to rehabilitate the pumping station, which draws water from the Wami River. There may be some institutional confusion in relation to the legal classification of UWAWAKUDA. The Wami-Ruvu River Basin Office (WRRBO) views it as a formal and registered WUA. However, other key informants suggest that UWAWAKUDA is a cooperative society and so is regulated by a different constitution and law. As a society, UWAWAKUDA would have a formal relationship with government; as a WUA it would be more akin to an NGO.

Farmers within the Dakawa Rice Farm have benefited in the last few seasons from the inputs of the USAID NAFAKA project and from other projects delivered through the Chollima Research Centre. There has been a move to using the SARO5 hybrid rice variety and to transplanting rather than broadcasting rice seed.

The Chollima Research Centre (CRC) is also located in Dakawa and uses 100 acres of land within the scheme. It produces rice seed for the national Agricultural Seed Agency (ASA). This centre is under the

Ministry of Agriculture, Food and Cooperatives. The current Chairman of UWAWAKUDA is also an Agronomist in CRC. Agricultural Officers from CRC work with local farmers on improving the productivity of rice production. CRC has a number of externally funded donor projects relating to rice productivity, such as an Australian-funded initiative on the 'System for Rice Intensification'.

Dakawa is also the location for the Demonstration Centre of China Agricultural Technology in Tanzania. Opened in 2009, the centre has 62 hectares of land and is experimenting with the production of Chinese hybrid varieties of rice, maize, vegetables, as well as intensive poultry production. This centre draws water from a borehole, not from the Wami River. The centre works in partnership with the Tanzanian staff of CRC and hosts farmer extension activities. Outside of the Dakawa Rice Farm, land registration, allocation and agricultural extension work comes under the Mvomero District Council and the Dakawa Ward Office. The Wami-Ruvu River Basin Office (WRRBO) oversees the use of water from the Wami River and can issue water rights.

Costs and Benefits of Rice Farming

Rice is the only crop produced within the scheme. Several farmers report increases in productivity owing to inputs from USAID, CRC and the efforts of farmers themselves. Farmers report the potential to get up to 45 50 kg bags of rice per acre with current irrigation techniques. However, a number also report that in 2012 they were able to get Tsh. 100,000 (£40) per bag of rice, and that in the 2013 season they received only Tsh. 50,000 (£20). Therefore the increasing productivity has been offset by a decline in price. Interviews with farmers suggest that many farmers who had taken loans for their production costs were now concerned about their repayments given the drop in price they were able to get for the rice. There were also complaints that payment for rice came very late.

According to key informants, all rice is sold at the farm gate, with buyers coming to Dakawa. The farm currently has no storage facilities, processing capacity or transport. UWAWAKUDA staff and members argue that these are needed to increase the profitability and sustainability of the scheme. Another key informant explained further that the only milling machine was owned by the scheme under TANRICE,[6] but this was sold off to a private investor.

Some farmers reported their belief that rain-fed land could produce greater profits on rice production than irrigated land in a good year, as the land outside the scheme could be farmed with lower inputs and so had a lower production cost. They reached this conclusion without

---

[6] TANRICE was a project supported by JICA: see http://www.ippmedia.com/frontend/?l=45983.

reference to records of costs of production and sales. However, financial analysis (based on further farmer interviews) of inputs and outputs supports the different conclusion that in fact the irrigated land is more financially profitable (Mdee 2014).

The overall profitability calculations for the individual farmers in the Dakawa scheme do not include the full cost of electricity and maintenance for the scheme as a whole, so their profits are effectively subsidized. Analysis of the accounts for UWAWAKUDA suggests that farmer membership contributions are not paying the full costs of production in the scheme and that large inputs of aid fill the shortfall (Mdee 2014).

Farmer interviews suggest that within the scheme there is a general satisfaction with the efficiency and effectiveness of their own production. They were able to articulate significant recent gains in productivity through access to better seed, fertilizers and improved cultivation techniques through USAID/NAFAKA. Most farmers interviewed also expressed that water-sharing (with some limitations) is as fair as it can be given the current difficulties with pumping operations.

Research Officers from CRC and USAID Project Staff confirm that a significant amount of work has been done with scheme members on improving productivity of production, for example on systems of transplanting seedlings, and the use of manure and other inputs. Access to credit has also improved farmers' ability to purchase inputs. On the other hand, USAID Project Staff also mentioned that farmers were vulnerable to being sold unsafe chemicals. An example was cited of a case where Chinese sales people sold a contaminated pesticide to one farmer, who then lost his whole crop as a result.

Managing Dakawa: A Turbulent History and a Complex Present

The Dakawa Rice Farm has had quite a turbulent political history, and the current operating arrangements are the latest in a succession of attempts to manage it. Built in 1981 with aid from North Korea, it was originally a state rice farm under the National Agriculture and Food Corporation (NAFCO) (Chachage & Mbunda 2009). NAFCO collapsed in 1996 and the farms under its control were sold or transferred to the Parastatal Sector Reform Commission (PSRC). Reportedly the farm was unused for a period of ten years before this.

After the intervention of PSRC, the farm was handed over to a number of high-profile police or political figures ('the group of 6'), and they invited other villagers to join them. An organization called DAKCOP emerged in 1999 to take over the farm. At this time PSRC issued a letter to order the farm to be handed over to the villagers of Dakawa. The then District Commissioner ordered the farm to be divided between the Dakawa Village Council, Government Officers and DAKCOP. This led to the breakup of DAKCOP, and UWAWAKUDA was established.

This period coincides with an increase in the population of Dakawa according to Local Government Officials, but it is not captured in census data. Since then there have been numerous allegations of corruption and mismanagement. The first Chairman of UWAWAKUDA was deselected after two years as members were not satisfied that some plots were inaccessible and did not receive water. The second Chairman, elected in 2005/6 for two years, was accused of giving plots to more than one person:

> At this point the Village Council decided that they wanted to take control of the farm and they installed their candidate to become the Chairman. (Farmer interview (male), September 2013)

However, this new Chairman was also accused of corruption and mismanagement:

> Another conflict emerged because water availability become more scarce and people who paid their money to get the plot didn't get any. There was a lot of conflict about money as it seems the money was not deposited in the bank. Therefore some people took the matter to the Ministry of Agriculture and they conducted an investigation. (Farmer interview (male), September 2013)

Following an investigation, the previous chairman was removed and the current leadership put in place. The current chair is an employee of the Ministry of Agriculture and Food Security. He was appointed by the Ministry alongside a Deputy Chair, Bursar, Farm Manager and Pump Attendant, all installed for a period of three years to get the farm back on track:

> Since they took over there hasn't been a problem, money is available and the productivity has increased from 15–19 bags per acre to 30–35 bags. (Farmer interview (male), September 2013)

It may be significant that this period coincides with external intervention by USAID under the 'Feed the Future' Programme, which has significant inputs for increasing farmer productivity. Work on clearing irrigation channels and a feasibility study for the replacement of the existing pumps has also been undertaken. Nonetheless, there are continuing suggestions that the management of the scheme has been politicized, with positions of influence reflecting political party allegiances. In this account, the 'real' small farmers of Dakawa are marginalized by less visible but more powerful political interests:

> If the Regional Commissioner wants his plot's water then all he needs to do is to call the office here and it will happen, even if it is not in the planned watering cycle. (Farmer (female), November 2013)

According to UWAWAKUDA, the farm is divided into 12-acre blocks, and the maximum area of land that can be farmed by one person is 12 acres. However, there is evidence that there is great variation in plot size. Some of the blocks are in fact farmed by more than one family given constraints in capital for investment (hence the average of 3.5 acres per farmer in our survey). However, it is also reported that some families control several blocks by registering them under the names of different family members. Further it has also been asserted that large blocks of land are owned by significant individuals working in government and the armed services.

Current membership of UWAWAKUDA is reported to be just less than 954 farmers. However, these figures cannot be verified and several interviewees (including USAID Project Staff) mentioned that access to member lists is neither open nor transparent. Some went as far as to suggest that in reality many 'farmers' are simply 'labourers' on other people's land.

All of the water for the Dakawa Rice Farm is taken by pumping station from the Wami River, which flows through Dakawa. Tsh. 15 million (£6,000) per month) is paid by UWAWAKUDA to TANESCO for electricity. Another USAID-funded project is under way to rehabilitate and install new pumps in the pumping station to make this operation more efficient.

A number of interviewees (UWAWAKUDA Staff and USAID Project Staff) report that the flow of the Wami River restricts the operation of the scheme. In 2013 only one crop of rice had been cultivated as the level of the river was too low to run the pumps outside of the rainy season. This is attributed to competition from upstream users including large commercial investors who, it is said, are also taking water from the Wami (USAID Project Staff, WRRBO Officials).

Water access from the river outside of the scheme is in theory regulated by the WRRBO. The local Wami-Ruvu River Basin Ward Officer explained that at the local level he is only responsible for registering new groups of Water Users and informing them of the regulations that are in place under the 2009 Water Users' Act. He is also responsible for enforcing this act but said that no one has yet been prosecuted under it:

> Water usage has increased due to irrigation. Long ago people did not know how to irrigate. We are trying to control this by giving permits and educating those who are water thieving. The river level has gone down due to the lack of rains and not due to the number of users. (WRRBO Local Officer, October 2013)

Officials of WRRBO confirm that in the Dakawa area, work on registering WUAs is well advanced and they are functioning to issue water permits. As in the Choma case, they suggest that WRRBO has limited capacity to regulate or control the quantity of water that users take once their permit has been issued. It was further said that there was an upstream water use issue with the Wami River, where it is believed that the river has been diverted by a large investor, for irrigation use. This was also suggested by a retired commercial farmer with long experience of the area. Other large water users on the Wami in the Dakawa area are Mtibwa Sugar and EcoEnergy – producing sugar and renewable energy.

All farmers using the scheme are members of UWAWAKUDA and can apply to become members of the Board that oversees the operation of the irrigation scheme. All members are entitled to attend the General Meeting, where the Board Members, Chair and Secretary are selected by a vote. The Chair and Secretary are salaried positions. To access land in the scheme a membership fee (referred to as HISA) must be paid. There is currently a waiting list for membership. Members are required to have 10 shares (HISA) costing Tsh. 10,000 (£4) each. The share does not generate a dividend.

The current Chairman of the Board is also an Agronomist at the nearby Chollima Research Centre. The Board also employs a professional Farm Manager to supervise pumping operations. Members of UWAWAKUDA pay Tsh. 60,000 (£24) per acre per year to cover the cost of electricity to operate the pumping station. Water is drawn from the Wami River by the pumping station, and it is the Board who make decisions on when water will be pumped, and the cycle by which it reaches the different blocks. This charge does not cover the costs of electricity or the maintenance of irrigation channels. The management is responsible for the maintenance of the main canals and pumping the water. In theory these activities are covered by the fees paid by members, but accounts show a shortfall.

Within the 12-acre plots, the users are responsible for the maintenance of channels and water flows. Where multiple farmers share a block they elect a leader and must cooperate with one another on deciding when water is allowed into the plots. Irrigation water is pumped according to a cycle agreed by the Farm Manager and the Board. Given the problems with the level of the Wami River, in the 2013 season, water was pumped to the farms from April to July. The plots of land nearest to the pumping station are the first to receive water. Those plots farthest away from the pumping station do not receive water until several weeks after the first plots, and therefore the timing of tasks and production varies according to the position of the plot within the scheme. There are four sections to the farm and gates across the irrigation canals are open and shut to control the flow of the water.

It was reported that the timing of the flow can disadvantage those farmers with plots at the furthest corner as, by the time they receive the water, the weather is already becoming colder (June/July). Farmers interviewed see this as unfair and note cases where some with the plots furthest away have failed to produce a crop.

Farmers within each 12-acre block need to decide collectively when they will open the gates to water the plot. They can make this decision when the water is flowing to their section of the farm. In principle anyone who is found to be stealing water can be expelled from

UWAWAKUDA, and there are one or two examples of farmers being expelled as a result of physical conflict over water stealing during the night. Farmers uniformly say that fairness is important as a principle, and on the whole agree that the formal system tries to be fair. Most farmers interviewed report that the current arrangements are working well. Given the turbulent political history of the farm, it was said by several interviewees that, in the past, pressure might be brought to bear on the farm managers to divert water to plots belonging to powerful individuals.

The main reported limitation of this system is where many farmers sharing a 12-acre plot may be at different stages of cultivation or may use different methods of rice production (broadcasting vs transplanting) and may require water at different stages. Some farmers may also be more organized than others. Farmers within the blocks must have a high degree of cooperation. Many farmers reported this as an issue. Some said that they had worked with their co-plot holders for several years, and so they had a high level of cooperation and trust. They could meet and agree when they need to allow the water into the plot:

> We have worked with each other for some time and so we know how to co-operate! (Farmer interview (female), August 2013)

However, most farmers also cited this arrangement as a reason for conflicts and disagreements. Levels of trust between plot holders clearly vary, as shown in the quotation below:

> We don't trust each other because everyone is looking after their own interest. Although we might be talking and sometimes do things like ploughing and harvesting together, deep down no one trusts anyone. (Farmer interview (female), September 2013)

There is no evidence of open conflict over the allocation of land within the scheme, but there are allegations of issues around membership of UWAWAKUDA, which itself confers access to land. It is alleged that some people have been allocated plots without having to move up the waiting list. Further some families have gained access to multiple plots by registering them to a series of their relatives. One farmer expressed frustration that the farm is not for the people of Dakawa:

> For your information, there are many villagers 'Dakawa dwellers' who are in need of land in the scheme but don't have access to it, therefore the issue of land accessibility is becoming complex as time goes on. (Farmer interview (female), January 2014)

More instances of conflict relate to the water-sharing arrangements in the 12-acre blocks. Farmer interviews suggested that such conflicts are common, and where they cannot be resolved they are brought to the farm manager and Chairman for adjudication. Examples were cited in the 2013 season of two members who were expelled for stealing water from others at night. One interviewee attested that physical conflict had erupted on occasion, and that there had once been a fatality as a result.

Another interviewee says that water theft is common:

> There is also water thieving, which is very problematic. It gives me as a leader of a block a moral dilemma as to whether to report them, as it warrants the cancellation of their membership. These are people we know therefore we tend to let them off, which can only encourage such behaviour. (Farmer interview (male), November 2013)

Another farmer also alleges bribery:

> People are very corrupt, some people give as much as Tsh. 50,000 (£20) to irrigators so that their plots get water but you can give as little as a loaf of bread. The management never come to inspect if the plots were watered or not and therefore this gives the opportunity for corruption to continue. (Farmer interview (male), October 2013)

There is a range of views from the farmers within the scheme as to the 'fairness' of the systems for managing irrigation. Some people argue that the tight schedule for pumping water is too rigid and has no flexibility. Others suggest that the flat rate of Tsh. 60,000 per acre is not fair as those who only have 1 acre are likely to be much poorer than those with 12 acres. The management accept that there are members who may have insufficient capital to pay the fees and may be forced to rent out their plots to others.

One female farmer reported in January 2014 that:

> there are rumours that next season each farmer will pay almost double per acre as compared to last season. It is expected to exceed Tsh. 100,000 per acre. This will be a disaster to most of us. If we don't pay the expected amount then we will be considered ineligible and our land will be granted to other people – for that land access for us small farmers is not guaranteed.

Financial analysis, in combination with key informant interviews, suggests high levels of borrowing by farmers to fund production. Further analysis is needed to investigate if an increase in water payment would impact heavily on the viability of production.

Questions of Sustainability

The UWAWAKUDA Chairman articulates an impressive vision for expansion of the scheme, including concreting the irrigation channels to improve water retention and efficiency, construction of on-site storage and processing facilities, and the purchase of transport that would enable farmers to sell rice at a much higher price. However, it is clear from scrutiny of the farm accounts that, with the current level of farmer contributions, it is unlikely that UWAWAKUDA could raise the capital for this type of development without further donor intervention. It appears therefore that the scheme is not sustainable from internal resources.

There are also differences of opinion in relation to the issue of 'smallness' and efficiency. The registration of several plots to the same families (using relatives' names) is seen by some as subverting the ethos of 'smallness' and preventing poorer farmers from accessing the scheme. However, one USAID-connected aid worker with experience of several aid-funded attempts to revive the Dakawa Rice Farm over a number of decades, argues that at least those with large acreages can afford to invest in the irrigation infrastructure, such as concreting channels. Large owners in this view are successful entrepreneurs.

The greatest limitation to the long-term sustainability of the scheme is the insufficient level of the Wami River. If water levels were adequate at least two crops per year could be produced. This is the baseline assumption of donors looking at the rehabilitation of the scheme. Without this, several key informants have expressed concern that the scheme is not viable. Similarly, the high cost of electricity to operate the pumps is also a significant issue for the scheme and a limitation in terms of cost-effective production.

External partners have played a significant role alongside the political and business entrepreneurs in reviving the ailing NAFCO farm. The farm would not be operational without a significant aid subsidy from USAID (and before them JICA through TANRICE). The current aid fashions around agriculture and the location of Dakawa (a day trip from Dar es Salaam) makes it an ideal 'photo op' for aid visitors. As one Dakawa farmer put it:

'All the world is coming to Dakawa ... even the Queen of Denmark has been there.'

Conclusions

While the two study locations offer examples of very different types of irrigation management structures, technology and scale, they point to the possibility of several conclusions:

Formality and informality
The Choma case suggests that Tanzanian water policy and management institutions are not effective at dealing with the reality of institutional plurality. Instead, Choma shows informal and traditional irrigation practice simply branded as 'illegal'. The evidence suggests that despite the small scale and illegality of their irrigation, the Choma farmers are successfully able to produce commercial vegetable and fruit

crops. They also show high levels of interest in organic and conservation agriculture where supported by effective local partners such as NGOs. The Tanzanian water institutions appear unable to engage at all with informal water use, and the farmers themselves are resistant to being required to formalize their traditional and longstanding water use.

In Dakawa, the formality of the water access by no means solves internal conflicts over the use of water. Membership of UWAWAKUDA is political and contested, and a lack of transparency and accountability is in evidence despite the formal democratic and reporting structures.

Contested water use narratives

In the Choma case there appears to be very clear contestation over the rights to water. The WaLuguru farmers, who have lived in and farmed the Uluguru Mountains for centuries, believe that they can use the water from the rivers without governmental interference. The wider regional politics of water supply acknowledge that the Uluguru Mountains form the main water catchment for Morogoro Municipality, as well as for Tanzania's largest city, Dar es Salaam. For some the Choma farmers are making a good living in a difficult terrain and can be encouraged (both financially and productively) to manage their environment to conserve water. For others, the farmers are destroying and polluting important water sources and they must be moved. The political ecology of water use in Choma is explored in depth in Mdee (2017).

In Dakawa, the right of the Dakawa scheme to take water from the Wami River is not in doubt; the scheme holds an official permit. However, the levels of the Wami River have fallen to the extent that the pumping station can only be used in the rainy season, and therefore the scheme cannot operate at full capacity. There is no doubt that there are increasing numbers of legitimate water users (alongside illegitimate ones), but the needs of all these users are not being met. Within the scheme itself we also see a fairness narrative around who accesses water and when. Throughout the recent history of the scheme this has proved a critical factor in the perceived effectiveness of the management and in allegations of corruption and political interference, which might give preferential water access to certain farmers (Harrison & Mdee 2017).

Lack of capacity to monitor and track water use

It follows from the points above that the inability of current formal water user institutions to monitor and regulate the water use of even legal water users is a serious limitation. The Choma farmers become an easy target for blame for their 'excessive use', and the falling levels of the Wami River in the Dakawa case can be attributed to the increasing numbers of legitimate but ultimately competing users. One WRRBO employee, in brushing off a request for an interview says 'we simply sell water, that is all we do'. Ultimately, this unregulated and unmonitored selling of water distorts access to and use of water resources (see Van Eeden et al. 2016).

Doubts over scale, efficiency and sustainability

This research investigates how small-scale irrigation can improve farmer productivity and how farmers can receive, construct and share knowledge and information that will allow them to enhance production. In this sense, both study locations show some success. In Choma, the farmers produce high-value commercial crops from very small plots. This has improved their livelihoods and well-being. The success of local NGOs, such as Sustainable Agriculture Tanzania, in working with farmers on organic and soil conservation techniques, has shown farmers to be willing to learn where techniques are low-cost and benefit their productivity.

In Dakawa, rice production levels have doubled or even tripled. Effective inputs of resources and techniques from external donors (USAID, JICA) have produced good productivity gains. Rice production is a profitable enterprise under the current Dakawa model. The increased adoption of transplanting and the use of the 'system of rice intensification' shows that farmers are willing to learn and implement new techniques where the resources are available for them to do so.

However, in both cases, longer-term sustainability is a concern. In Choma, the narrative of rights to the river water must be resolved. Ways need to be found to facilitate institutional engagement and to give the farmers a meaningful voice.

In Dakawa, inputs of aid subsidize the true costs of production. Rice productivity has increased but the market price has declined, and therefore incomes have not risen. Many farmers take on high levels of credit to invest in rice, and many struggle from year to year to obtain the inputs costs. Already some of the bigger farmers are seeking an escape to more profitable projects if the contribution of farmers to the scheme has to rise. The darker politics of who really benefits from the Dakawa rice scheme also cast doubt that such grand schemes, farmed by 'small-farmer' cooperatives, can really deliver the transformation of Tanzanian small-farmer interests that they are assumed to promise.

The existing institutions of water management, irrigation management and agriculture are seemingly unable to resolve the dilemmas outlined above while in their existing forms. It is essential that they do so. With increasing populations, the uncertainties of climate change and a national strategy of structural economic transformation, it is imperative for the Tanzanian state to address competing demands for water in an inclusive and sustainable manner.

8

The Industrial Development of Tanzania in Comparative African Perspective

Peter Lawrence

Following decolonization throughout much of Africa, early development plans and policies focused on how to move rapidly from a raw material-exporting economy to a manufacturing industrial economy. Tanzania, although emphasizing the importance of rural development and domestic food production, was no exception in setting out ambitious plans for manufacturing growth. This chapter will try to situate Tanzania's industrialization experience in the context of the wider African experience in order to address the question of why, in Tanzania, as across the continent, economies have not produced the kinds of structural changes that have characterized the growth of manufacturing in other parts of the world.

This chapter will first review Tanzania's manufacturing growth performance over the five decades since independence in comparison with other African countries and the Global South; secondly, consider various explanations that have been given for the performance of Tanzania and countries across the continent; and thirdly, discuss the relatively new theorization and associated policy proposals for more rapid structural change. The chapter will conclude that Tanzania's manufacturing performance has mirrored that of the continent as a whole and, like even the best-performing African economies, Tanzania has yet to develop a strategy for changing its economic structures in order to break away from being predominantly dependent on the export of industrial and agricultural raw materials to service manufacturing elsewhere in the world. However, the advent of a new administration prioritizing such a strategy could significantly change its rate of transformation.

The Early Strategy: Import Substitution

As Weiss and Jalilian explain in Chapter 9 of this volume, the conventional view in the period leading up to decolonization and afterwards was that a key part of the development process was manufacturing industrialization. The growth of manufacturing was expected to begin with the first stage processing of agricultural and mineral raw materials produced by these other sectors, so that more of the value added to products remained within the domestic economy. Consequent upon the accumulation of capital from these industrial activities, investment would take place in intermediate and producer goods industries so that the necessary inputs of machinery and parts would be produced domestically and deepen the industrialization process.

At Independence some minor industrial processing of agricultural raw materials had already taken place, the most notable examples in Tanzania being the decortication of sisal leaf, which produced sisal fibre, and the ginning of cotton to separate seeds from fibre. But, instead of total fibre production being turned into the final products of ropes and agricultural twine in the case of sisal or textiles in the case of cotton, the majority of the output of fibre was exported to be processed in the developed countries' factories. Nevertheless, the sisal plantations were still referred to as the sisal industry because of this first-stage processing of leaf into fibre by the mechanical decorticators in the 'factories' on the estates, and cotton ginneries were also counted as an industry, and thus included in the industrial statistics.

At Independence in 1961, Tanganyika, as it then was, had 220 industrial establishments employing 10 or more people, with an aggregate labour force of 20,000 workers in a population of nine million. Manufacturing industry constituted 4 per cent of total GDP (Skarstein & Wangwe 1986: 2). The sector was dominated by food processing, beverages and tobacco, with some furniture manufacturing and transport equipment repair, but also included first stage processing of primary commodities – principally sisal decorticating and cotton ginning.

The early development plans of the 1960s, the Three-Year Plan (1961–4) and the First Five-Year Plan (1964–9), set out a wish list of manufacturing projects that represented the acceleration of the process of import substitution, a process that had already begun under the colonial administration (World Bank 1961). These plans were less about a planning process in which there were clear organized interlinkages between the sectors of industry that were to be promoted, but rather a reading from the list of imports of manufactures to identify what might be produced locally. In theory this would result in a fall in demand for imports and help to balance the trade account of the balance of payments. The first plan proposed the manufacture of 'simple consumer goods' (Skarstein & Wangwe 1986: 4), to be instigated by private foreign investment, encouraged by policy incentives such as tariff protection from competing imports (Rweyemamu 1973). The first five-year plan of the newly constituted United Republic of Tanzania built on the three-year plan, and like the first, expected the investment in industry to be largely funded by foreign capital.

By the end of the 1960s and the publication of the second five-year plan, Tanzania could show impressive manufacturing growth rates averaging over 10 per cent a year throughout the decade, with manufacturing's share of GDP at over 9 per cent (Skarstein & Wangwe, 1986: 10). Some of this growth could be accounted for by the Kampala Agreement between Kenya, Tanzania and Uganda, which tried to redress the concentration of industry in Kenya by allocating new industrial projects to the other two countries to service the combined market of all three. Tanzania was allocated aluminium sheets and foil, tyres and tubes, radio assembly and parts production (Rweyemamu, 1973: 119). The subsequent formation of the East African Community was part of a strategy to share the market for manufactures and take advantage of scale economies.

There was also some change in the structure of manufacturing over this first decade. Although food beverages and tobacco remained the largest group, other sectors grew in relative importance, especially textiles and clothing, and chemicals, and there was also a slow relative growth of the capital goods sector (machinery and transport equipment). However, this was a period of 'perverse capitalist industrial growth' (Rweyemamu 1973). Rweyemamu characterized this as the use of capital-intensive techniques to produce largely luxury consumer goods in a manufacturing sector dependent on foreign investment and technology. Thus little of the abundant labour force was employed, few linkages were created with other sectors of the economy, the distribution of enterprises was locationally unbalanced and the whole process created a non-competitive monopolistic or oligopolistic market structure. Further, the manufactured goods, protected as they were against foreign competition, could not be exported because they were not internationally competitive. Historically, what could be exported were largely raw materials that had no domestic market base (Rweyemamu 1973: 245).

However, in the early 1970s, there was an attempt to shift policy towards deepening industrial development by effecting the very structural change that Rweyemamu had identified as perverting development. The emphasis was now on building an economy where industrial production was geared towards the production of commodities that satisfied domestic demand and the production of capital goods to yield these. The subsequent Basic Industry Strategy, influenced by the work of Rweyemamu and the Guyanan economist Clive Thomas, who had taken a chair of economics at the University of Dar es Salaam, was a 20-year plan (1975–95) to set up industries that would, in Thomas's phrase, 'effect a convergence of the pattern and rate of domestic resource use and domestic demand' (Thomas 1974: 125). Service of a consumer goods sector that would satisfy the basic needs of the population required an intermediate and capital goods sector whose output would provide inputs into the consumer goods industries, especially machinery produced by the metalworking and engineering sector (Skarstein & Wangwe 1986).

The pressure of increasing debt and chronic balance of payments crises pushed Tanzania into the arms of the IMF and World Bank whose objective in the 1980s was to 'get prices right' .This essentially meant opening economies such as Tanzania's to the global market to incentivize domestic producers to compete successfully with global manufacturers at 'world' prices. However, the so-called Structural Adjustment Programmes that followed and were required in order for countries to receive aid made no long-term improvement in manufacturing growth. Indeed, it was unlikely that they would, since trade liberalization was bound to result in some domestic de-industrialization, at least in the short run, as uncompetitive enterprises went out of business. There was little attempt at industrial rehabilitation and building on acquired manufacturing experience; rather there was a renewed emphasis on exportable primary products, both food and minerals.

Trade liberalization was supposed to make manufacturing competitive and therefore give African producers access to world markets and enable them to take advantage of economies of scale, with the ultimate effect of changing the export structure in favour of manufactured exports. However, the evidence from East Asia suggests that a strongly protected domestic market is a first step in manufacturing development after which successful firms will move into export markets as they become more competitive (Wade 2004). Tanzania and many other African countries have large enough populations and domestic markets, especially if they are in economic unions such as the East African Community.

However, the Basic Industry Strategy failed to change, to any significant extent, the structure of Tanzanian industry. The 1970s and 1980s were characterized by highly volatile rates of growth swinging from over 15 per cent to minus 10 per cent. The 1973 oil price hike and the concurrent droughts,[1] exacerbating a policy-induced fall in agricultural output, followed at the end of the decade by a further oil price hike and a world recession, meant that much of Tanzania's foreign exchange went into importing food and petroleum and there was little available to support industry, resulting in shortages, especially of spare parts for industrial equipment. Growth rates fell sharply and became negative from 1978, such that by the mid-1980s, manufacturing contributed around 5 per cent to GDP, which itself was stagnating.

Throughout this period the resistance of Tanzania to the liberalizing reforms championed by the international financial institutions (IFIs) persisted and has been well documented. The state-directed model, which rejected liberal markets on the grounds of their previous failure to generate a foreign investment-led growth back in the 1960s, was regarded as still valid. By 1984–5, resistance began to weaken and the

---

[1] Some accounts downplay the effects of the droughts, arguing that the decline in food production was the result of the rural villagization policy (Lofchie 2014: 31).

currency was devalued. There followed various price and trade liberalization measures, but there was some slippage as vested interests slowed the pace of liberalization and it was only by the middle of the 1990s, and further crises, that resistance collapsed and Tanzania adopted a new round of liberalization measures, which involved further reducing the state's role (Mwase & Ndulu 2008). For manufacturing industry, this meant privatization and often foreign ownership. Manufacturing growth moved from a negative rate at the beginning of the 1990s, to grow rapidly over the next two decades, fluctuating during the 1990s one or two points below the 10 per cent mark. Much of this growth, as we shall see, was in first-stage processing of minerals and not in the high-value-added sections of the manufacturing process.

Performance

This section tracks various indicators of manufacturing performance in Tanzania in comparison with African regional economic groupings. The usual cautions apply to the data on which Table 8.1, and those that follow, are based. Some runs of data only start in 1990, and in many cases there are years with missing data. The country group averages are weighted by population and grouped broadly along the lines of the economic unions, avoiding overlapping membership.

As Table 8.1 shows, manufacturing growth rates, both of Tanzania and the rest of Africa, varied from around −10 per cent to over 20 per cent in the 1970s and 1980s, but began to cluster around 5 to 10 per cent in the later 2000s. Tanzanian manufacturing growth showed large improvements after the 1985–6 reforms, but these returned to negative growth in the early 1990s, settling through the 2000s at a consistent 8 to 9 per cent a year, credited to the reforms of the later 1990s but clearly with a lag of five to seven years, though slowing again in the early

Table 8.1 Africa and Tanzania: Manufacturing Growth Rates, 1971–2012 (five-year average per cent per annum)

	1971– 75	1976– 80	1981– 85	1985– 90	1991– 95	1996– 2000	2001– 05	2006– 10	2011– 15
EAC	9.6	8.9	2.9	5.2	0.4	6.6	6.8	5.4	4.5
North East	0.2	5.3	2.8	2.3	2.1	5.4	2.3	4.1	9.0
Central	7.3	1.8	10.6	−1.8	−3.4	−0.8	12.0	5.0	7.2
West Africa	4.4	2.9	6.1	3.3	2.6	3.7	3.6	1.3	3.5
Southern Africa	16.0	14.4	14.4	16.5	15.9	14.6	14.7	14.7	1.5
Maghreb	9.4	11.3	6.4	1.8	1.8	2.7	2.7	2.1	1.7
Tanzania	7.9	−3.1	−3.6	7.7	0.0	5.7	8.1	8.6	6.0

Source: World Bank, *World Development Indicators*

2010s. The one exception to this volatility story is the Southern African group, heavily dominated by the already much more industrialized South Africa and Botswana, with a first-stage industrial processing based on the mining of its rich deposits of diamonds.

Table 8.2 compares the trajectory of shares of Tanzanian manufacturing in GDP with other African regional country groups, including the countries of the current East African community. In 2015, Tanzania's share of manufacturing in GDP was much the same as it was in 1971, but, as for many country groups, it has fluctuated over time with changes in international conditions and domestic political upheavals. North East Africa, dominated by Egypt and Ethiopia, shows long-term share increases to 15 per cent of GDP or above, while Southern Africa consistently hovers around that 15 per cent level throughout, dominated of course by the historical strength of manufacturing in South Africa, Zimbabwe, Lesotho and Swaziland.

Another indicator of changes in economic structure brought on by manufacturing growth is the proportion of manufactures that are exported, an expression of the competitiveness of domestic manufacturing, and shown in Table 8.3. Tanzania's share of manufacturing exports in total exports has been the fastest-rising in Africa in recent years, though this starts from a low base and may be distorted by the inclusion of semi-processed raw material exports with very little manufacturing value added.[2]

Nevertheless, at the aggregate level, Tanzania's performance in the 2000s outstrips other country groups by a distance, especially remark-

Table 8.2 Africa and Tanzania: Shares of Manufacturing in GDP, 1971–2012 (per cent and five-year averages)

	1971– 75	1976– 80	1981– 85	1985– 90	1991– 95	1996– 2000	2001– 05	2006– 10	2011– 15
East	6.3	6.4	6.6	7.4	8.9	9.9	9.4	9.5	8.7
North East	9.8	11.7	4.6	11.8	15.7	17.8	16.8	14.2	14.0
Central	2.2	3.9	11.4	10.5	5.3	6.8	5.5	4.4	6.7
West Africa	4.3	3.8	4.3	5.4	5.8	6.1	6.9	6.5	7.4
Southern Africa	16.0	14.4	14.4	16.5	15.9	14.6	14.7	14.7	13.5
Maghreb	12.2	12.2	15.3	16.9	16.9	15.2	14.0	14.4	16.6
Tanzania	9.9	9.1	6.9	7.8	7.8	8.8	8.8	9.0	8.4

Source: World Bank, *World Development Indicators*

---

[2] Some datasets, especially the World Development Indicators, have much higher manufacturing export shares for later years, which may result from category differences.

able given the performance of the earlier decades. However, it has been suggested that,

> ... there is some lingering doubt whether Tanzania can sustain this impressive MVA growth trend, especially if it continues to focus on natural resource-based activities, notably metal and extractive industries whose value added growth is limited. It has been suggested that one of the strategic options for the country is to move to higher value added activities. The structural change necessary for improving the country's economic development has to be based on its comparative and competitive advantages. Increasing value addition through enhanced processing of agricultural products and natural resources can be a possible starting point for Tanzania's structural transformation. (Wangwe et al. 2014: 17)

An indicator of deepening economic development is the increasing importance of capital goods manufacture relative to consumer goods in total manufacturing output. Table 8.4 tracks the structure of manufacturing output over the last four decades. It shows that the manufacturing sector is dominated by processed Food, Beverages and Tobacco (FBT), more so for Tanzania than for Africa as a whole. Textiles and Clothing shares in output have fallen considerably in Africa as a whole while, in Tanzania, there has been a recent revival, albeit from a low base.[3] The share of Machinery and Transport Equipment (MTE), a proxy for the capital goods sector, has remained low both in Tanzania and Africa, although Table 8.4 suggests that this is

Table 8.3 Africa and Tanzania: Shares of Manufacturing Exports in Total Merchandise Exports (per cent)

	1971–75	1976–80	1981–85	1985–90	1991–95	1996–2000	2001–05	2006–10	2011–15
EAC	0.9	7.7	4.0	4.3	9.4	14.9	15.7	25.8	26.9
North East	9.8	11.8	4.7	11.8	15.8	18.0	16.8	14.2	28.7
Central Africa	6.4	4.6	0.7	0.6	1.5	3.1	2.2	1.8	19.9
West Africa	4.5	2.5	1.8	1.7	1.9	7.3	8.4	10.1	18.1
Southern Africa	6.1	13.3	7.7	2.2	17.0	28.8	31.8	30.1	37.7
Maghreb	9.1	14.5	22.3	29.6	32.0	35.1	36.2	34.4	48.4
Tanzania	7.8	8.2	20.1	8.0	7.2	9.6	8.4	15.8	26.1

Source: World Bank, *World Development Indicators* and UNCTADSTAT

---

[3] The performance of this sector has not been helped by the commercialization of imported second-hand clothes, originally donated through charities, which accounted for over a third of all Tanzania's textile imports by 2002 (Wangwe et al. 2014).

Table 8.4 Africa and Tanzania: Shares in Manufacturing Output (per cent, selected years)

		1970	1980	1990	1995	2000	2005	2010	2015
Food, Beverages & Tobacco	Tanzania	36.0	23.2	51.2	45.1	55.9	64.8	53.3	70.0
	Africa (median)*	36.6	35.3	37.7	39.2	25.2	28.2	30.5	40.5
Chemicals	Tanzania	4.2	5.8	11.0	7.1	5.93	5.49	7.7	8.2
	Africa (median)	5.6	5.8	8.6	8.8	7.77	5.43	8.5	10.6
Machinery & Transport Equipment	Tanzania	4.3	6.1	3.4	1.9	1.87	1.1	4.8	1.9
	Africa (median)	3.7	3.8	2.3	4.3	6.71	5.65	5.0	5.7
Textiles and Clothing	Tanzania	28.1	33.1	2.8	0.1	5.0	8.1	4.3	3.8
	Africa (median)	15.7	14.3	11.5	11.0	10.2	10.1	4.1	7.8

*Africa medians are for 2012–13
Sources: World Bank, *World Development Indicators* and United Republic of Tanzania (2016)

rising from its low base. Tanzania has entered into a partnership with a Chinese company to build an iron and steel complex in the Southern Highlands, based on coal and iron ore mining projects in the region, which should be producing iron and steel products in 2018/19 (NDC 2017).

Finally, manufacturing, and overall economic growth, is crucially dependent on investment in capital stock. Table 8.5 compares capital formation in Tanzania with the median of that in Africa as a whole over the last four decades. In only one of those decades has Tanzania's gross fixed capital formation relative to GDP been significantly below the median for the continent, and during the latest growth spurt, it has reached a proportion of GDP more than 50 per cent higher than the median for Africa.

As the data in the above tables show, Tanzania has seen very little structural change as indicated by the development of the manufacturing sector as an important contributor to GDP and exports, being in much the same position as at the start of independence. Manufacturing's contribution to exports has only recently shown substantial increases, though there may be some categorization problems here. The structure of manufacturing has, however, shown little change, with the very slow development of the capital goods sector.

Table 8.5 Gross Fixed Capital Formation in Tanzania (percentage of GDP)

	1970–79	1980–89	1990–99	2000–09	2010–13	2014–16
Tanzania	20.1	18.35	21.60	23.80	31.33	29.0
Africa (median)	24.86	18.58	16.90	16.83	20.39	22.1

Source: World Bank, *World Development Indicators* supplemented by calculations from *Tanzania, Statistical Abstract 2015*

Tanzania's Sustainable Industrial Development Policy: A New Approach?

The end of the period of the Basic Industry Strategy and the reaffirmation of a liberalization strategy, involving a more limited role for the state and a concomitant major role for the private sector, were the two main reasons given for the introduction of the Sustainable Industrial Development Policy in 1996 (URT 1996). Recognizing that the industrial sector contributed only a small proportion of GDP, the new policy emphasized the importance of investment in such a potentially dynamic sector that could drive up Tanzanian growth and productivity rates by enhancing the technological levels embodied in industrial production. The priority now would be the development of agro-allied industries and of intermediate and capital goods industries to support each other and the consumer goods sector. Emphasis would be placed on achieving a balance between import substitution and export promotion based on competitive advantage. A priority was given to the development of the small and medium-sized (SME) sector and assisting the informal sector activities to become SMEs and promoting their links with large enterprises.

The sequencing of the plan was as follows. The first five years would involve the rehabilitation of existing plant; the following ten years would comprise investment in intermediate and light capital goods manufacture as well as the technical and economic preparation for the exploitation of iron ore resources. The last ten years to 2020 would see the development of a basic capital goods sector and especially an iron and steel industry. The role of the government during these phases was seen as one that enabled investment and supported the sector through the appropriate liberal macroeconomic and trade policies. Furthermore, the government's role was to address the problems associated with education and training and research and development noted above.

Proposals for a basic capital goods sector relying on the domestic resource base had been made before, most notably by Thomas (1974), while a plan for an iron and steel industry using domestic resources had been mapped out, in considerable detail, by Luttrell (1986) based on Thomas's strategic principles. Although this had support from some sections of the political leadership, the plan had never been seriously considered. As Luttrell himself noted, the alliance of state bureaucracy, foreign capital, foreign consultancies and donor agencies fed the persistent dependency relationship that militated against the very self-reliant strategy embodied in the Arusha Declaration back in 1967, and therefore against an industrial strategy that did not depend on foreign resources. This dependency relationship was no better exemplified than in the choice of technique in industrial plants established so far. The foreign partners in the industrial plants determined the technique of production, which invariably required importing machines and other inputs from the very investor, who, after nationalization, became a managerial partner of the state (Barker et al. 1986).

The priority placed on the development of SMEs has significance for any deepening of manufacturing, given the importance of SMEs as producers of specialist inputs that go beyond the capacity of large manufacturers to produce. A recent survey of micro, small and medium-sized enterprises (MSMEs) found that 13.6 per cent of these were in the manufacturing sector (URT 2012). Over 40 per cent of the manufacturing enterprises were located at home. However, the survey also found that very few of the MSMEs' customers were among the large enterprises. Their customers were usually local to their area and were either individual consumers or other producers and traders. There was little evidence that any of these enterprises were growing and moving beyond the SME category, and plenty of evidence that they were not raising their technological levels – indeed, it appears that their small size is often given as the reason for not using machines at all. Even when technology is used it has been found to be old, with producers depending on foreign technology and having inadequate technological knowledge to find suitable equipment let alone to innovate themselves (Mahemba & Bruijn 2003).

The election in 2015 of President Magufuli on an anti-corruption and pro-industrialization platform has meant a renewed emphasis on investment in infrastructure, education and the mobilization of domestic resources through better tax collection and the elimination of corruption so as to increase investment. The budget for 2016–17 increased development expenditure to an amount equal to 10 per cent of GDP (World Bank 2017). It is too early to assess the impact of the new government policies, but Magufuli has replaced the top management and boards of directors of parastatal enterprises in the quest for greater financial discipline, although it has been suggested that he is simply strengthening the position of his faction of the ruling elite (Jacob 2017).

Comparative Experience

Tanzania's experience is similar to that of much of sub-Saharan Africa as the tables presented earlier in this chapter indicate.[4] However, there are signs that some countries are pursuing more transforming industrial strategies. Ethiopia,[5] for example, has enjoyed consistently high manufacturing growth rates, especially in recent years, sometimes into the teens, with significant increases in the share of manufacturing in GDP and in the share of capital goods in manufacturing value added (World Bank, *World Development Indicators*). The Ethiopian state is increasingly characterized as a 'developmental state' in the sense that the state has a clear strategy directed towards development and an industrial policy in which investment is prioritized for specified industries. There is an emphasis on the production of manufactured goods that are linked to agriculture, of ensuring that supply chains function effectively, that levels of technology match domestic capabilities and that finance is supplied by state banks, with foreign banks not permitted to operate. There has been a strong emphasis on education enrolment and infrastructure, especially roads and power. Foreign investors have been attracted to provide capital and technology. They have also been incentivized to export competitively by subsidies and credits, import duty exemptions and tax holidays (UNECA 2016).

Rwanda is another case where there has been rapid GDP growth of 7 to 8 per cent per annum over the last decade or more. There have been some years over the last two decades where manufacturing growth rates have hit double figures, but these have usually been around 5 to 8 per cent per annum. Where Rwanda has seen more rapid growth has been in the service sector, and especially in the information and communication technologies (ICT) and tourism sectors. The extremely rapid growth of the ICT sector saw mobile phone use increase 17-fold between 2006 and 2012, and an expansion of electronic services in banking, trade and agriculture. The growth in tourism has also been rapid, with the state assisting this process through, for example, training in such tourist services as hotel management and catering, the expansion of infrastructure, especially roads, and exemptions from import duty for those investors bringing in modern hotel equipment not produced in Rwanda. However, there will need to be sustained investment in manufacturing to achieve structural transformation (UNECA 2016).

In both Ethiopia and Rwanda, a 'developmental authoritarianism' has been driving this growth, characterized by the state interventionism described above and political control over people's lives in which the

---

[4] Excluding South Africa, although here, there has been some evidence of de-industrialization and a failure to deepen manufacturing.
[5] A comparison of Tanzania and Ethiopia in terms of exchange rate policy and export competitiveness is provided in Chapter 12.

democratic freedoms of association and independent political activity are restricted through a strong state single-party regime directed to specific development goals and against the growth of powerful vested interests (Matfess 2015).

Explanations for Tanzania's Manufacturing Performance

Tanzanian manufacturing performance was not untypical of the rest of the continent in lacking the development of a structurally mature manufacturing sector. Relying on the neo-liberal macroeconomic adjustment strategies promoted by the World Bank and the IMF was not enough, and it was recognized that an industrial strategy that addressed the shortcomings of the industrial sector was regarded by some as essential to achieving structural change (Wangwe 2001).

According to Wangwe, there were several reasons why Tanzania had not yet established a competitive industrial sector. The ISI strategy effectively required protection for new manufacturing enterprises and gave the firms a monopoly of the domestic market behind that tariff wall. In spite of the respectability of limited period protection for 'infant industries' while they became competitive internationally, the vested interests created in the process perpetuated this protection. Competitiveness was also not helped by the overvalued exchange rate, which of course lowered the prices for imports and imported inputs, thus, along with low interest rates, encouraging more imported capital intensive techniques in an economy where employment creation was critical. As Wangwe observed, low real interest rates also led to credit rationing, in which those who had more political clout were able to divert investment from more profitable activities.

The lack of adequate institutional support in the case of research and development also hindered manufacturing development. The failure to create or exploit linkages with other sectors reduced the impact of such investments on the economy in general by not maximizing the linkages to generate new output elsewhere, most famously in the case of a fertilizer factory that did not use domestic sources of inputs, such as phosphates, but imported all of them (Coulson 1979). The lack of adequate infrastructural development in power supply and communications, both transport and telephonic, added to the cost of doing business, one of the obstacles to increased foreign investment and a growing manufacturing sector experienced across the continent.

As Wangwe (2001) further argued, manufacturing development did not involve continuous development and adaptation of the technology embodied in initial capital investments. It was more important to acquire foreign investment with its given technology than to develop new technologies based on the original investment. Programmes intended to rehabilitate Tanzanian manufacturing, were found to have paid little attention to the question of raising the level of technological capability, ... technological learning and acquisition of technological capability were not an important part of the process of industrial deepening and the implied qualitative changes in the structure of production. With regard to technological development and growing industrial complexity, there was a reversal characterized by industrial shallowing, e.g., in textiles (producing grey material instead of printed products). (Wangwe et al. 2014: 7–8)

The technology problem was related to the low level of skills of the labour force, especially in respect of technical education, and the lack of exploitation of learning by doing and on-the-job training. Generally low levels of education of the skilled and semi-skilled workers and middle managers, a lack of technically trained managers, as well as a lack of capacity in engineering and design, perpetuated a high level of dependence on the foreign investors and their expatriate staff (Barker et al. 1986).

Many of these explanations for the poor performance and lack of deeper development of Tanzanian manufacturing have been offered for the wider African experience.[6] The adoption of import substitution strategies of industrialization in the way in which they were implemented simply changed the composition of imports and increased rather than reduced the demand for imports, and did nothing to create a sector that could orient its market towards exports. Structural adjustment packages, which liberalized imports and removed the protection enjoyed by domestic industry, had substantial negative effects on domestic production rather than giving rise to a more internationally competitive sector. The relatively high costs of 'doing business', largely laid at the door of inadequate power, transport and telephone and electronic communications (transport links still heavily skewed towards ports rather than towards improving links within countries), and bureaucratic delays in completing contracts, are common throughout the continent.

The labour market issues referred to in Wangwe's explanation for poor competitiveness, such as low skill levels and inadequate training, have affected productivity and innovation everywhere on the continent. Paradoxically, it has been argued that the monopoly position of many domestic enterprises has allowed such enterprises to raise wages to a level that is uncompetitive with other developing economies, although the evidence that African industrial wages are too high is scanty.[7]

Credit and investment constraints, despite the financial liberalizations that should have directed finance to the most productive projects,

---

[6] See Lawrence (2005 and 2015) for continent-wide surveys of manufacturing development from which much of the following is drawn.

[7] See Chapter 9 of this volume for a detailed analysis of Tanzanian manufacturing productivity in comparison with a selection of other African countries.

also appear to have slowed manufacturing development, although there is plenty of evidence from around the world that well-developed financial sectors do not necessarily lead to manufacturing growth.

Although privatization of state-owned enterprises was at the fore-front of liberalization policies, it has been argued that the slow pace of privatization has slowed the recovery of the industrial sector. In Tanzania, only after the reforms following the election of President Mkapa in 1995 did the speed of privatization pick up and start to turn around poorly performing enterprises (Moshi 2001; Edwards 2014). The slow speed of privatization was the result of governments, like Tanzania's, not wanting to see privatization ending up with foreign ownership. From the literature on the subject it is not clear that privat-ization has resulted in greater competitiveness, or indeed that owner-ship, rather than competition, makes much difference to performance (Grenier et al. 2000), rather it has increased the dependence of domestic economies on foreign capital and the growth of vested interests in maintaining an essentially dependent industrialization. Moreover, as Gray (2013) points out, such liberalization policies did not enable the state to exert any control of newly privatized enterprises' rents.

The Political Economy of Industrialization

While many of the economic explanations for the failure of Tanzania, and other African countries, to achieve structural transformation through industrialization hold water, they beg the question of why after fifty years there had been little change in the largely political-economic factors that determined the pace of transformation. One early expla-nation argued that majority or total state ownership of manufacturing projects accelerated the formation of a layer of management that became the basis of a 'bureaucratic bourgeoisie' (Shivji 1976). This managerial class, which interchanged regularly with government bureaucrats, was not the productive accumulating (capitalist) class nor the socialist accumulating state that characterized the development of capitalism in the developed countries, and in the latter case, the rapid industrialization of the then actually existing state socialist countries of Eastern Europe and Asia. Rather, Shivji argued, it was a dependent class that could not, as individuals, accumulate for the whole class but a class that could only reproduce itself by means of its control of the state and the state's ownership of a large proportion of the means of production.

As others have noted, the only basis for an accumulating capitalist class lay in the mainly Tanzanian Asian business community, which for obvious political reasons could not be aided, other than infor-mally, by a Tanzanian state pursuing an East Asian-style development strategy (Gray 2015). So, although the state owned many enterprises, its degree of real control was tempered by the ability of enterprise senior managers to sidestep any industrial policy. Power was relatively equally distributed between the different class factions of the state, and alliances were formed between state, party bureaucrats and enterprise managers to maintain rents even when the enterprises were performing poorly, rents that were enhanced by corrupt pricing and sales practices (Gray 2013).

This 'political settlement' meant that, as Gray and others have noted, the ruling party, CCM, did not have the level of centralized power necessary to discipline the relevant actors such that the rents accrued from corruption were channelled into investments in manufacturing activities and the infrastructure required for their success (Kelsall 2014; Gray 2015). As Kelsall concluded, while the management of rents had been centralized in the Ministry of Finance, there were a number of factors that impeded a successful industrial policy, which included 'opportunistic rent seeking' and 'endemic corruption in the country's ministries, departments and agencies'. This resulted in resources not being directed to the production of effective services, and in corruption in the regulatory and tax-collecting agencies, which both diverted resources and made doing business more hazardous (Kelsall 2014). One factor underlying the rent-seeking behaviour that helped to fund the ruling party was the imperative of the party to have the resources to win elections. This aspect of rent-seeking, as well as the need to maintain political support between elections, meant that funds that could have been used to invest in productive activities were siphoned off, and resulted in investments operating at lower than optimal efficiency levels and inhibited the success of such developments as the Investment Promotion Centre and the Special Economic Zones (Kelsall 2012).

Within the ruling elite are factional interests allied to particular branches of the economy, and in particular to the different economic actors within those branches who can help finance the political activity that keeps the politicians in office (Whitfield & Buur 2014). For example, the development of manufacturing in Tanzania may be inhibited by mineral resource interests, both domestic and foreign, which prioritize the exploitation of such commodities as coal, against clean sources of energy with their manufacturing linkages, not to mention their environmental benefits (Jacob 2017).

A further explanation for the systemic corruption referred to above impeding the development of industrial policy has been based on the concept of 'neo-patrimonialism', often invoked as the main characteristic of governance in Africa. This encompasses the combination of, on the one hand, informal relationships between those at the top and those operating below and on the other, the formal trappings of the legal state. The informal relationships are characterized by corrupt practices in the appointment of key personnel, or in side payments to ensure that certain policies are pursued. Either way, the possibility of a rationally directed industrial policy is severely reduced. There is considerable debate in the literature as to whether 'neo-patrimonialism' not only adequately explains these relations and accounts for the distribution of the rents derived from state activity, but also accurately reflects Weber's 'patrimonialism' from which it is derived (Pitcher et al. 2009; Kelsall 2013). It is also not clear that aspects of this ideal type neo-patrimonialism, such as patron–client relations and rent-seeking, impede development, rather than providing, in specific circumstances, the institutional structures to allow growth (Kelsall 2012).

What the above explanations are pointing towards is the failure to establish the state as a developmental force creating the conditions, whether initiated by the state or by the private sector, for enterprise to flourish. Such seemingly straightforward state investments in better port, airfreight, warehousing and other facilities to reduce the costs of exporting and importing, in building and maintaining roads and rail transport, in supporting educational research and development institutions so as to provide a better-trained labour force and in measures to ensure support for enterprises is repaid in enhanced performance are examples of the 'developmental state' at work and characteristics of state support for industrialization in the successful East Asian economies (Wade 2004, 2012; Chang 2012). As important as infrastructural support for manufacturing has been for the successful Asian economies, so has investment in agriculture to raise productivity and, here again, in Tanzania, policy has failed to deliver. This is ironic given that the basis of President Nyerere's *ujamaa* strategy was to reorganize production so as to raise output and secure the necessary food surpluses for the increasing urban populations.

What is to be Done? Global Value Chains, the New Structural Economics and the Developmental State

The successful transformation of many of the East Asian economies through manufacturing industrialization has led to a new consensus that this is the way forward for African economies. Much of the early transformation observed in East Asia took place at a time when national economies were still the units of analysis and nation states played an active role in supporting domestic manufacturers while utilizing foreign technology and expertise to build up their capacity in manufacturing and the human capital required for its maintenance and expansion. More recent manufacturing growth in that region, especially in China, has come from enterprises, whether domestically or foreign-owned, inserting themselves into global value chains (GVCs) as producers of components required for the final product and as producers of the final product not only for their domestic market but also for regional markets, and so developing regional supply chains, but in both cases as part of global corporate producers or as suppliers to them (Gereffi 2014).

In the case of African countries such as Tanzania, industrialization has largely involved the production of basic consumer goods or final assembly of advanced consumer goods and of capital goods using imported components. This has resulted in little of the final products' value added accruing to the national economy. Capturing greater value from the GVC is a favoured strategy either by inducing foreign investors to produce their intermediate goods for final assembly elsewhere or producing the whole product for export to high-income markets. The advantages and disadvantages of trying to participate in GVCs are well known, with inflows of capital and technology allowing for the possibility of countries specializing in products that could be internationally competitive, on the one hand, but with powerful global corporations taking much of the value added on the other. With the kind of industrial policies that provide the necessary education and infrastructure it is possible, as East Asian experiences showed, to capture the whole GVC (Gereffi 2014; UNECA 2016). This might be more possible in low income regional markets where the global corporates lack local knowledge, though as these markets become more known to the global players, this local advantage dissipates (Gereffi 2014).

The industrial policies required to capture more of the value chain can be carried out by a different kind of active state, depending on how far the market is regarded as the central institution of resource allocation or how far the market itself is subject to regulation by the active state. The new structural economics asserts the primacy of the market but advocates government facilitation in making the markets work, by 'coordinating investments for industrial upgrading and diversification and in compensating for externalities generated by first movers in the dynamic growth process' (Lin 2012). Factor endowments determine comparative advantage, and thus which industries to develop and relative factor prices must reflect relative endowments in order to achieve this comparative advantage, while adapting imported technologies can assist in the process of moving from a labour-abundant to a capital-abundant economy. Government's role is to coordinate the necessary investments and supply the necessary incentives and compensation where market signals are distorted.

To what extent the political conditions for such kinds of industrial policy exist will depend upon an effective alliance of a political class or dominant fraction of that class and its tight control of the machinery of the state together with industrial, and especially manufacturing, capital. As Whitfield and Buur (2014: 128) suggest, those elites pushing an industrial policy need to be able to resist competing demands from other interest groups. They must be able to provide the appropriate incentive structure to enterprises so that they deliver when the infrastructure they need is financed by public expenditure, and the government subsidizes investment costs, waives import duties and provides other financial incentives, as well as negotiating preferential trade arrangements for the final products.

Does the combination of market and strong government facilitation under the necessary political conditions produce the 'developmental state', the characterization given to the successful East Asian 'tigers' and now even to China? As Mkandawire (2010) observes, characterizations of the developmental state tend to regard all aspects of successful transformed economies such as those of East Asia as having been directed to the development objectives that they achieved. However, as he points out, with reference to studies of Japan and Taiwan, more historically accurate is that much of the process was making mistakes and learning from them to find a path that was effective, but hardly optimal in the sense of neoclassical economics. So when the developmental state is invoked as the solution to achieving structural change, this is more an indication rather than a blueprint of what such a state might look like.

If a developmental state is one that expands capabilities (Evans 2010), by universalizing a well-functioning education and health care system at all levels, then Tanzania has a new government anxious to do this (Magufuli 2015). Whether it has the capabilities to effect an industrial strategy that leads to the objectives discussed earlier in this chapter is another matter. Certainly there are indications that the emphasis on industrialization may mark the beginning of a process of serious structural change. Whether the way in which these developmental objectives are introduced 'embed' them in popular consciousness and action so that they are embraced as common objectives may depend on the degree to which the development strategies are democratized (Evans 2010; Mkandawire 2010), although as noted earlier in the cases of Ethiopia and Rwanda it would appear that a more authoritarian approach is favoured even if it is not sustainable.

Conclusion

This chapter has provided an account of Tanzania's industrialization and attempted to make some comparison with other African country groups' performance since decolonization. The Tanzanian experience has proved to be no exception in the African context. As has been the case for much of the continent, Tanzania has lacked an overall strategy that would not tie in the country to a dependence on imported technology and capital. The three phases of industrial strategy have all effectively depended on foreign capital and been unable to make serious links between industrial development and the domestic resource base. Only with the recent development of plans to produce iron and steel in cooperation with China, is there evidence that there will be a shift in strategy away from simple import substitution to the local production of capital goods that can substitute for imported capital equipment. However, given the ownership of those local consumer goods enterprises, and their position in the global value chain, this may be resisted. Resistance may also come from those factions of the ruling political elite that have vested interests in industrial primary commodities. What the Tanzanian experience also demonstrates is that the question is not whether enterprises are state owned or privately owned, but whether the state is able to regulate enterprises in such a way that they operate efficiently and that the state can enforce this efficiency by effectively controlling the monopoly rents that many of these enterprises can appropriate for themselves.

This chapter has further considered the different explanations, both economic and political-economic, for Tanzania's manufacturing performance and the new theorization which, incorporating some of the elements of an ideal type 'developmental state', tries to synthesize the state–market dichotomy by proposing industrial policies with specific facilitating roles for the state and lays out the political conditions for the proposed policies to be effective. There are indications that the current, relatively new, Tanzanian administration, like some others in Africa, is taking these policies seriously. However, achieving the 'developmental state' (if that is indeed a meaningful term) is still a challenge for African countries, and Tanzania is no exception.

9

Competitiveness in African Manufacturing: Some Evidence from Tanzania

John Weiss and Hossein Jalilian

Introduction

There is a long tradition in economics that argues that manufacturing industry is critical for economic growth, particularly at relatively low income per capita (Weiss 2011). This 'engine of growth argument' rests on several features of the sector:

- Output per worker (productivity) is normally considerably higher than in agriculture or services (although not in mining) so that structural change in favour of manufacturing raises the overall productivity of an economy.
- Productivity growth in manufacturing has historically been more rapid than in other sectors owing to greater technical change and learning effects.
- Manufacturing is the sector where there is greater scope for specialization as outputs grows.
- Its linkages with other parts of the economy are greater than for any other aggregate sector.
- As a key tradable sector, manufacturing expansion allows access to the world market and faces better demand prospects there than primary exports.

The normal historical pattern has been that, in poor countries, the share of manufacturing in total economic activity is very low, but that as growth occurs and workers move out of agriculture, it rises rapidly. Once a threshold income level is passed the relative share of manufacturing starts to decline as demand shifts towards services. Thus for example, in 2005, manufacturing was 9 per cent of GDP in Ghana, 30 per cent of GDP in a middle- income economy like Malaysia and averaged 16 per cent in the OECD economies (Smirzai 2013: Table 1.2). It is at the transition from low to middle income status that the engine of growth effect can be expected to be greatest owing to the greater scope for a productivity boost as workers shift out of agriculture.

Experience in sub-Saharan Africa has not matched this positive story. The sector remains relatively small with much of it vulnerable to competition from imports. This chapter discusses evidence on recent Tanzanian experience in the context of industrialization in Africa more generally, drawing in some instances on empirical work by the authors. It considers industrialization in Tanzania from the perspective of economic competitiveness, and therefore should be seen as complementary to the broader discussion of the political economy of industrial development in Tanzania given in Chapter 8. We look at African experience, before turning to the Tanzanian case, and then present some empirical evidence from firm-level surveys of manufacturers in Tanzania before concluding the chapter.

African Industrialization: Unfulfilled Expectations

The disappointing performance of industrialization in sub-Saharan Africa is now well known. When African economies emerged as independent states in the 1960s they were largely based on primary products, minerals and low productivity services. There are estimates that suggest that for sub-Saharan Africa in 1960 agriculture took 42 per cent of GDP and manufacturing 8 per cent, with most of this small-scale informal sector activity (UNIDO 2013: Table 1.1). By 2011, while the share of agriculture in economic activity had declined and that of services had risen significantly, that of manufacturing was no more than 10 per cent, and if South Africa is removed from the calculation, the average falls to 7 per cent.[1] Consequently Africa's share in world manufacturing value added has remained very small at around 1 per cent of global production over this period, and Africa's share in manufacturing value-added in the 'industrializing country' group has fallen. Even though sub-Saharan Africa has had relatively strong GDP growth since 2000, in part because of favourable international commodity prices, only seven countries out of 23 have had a growth of manufacturing value added over 2001–12 in excess of 5 per cent annually so, while there has been a recovery in manufacturing, it is modest and is not spread widely across the region.[2]

Since the 1970s much of the labour migration out of agriculture has been either to low-productivity services or to low-productivity informal manufacturing rather than to the formal higher-productivity segment of manufacturing on which the 'engine of growth' case is

---

[1] South Africa is very much an outlier in the region, with manufacturing value added per capita in 2011 of $897 (2005 constant dollars). In contrast the figure for Tanzania is $40 and in Ethiopia it is as low as $11; see UNIDO 2013: Table A 3.1.

[2] World Bank: World Development Indicators; world manufacturing grew at 3.5 per cent annually over this period.

based. It has been argued that the shifts in economic structure that have occurred in Africa have retarded growth as labour has not moved from agriculture to higher-productivity activities, and thus overall levels of productivity have increased only very modestly and in some cases have declined (McMillan & Rodrik 2011). However, it appears that the revival of growth post-2000 has altered this picture in Africa, with evidence that, in at least some countries, the structural shift of labour has been into higher-productivity activities in either manufacturing or services, so that the structural change that has taken place, while still modest, has become growth-enhancing rather than growth-reducing.[3]

There are different interpretations of this story of the relative failure of industrialization in Africa.[4] In one, African industrialization was always going to be limited by a number of unfavourable initial conditions, many of which still exist today. An interesting very early statement of this position is from one of the pioneers of Development Economics, W.A. Lewis, in his policy document on the prospects for industrialization in the Gold Coast written in the early 1950s (Lewis 1953). In putting forward a series of policy ideas to support industrialization in the Gold Coast, Lewis was clear that while industrialization is a useful way to diversify the economy and create employment, a major programme to support industrialization would be premature. He regarded low-productivity agriculture as the key bottleneck to successful industrialization, and without rising productivity in agriculture, the home market would be small, with little surplus income for investment. Hence he saw raising agricultural productivity combined with improvements to infrastructure and public services as the key priorities. Policy for industry should focus selectively on activities that could be competitive in a relatively brief period with modest levels of support.

In addition to a stagnant agricultural sector, Lewis identified key features of the Gold Coast that hindered its industrialization and remain relevant to contemporary policy debates. First there is the issue of factor endowments and whether those of African economies imply that a specialization in industry is justified. Lewis argued that the land–labour ratio is such that in the Gold Coast it is land not labour (or at least not male labour) that is the surplus factor.[5] This means that for male workers, while money wages are low by European standards,

---

[3] McMillan et al. (2014) update their original analysis for Africa by splitting the time periods pre- and post-2000. In half the African countries in their sample post-2000 the shifts of labour into manufacturing were sufficient to create productivity-enhancing structural change.

[4] Lawrence (2015) examines African industrial experience in detail.

[5] '... there is a shortage of labour in the sense that at the current level of wages employers cannot get all the labour they want, in spite of the fact that there is considerable immigration from the French Territories' (Lewis 1953: para 223).

they are high by the standards of other underdeveloped countries, and this poses a key constraint on using the export market as the basis for industrialization.

This argument from the early 1950s has been used many times since then to assess Africa's comparative advantage in manufacturing and explain its continued relatively low level of manufacturing production and exports (Wood & Berge 1997; Collier 2000). Cross-country firm-level surveys confirm relatively high African wages in some, but not all, countries relative to competitors at similar income levels (Clarke 2012). Furthermore, even where African wages are below those in emerging economies like China and Vietnam, they are offset by the productivity differentials, so that unit labour cost of production is higher in most African producers than in these key competitors (Dinh et al. 2012).

The second disadvantage highlighted by Lewis is the high cost of what he terms public services – which he listed as electricity, water, gas, telephone and transport facilities. Discussion of the inadequacy of infrastructure in most of sub-Saharan Africa continues, and it is commonly accepted as a continued constraint that has still not been addressed (Page 2013). Firm-level data suggest that high costs of logistics and infrastructure are more serious disadvantages than wage costs (Clarke 2012). The interpretation placed on these results is that the key to understanding Africa's failure to break into export markets for manufactures lies not in its wage or labour productivity levels, but in indirect costs linked with the 'business environment'.[6] The latter is a term typically defined very broadly to include weak governance, which makes it difficult to enforce contracts and property rights, including rights to land, lack of access to finance through an underdeveloped system of financial intermediation and excessive regulation and bureaucratic control. The combination of relatively high wages and high transaction, and infrastructure costs has meant that sub-Saharan Africa has largely been excluded from global manufacturing value chains (although there is evidence of successful links with food and horticultural-based chains for international retail sales).[7]

This interpretation of the difficulties of industrializing Africa can be contrasted with the view that policy can create its own opportunities and overcome obstacles like those listed above by sheltering local producers from foreign competition and by building linkages within the domestic economy. This implies that the import substitution era of

---

[6] On average across firms in the low- and middle-income countries in Africa these 'business environment' costs account for 9 per cent of sales, as opposed to less than 3 per cent in upper middle-income African economies and less than 2 per cent in successful East Asian exporters (Clarke 2012: Table 9).
[7] As a crude indicator manufactured exports were only around a quarter of total exports for sub-Saharan Africa (SSA), excluding South Africa, in 2011, as compared to over 70 per cent for all industrializing economies (UNIDO 2013: Table A.6.6).

the 1970s and early 1980s should have been built on to provide the base for later export expansion in the same way as occurred in East Asia. In this view the import liberalization that occurred as part of structural adjustment lending was an opening of the region's economies from a position of weakness, not one of strength (as in East Asia), leading to a loss of manufacturing skills and capabilities that have taken decades to rebuild.[8] This type of counterfactual argument is difficult to resolve. What we know is that much of the manufacturing sector in Africa in the 1970s and 1980s was high-cost by international standards, often due to many of the factors listed above. Trade liberalization alone was insufficient to reverse this trend, and it may well be that a more phased approach combined with supply-side support to resolve some of the key constraints, particularly a lack of finance, might have yielded better results.[9]

Is Africa an Outlier?

Regions of the world economy are different. As noted above, Africa has a much higher land–labour ratio than Asia, with relatively high levels of exploitable natural resources, which affect relative factor prices and the cost of non-traded activities, which in turn push up real exchange rates and thus penalize tradable activities like manufacturing. Other distinctive features in Africa include a disproportionately large share of small informal firms and a 'missing middle' of medium-sized firms, within the sector, both of which will create a wide range of productivity levels between firms within a sector, with some African firms operating close to the best practice frontier and others, usually considerably smaller, operating well within it (Gelb et al. 2014).

There is a wealth of statistical evidence illustrating these trends and highlighting the distinctive experience of Africa. Earlier work by the authors looked at the period 1975–93, and found that, while there was a tendency for the manufacturing share in GDP to fall over this period, there was considerable heterogeneity among African economies; for 16 African countries as a group there was no evidence that this decline was any more marked than in other regions once trends in income and population were controlled for. However, the Africa sample as a whole appeared to behave differently from the other

[8] As Lawrence (2015) puts it, 'Had interventionist policies to rescue and rehabilitate failing enterprises been rigorously followed rather than allowing import liberalisation to put them out of business altogether, it could be argued that SSA's manufacturing sectors would have been able to build on the previous 20 years of accumulated experience.'
[9] The potential for industrial policy to support industrialization in Africa is explored in several of the chapters in Stiglitz et al. (2013); see particularly Chang (2013).

developing countries, with individual country factors dominating (Jalilian & Weiss 2000).

Rodrik (2015) has updated this analysis. Now controlling for income and population, a smaller sample of 11 African countries behave similarly to the full sample, with the exception of a higher than expected share of manufacturing value added in GDP in the 1970s and 1980s, given these countries' income and population. However, the result for African countries is very strongly influenced by the inclusion of Mauritius, which is an outlier, given its successful focus on manufactured exports. When it is excluded, the positive impact on manufacturing share remains only for the 1970s, which is the effect of protected industrialization through import substitution. In the decades of the 1990s and 2000s for the African countries there is a strongly significant negative trend of a declining manufacturing value added and employment share, after controlling for income and population.[10] These results match the analysis in McMillan et al. (2014: Table 5), which shows that, in explaining the growth of labour productivity owing to labour reallocation between sectors, what they call the structural change term, the dummy variables for African and Latin American countries are negative and significant, reflecting the relative decline of manufacturing in these economies.[11] The key explanation offered for the success of manufacturing in Asia, in terms of maintaining its share in output and employment, is its success in developing manufactured exports, since, when the data are split between economies that export manufactures (more than 75 per cent of merchandise exports) and those that do not, the time period effects are different, with the exporting economies showing positive rather than negative signs for the time period dummies (Rodrik 2015). Hence Africa's well-known failure to develop major exports of manufactures through links with global value chains has a pivotal role in this interpretation of relatively weak performance.

In terms of development within the sector there is evidence that, owing to the wide dispersion in productivity between firms in Africa, it is intrinsically less dynamic than manufacturing sectors elsewhere. Rodrik (2013) has raised the issue of convergence in productivity growth within a sector as producers learn to catch up with the technology frontier. Convergence can be either unconditional, so there is

[10] For African countries in the 1980s the period term for the manufacturing share is negative but insignificant, while the employment share remains both negative and significant, indicating a greater than expected decline in the share of manufacturing employment in GDP. Broadly similar trends are found in the Latin American case, but not for the Asian countries in the sample, where all the time period effects are positive.

[11] It is notable that this must in part reflect resource endowments since when a variable for the share of raw materials in exports is included the country regional dummy for Africa (and also for Latin America) loses its significance and its negative sign.

catch-up, or conditional, with the size of the catch-up conditioned by the initial position.[12]

Rodrik conducts this analysis at a disaggregated level, with manufacturing alone showing considerable scope for both types of convergence with the conditional coefficient typically double that of the unconditional, as country-specific conditions play a large role. The significance of this is that catch-up productivity growth in the sense of approaching best practice levels holds regardless of the country's policy environment, although the speed of convergence will be affected by policy. He finds that convergence applies only within manufacturing, not elsewhere. In Rodrik (2014) he confirms that convergence within manufacturing is found in African countries as well as internationally.

Weiss and Jalilian (2016) repeat this analysis with a slightly different data set and find evidence that the pattern is different for African as compared with non-African economies. The focus is not on intra-manufacturing differences, but on whether manufacturing is different from other sectors in terms of convergence potential. Unconditional convergence is not confirmed for any of the productive sectors for the whole dataset, as there is no statistically significant relationship between the sectoral growth of labour productivity and its initial level. However, if African countries are excluded there is now some weak support for unconditional convergence with negative coefficients on initial productivity for manufacturing, mining and public utilities. Once a test for conditional convergence is applied the picture changes.[13] For the full dataset the sign on initial labour productivity is now always negative and is significant in public utilities, construction and transport and communications and in the aggregate. When African countries are excluded conditional convergence is confirmed strongly for manufacturing, public utilities and in the aggregate. In the non-African sample, once we control for institutional quality, convergence is faster and more significant in manufacturing than in public utilities. Thus, outside Africa, catch-up productivity growth is found in manufacturing and, unlike the results of Rodrik (2014), Africa does appear to behave differ-

---

[12] Unconditional convergence is formulated as:
$$cg_{ij} = \alpha + \beta 1\, ny_{ij} + \varepsilon$$
where cg is the compound rate of growth of labour productivity for sector j in country i, y is the initial level of labour productivity for the sector and ε is the stochastic term.

For unconditional convergence to hold, β should be negative and significant. Similarly, conditional convergence, controlling for features of an economy, is tested by an equation of the form:
$$cg_{ij} = \alpha + \beta_1 ln y_{ij} + \mu Z_i + \varepsilon$$
where Z_i is a set of country-specific controls. Conditional convergence requires that β_1 be negative and significant.

[13] Only one control variable, a composite institutional quality measure, is applied on the grounds that this is correlated with other plausible controls.

ently from other regions in terms of productivity convergence. This suggests that, even where manufacturing is established in Africa, it is less dynamic in relation to productivity than in other regions.

Tanzanian Experience with Industrialization

Tanzanian experience mirrors much of that of the rest of sub-Saharan Africa. At independence in 1961 the manufacturing sector was very small, with 220 registered manufacturing enterprises employing 10 or more workers, and a few large firms like Coca-Cola, East African Breweries, Tanganyika Packers, British American Tobacco, Metal Box and Bata Shoes foreign-owned and the remainder small local enterprises. Industry, including mining as well as manufacturing, was estimated to contribute no more than 4 per cent of GDP (Skarstein & Wangwe 1986). Discussions of industrial performance in Tanzania conventionally divide the post-independence period into four phases:

- Early post-Independence (1961-67);
- State-led industrial development (1967–85);
- Industrial development under Structural Adjustment (1985–95);
- Post-reform development agenda (1995 onwards).[14]

In the early 1961–67 period there was no attempt to change the structure of the economy or the pattern of ownership. Two development plans were introduced to encourage diversification of the economy, but there was little regulatory control, a relatively open trade policy and foreign investment was promoted, through tax incentives and import tariff protection. There was some expansion of manufacturing, with a 50 per cent increase in the number of manufacturing establishments in 1961–65 and a rise in manufacturing's share in GDP to 6.6 per cent in 1966 (Wangwe et al. 2014).[15]

In the early 1960s more than 75 per cent of industrial investment came from the private sector. However, the indigenous private sector was very weak so that ownership was concentrated in either foreign investors or ethnic minority nationals. The phase of state-led industrialization was to address the problem of who would mobilize the necessary resources by giving this role to the state. The Arusha Declaration in 1967 ushered in a major shift in policy with its emphasis on socialism and self-reliance. In the phase of state-led industrial development there were a number of major changes affecting manufacturing. A signifi-

---

[14] This categorization comes from Wangwe et al. (2014); see also Morrisey & Leyaro (2016). This section draws heavily on both of these sources.
[15] Over the period 1961–66 manufacturing averaged around 5 per cent of GDP (Morrissey & Leyaro 2016: Table 21.2).

cant proportion of new investments were made by parastatals, foreign investment was limited to joint ventures with the government, import tariffs were increased and controls on access to foreign currency were introduced. Private sector activity was regulated through industrial licensing, and a system of price controls was introduced for selected manufactured goods. While the economy was not centrally planned the role of the state in industrialization increased dramatically, with the public sector responsible for 47 per cent of manufacturing employment in 1973, as compared with 15 per cent in 1967 (Skarstein & Wangwe 1986).

This can be seen as the real commencement of the import substitution programme in Tanzania, and growth in the protected home market was initially relatively rapid, with real manufacturing value added increasing at an average of just below 6 per cent annually in 1967–79. The sector reached a peak of 10 per cent of GDP in 1972, as compared with 8.4 per cent in 1967, although it had fallen back again to 8.5 per cent by 1979.[16] The 10 per cent share of GDP for manufacturing has still not been exceeded more than 35 years later.

There were limits to this expansion in part through its reliance on imported inputs. This was recognized in the launch of the Basic Industry Strategy at the end of this period, which aimed to strengthen domestic linkages, shift production towards intermediates and capital goods and reduce reliance on imported inputs. The strategy was to run for 20 years from 1975, with the ambitious targets of an annual average industrial growth rate of 8.8 per cent and a major structural transformation such that manufacturing's share in GDP would reach 18.8 per cent by 1995. The Basic Industry Strategy reflected one response to what emerged in the late 1970s as a serious balance of payments constraint on growth. However, its implementation would have required heavy investment in a range of producer goods, and by the late 1970s the macro problems facing the economy meant that such a programme was financially unsustainable for the government (Lall & Wangwe 1998).

On the other hand, there were also limits to the expansion in the 1970s created by a combination of trade policy, exchange rate management and unfavourable external shocks, particularly the rise in the oil price. Manufacturing was aimed at the domestic market and exports of manufactured goods were no more than 10 per cent of total merchandise exports in the 1970s; the sector was a strong net user of foreign exchange. The exchange rate was managed by relatively high import tariffs and controls on access to foreign currency for both current and

---

[16] Morrissey & Leyaro (2016: 387). The World Development Indicators have different figures. They show manufacturing growing on average by 5.1 per cent for 1965–80 and averaging 11.9 per cent of GDP for 1971–80; see Lawrence (2015): Table 20.1. NBS also has different figures and shows a peak share of 13 per cent in 1975; see Wangwe et al. (2014): Figure 5.

capital account purposes. This created high effective protection for manufacturing, and, by the early 1980s, increasing overvaluation of the currency, both of which exacerbated the foreign exchange problem. One estimate put the overall effective protection for manufacturing as high as 470 per cent in 1984, which suggests that the growth rate of the 1970s had been artificially inflated by the excess of domestic prices over world levels (Lundahl & Ndulu 1987). Similarly, there are estimates of exchange rate overvaluation from 1980 onwards that put the overvaluation rising from around 40 per cent in 1981/82 to as much as 80 per cent in 1985 (Hobdari 2008). As an import-intensive activity manufacturing was bound to be seriously constrained in this macroeconomic climate.

Initially the government addressed these macro problems with a 'home grown' adjustment programme and an export retention scheme allowing exporters to access some of their export earnings to import intermediate goods. After the weak response to these measures the government turned to the international financial institutions and committed to a Structural Adjustment Programme in return for balance of payments support and funds for enterprise restructuring. The programme reforms were embodied in the Economic Recovery Programme (ERP), which commenced in 1985. While the thrust of the reforms was primarily macro, the change in trade policy in particular created a new environment for industrialization for the period 1985–95. Import tariffs were reduced, the foreign exchange licensing regime was liberalized and a crawling peg exchange rate was introduced to reduce the overvaluation. The focus on state-led industrialization was reversed with privatizations of the manufacturing parastatals where buyers could be found.

The initial outcomes for manufacturing were modest at best. Its GDP share averaged 8.7 per cent for 1986–95 and its average annual growth from 1981 to 1990 was 3.6 per cent, falling to 2.6 per cent for 1991–2000.[17] Some enterprises were restructured, but some closed. The textile sector was particularly badly hit by the influx of low-cost, some second-hand, textile and clothing imports with the closure of 22 out of 24 mills by 1993 (Wangwe et al. 2014: 12). Privatization reduced the number of state-owned enterprises so that, by the mid-2000s, they accounted for no more than 10 per cent of all manufacturing enterprises (cited in Morrisey & Leyaro 2016: 388).

The period from 1995 onwards is described as a 'return to industrial development as a development agenda' (Wangwe et al. 2014) on the grounds that it reflects a renewed emphasis on industrialization but in the post-Structural Adjustment context of a focus on markets and private sector development. The planning framework for industrial

---

[17] The GDP share comes from Morrisey & Leyaro (2016): Table 21.2; annual growth comes from Lawrence (2015): Table 20.3, but the original source is the World Development Indicators.

development was to be the 25-year Sustainable Industrial Development Policy for Tanzania (SIDP 2020) launched in 1996 (URT 1996). This had short-, medium- and long-term components. In the short term (1996–2000) the aim was to rehabilitate and consolidate existing capacity. In the medium term (2000–10) the goal was to create new capacity in areas with the potential for competitiveness, with an emphasis on intermediates and light industry. In the longer run (2010–20) the aim was to develop more sophisticated products, including capital goods.

The private sector was to be the driving force behind this programme and incentives, such as those enshrined in the Export Processing Zones Act passed in 2002, were offered to increase private sector investment. To support these investments, measures were taken to improve the 'business environment', for example by investing in infrastructure and revising regulatory controls. Although ambitious targets such as the creation of a semi-industrial economy comparable to that in a middle-income economy by 2025 have been set, it is unclear how far the government has managed to influence industrial performance through this type of planning.

The current national plan document (URT 2016a) points to some of the implementation failures of earlier plans, for example, in relation to an inability to secure funding, bureaucratic delays in the planning process and a failure to improve aspects of the business environment. Although they do not necessarily impact directly on investment decisions country rankings by the World Bank *Doing Business Report* are taken seriously by the government, and the plan highlights a slippage in Tanzania's overall ranking in 2016 and the need to improve on this is highlighted as a key objective.[18] The plan retains ambitious targets such as a 10 per cent annual growth of manufacturing up to 2025 and a share in GDP of 18 per cent by 2015. In line with thinking on 'modern industrial policy' (Felipe 2015) the role of government is largely envisaged as a facilitator of private sector initiatives. There are plans to establish Special Economic Zones and Industrial Parks to draw on agglomeration economies, as well as initiatives to support SMEs and to encourage diversification within manufacturing. This is principally through support for the development of petro-chemicals utilizing locally available natural gas and iron and steel production utilizing local iron ore and coal.[19]

Manufacturing performance after 1995 was initially weak, but started to improve after around 2000, averaging around 8 per cent annually for 2000–15 as compared with 2.6 per cent annually for 1991–2000

---

[18] The previous plan set a target for Tanzania to reach the top 100 countries by 2015, while the actual ranking for 2015 is 139 out of 189 countries. Tanzania rates particularly poorly for time to receive construction permits and paying taxes (URT 2016: 12).

[19] The Mchuchuma coal mine and the Liganga iron and steel complex are to be developed by a Tanzania–China joint venture, reflecting a major involvement of China in restructuring the manufacturing sector.

(Lawrence 2015: Table 20.3). Since 2010, however, growth has slowed a little, averaging around 6 per cent annually for 2010–15.[20] In part this modest revival would have been due to a stronger macroeconomic performance, in turn partly linked with favourable commodity prices for traditional exports. Nonetheless the contribution of this growth to structural change has not been very significant. Manufacturing as a share of GDP was estimated to be still below 9 per cent in 2011, which was a little below Kenya, Malawi and Mozambique, but above that of Uganda, although recent growth rates have been higher in Tanzania as compared with these comparators.[21] More recent estimates based on rebased constant prices suggest a manufacturing share in GDP of around 7 per cent annually over 2007–13, but no more than 5.2 per cent in 2015 (URT 2016: Table 3.2). Manufacturing structure is based around 'early' industries with agro-processing activities food, beverages and tobacco taking around 35 per cent of value added, textiles and clothing 10 per cent and leather goods 8 per cent.[22] Growth since 2000 has been concentrated in activities using local inputs like paper and paper products, food and beverages, textiles, tobacco and non-metallic minerals. Activities like electrical machinery, engineering and vehicle repair have declined (Morrissey & Leyaro 2016: Table 21.3). Employment growth is recognized as slow, with formal manufacturing currently employing less than 5 per cent of the workforce. It is also skewed within manufacturing with the largest 40 companies employing 36 per cent of manufacturing workers, which is estimated to be the employment created by 24,000 micro enterprises (cited in Morrisey & Leyaro 2016: 388). Production remains highly import-intensive.[23]

In terms of specific policy for manufacturing Wangwe et al. (2014: 43) list five major challenges, which are very similar to the points made earlier in relation to industrialization in sub-Saharan Africa in general:

- Technical challenges relating particularly to unreliable power supply, outdated equipment and lack of skilled workers;
- Administrative challenges relating to weak enforcement of laws and regulations;
- Financial challenges in relation to access to and cost of credit;
- Market challenges in relation to strong import competition;
- Policy challenges relating to intrusive government regulation.

[20] The most recent five-year national plan reports manufacturing growth for 2005–15 averaging 8 per cent annually over the whole period and 6 per cent for 2010–15 (URT 2016: Table 3.2).
[21] UNIDO (2013): Table A 3.1. Morrisey & Leyaro (2016) cite a similar figure for 2010.
[22] These figures come from the 2008 industrial survey; see Wangwe et al. (2014): Table 1. The survey covers 729 registered industrial establishments.
[23] Wangwe et al. (2014: 43) report that for the firms they survey on average 70 per cent of inputs are imported.

Evidence on some of these challenges is provided by the survey of Fafchamps and Quinn (2012), which compared small and medium enterprises (SMEs) in five subsectors of light manufacturing in China and Vietnam with three African countries, Ethiopia, Tanzania and Zambia. Tanzania stands out in a few areas, even relative to the other African countries.[24] Firms tended to be smaller, with a very low share of limited liability companies and the highest share of unregistered firms. Firm owners have the lowest rate of educational attainment. Reflecting these characteristics, the Tanzanian firms have a much lower rate of innovation, both product and process innovation, than do firms elsewhere. Also firms in Tanzania have a much larger share of casual workers, which is not due to the effect of smaller firm size, with nearly 80 per cent of workers having no more than primary education. The incidence of power outages is high, and a high proportion of firms report competition from imports.[25] The bulk of funding for investment comes from internal funds and retained earnings, although the share is not much out of line with that in the other four countries, with a very low proportion of firms in each of the African countries having borrowed from a bank. The nominal cost of finance for those that do was considerably higher in the African countries than in China.[26]

Firm-Level Evidence on Manufacturing in Tanzania

To provide detailed information on the cost competitiveness of manufacturing in Tanzania this chapter draws on firm level data collected as part of the World Bank study *Light Manufacturing in Africa* (Dinh et al. 2012). This involved detailed firm surveys from a number of East African economies in an attempt to assess competitiveness of these firms relative to imports of competing manufactured goods from China and Vietnam. The surveys were not comprehensive and the results are not necessarily representative, but the general picture is that many local manufacturers in Africa, although possibly less in Tanzania, are struggling against Chinese competition. The exercise reported here covered three or four firms per product line in Tanzania, and the cost data examined are a weighted average for each line. Hence no more than 20 firms were examined.[27]

[24] The focus here is just on SMEs, but given differences in size across the sample the authors caution that the impact of size needs to be controlled for statistically.
[25] The proportion is higher than in Ethiopia and Zambia, although both of these are landlocked countries that receive natural protection.
[26] The averages rates reported are 4.7 per cent in China, 14.0 per cent in Tanzania and Vietnam, 10 per cent in Ethiopia and 21 per cent in Zambia.
[27] One of the authors was involved in the analysis of this data, which was published originally on the World Bank website as volume 2 of Dinh et al. (2012).

Table 9.1 gives data on wages in a number of East African economies relative to those in China and Vietnam taken from surveys of formal sector firms in 2009/10. Tanzania emerges as the highest wage of the three African economies, with wages well above those of Ethiopia. Average wages vary between firms producing different products, but all African wages are well below the level in China. For Tanzania, apart from wheat processing, wages are less than half the Chinese level. However, in some instances Tanzanian wages are above those in Vietnam.

Table 9.2 gives data from the same survey on productivity levels (in terms of pieces per employee per day). China has double the productivity of Africa in the manufacture of polo shirts and an even greater advantage in the manufacture of chairs. Tanzania has the highest labour productivity of the African firms in wheat processing and leather causal shoes. In both of these goods its productivity is higher than in China. Hence in relation to Tanzanian competitiveness in terms of relative wages and productivity the picture appears mixed.

Table 9.1 Wage Comparisons

Wages/ month US$	Ethiopia	Tanzania	Zambia	Vietnam	China
Polo shirts	39	128	n.a.	103	269
Wooden chairs	46	100	127	112	231
Leather loafers	26	113	n.a.	91	308
Metal working	n.a.	n.a.	n.a.	129	231
Wheat processing	42	116	83	56	120

Source: Dinh et al. (2012), unpublished Volume 2, Table A1; n.a. is not available

Table 9.2 Productivity Comparisons

Pieces/ employee/ day	Ethiopia	Tanzania	Zambia	Vietnam	China
Polo shirts	12.1	11.7	n.a.	12.3	24.8
Wooden chairs	0.3	0.5	1.2	1.6	4.9
Leather loafers	3.4	4.7	n.a.	3.6	3.9
Metal working	10	n.a.	n.a.	26	17
Wheat processing	1.1	11.6*	0.9	0.9	0.2

*Highly automated
Source: Dinh et al. (2012), unpublished Volume 2, Table A2

Differences between countries in input and logistics costs must be added to obtain a comparison of factory-gate costs. Once this is done it is clear that for most products the advantage of low wage costs is offset by a combination of lower labour productivity and higher input and logistics costs. Only in the case of leather goods can African firms in all countries compete on cost terms with China. Tanzanian firms have a slight cost advantage over Chinese firms in the metal product covered.

Table 9.3 summarizes the cost differences – distinguishing between the impact of labour, productivity, input costs and logistics costs between African firms and Chinese firms making a comparable product. The difference between firms in the different African countries by these categories and Chinese firms is given as a percentage of the average cost in China. Hence, for example, on average across all products covered, lower wages give a cost advantage of 16 per cent of total Chinese costs in Ethiopia, 9 per cent in Tanzania and 8 per cent in Zambia. In the case of Tanzania and Zambia this advantage is offset by the labour productivity differential, which is 13 per cent and 9 per cent of Chinese costs, respectively. In all cases input costs and logistics costs are higher for African firms, so these reinforce the productivity disadvantage.

In the case of Tanzania the net effect of lower wage costs but lower productivity and higher input and logistics costs was to make two product lines, leather shoes and wheat processing, cost competitive with Chinese goods. The comparison here is costs in Tanzania against costs in China so trade costs and import tariffs will give a natural protection to local producers.

Economic efficiency assessments of this local production require efficiency pricing of inputs and outputs. To assess this, the study used a version of the domestic resource cost indicator (DRC), which estimates the domestic resources at efficiency prices required to generate a dollar of foreign exchange either through import substitution or export (Krueger 1966; Bruno 1972). The efficiency pricing approach applied was approximate and involved removing all identifiable taxes and subsidies, deducting all identifiable imported inputs from the foreign exchange value of output and applying a capital recovery factor to estimate an annual capital charge. In this analysis Chinese costs are at c.i.f. prices but exclude any import tariff. The value of domestic resources was converted into dollars at the actual exchange rate and compared with the net foreign exchange effect from production.

Thus DRC is $(DR*ER)/FE$ and efficiency requires $DRC < 1$

where DR is the per unit domestic resources used in production, ER is the exchange rate and FE is the per unit net foreign exchange effect.

In theory ER in this calculation should be the long-run sustainable real value (the 'equilibrium exchange rate'), and misalignment of the actual rate ER can give misleading results. The analysis tested for the sensitivity of the efficiency results to future values of ER.

Table 9.3 Cost Differences Relative to China

Product		Polo shirts	Leather goods	Wooden chairs	Metal working	Wheat processing	Average
		Differential as % of Chinese production cost					
Wages	Ethiopia	−8	−37	−17	−10	−10	−16
	Tanzania	−4	−24	−8	−4	−4	−9
	Zambia	−5	−24	−5	−2	−2	−8
		−6	−28	−10	−5	−5	−11
Average Productivity	Ethiopia	3	2	40	5	−1	10
	Tanzania	6	0	60	0	−2	13
	Zambia	4	0	50	−10	−1	9
		4	1	50	−2	−1	10
Average Inputs	Ethiopia	4	2	87	14	28	17
	Tanzania	3	1	14	n.a.	32	12
	Zambia	4	3	50	25	49	26
		3	2	50	19	36	22
Average Logistics	Ethiopia	6	5	15	6	18	10
	Tanzania	3	3	n.a.	n.a.	7	4
	Zambia	7	3	18	8	21	12
		6	4	17	7	15	10
Average Total cost	Ethiopia	5	−28	125	15	35	30
	Tanzania	8	−20	66	−4	33	27
	Zambia	11	−16	113	20	67	39
		8	−21	107	19	45	31

Note: negative sign indicates cost lower than that of China
Source: Dinh et al. (2012), unpublished Volume 2, p 32

Table 9.4 DRC Summary: Tanzania

Product	Current DRC	ER adjustment for competitiveness
Polo shirts	0.61	Competitive
Leather loafers	0.96	Competitive
Wheat milling	1.09	9%
Wooden chairs	2.65	1657%

Source: author's calculations

Table 9.4 gives the summary DRC results for four of the product lines. Two of these were competitive at the time of the study (DRC<1) and one, wheat milling, required only a very modest productivity improvement or real exchange rate adjustment of 9 per cent to be so. The other product, wooden chairs, was uncompetitive on the basis of any realistic assessment of the future real exchange rate.

Conclusions

Broadly manufacturing retains a potential to contribute significantly to economic growth at Africa's income level. There are many arguments to explain why Africa tends to remain an outlier in discussions of industrial performance. Wage costs are often not low enough to offset a combination of low productivity and high infrastructure and related transaction costs. In addition lack of skills and access to modern technology contribute to lower quality levels. Tanzania shares many of the challenges faced by other sub-Saharan African countries. Nonetheless the firm level evidence presented here suggests that, in parts of manufacturing in Tanzania, performance is perhaps not as weak as is sometimes suggested. In relatively simple labour-intensive activities (shirts and leather goods) and resource-based (wheat milling) the 'representative firm' data once adjusted to economic terms suggests underlying efficiency and thus competitiveness in relation to imports from China. This is a competiveness in 'early' industries that is expected at relatively low income levels and is a far cry from the expansion of more technologically sophisticated goods, but does suggest that there is potentially a competitive core of activities that can be built on in the future. It will not be easy be to move into more sophisticated products that require a more sophisticated range of production capabilities, and the challenge for policy in Tanzania is to create a framework that both allows access to foreign technology and investment, while at the same time supporting the development of local production capability. The current national plan document highlights most of the key issues, but past experience suggests that translating a diagnosis of the problem into effective policy measures remains a daunting task.

10

'Good Life Never Comes Like Dreams': Youth, Poverty and Employment in Arusha

Nicola Banks

Introduction

Two demographic trends are changing Africa's population and poverty dynamics. Its population is forecast to treble over the next forty years (UNDP 2012), and its populations are increasingly urban and increasingly young. All but three African countries have over 40 per cent of their adult population in the 15 to 29 age category, and by 2035 the majority of Africans will be living in cities (Guengant & May 2013). The 'power' of youth brings both possibilities and challenges, nowhere more evident than in sub-Saharan Africa, and governments must prepare more effectively for their futures (Burgess 2005).

Cities, in particular, are a main stage for young lives across the continent (Hansen 2015). Dynamic city contexts heighten youth aspirations through their offer of economic opportunities and higher wages, infrastructure, better access to education and services, and perceptions of 'modernity'. These factors make migration a phenomenon closely linked with youth, particularly young men (Crivello 2011; Jeffrey 2011; Honwana 2012). But a 'crisis of youth' looms as an increasing number of young Africans find it difficult to gain education and employment or meet standard of living aspirations (Jones & Chant 2009). Young Africans are not finding that these urban benefits and promises are translating into better social and economic mobility for their generation. Unemployment rates for youth are higher than for adults across the whole continent (Thurlow 2015). The new labour markets, education systems and consumer cultures that have accompanied urbanization mean that traditional, linear moves from youth to adulthood are unlikely (Valentine 2003; Worth 2009).

Tanzania's youth population will not peak until 2030, and with half of its population already under the age of 25, it already has the tenth largest youth population in the world (Lam 2006). Ambitions and aspirations have fuelled a wave of youth migration to urban centres (Burton 2010). One in every three children born in Tanzania today will be living in towns or cities by the time they are 20 years old (Riggio 2012). Yet cities are difficult places to be young and poor. Tanzania has struggled to translate its economic growth into significant poverty reduction (Arndt et al. 2015). Despite growth performing more strongly in urban areas (Arndt et al. 2015), job creation has not kept up with rapidly growing urban populations, which remain dependent on the informal economy (Guengant & May 2013). Unemployment is predominantly an urban phenomenon. At 16.3 per cent – and increasing to 31.3 percent in Dar es Salaam – urban unemployment rates are significantly higher than the national average (NBS 2006). Young people in particular are overrepresented in under- and unemployment rates. They constitute 60 to 65 per cent of the country's unemployed population (Lintelo 2012), and the youth (15–24) unemployment rate is four percentage points higher than the national average (NBS 2006).

This chapter explores the experiences of Arusha's youth from one low-income community as they try to navigate the school-to-work transition in a context of poverty, hardship and a challenging labour market. Employment insecurity is not unique to low-income youth, but shared by young people of all ages and education levels; however, for the purposes of this chapter we look at this group in particular and the additional challenges that this background brings in the transition to adulthood. We discuss how 'youth' has been defined and conceptualized from African and academic perspectives, before outlining the research methodology. We then unpick the 'urban advantage' for young people in Arusha, before examining the forms of support they receive from households and the community and how this influences their hopes and aspirations.

Definitions and Frameworks

How we frame 'youth' is important for deciding what our research captures or leaves out.[1] Common framings of 'youth' are by age and transitional status. While the United Nations defines 'youth' as those between 15 to 24 years, in the majority of African countries (including Tanzania) this stretches to 35 years given the difficulties young people face in accessing employment, moving into their own housing, starting a family, and being socially recognized as adults (Gupte et al. 2014). Hence, the concept of 'youth' is increasingly seen as a period of transitional limbo, where young people are 'stuck' or 'waiting' indefinitely (Hansen 2005, 2015; Locke & Lintelo 2012). Several ethnographic studies give rich insight into the frustrations and dilemmas of this period of physical and social immobility (Jeffrey & McDowell 2004;

---

[1] Honwana (2012) gives the most comprehensive overview of how 'youth' has been defined, both generally and more particularly in an African perspective.

Mains 2007; Ralph 2008; Sommers 2012; Honwana 2012). Young people are not passive in their attempts to achieve these goals, but they remain hard to reach.

This temporal extension of youth-hood resulting from an inability to achieve the social markers or adulthood lends itself to the 'transitions' conceptualization of youth popularized by the World Bank. The 2007 *World Development Report* defined youth as a process of transition on the path to adulthood, which requires passing through five key transitions: learning, work, health, family and citizenship (World Bank 2007). These transitions are set against a backdrop of other changes, including the increasing independence and agency of youth, the diminishing influence of parents and families, and the increasing influence of other external factors – such as peers, the media, global connections and the broader economic, social and cultural environments that have heightened aspirations across Africa (Juarez et al. 2013; Resnick & Thurlow 2015). The idea of 'youth' as a period or temporal process again is central, linked closely with ideas of 'navigation' and a process of 'becoming' on the journey to adulthood (Christiansen et al. 2006; Worth 2009; Van Dijk et al. 2011).

It is helpful to view youth as more than a process of transition if we want to accurately assess opportunity and vulnerability across these changes. There is huge heterogeneity across age spectrums in both vulnerability and opportunity, and few opportunities allow youth to follow a linear progression from school, to work, to marriage and family (Grant & Furstenberg Jr 2007; Honwana 2012). Understanding youth as an accumulation of these five transitions does not embed them in a conceptual framework that recognizes the inter-linkages between them and the overlapping social, political and economic exclusion young people face across them.[2] We are encouraged to view each transition independently, when the reality is that they are highly interconnected. A better understanding requires us to identify the cross-cutting themes and influences across *all* transitions or life phases, exploring how they compound one another to lead to positive or negative outcomes. This will help us to identify the support that young people need to assist them and the vulnerability factors that constrain their own developmental efforts.

Banks and Sulaiman (2012) propose an alternative conceptualization of youth opportunity and vulnerability. They argue that we must attempt to reconcile the role of young people's agency alongside the broader structural environments that heavily influence this. That is, we must look at the assets, resources and capabilities that young people have to draw upon in their search for livelihoods, the forms of institutional support they can draw upon, and the structures and processes

---

[2] Furthermore, I would argue that 'health' is not a transition, per se, but a heightened vulnerability as young people navigate the other transitions.

that may assist or impede their attempts to succeed today and plan for the future.

These authors also highlight the importance of investigating how the combination of these factors (assets, support and structures) shapes the aspirations of young people and the opportunities they perceive to be available. The importance of hope and 'psychological agency' is beginning to make its way into conceptualizations of poverty and livelihoods (see, for example, Klein 2014), and arguably, nowhere are hopes and aspirations more important than among young people working towards a better future. In this, the framework provides the foundations for the third component, which recognizes that 'outcomes', both positive and negative, are influenced dynamically by the interplay of the first two (Banks & Sulaiman 2012). Individual outcomes are not just a result of individual assets or capabilities, they are heavily influenced by the household, community, and social and economic structures that they are embedded in. We cannot understand vulnerability, or negative outcomes such as risky behaviour, without recognizing them as rooted in much deeper problems of poverty and unemployment, limited assets and social support systems, and a limited ability to hope for a better future.

Research Methodology

The research here is based on in-depth research in one low-income ward in Arusha,[3] known throughout the city for its 'troubled' – and 'troublesome' – youth. This reputation means that young people believe they will be disqualified for jobs when employers find out their address, immediately judging him or her as a loiterer, criminal or drunkard. The ward is comprised of six 'Streets'.[4] A census listing was completed across all six streets followed by focus groups with young men and women (aged 18 to 24) that explored local definitions and experiences of youth poverty and the types and sources of support that young people receive. In-depth interviews were carried out with 48 young people in one of the six Streets, disaggregated by age, gender, educational and employment statuses. This allowed us to compare the experiences of unemployed and employed young men and women making the school to work transition across three age groups (18–19; 20–21; 23–24) and

[3] This research is part of a broader three-year project exploring youth, poverty and inequality in urban Tanzania. It is funded by the ESRC under grant reference number ES/K009729/1.
[4] These six 'Streets' are not singular roads as we would define 'street' in most circumstances. They are instead six different divisions within the ward, clearly delineated by local markers such as bridges and river crossings. Each street covers a large area, comprising multiple streets and pathways and, in some areas, forested areas and banana plantations.

across two educational categories (those leaving after Standard 7 and those leaving after Form 4[5]).

Employment is central to all aspects of young people's lives: their ability to meet their basic needs and invest in the future, to gain social legitimacy and respect, to live up to their personal ideals of contributing to their household's well-being, to secure their independence and to start their own family and move towards adulthood. Consequently, in-depth interviews focused on how young people navigated their school-to-work transition, but contextualized this within their household and individual circumstances. The interviews also explored their happiness, satisfaction and hopes for the future. Additional interviews were conducted with local leaders and parents, alongside focus groups with male and female community elders. These enabled us to contextualize young people's experiences within the household and to explore how the broader social, political, cultural and economic context in which individual outcomes are so deeply embedded influence young people's experiences and life chances.

There is huge diversity in young men and women's experiences across the Street. Each young person has a unique story. But there is also a distinct shared story of struggle, regardless of whether a young person is employed or unemployed. Arusha's economic decline means that young people are entering a challenging and competitive labour market with low- and poor-quality educational qualifications. Large and abandoned textile and food factories line one of the roads leading up to the ward, a stark sign of the collapse of Arusha's industry that began in the 1990s. Prior to this, local leaders say that it was 'easy and smooth' to get a job, even for young people. Now, with only a handful remaining, it is hard. Difficulties accessing work are not unique to young people from low-income areas. However, they are compounded by several factors, including a background of household poverty, a lack of community trust, cohesion and support, and social exclusion within and outside the ward as a result of negative stereotypes of young people. 'The city is driving youth crazy,' explained young men in an early focus group, as we go on to explore.

Education and Employment: Unpicking the 'Urban Advantage'

The urban advantage in education and employment is often highlighted. Tanzania's towns and cities benefit from a greater number of

[5] Standard 7 marks the completion of primary education and completion of Form 4 marks the end of lower secondary education. If a student passes their Form 4 exam they are eligible to go on to Forms 5 and 6, which constitute higher secondary education.

and shorter distance to schools, and a greater volume of and diversity in non-agricultural employment opportunities (Bryceson 2015). They also experience higher rates of consumption growth and poverty reduction (Arndt et al. 2015). But this has not translated into better social or economic outcomes for Arusha's youth in this low-income ward. A declining industry means there is a critical lack of decent jobs, and the quality of education is insufficient.

Education has not equipped young people with the knowledge or skills they need. Schools are locally called 'Saint Kayumbas', making a mockery of how they teach students about modern realities, such as computing, without any equipment (see Banks in Death et al. 2015). Parents, too, lamented the quality of schooling. Mothers emphasized that employers do not value lower secondary education (Form 4) any higher than primary education, meaning that even those leaving with these additional qualifications are unable to get a job. Form 4 education, the only realistic achievement for most youth here, is simply not enough to make your way in the job market.

Household poverty and familial responsibilities both make staying in school difficult. Parents struggle to pay school fees for all children, investing in their elder children in the hope that they will contribute to fees for their siblings when they start working. Most young people in the Street complete primary education, with only five (of 252) school leavers not able to reach this level. Less than half of young people continue on to secondary education, and its completion is less assured for those who start it, with a mixture of exams and school fees forcing early drop-out. Of the 42 per cent of young people who start secondary education, less than one-third (30 per cent) complete Form 4. Only three per cent of the Street's youth continue on to college or vocational training institutes for further learning. Pressures to drop out are higher for young women, given their familial responsibilities. 'Boys are allowed to do everything and anything,' one focus group of fathers explained, 'but girls have to squeeze all of these things around their responsibilities at home.'

Young people are well aware that their qualifications are insufficient to access decent employment. As one young woman explained:

> There is no opportunity. So for many, you finish school, you have bad luck, and then you don't make it to the next stage [of employment]. Then there is no option for youth but to be on the street.

Unsurprisingly many youth display aspirations for further education. But, in the meantime, challenges are exacerbated by the fact that parents stop supporting their children after school completion. They are expected to pay their own costs and contribute to the household. The main work opportunities, where available, are factory work, employment in shops, bars or businesses or unskilled casual labour. Young people rarely referred to themselves as 'employed'. The majority receive small informal jobs here and there, but not enough to constitute 'work'. Young people primarily do their job search through their parents or relatives, waiting until they hear of an available opportunity through them. There were regular complaints that most jobs require bribes to secure: cash or, for young women, the demand for sex. Young people also spoke about getting exploited for their work, low pay and non-payment, and getting treated badly by their employers.

Parents and young people both highlighted that the best – if not only – option within such a challenging environment is self-employment. As young women explained, 'There are no opportunities here except for making your own business.' Self-employment is viewed with more esteem since it enables you to be self-reliant. But it is not without its challenges, first and foremost, a lack of capital. Without a stable income stream that allows them to save or parents that can help, young people do not have the financial capital they need to get started and are unsure of where to get it. Focus groups were happy to say entrepreneurship was a goal they were working to meet, but hesitant when asked where they would find capital. Business skills, knowledge of the market and innovation were also highlighted as skills that are critical to success, but lacking in youth. Young men argued that, 'If one person is seen to be successful another will start up next to him', and this competition was also seen as a constraint on starting and sustaining a successful business.[6] A strictly regulated business environment, requiring licences and permits, also increases the costs and risks of business. Mothers emphasized that problems with regulation – and as a consequence, police harassment – are greater today. This was evident talking to one young man who made beaded handicrafts but was unable to sell them easily:

> I have tried everything ... The problem is the police and guards, they hassle you and chase you away because you're not allowed to work there. Sometimes they take all your goods, which makes it much worse.

His only option was to sell through intermediaries, avoiding these risks even if it means less profit. With over half (54 per cent) of non-school-going youth (aged 18–24) declaring themselves unemployed in our

---

[6] This is evident walking the streets of Arusha: pavements in front of the shops are saturated with miniature mobile small businesses selling all variety of goods – DVDs, mobile phones, phone credit, bracelets and handicrafts, sunglasses, hats, beaded shoes – and services, like mobile phone or watch repairs. On the other side of the pavement, near to the road, are frequent vendors roasting corn atop small barbecues, women selling avocados or grilled yams. On top of this are the more mobile businesses: young men pushing makeshift wheelbarrows around the street selling peeled oranges or watermelons, carrying large trays of sunglasses, armfuls of T-shirts, rolled-up pieces of artwork for targeting tourists, or a precariously balanced selection of shoes or rucksacks, all vendors wandering around the streets looking for customers.

survey, other forms of support are critical for them to cope with these difficult circumstances. As we go on to explore, however, this is limited from all directions.

Safety, Security and Support:
The Relative Isolation of Arusha's Youth

Support from the household

Household poverty, and in some cases, 'poor' parenting reduce the levels of support young people can expect – and get – from the household. In one focus group, young men highlighted the Swahili proverb, '*mtegemea cha ndugu, ufa masikini*', loosely translating to 'if you depend on your relatives you will die poor'. Youth poverty starts in the household, and if your poor relatives are the only opportunity for you in terms of income, access to job opportunities and social networks, then you will be unable to improve your situation. Household poverty influences both the material and emotional support young people receive from parents.

As the previous section outlined, parents and youth are aware that education provisions are not enough to provide value in the labour market. This can exacerbate tension between parents and children. As one community leader explained, 'Some parents may have failed to give them enough education, so there is no job when they finish. So they will say, "Leave me alone, you haven't given me the education I need so I have to fight for myself now."' Fathers highlighted the powerlessness they felt, saying that, 'We know education is key to life. But as a parent if you don't have anything to support your child through school, then what can you do? Nothing, you have to sit and wait and see what happens with them.'

For parents struggling to make ends meet, school drop-out marks the end of full parental support. Pressure is put on young people to start becoming financially independent, especially for young men. Young men lamented that 'Once you turn 19, your parents don't want to see you anymore and will chase you out.' One focus group highlighted this as the moment that differentiated between adolescents and youth, when they stop depending on parents for food, clothing and other needs and start depending on themselves. Mothers said that young people have no choice but to find some way of making money, regardless of what this may be. 'They need to do this so that they can help their parents, including covering the school fees for their younger siblings.'[7]

[7] Implicit in the contract between parents and children is that they will invest in their education for as long as they can, but in return, they must then do the same so that their siblings can access as much education as possible. 'Mostly the first child gets opportunity to go further with their education. The second and third children face more troubles finishing. It might be economic troubles at home that mean parents cannot afford to keep schooling them. We are

This is a considerable source of pressure and tension: for young men who cannot access the work they need to cover their costs and meet their household obligations and for parents who feel sons are not contributing enough. While girls were seen to be more 'kind-hearted' in their concern for the household, mothers and fathers argued that young men, despite being expected to contribute to the household's upkeep, find ways to avoid this responsibility. 'If a young man gets 10,000 shillings, he will keep it himself,' mothers argued. 'He may come home and say he hasn't earned any money or he has given it all to his girlfriend.'

This leads to a contradiction between gender values and realities. Young women do not face the same pressure to reach financial independence, in part owing to their domestic contributions and in part, a protective factor. For young women forced to support themselves one of the only options may be to enter transactional sexual relationships that end in sexually transmitted diseases and early pregnancy. But poverty still leads to households depending on their daughters. As mothers illustrated, 'Girls have to take some of the burden of the family, and the only way is to endanger herself. Then in the end things become much worse for her and the household. Because we were struggling already, and then she brings a new baby to feed.' Fathers argued that this was a result of poor parenting as well as poverty, placing too much responsibility on young women when few opportunities exist. Yet at the same time, there is an overwhelming sense that, while parents should – and want to – do more, their hands are tied because of poverty and hardship.

Household poverty also leads to a lack of emotional support. By and large, mothers and fathers must both work to meet living costs, reducing the time they are at home to monitor, support and spend time with their children. Young people are often reluctant to magnify their parents' burdens by bringing their problems to them. One unemployed young man explained, 'I can't go to my parents. If I go, there won't be food and they will cry for me. I don't want this, so I will go to bed hungry if I cannot pay for food myself.' For other youth it is poor parenting, as well as household poverty, that is the problem. In focus groups, both parents and youth spoke widely of this issue, which demonstrated itself in a lack of interest in youth, parents speaking badly to them, alcoholism and domestic violence. One mother interviewed said that breakdown in parenting was largely due to capability. 'Some parents aren't capable of raising kids, others aren't serious about it,' she said. 'But it's also a lack of education, knowledge and stability. Parents, too, have grown up in hard times, so they received the same [minimal] support from their family.'

---

investing in our first child in the hope that they will then assist their younger sisters and brothers to go to school in the same way' (mothers, focus group).

Against this backdrop it is no surprise that there are intergenerational tensions within the household. Parents have given what they can within their constraints, but it is still not enough. Despite being better educated than their parents, young people face the additional frustration that this has not translated into better outcomes for them. Parents spoke of their frustration that 'Many young people have decided to select globalization to be their parents.' Fathers reflected that 'most young people are "copying and pasting" bad things from abroad', and no longer want or will accept advice and guidance from their parents. These frustrations are particularly acute for young men, who are not only less likely to listen, but are also more mobile and absent from the household. It is the pathways that they see through their connections with the modern world that young people want to follow, not the ones outlined by their parents and within the narrow and restricted opportunity landscape that the ward and broader city offers them.

Support from the community
A lack of community support stems from the large population of unemployed youth. Young people are characterized as a homogenized, lumpen, trouble-making category and excluded from community activities and decision-making. One local leader explained, 'There are so many youth here that don't have jobs ... So all day they don't go anywhere, they stay in the streets around their home area. But people don't like these young people sitting in the streets near them all day ... If anything happens, then straight away they will blame those sitting there.' Young men spoke their frustrations that if a youth in the community is seen to be successful, it is assumed they have done something illegal to achieve it. This has led to young people withdrawing from attempts to speak to elders or give their opinion in community matters. 'There is nowhere that you can go and present your needs, your desires, your plans,' they explained. 'If you try to speak to people, it goes badly. Someone will say "Look at this boy, he thinks he knows each and every one – put him in a cell!"'

Local leaders highlighted that for young people to be more supported at the community level required them to be more visible, being seen to do positive things and disproving stereotypes. One highlighted how important it was for young people to be mobilized. 'It is also upon the community to help [youth] overcome their challenges, to help mobilize youth and educate them on how to stay in a group, and how to start small businesses and succeed, as individuals and together.' Fathers, too, said that one of the major challenges for youth is that they 'are not seen'. These perspectives suggest that, through mobilization, young people and their needs can be more clearly seen and separated from the negative stereotypes of young people that dominate.

However, it is important to highlight the tension that despite 'youth mobilization' being seen as the solution,[8] the reality is that groups of young people are viewed as a threat and broken up. In one focus group, young men highlighted that, while there is a youth development officer that is meant to help young people in the ward, their door is still closed to youth. 'They aren't open to young people,' they explained. 'But worse than that, they fear them. So if we approached them, especially in a group, they would call the police.' They said that local political figures, too, see groups of young people as a threat. 'They are calling the police, saying there is a bad group here. They don't want young people to come together as they think they are a threat to them, plotting against them.'[9] Local politics is actively fracturing the ability of young people to mobilize or even socialize in small groups.

For support at the community level, it is important to emphasize that it is not just about the 'social' in terms of support and guidance. It is also about a lack of physical space where young people can come together and build peer support networks. Focus groups with young men and women highlighted that there is no opportunity for them to 'enjoy being young', and expressed a desire for clubs or playgrounds where they can escape the hardships of everyday life, draw strength from each other and develop their talents, self-esteem and confidence. Mothers said that the third priority for youth (behind employment and entrepreneurship) was clubs where young people can be provided with skills training. Likewise, fathers emphasized the need for a space that would enable young people to be mobilized and mentored. The benefits of a youth centre go beyond providing a place that young people can safely inhabit, providing a platform for delivering other services and support, such as skills training and mentoring.[10]

---

[8] Here we are talking about youth mobilization being seen as a solution at the community level, but it is also more widely recognized as a solution, at the city and national levels, as well as in international policy and rhetoric.

[9] Being an election year, these young men were also confident that these same local politicians that felt threatened by them and called the police on them would soon be coming to the Street and changing their behaviour towards them. 'It's different during an election time', they said. 'These leaders are always interrupting youth when they want something from us, and they will be good to us during elections so that we vote for them. But they will forget us after the vote. When a leader wants to be voted you see him all the time and he will help you if you ask. But once he becomes a leader, he will put tint on his car windows so you cannot even see him!'

[10] Banks (2015) explores one example of a youth development programme in Tanzania and neighbouring Uganda, which, through the provision of a club house or a 'safe space', mobilizes young women from around the community and provides them with life skills and vocational training, assets and access to microfinance and a mentor, and builds social networks that club members rely upon for support and advice. Key to the programme's success is its integrated approach and the provision of this physical space. Together, these

Hopes and Aspirations for the Future

These findings illustrate a bleak environment in which young people are ill-equipped with the skills and assets they need. This is compounded by a lack of institutional support from all directions, and the tensions arising between young people and their parents, as well as the broader community. We cannot extricate an individual young person's outcomes or struggles from these broader environmental influences, which impact strongly upon their lives and opportunities, from the household, community and societal level, and we must recognize the impact that these compounding factors have on young people's happiness and mental well-being and, in turn, their hopes and aspirations. 'I had a desire to have a good life,' explained one young man, 'but life is kicking me out of the way.'

Goals for the Future

To a certain extent, young people remain defiant in their day-to-day struggles and in their hopes and goals for the future. Future goals hinged around the desire to further their education or start some form of business. These two goals are closely aligned with the pressures of Arusha's labour market: further education is a must if any form of decent employment is to be secured, and for those who cannot achieve this, labour market opportunities are so limited that many see self-employment as the only means of securing a decent income. Yet financial barriers to both remain high in terms of fees or capital. It is also important that, while many young people specify a goal, such as 'I want to do business', few can outline specific plans to get there or even specify details such as the kind of business they want to do. Critical here is that there are almost no success stories of young people in the community to inspire, guide or mentor young people.[11]

---

improvements have generated significant social and economic improvements, with social improvements having a knock-on effect to other young women in the community that are not members (Banks 2017).

[11] Of the 24 interviews in this Street, only one young woman had created – and stuck to – a medium-term plan for improving her future. She had been working in a nearby factory for close to five years. I asked how she had managed to stick with this job for so long, since many young people leave after short periods of time working. 'It's because I have a plan,' she explained. 'I have always planned to work there for five years and through this save enough money for college or further schooling.' This commitment and planning that has motivated her to persist with a difficult job is absent in the majority of young people we spoke to.

Reinforcing Stereotypes

The previous section has illustrated the pressures young people – especially young men – face from the pressure to be self-reliant where work is so scarce. As fathers explained, 'It is when you can't get a job that the problems start.' This causes young people to have low self-confidence and resort to other means of relieving the pressures they face. Parents argued that this led young people that have 'given up' to drink alcohol and take drugs, or join gangs and turn to crime when there is no other option for supporting themselves. In one focus group, young men were asked to write down their three main concerns. One wrote, 'I am worried about becoming a thief like others here.' This link between a lack of opportunities and youth involvement in gangs, crimes and risky behaviour was highlighted across the board, by parents, community leaders and youth themselves.

This has also led to a breakdown in friendships and peer support networks, which are all the more important in a context of limited social support from parents, community members and local officials. Levels of trust for other young people in the community were strikingly low. There is a clearly identifiable fear associated with friendship in this low-income ward where time is plentiful but getting ahead is hard. Both sexes said it was dangerous to make friends nearby for fear of being led towards drinking, drugs or criminal activities. One young man we interviewed found himself stealing with a group of youth in order to help feed his family. 'This way I got involved with bad groups,' he said. 'I was drinking and smoking with them.' It was only after his mother intervened that he could detach himself from these groups. The pressures from the group remain even though he has cut off relationships with them. 'It has not been easy,' he said. 'They don't look at me well and use hard language towards me.'

Hopelessness and Disillusionment

It is important to contextualize the position of Arusha's young people today within the environment in which they have grown up. Heightened aspirations from higher education levels and global connections are widespread. Economic opportunities – where available – are not enough to fulfil these, whether from low paid factory work, exploitative wage labour, survival activities like collecting scraps, or businesses started with limited capital. Disillusionment is widespread. For some, this results from the pressures of unemployment and its implications for self-esteem. For others, even where some form of work is secured, demeaning jobs, low salaries and poor treatment are equally disillusioning. Neither scenario allows young people to feel secure in their personal identity, so strongly tied up in self-reliance and providing to the household, let alone to enable them to fulfil their modern and global aspirations.

Interviews asked young people to rate their happiness on a scale of 1 to 10, and whether their lives were better or worse than expected. No young men or women reported their lives as better than expected. Two-thirds of young men interviewed said their lives were 'worse' than expected, as did 60 per cent of young women. Young people asked how this could not be the case when their earnings were so low, the pressures upon them were so high and opportunities that might change this so few. 'My life is worse than I expected because I have no direction,' explained one young man. Another asked, 'Of course it is worse, because I have no job, little education. What else is there?'

In terms of happiness, too, young people expressed more disillusionment and fear than optimism, especially young men. With 1 representing 'very unhappy' and 10 representing 'very happy', 60 per cent of young men reported themselves between scores of 1 and 5 (and half of these placed themselves at only 1 or 2). In their explanations they highlighted uncertainty about the future, unhappiness at being unemployed and the pain of watching their families struggle without being able to help. 'I have not fulfilled my goals and have no money in my pocket,' explained one man. 'I don't even have time to laugh, how can I be happy?' said another. Young women reported slightly higher happiness levels. Only 50 per cent reported scores between 1 and 5, and only one-fifth of these gave themselves a score of 1 or 2. Those reporting higher scores were those who were those supported by their parents or who could envision some improvement in the future, whether through further education, work, or, for young women, marriage. Higher levels of happiness for young women may be explained by the fact that they face less pressure to be self-reliant and have hopes that somehow life will change after marriage – whether or not this occurs.

Conclusions

Good life never comes like dreams was a quote written on the wall of a youth centre in Dar es Salaam in the initial phase of the research, and its spectre followed me throughout the research process. While situated in dynamic city environments and at an age where they are dreaming of a better future, Arusha's urban youth are stuck in a transitional limbo, focused on staying afloat in today's difficult circumstances rather than looking forward to future plans. While popular conceptualizations of youth are based on the idea of transition, the research finds that there are few transitions taking place. Instead, there is a gaping limbo after school completion, where the main forms of work available to young people are limited in number and, where available, low-paid and insecure. The idea of a transition, too, is implicitly suggestive of support through a period of change, but this is strikingly absent. School is not preparing them to make this transition, nor are the majority of low income households able to better support them in the process. Community support is limited owing to widespread negative perceptions of young people.

Despite improvements in education and the perceived opportunities the city has to offer, both young people and parents report that today's urban youth have considerably *less* opportunity than their parents and older generations did. There remain few avenues through which personal ambitions can be realized in a context of fierce economic competition, limited state support and declining support from households and communities. We have to recognize all of these critical factors – the limited skills and capabilities, the lack of institutional support young people receive, and their adverse effects on psychosocial well-being in terms of happiness and self-esteem – as background information to any understanding of young people's labour market readiness and preparedness for the transition to adulthood. Dashed hopes and aspirations, limited friendship circles, leaving school feeling like a failure: all of these experiences will have huge implications on a young person's ability to build and take advantage of the networks that they need to carve out a better future.

11

International Aid to Tanzania – with some comparisons from Ghana and Uganda

Michael Tribe

Introduction

This chapter analyzes international aid (Official Development Assistance or ODA) to Tanzania over the period from 1980 to 2012 and makes comparisons with Ghana and Uganda, countries that are also significant recipients of aid and have experienced similar pressures from donors for policy reform. It considers the implications of some issues arising from the ODA statistics and reviews relevant literature, including official publications, relating to the Tanzanian 'aid experience'. Particular attention is paid to the impact of aid on economic growth and poverty reduction. Specific Tanzanian 'aid issues' are discussed including Budget Support, corruption and alignment with the principles of the Paris Declaration.

The cases of two of the three countries referred to in this chapter, Tanzania and Ghana, are also discussed in Whitfield (2009). The growth experiences of all three of the countries discussed in this chapter are also referred to in Chapter 1 of this volume. Whitfield and Fraser (2009) make the point that the economies of some of the countries previously regarded as highly aid-dependent have experienced rapid economic growth and are now both less aid-dependent and have access to other sources of funding, particularly China and India. Such changes in the availability of funding options have implications for issues such as policy conditionality, although the reforms already carried out imply that such issues are no longer a major source of disagreement.

Initially this chapter presents the aid statistics for the three countries in recent years. It then considers their respective records in terms of economic growth and poverty reduction and makes comparisons of the aid experiences and growth outcomes for the three countries. The chapter then proceeds to examine the specific case of Tanzania in detail in relation to the issues of Budget Support, corruption and the specific aid strategies adopted over time before concluding on the Tanzanian experience.

Aid to Tanzania, Ghana and Uganda

Table 11.1 shows summary data from the OECD DAC's website (OECD DAC 2014a) for the years 2010 to 2012. In current US$ prices Tanzania's per capita Gross National Income (GNI) has recently been about 20 per cent higher than that of Uganda, and Ghana has a per capita GNI about 2½ to 3 times that of Tanzania and Uganda.[1] Despite this relative GNI per capita data, ODA has been running consistently higher in Ghana than in Uganda, and ODA to Tanzania has been around 50 per cent higher than to Ghana and Uganda over this period. ODA to Tanzania as a proportion of GNI was about the same as that of Uganda at around 10 per cent and about twice that for Ghana.[2] The recent lower proportional

Table 11.1 Recent Comparative Aid Statistics – Tanzania, Ghana and Uganda

Country	Tanzania			Ghana			Uganda		
Year	2010	2011	2012	2010	2011	2012	2010	2011	2012
Net ODA ($US million current prices)	2,958	2,446	2,832	1,693	1,810	1,808	1,723	1,578	1,655
Bilateral share (%)	56	68	63	53	49	48	60	62	56
Net ODA / GNI (%)	13.1	10.4	10.1	5.3	4.8	4.7	10.9	10.1	9.9
Population (million)	45.0	46.4	47.8	24.3	24.8	25.4	34.0	35.1	36.3
GNI per capita (US$ million current prices)	530	540	570	1,260	1,410	1,550	460	470	440

Source: OECD DAC, 2014a
Note: See note 1 on the re-estimation of Ghana's national income

[1] The increase in Ghana's GDP is partly explained by the 2010 revision of Ghanaian GDP statistics (GSS 2010). The old series, based on the 1968 UN SNA system, was replaced by a new series based on the 1993 UN SNA, resulting in a 60.3 per cent increase. Updating of GDP statistics across sub-Saharan African countries, applying more recent UN SNA approaches, is ongoing. The Tanzanian National Bureau of Statistics has revised its GDP statistics several times, most recently in 2014 (URT 2014a). The main problems arising from the revision of national income statistics relate to cross-section (inter-country) and intertemporal (time series) comparisons. Inter-country comparisons of GDP levels are made on the assumption that statistical methodologies and sources permit realistic comparisons (Morgenstern, 1963; Devarajan 2013; Jerven, 2013a, 2013b, 2014). In September 2018 a further new series of Ghanaian GDP statistics based on the 2008 UN SNA and giving another 30 per cent increase in GDP (GSS 2018).
[2] Using proportions (rather than current price values) avoids the problems associated with variations in the reliability of individual country price deflators and changes in international currency exchange rates. The basic data in this chapter are expressed in constant prices sourced from both international and national sources.

international allocation of ODA to Ghana reflects the higher per capita income when compared with the two East African countries. The bilateral share of ODA has ranged from a low of 48 per cent (Ghana for 2012) to a high of 68 per cent (Tanzania for 2011), illustrating the significance of multilateral ODA in recent years (coincidentally demonstrating the limitations of ODA data which include only bilateral aid).

Table 11.2 shows average 2010–12 data for ODA from major donors to Tanzania, Ghana and Uganda. Broadly, it can be seen that the major donors for all three countries are very similar in terms of both the range of countries/institutions and the rank-ordering. The USA tops the list for Tanzania and Uganda and is in second place for Ghana.[3] Table 11.2 also shows the significance of the principal multilateral donors (the International Development Association [World Bank], the African Development Bank (AfDB), the European Union (EU), the Global Fund,[4] and IMF Concessional Trust Funds).

The OECD data used do not include the sectoral distribution of bilateral ODA disbursements before 2005, or for multilateral aid. Chang (2014) has criticized the extent to which the focus of the MDGs on poverty reduction and social sectors has tended to take attention and resources away from the more directly productive sectors of the economies of developing

Table 11.2 Major Donors to Tanzania, Ghana and Uganda (2011–12 average US$ million current prices)

	Tanzania	Ghana	Uganda
USA	555	268	396
IDA	404	401	188
UK	224	129	149
AfDF	146	171	144
EU Institutions	145	89	160
Japan	134	81	63
Global Fund	125		87
Sweden	121		
Denmark	119	80	66
Norway	105		70
IMF (Concessional Trust Funds)		185	
Germany		89	55
Canada		86	

Source: OECD DAC 2014a

---

[3] The USA is the largest ODA donor country internationally despite having one of the lowest ODA/GNI ratios, reflecting the high level of the US GNI.

[4] The Global Fund is a comparatively recently established 'umbrella' organization mainly focused on the health/medical sector and which represents the phenomenon of 'blending' of development finance.

countries, thus handicapping the internal capacity for poverty reduction.

Table 11.3 shows the sectoral distribution of bilateral ODA to Tanzania, Ghana and Uganda for 2005 and 2012. For all three countries, the preponderance of Social Infrastructure and Services (SIS) in the sectoral allocations of bilateral ODA is remarkable. For Tanzania there was an increase between 2005 and 2012 from about 40 per cent to just over 60 per cent. For Ghana the data are skewed by the impact of significant debt relief but, by 2012, SIS received about 45 per cent of bilateral ODA. For Uganda the proportion of bilateral ODA allocated to SIS amounted to about 55 per cent in both 2005 and 2012.

Economic Infrastructure and Services (EIS) allocations have significant variations over time and between countries for the two years shown in Table 11.3. For Tanzania in 2005 EIS received 18 per cent of

Table 11.3 Sectoral Distribution of Bilateral ODA Commitments – Tanzania, Ghana and Uganda (percentages)

	Tanzania		*Ghana*		*Uganda*	
	2005	*2012*	*2005*	*2012*	*2005*	*2012*
Bilateral ODA Commitments (current US$ million)	1031.35	1314.83	846.15	1069.78	840.12	824.5
Social Infrastructure and Services	40.38	61.38	12.77	45.11	53.75	56.75
Economic Infrastructure and Services	18.19	8.39	6.02	22.03	3.17	12.36
Production Sectors	2.39	11.00	5.57	18.75	4.49	18.19
Multisector	3.73	6.65	2.38	4.18	2.43	4.27
Programme Assistance (including Food Aid)	19.39	0.12	11.82	8.71	7.66	3.99
Action Relating to Debt	9.22	0.00	56.89	0.00	11.28	0.00
Humanitarian Aid	3.64	1.34	0.59	0.21	15.99	3.98
Unallocated/ Unspecified	3.06	0.91	3.96	1.01	1.23	0.46

Source: OECD DAC 2014a

Note: Data for 'action relating to debt' bias the results in this table for Ghana relative to Tanzania and Uganda. Bilateral debt relief peaked in 2007 for Tanzania and in 2005 to 2008 for Uganda allocations, falling to about 8.5 per cent in 2012. However, for Ghana and Uganda there were substantial increases in allocations to EIS, in the case of Ghana from 6 per cent to 22 per cent, and in the case of Uganda from 3 per cent to about 12.5 per cent. Although the allocations to SIS were very much higher than those to EIS, Tanzanian experience differs from that of Ghana and Uganda, while all three countries fit the pattern identified by Chang for SIS.

Data for the Production Sectors in Table 11.3 show significant increases between 2005 and 2012 for all three countries: from about 2.5 to 11 per cent of allocations in the case of Tanzania, from about 5.5 to nearly 19 per cent in the case of Ghana, and from about 4.5 to just over 18 per cent in the case of Uganda. Programme Assistance (including Food Aid) has only been substantial in the years covered by Table 11.3 in Tanzania, but all three countries show declines for this sector. Humanitarian Aid has only been substantial for Uganda, with all three countries, again, showing significant decreases.

In many respects the story revealed by Table 11.3 is somewhat at variance from that unfolded by Chang, with sectors other than SIS receiving substantial allocations of bilateral ODA in 2005 and 2012 for these three countries. However, there can be no doubt about the over-riding emphasis of bilateral ODA on SIS, with its focus on a form of 'poverty reducing' objective contrasting significantly with a poverty reduction strategy based on the generation of economic growth.

Table 11.4 sets ODA into a wider economic focus for all three countries included in this review, with two specific dimensions – ODA receipts as a percentage of Gross National Income (GNI) and ODA as a percentage of Government Expenditure.[5]

Table 11.4 ODA in Context

	ODA as % of GNI		ODA as % of Govt Expenditure	
	1990	2011	2001	2012
Tanzania	28.56	10.32	78.59 (2004–05 Budget)	70.31 (2009–10 Actual)
Ghana	9.69	4.75	64.42 (2001)	21.52 (2012)
Uganda	15.69	10.10	65.30 (2001)	49.62 (2012)

Sources: World Bank (2014a) except for Tanzanian ODA as % of Govt Expenditure (URT 2005b: Table 8.1 and URT 2010a: Table 7.2)
Note that Government Expenditure includes both Recurrent and Investment Expenditure

[5] In the notes to Table 11.4 the citation to official Tanzanian government publications refers to 'URT' – the United Republic of Tanzania. This acronym has been used throughout.

It can be seen that, in 1990, ODA was only just below 30 per cent of Tanzanian GNI, an exceptionally high ratio and indicative of Tanzania's low level of income. By 2011, this figure had fallen to just over 10 per cent, reflecting strong economic growth in the intervening two decades rather than a significant reduction in ODA. For Ghana, ODA as a proportion of GNI approximately halved over the same period, falling from about 10 per cent to about 5 per cent. For Uganda, there was a 50 per cent fall in this ratio, reflecting both strong economic growth and a sustained high level of ODA. Even at 10 per cent of GNI the level of ODA to Tanzania and Uganda in 2011 can be regarded as considerable.

For the second dimension, it can be seen that, in 2004–5, ODA as a percentage of government expenditure was around 80 per cent in Tanzania, falling to around 70 per cent by 2012, reflecting the fact that total government expenditure includes both non-recurrent ('development' and capital investment) expenditure, encompassing many activities supported by ODA, and recurrent expenditure (regular government activity). For Ghana ODA as a percentage of government expenditure fell from 64 per cent in 2001 to 21.5 per cent in 2012, while for Uganda the equivalent figures were 65 per cent in 2001 and 50 per cent in 2012. In this respect the Ghanaian data suggest greater reduction of the significance of ODA by comparison with Tanzania and Uganda, but for all three countries ODA has had a very considerable role in funding government expenditure.

Figure 11.1 shows the relative significance of different types of Tanzanian government financial sources. Budget Support provided about half of 'foreign revenues' for the period reviewed. Foreign revenues provided about 42 per cent of the sum of foreign and tax revenues for both periods included in the figure, and about 40 per cent of the sum of foreign and domestic revenues for both periods. This confirms the very significant position of foreign financial inflows in the funding of Tanzanian government expenditure.

To put ODA into another form of 'context', Table 11.5 sets out the main elements of international financial flows for the three countries.[6] One interesting aspect of the data in Table 11.5 is that, for Tanzania and Ghana, the net effect of ODA, NGO aid, 'umbrella organization' aid, personal remittances and foreign direct investment on the balance of international payments is approximately neutral. Only in the case

[6] In preparing this chapter an attempt was made to include data on illicit financial flows, particularly relating to over-invoicing of imports and under-invoicing of exports (in other words, 'transfer pricing'). The principal contemporary source for these data is the work of Global Financial Integrity (GFI). A recent detailed study of several African countries (including Tanzania, Ghana and Uganda) breaks new ground in this respect (GFI 2014). However, because the research focus of GFI differs significantly from that of this chapter the GFI data are not directly comparable with other financial flows as defined.

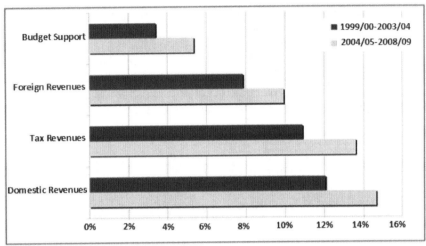

Source: Irish Aid/DFID 2010: 21
Note: The sources for the data in this figure were World Bank and IMF documents

Figure 11.1 Tanzania: Five-Year Comparison of Revenues by Type (as a proportion of GDP)

Table 11.5 Net International Financial Flows: Tanzania, Ghana and Uganda, 2012 (US$ millions)

	Tanzania	*Ghana*	*Uganda*
Net ODA Inflows	2,436	1,800	1,582
'NGO' Inflows	40	30	55
'Umbrella Organization' Inflows	159	98	165
Personal Remittances (inflows)	59	121	642
Foreign Direct Investment (net inflows)	1,706	3,294	1,721
Net Financial Inflows	4,399	5,343	4,165
Imports – Exports (Goods & Services)	– 4,140	– 5,196	– 2,895

Sources: Row 1 – Table 11.1 above; Row 2 – d-portal.org, 2014; Rows 3, 4 and 6 – World Bank 2014a
Notes: 'NGO' inflows relate to 'traditional' NGOs – excluding 'umbrella organization' aid – see Table 11.7 below. See footnote 6 on the problems associated with including comparable data on illicit financial flows

of Uganda is there a substantially positive net impact from these five flow series. The net ODA inflows have already been presented in Table 11.1. The international NGO inflows were surprisingly difficult to locate,[7] but it can be seen that the overall financial impact is very small when compared with ODA (1.6 per cent for Tanzania and Ghana, and 3.4 per cent for Uganda). This is not to belittle the importance of international NGO contributions to the three countries, part of which involves acting as instruments for the implementation of some types of ODA that donors have judged to be more effective if handled by NGOs.

Within changes to 'aid architecture' there has been a concern by donors to make inter-country ODA allocation more systematic, reflecting international development objectives. In 2010–11 the UK's DfID undertook Bilateral and Multilateral Aid Reviews (DfID, 2011a, 2011b, 2011c). The Bilateral Aid Review aimed to cut the number of countries to which the UK contributed ODA from around 87 to around 27 countries. A central part of the allocation process was the application of a 'Needs and Effectiveness Index' – 'Needs' being based largely on poverty-reduction criteria and 'Effectiveness' being based on governance criteria (Tribe 2017). Following this review all three countries remained within the 27 'survivors' as "DfID priority" countries. The projections of DfID ODA allocations are shown in Table 11.6. It can be seen that all three countries were to experience slight falls in the proportion of UK Aid allocated to them. However, in money terms Uganda was scheduled to have a slight increase and then a slight fall in actual ODA allocations over the period 2010–11 to 2014–15, while Tanzania and Ghana were scheduled to have a slight increase in UK ODA allocations (DfID 2011b: Annex F).

During the period 2010–11 to 2014–15 UK ODA was scheduled to increase from 0.57 per cent to 0.70 per cent of Gross National Income (House of Commons 2013a: 14). The Technical Report relating to the DfID Bilateral Aid Review gives the basis for the changes to ODA allocations between countries (DfID 2011b). The DfID Multilateral Aid Review (DfID 2011c) examined the 'alignment' between the priorities

Table 11.6 UK Aid to Tanzania, Ghana and Uganda before and after the 2011 Bilateral Aid Review

	Tanzania	Ghana	Uganda
2010–11 % UK Aid	5.17	2.93	3.10
2010–11 UK Aid £m	150	85	90
2014–15 % UK Aid	4.08	2.43	2.18
2010–11 UK Aid £m	168	100	90

Source: DfID 2011a, 2011b

---

[7] Most accessible NGO aid statistics have been based on reporting outflows from donor countries rather than inflows by recipient countries. A new data source is now available that corrects this data 'gap', and has been used for Table 11.5 (d-portal.org, 2015).

Table 11.7 Umbrella Organization Aid to Tanzania, Ghana and Uganda, 2012 US$

Organization	Tanzania	Ghana	Uganda
GAVI	30,761,553	44,831,988	12,527,115
Global Fund	120,419,497	63,941,515	148,522,014
HIROs	3,938,872	–	4,265,490

Source: d-portal.org, 2014

of multilateral bodies to which UK ODA had been allocated, their performance, and the priorities of DfID. This review itself was subjected to close scrutiny by the International Development Committee of the House of Commons (House of Commons 2013b).

In recent years there has been a significant increase in the financial flows associated with what have been termed here 'umbrella organizations'. Bodies such as GAVI, the Global Fund and HIROs,[8] included in Table 11.7, receive funding from a range of organizations, including bilateral and multilateral ODA donors, international NGOs (both conventional and 'new', such as Comic Relief), private charities (such as the Bill and Melinda Gates Foundation) and the corporate sector (e.g. Vodafone), and they commit their aid contributions to specific objectives relating to medical campaigns. The three organizations identified in Table 11.7 have accounted for around 5 to 10 per cent of the value of ODA receipts for Tanzania, Ghana and Uganda in recent years. While the international collaboration reflected in Table 11.7 relates particularly to the medical/health sector, this type of multi-agency funding model has become more common across the 'aid' spectrum and has been referred to recently as 'blending' (Africa Progress Panel 2014: Chapter 4). The range of organizations involved in 'blending' also includes the Eurobond market and other forms of finance that are not included in ODA but which are included in ODF.[9] A higher proportion of international development investment, project financing and management and sector development now involves collaboration and co-financing between these groups. Private–public partnerships are one example.

[8] GAVI is the Global Alliance for Vaccination and Immunisation; the Global Fund is the Global Fund to Fight AIDS, Tuberculosis and Malaria; and HIROs is the Heads of International Research Organisations (Viergever 2011).
[9] The definition of ODF given by the OECD is: 'Used in measuring the inflow of resources to recipient countries: includes (a) bilateral ODA, (b) grants and concessional and non-concessional development lending by multilateral financial institutions, and (c) Other Official Flows for development purposes (including refinancing loans) which have too low a grant element to qualify as ODA' (OECD DAC 2014b).

Aid, Economic Growth and Poverty Reduction

Although the objectives of international aid are much wider than simply to contribute to economic growth, economists' judgement about aid effectiveness have mainly focused on analysis of the relationship between ODA and economic growth (Griffin 1970; Mosley 1980; Easterly 2003; 2006; Easterly et al. 2004; Gomanee et al. 2005; McGillivray et al. 2006; Rajan & Subramanian 2008; Clemens et al. 2012; Arndt et al. 2015; Lof et al. 2015; Arndt et al. 2016). Over the more than forty years covered by these references the focus of research has, inevitably, changed. However, the basic methodology has remained stable, being based on cross-country quantitative analysis using multiple regression techniques. There do not appear to have been any parallel, high-profile, single-country or grouped countries case studies. In addition, there have been few economic studies that aspire to trace the relationship between ODA and economic growth based on growth theory, particularly on modern, or endogenous, growth theory.[10] The most recent cross-country studies on the ODA–economic growth relationship have been particularly careful to distinguish between ODA that is focused on contributing to economic growth within a relatively short time horizon, and ODA that is either not focused on economic growth per se (e.g. humanitarian and/ or disaster aid) or is directly focused on poverty reduction and does not have an economic growth objective. More recent economic analysis has allowed for a time-lag between ODA receipts and impacts (Clemens et al. 2012; Arndt et al. 2015; Lof et al. 2015; Arndt et al. 2016) and for the long-term (rather than short-term) impact of aid. The results from these recent studies conclude that ODA has a relatively modest, but significant, positive role in contributing to economic growth in recipient developing countries, while earlier studies based on less complex interpretations of the statistics came to considerably more negative conclusions.

In the context of systematic analysis of the impact of ODA one of the most important analytical issues is to compare the outcomes based on actual ODA receipts (i.e. ODA disbursements and programme implementation rather than simply ODA commitments) by developing countries with the 'counterfactual' (what would be likely to have occurred in the absence of ODA receipts). While such analysis based on comparison of actual with counterfactual outcomes is notably rare, the counterfactual approach is the fundamentally correct methodology.

Some recently published empirical work on African economic growth is very instructive on the ODA–economic growth relationship. Rodrik opens his 2014 National Bureau of Economic Research paper thus:

[10] A good source for endogenous growth theory is Romer's seminal article in the *Journal of Economic Perspectives* (Romer 1994). Gomanee et al. (2005) point to the dearth of studies linking economic growth theory with the contribution of ODA to economic growth.

It is clear that Africa has benefited from a particularly favorable external environment during the last two decades. Global commodity prices have been high and interest rates low. Private capital flows have supplemented increased official assistance. China's rapid growth has fuelled demand for the region's natural resources and has stimulated direct investment in African economies. The global financial crisis, meanwhile, had little direct impact, given African countries' weak financial links with the rest of the world and low levels of financialization. (Rodrik 2014: 1–2)

Rodrik emphasizes the significance of economic reform, institutional quality and reduced civil conflict as factors explaining the better African economic performance during the period covered by Table 11.8. The first two of these favourable factors have been associated with ODA programmes (and what might be regarded as 'leverage' by the IFIs and the donor community) but would not necessarily show up in some of the regression analysis focused on the ODA–economic growth relationship. McMillan, Rodrik and Verduzco (2014) focus on structural change and productivity growth and the importance of economic reform and 'improved' governance in contributing to accelerated African economic growth. A tantalizing question therefore relates to the distinction between African economic growth that would have occurred with significantly less ODA, and that part of economic growth thath has resulted from the ODA inflows. Given the high and sustained levels of ODA to Tanzania, Ghana and Uganda, it would be difficult to conclude that ODA has not been a major factor in the improved economic performance.

Apart from the relationship between ODA inflows and economic growth, considerable attention has been given to the contribution made by ODA to poverty reduction in recipient countries. The role of ODA (and of the 'donor community') in reducing the extent of poverty in developing countries was given additional emphasis with the introduction of *Poverty Reduction Strategy Papers* in the mid-1990s (World Bank 2014b) as mandatory instruments of development planning, together with the PRSP Sourcebook (World Bank 2002a).[11]

Table 11.8 GDP Growth for Tanzania, Ghana and Uganda, 1990–2012

	GDP 1990 (constant 2005 US$ million)	GDP 2012	Annual average % GDP growth	2012 GDP as a % of 1990 GDP
Tanzania	7,454	22,432	5.24	334
Ghana	5,509	18,374	5.55	362
Uganda	3,466	14,735	6.81	481

Source: World Bank 2014a and author's calculations
Note: See footnote 1 on Ghana's national income data

[11] PRSPs were mandatory conditions for the application of the HIPC debt relief programme, but have also been widely adopted as economic development planning documents (World Bank 2014b).

Table 11.9 Poverty Headcount (per cent) <US$1.90 PPP per day

	Tanzania	*Ghana*	*Uganda*
1991/2	70.4	47.4	68.1
Most recent	46.6 (2011)	25.2 (2005)	33.2 (2012)

Source: World Development Indicators November 2016

Table 11.9 shows poverty headcount data for the three countries, comparing data for 1992 with the most recent data from *World Development Indicators* (World Bank 2016). The poverty headcount is the number (or proportion) of the population whose daily income is below the specified international poverty line, below which people are deemed to be in 'extreme poverty', currently US$1.90 (2011 prices). In the case of Tanzania, World Bank data show that in 1991 slightly more than 70 per cent of the population were in extreme poverty, with the proportion falling to just under 47 per cent in 2011. For Ghana the comparable proportion had fallen from 47 per cent in 1991 to just over 25 per cent in 2005, while for Uganda the comparable data were 68 per cent in 1992 and 41 per cent in 2009. This poverty indicator is open to a number of caveats, not only concerning the validity of the value of US$1.90 per day (in 2011 PPP$), but also because the data are based on periodic household surveys undertaken with World Bank support, with data being generated for different years in different countries. However, this is the best that we have. The implication of the data in Table 11.9 is that the extent of extreme poverty is somewhat higher in Tanzania than in Ghana and Uganda, but that there has been some success in reducing the extent of extreme poverty.

The poverty line is rather a 'blunt instrument' since it relates to an economic or 'income-related' definition of poverty (with all of the associated limitations), and also gives little indication of the shape of the frequency distribution lying below the poverty line so that it does not tell us anything about the depth of poverty below the poverty line. Table 11.10 contains data relating to two multidimensional poverty indices that have been included in the UNDP's Human Development Reports over the last twenty-five years.

For the Human Poverty Index there are data for 1998 and 2009, with a higher index value indicating a greater degree of multidimensional poverty. The data for all three countries confirm the steady reduction in poverty since 2006 shown by their poverty line data. While the poverty line data are essentially a measure of income poverty, the Human Poverty Index data included equal weighting of three measures relating to (i) the percentage of people not expected to survive to age 40, (ii) the percentage of adults who are illiterate, and (iii) a combined measure based on (a) the percentage of people without access to safe water, (b) the percentage of people without access to

Table 11.10 Human Poverty Index and Multidimensional Poverty Index

	Tanzania	Ghana	Uganda
HPI – 1 1998	29.2	35.4	39.7
HPI – 1 2002	32.7	28.7	40.8
HPI – 1 2006	36.3	33.1	36.0
HPI – 1 2007/8	32.5	32.3	34.7
HPI – 1 2009	30.0	28.1	28.8
MPI 2006-2008	n.a.	0.186 (2008)	0.399 (2006)
Population in MPI 2006–2008 (%)	n.a.	39.2	74.5 (2006)
MPI 2010–2011	0.335 (2010)	0.144 (2011)	0.359 (2011)
Population in MPI 2010–2011 (%)	66.4 (2010)	30.5 (2011)	70.3 (2011)

Sources: HPI – 1 UNDP HDR 2000, 2002, 2006, 2007/8 and 2009; MPI – UNDP HDR 2014
Note: Values for the Human Poverty Index were published by UNDP for about ten years starting with 1997, and the final round of published data is for the most recent year's data available at the time of the preparation of the Human Development Report 2009. There appears to have been no attempt to provide any reconciliation or overlap between the HPI and MPI series, making comparisons over longer periods of time very difficult or impossible

health services, and (c) the percentage of moderately and severely underweight children under five years of age (from UNDP 1998: 110 – see UNDP 2015).

The data in Table 11.10 for the Multidimensional Poverty Index (MPI), which replaced the Human Poverty Index in 2010, also show higher degrees of poverty the higher the index value, but also include an 'MPI Poverty Line' indicating the proportion of the population living in multidimensional poverty. The data for the MPI were incomplete for Tanzania at the time of writing but with this measure Ghana clearly has a degree of poverty lower than that for Tanzania and Uganda in this period, and for Ghana and Uganda the period between the middle and the late 2000s shows a drop in the extent of poverty, which is consistent with other measures.

Table 11.11 shows data for the Human Development Index (HDI), generated by the United Nations Development Programme, for 1990 and 2014.[12] The HDI, which was the original composite 'development index'

[12] The HDI is a composite index which has changed slightly over time. It is based on three elements: (i) life expectancy at birth, (ii) the average of mean years of schooling and expected years of schooling, and (iii) per capita income at PPP US$. Refer to Technical Note 1 (UNDP HDR 2014 – UNDP 2015). In many respects the HDI is conceptually the obverse of the HPI and MPI. The HDI, and many other measures of 'development' and of 'poverty', raise technical questions over the inclusion of averages and distributions in complex indicators.

Table 11.11 Human Development Index, 1990 and 2014

	Tanzania	*Ghana*	*Uganda*
1990	0.353	0.427	0.306
HDI Rank 2001	140	119	141
2014	0.521	0.579	0.483
HDI Rank 2014	151	140	163

Source: UNDP 2015 for 2014 data; UNDP 2001 for 2001 data – see UNDP 2015
Note: The ranking for 2001 is the oldest that is readily available

produced by the UNDP, shows a significant increase over the period 1990 to 2014, indicating an advance in the standard of living for all three countries. In general we would expect that an increase in the HDI would be associated with a reduction in the level of absolute poverty. The global ranking figures for 2001 and 2014 reflect an increase in the number of countries included in the ranking, but the data in Table 11.11 also suggest that Tanzania, Ghana and Uganda have slipped down the international HDI league table over these years.

A 'soft' conclusion to the issue of the contribution of ODA to poverty reduction (and to improvements in the standard of living) is possible, as with the contribution of ODA to economic growth. Not only has strong economic growth over a period of thirty years had an opportunity to impact on poverty and the standard of living in all three countries, but there can be only a limited empirical connection between ODA and economic growth given the potential significance of economic reform and improved economic governance.

Tanzanian Aid Issues

Recent aid literature has focused on changes in the structures and procedures within which ODA operates. The contributions of Severino and Ray (2009, 2010) and Severino (2011), based on experience in the OECD DAC (Development Assistance Committee), have been very influential in suggesting changes in the ODA 'mindset'. Kaberuka (2011) outlines some shortcomings and opportunities relating to ODA in sub-Saharan Africa. Kharas (2007) provides an overview of long-term ODA trends to the middle of the first decade of the twenty-first century, while Hyden (2003) reflects on his East African experience in proposing changes to aid donor strategies.

The joint Irish Aid/DfID evaluation report covering the period

---

'Improvements' in average levels (for example of the HDI) could conceivably be associated with changes in the distributions, with a deterioration for the lower parts of the distribution and an improvement for the upper parts of the distribution.

2005–10 (Irish Aid/DfID 2010) makes frequent mention of the views of the 'DPs' or 'Development Partners'. The literature has tended to refer to 'recipients' and 'donors', but if both are development partners then it is necessary to find an alternative means to distinguish between the two groups. The joint report's references to 'DPs' refer to members of the 'donor community', while the Tanzanian 'Development Partners Group' includes both the donor community as well as the Government of Tanzania (URT 2005a). Clearly the Tanzanian document is more inclusive, while the joint Irish Aid/DfID report did not embody the changed perspectives and terminology of the Paris Declaration and successor international agreements.

In recent years the significance of environmental issues in the context of ODA has come to assume a more important role in the policies and allocations of the donor community. Kahyarara (2014) provides a comprehensive overview of environmental policy in Tanzania, including the role of ODA. He explains that

> focusing on the funding for environmental degradation projects, the study notes that budget expenditure allocation to these activities is around 0.04 per cent of Tanzania's total expenditure. This is a problem given that in the near future financing for climate change alone would need around US$1 billion per year (or nearly 10 per cent of the budget). Ultimately, aid money is critical for Tanzania, as over 90 per cent of funds for environment come from donors.

This section focuses on three main issues: Budget Support (BS), corruption, and alignment with the principles of the Paris Declaration. There is also brief consideration of the literature on the impact of ODA on Tanzanian development, and of recent Tanzanian policy relating to the management of ODA.

Budget Support

The December 2014 version of the DfID Operational Plan for Tanzania 2011–2016 (DfID, 2014: 7) stated that

> DfID Tanzania will reduce and eventually cease to use General Budget Support (GBS) during the period covered by this plan, as the 2010 independent Country Programme Evaluation suggested that GBS was not the most effective way to deliver results in the current circumstances.

This decision by DfID, purportedly based on the joint evaluation report, which considered BS and public financial management in great detail (Irish Aid/DfID, 2010: Chapter 3), appears to have been driven more by internal UK political factors than by the findings of the evaluation report. The wording of DfID (2014) gives a misleading representation of the evaluation's recommendations. To quote the evaluation:

There remains a continuing and important place for GBS in Tanzania, where substantial improvement in the coverage of public services is necessary to progress towards the MDGs. However, the evaluation supports a relative reduction in the scale of GBS and SBS until the issues of quality, efficiency and equity in public spending are addressed through a revitalised dialogue process. (Irish Aid/DfID 2010: 68 para 6.10)

There have been evaluations of BS by two UK public sector institutions, the National Audit Office (NAO, 2008) and the Independent Commission for Aid Impact (ICAI 2012), both of which concluded that BS should be used cautiously. However, there was pressure on the Conservative/Liberal Democrat Coalition Government from Conservative backbenchers to reduce or eliminate the use of Budget Support in the UK Aid programme (FT 2014; Daily Mail 2014). The NAO and ICAI reports, in which Tanzania features somewhat positively, find some improvement in achieving BS objectives over the period from around 2005 to 2010. The joint Irish/DfID evaluation actually found that some of the difficulties experienced with DfID's use of Budget Support in Tanzania had been due to poor communication between DfID personnel in London and in Dar es Salaam.

HQ appreciation of how the application of BS and Paris Principles changed and developed over time was insufficient for them to give advice and support. More mutual lesson learning round the realities of programme management would benefit both sides. (Irish Aid/DfID 2010: 64 para 5.38)

The UK ICAI focused on DfID BS in one of its early reports (ICAI 2012), which summarized an international consensus on BS that had been developed during the negotiations (in which DfID had taken a leading role) leading to the launch of the Paris Declaration in 2005. This consensus is reproduced in Figure 11.2. Tripp (2012: 17) has a telling discussion of BS, the conclusion of which is as follows:

Many donors in Tanzania suspect that a large chunk of the funds that disappear are lost through the GBS or through the basket-funding process. This is because, as Barkan (2009) cogently explains, GBS represents large amounts of funds in unaudited accounts or accounts for which audits are not available to the public. This allows a large portion of the budget to support corruption and to be used as political finance.

Nevertheless, the laudable objectives that led to the introduction of BS as an ODA 'modality' within the Paris Declaration framework (as summarized in the ICAI's report and in Figure 11.2) are also clearly articulated by Tripp.

Traditional projects
■ Donor-led
■ Undermines ownership and accountability
■ Fragmented assistance
■ Bypasses country systems
■ Supports capital expenditure and technical assistance
■ Donor support is more volatile
■ Higher aid-management costs
■ Sustainability more difficult to achieve

Budget support
■ Partner country-led
■ Strengthens national ownership and accountability
■ Facilitates donor harmonisation
■ Uses and strengthens country systems, including the national budget
■ Supports recurrent expenditure
■ Donor support is more predictable
■ Lowers aid-management costs
■ Generates more sustainable results

Source: ICAI 2012: 4

Figure 11.2 The 'Paris Consensus' on Budget Support and Aid Effectiveness

Corruption

Much of the literature relating to the Tanzanian ODA experience mentions corruption as a major issue, and this has been one factor accounting for a degree of 'aid volatility' (Guardian 2014; DfID, 2014). The joint Irish Aid/DfID evaluation study devotes a significant amount of space to the issue of corruption (2010: Chapter 2) but concludes that Tanzania's corruption profile is little better or worse than that of other countries in the region. The evaluation report concluded that further research and analysis was needed as the basis for the development of more robust anti-corruption measures.

The well-respected Helleiner Report of 1995 (Helleiner et al. 1995; Wangwe 2002) is cited in the joint Irish Aid/DfID evaluation report in the context of corruption:

The Helleiner Report acknowledged these problems and was strongly critical of GoT. However, it also considered the ways in which DP [i.e. donor community] behaviour had contributed to this situation, by undermining ownership, by lacking transparency and predictability and by pursuing aid modalities which burdened the limited administrative capacities of GoT. The report was well received and created a positive environment for reforms, culminating in the Tanzania assistance strategy, PRBS (Poverty Reduction Budget Support] and, later, the joint assistance strategy for Tanzania (JAST). (Irish Aid/DfID 2010: 30)

Rotberg (2007) discusses the issue of corruption in a 'development overview' of seven sub-Saharan African countries (including Tanzania, Ghana and Uganda). A shortcoming of this work is the lack of direct attribution of sources, but this is always likely to be a problem in research on corruption. Rotberg gives an overview of corruption from a respected academic institution (the John F. Kennedy School of Government in Harvard University). He cites Transparency International data showing Tanzania as 93rd out of 163 countries in 2006 on the Corruption Perceptions Index, and the Global Integrity Index for 2006, which gave Tanzania an overall score of 59 (described as 'very weak'). Other evidence of significant corruption assembled by Rotberg is significant. In the international sphere the Tanzanian purchase of an air traffic control system from the UK (see also BBC 2001; Guardian 2006) developed into a long-running saga involving alleged corruption on the part of British Aerospace. In the domestic sphere Rotberg cites a wide range of cases to substantiate his arguments.

The corruption phenomenon in Tanzania is highlighted by Tripp (2012). While the main statistics presented in her paper are sourced from Transparency International there is also other primary and secondary evidence about corruption in Tanzania and its relationship to ODA. Tripp cites the World Bank CPIA measure in her discussion, implying a significant deterioration in 'country performance' ranking (i.e. weakening of the governance standards), and suggests that 'some in the Bank feel the ranking should be lower but that would put it out of sync with countries that are regarded less favourably than Tanzania' (Tripp 2012: 13). This is consistent with the joint Irish Aid/DfID evaluation of 2010 finding that, despite its poor record on corruption, Tanzania is no worse – and probably better – than other ODA recipients in this respect. Tripp presents data for 'Donor support of political reform, 2000–10' demonstrating the extent to which ODA has had the governance and reform process as a key target of its funding (Tripp 2012: Table 1).

The World Bank's relationship with the current Tanzanian Joint Assistance Strategy is set out in a World Bank document which refers explicitly to the corruption issue:

> Corruption and accountability emerged as important themes during the 2010 election campaign. The president made strong commitments on both issues in his inaugural address. Seven high-level corruption

cases involving an estimated US$1 billion took place between 2000 and 2008, tainting Tanzania's reputation. The government took decisive actions that helped restore confidence, but definite solution of some of the cases remains a matter of concern. Renewed government commitment on these issues would help address the perception of increasing corruption. (World Bank 2011: 1–2)

As the lead member of the donor community World Bank views clearly carry considerable weight on this issue.

The suspension of UK and other countries' ODA provided on a BS basis in October 2014 appears to have been prompted by investigations of the Tanzanian Parliament's Public Accounts Committee into allegations of widespread corruption. The report in the *Guardian* newspaper (Guardian 2014) emphasizes the central role of Tanzanian opposition politicians in pressing for suspension of ODA, rather than the roles of the UK political system or of international evaluation reports.

The corruption issue is clearly significant, but has tended to be clouded by limitations of both a conceptual and empirical nature. The focus on international comparative indices of corruption (such as Transparency International's Corruption Perceptions Index – TI 2015) tends to cover only private sector views of public sector corruption, implying that the 'blame' lies with the public sector rather than with the private sector. This echoes the World Bank definition of corruption: 'the abuse of public office for private gain' (World Bank 2015b).

A more balanced view would be critical of both public and private sectors. From both an ethical and developmental viewpoint corruption entirely within the private sector is just as unacceptable as that covered by the World Bank definition. The case of the air traffic control system related to alleged corruption involving a private sector international source. New UK legislation was approved in 2010 covering all forms of bribery and corruption with, *inter alia*, the objective of getting better control over the activity of donor country private sector institutions (Guardian 2010; Ministry of Justice 2011). Bribery and corruption is an international issue on which the OECD has a continuing focus (OECD 2014).

A distinction is necessary between 'international' corruption influencing broad ODA allocations between countries, programmes and contractors and 'domestic' corruption, which affects the extent to which the intended beneficiaries of ODA programmes actually receive support (perhaps with resources being misappropriated). This 'domestic' dimension was the subject of a UK report by the Independent Commission for Aid Impact, which was critical of DfID's record on anti-corruption measures relating to poverty-reduction programmes (ICAI, 2014).

1. **Ownership:** *Developing countries set their own strategies for poverty reduction, improve their institutions and tackle corruption.*

2. **Alignment:** *Donor countries align behind these objectives and use local systems.*

3. **Harmonisation:** *Donor countries coordinate, simplify procedures and share information to avoid duplication.*

4. **Results:** *Developing countries and donors shift focus to development results and results get measured.*

5. **Mutual accountability**: *Donors and partners are accountable for development results.*

Source: OECD DAC 2005 and 2008

Figure 11.3 The Principles of the Paris Declaration

Alignment with the Paris Declaration

The central principles of the Paris Declaration of 2005 are shown in Figure 11.3. These principles apply to all donors and recipients within the ODA system.

There have been two main strands tracking the implementation of the new aid architecture represented by the Paris Declaration (OECD DAC 2005 and 2008). The first has been through a series of international meetings in Rome (2003), Paris (2005), Accra (2008), Busan (2011), Mexico City (2014) and Nairobi (2016) (OECD DAC 2015a; Global Partnership 2016). At the Busan meeting the Global Partnership for Effective Development Cooperation was established to monitor the process of securing alignment with the principles of the Paris Declaration by ODA donors and recipients (Global Partnership 2013). The second strand is represented by the major multi-country evaluation study undertaken by IOD PARC, funded by the OECD DAC Paris Declaration Secretariat and by the Danish Institute for International Studies (Wood et al. 2011; Betts & Wood 2013; Wood & Betts 2013). This evaluation study covered seven donor institutions and 21 recipient countries (OECD DAC 2015b). The ten African countries that were studied included Ghana and Uganda, but not Tanzania.

An overall conclusion from the Final Report of Phase 2 of this major evaluation (Wood et al. 2011) is that, although progress had been made towards implementing the principles of the Paris Declaration between

2005 and 2010, the implementation process was relatively slow and uneven, varying significantly between individual principals and individual countries. This relatively slow progress is not surprising given the political and administrative complexity of implementation. Also unsurprising is that the evaluation found that significant shortcomings among both the recipient countries and the donor institutions still need to be registered by the 'aid industry'. In particular, the tendency for donor evaluations to 'blame' recipient countries for slow progress while overlooking the slow progress of donor institutions (Irish Aid/DfID 2010: vi–xv) and for recipient country evaluations to 'blame' donor institutions for slow progress (URT 2009f), is rather unhelpful. It is clear that the international system significantly underestimated the complexity, and timescale, of the prospective implementation of the principles embodied in the Paris Declaration.

An early (i.e. pre-Paris Declaration) review of Norwegian ODA to Tanzania gives an interesting insight into the principles and practice of a leading 'Nordic' donor, with a particular focus on 'conditionality', which demonstrates that the Norwegian approach did not follow the more aggressive 'Washington consensus' approach adopted by other international donors (Selbervik 1999).

ODA in Tanzania

Over the years there have been many studies on the Tanzanian relationship with ODA and with the 'donor community'. One of the most comprehensive is that by Bigsten et al. (2001) published in a major World Bank study that included ten country case studies. This study was based on a series of data that ended in 1996, illustrating the time-lags associated with such comprehensive studies. The Helleiner Report (Helleiner et al. 1995) was based on data from a similar time period. Wangwe (1997) produced a comprehensive overview of 'The Management of Foreign Aid in Tanzania', prior to the development of the principles of the Paris Declaration, which highlighted the issues of aid ownership, joint ownership of aid, capacity building, resource budgeting, policy direction, aid coordination, aid conditionality and dealing with corruption. It is salutary to find that essentially the same set of issues were still current in 2016 without any question of 'reinventing the wheel'. Many of these issues were revisited constructively by Helleiner early in the new millennium (Helleiner 2001). Wangwe and Ndulu (1997) gave a brief and authoritative overview of Tanzanian economic development in the decade following the adoption of the 1986 Economic Recovery Programme, with sections dealing with international debt and with the relationship between economic growth and poverty reduction that are still of great interest. Nyoni (1998) reports a study that is relevant to the issue of 'Dutch Disease', finding that aid inflows had not signifi-

- GoT leadership and ownership has been strengthened

- The formulation of national priorities and processes in Tanzania Mainland and Zanzibar are not yet harmonised;

- Reasonably good progress has been made in rationalisation and harmonisation and alignment of processes with a view to reducing transaction costs;

- Public resource management has improved considerably;

- Participation by all stakeholders in policy dialogue has been broadened and is becoming more institutionalised;

- GoT needs to be more assertive in stating its preferred forms of aid modality. The GoT has expressed a preference for General Budget Support (GBS) as an aid modality;

- Concerns have been expressed about the risks of deepening aid dependence;

- TA [technical assistance] has continued to be most challenging in terms of being supply driven, with tied procurement and little built-in capacity building.

Source: Derived from URT 2005a

Figure 11.4 Summary of Findings of the 2005 Report of the Independent Monitoring Group

cantly impacted on the foreign exchange rate. However, this study was based on data from a period when the exchange rate was essentially 'administered', rather than being open to market forces, so that more recent studies with a similar focus might reach different conclusions.

In 2005 the Tanzanian 'Independent Monitoring Group' produced an evaluative review of ODA relationships in Tanzania (Killick 2004; URT 2005a). A summary of its conclusions appears in Figure 11.4. The broadly positive outcomes are from an independent evaluation, undertaken within Tanzania by an international group of experts,[13] which provides an invaluable comparator for external evaluations undertaken by the donor community. There are two areas that are of particular

[13] To quote the IMG Report: 'The IMG team comprised four persons: Prof. Samuel Wangwe (Chairperson), Mr. Dag Aarnes (Consultant/Senior Economist, Partner Assist Consulting AS), Prof. Haidari Amani (Executive Director of ESRF) and Dr. Alison Evans (Independent Consultant and Associate of ODI, London – who made her contributions through commenting and contributing to drafts at all stages of this work). In carrying out research for this work the team received contributions from Mr. Deo Mutalemwa, Ms Kate Dyer (on the Education sector) and Ms Moorine Lwakatare' (URT 2005a: iii).

interest. The first is that of the Sector Wide Approach – described as an 'approach (SWAp) to aid organisation and delivery which became popular in the donor community in the mid-1990s [and] was a response to the fragmentation, and perceived limited effectiveness of aid' (URT 2005a: 22). The main problem identified with the SWAp by the evaluation group was that the 'vested interests of sectors in collusion with DPs [ODA donors) leads to exaggeration of mistrust on MoF [Ministry of Finance] and engagement of lobbies to delay changing the system for the better. This observation is consistent with the observation made by Berke (2002) in the context of embedding sector programmes to the PRS process' (URT 2005a: 24). The second concerns the definition of 'harmonisation', a key concept within the Paris Declaration: 'It appears that DPG [the Tanzanian Development Partners Group] does not have a working definition of what it means by harmonisation' (URT 2005a: 28), and 'some donors continue to carry out practices, which are not consistent with the spirit of TAS [Tanzania Assistance Strategy], Rome Declaration, [and] developments in harmonisation and alignment agreements at OECD/DAC level' (URT 2005a: 29).

An ActionAid (UK) report published in 2004 focused on ODA conditionality as applied to the development of the water supply system in Dar es Salaam, and specifically to pressure applied by donors for privatization of the system. It particularly highlighted contradictions between the poverty-reduction objectives of social infrastructure development and cost recovery and other financial objectives of privatized systems. However, Tripp (2012: 20) reports that this attempt at privatization proved to be unsuccessful because 'the larger infrastructure enterprises, including Dar es Salaam Water Supply and Sanitation, proved more challenging and were unable to become financially sustainable through public-private partnerships. With the exception of Tanzania International Container Terminal Services (TICTS), they all reverted to public control.' This illustrates the limitations of some types of donor conditionality, suggesting that even from a pragmatic viewpoint it has not always been realistic.

The Tanzanian Assistance Strategy and Public Financial Management Reform

The Tanzanian Joint Assistance Strategy (JAST) followed the Tanzanian Assistance Strategy (TAS), which had been launched in 2002 (URT 2004; URT 2006a). A background document from the African Development Bank (AfDB) provides a summary of the history and processes associated with the TAS and its evolution into the JAST (AfDB 2006). The AfDB document also offers an invaluable commentary charting the way in which the Tanzanian government interacted with the donor community in attempting to apply the principles of the Paris Declaration.

Another AfDB document provides more insights into the process of implementing the JAST (AfDB 2007). A Memorandum of Understanding committing the Tanzanian government and its 'development partners' to the 2006 JAST (and to the principles of the Paris Declaration) was signed by representatives of Tanzania, the African Development Bank, Belgium, Canada, Denmark, the European Commission, Finland, France, Germany, Ireland, Japan, The Netherlands, Norway, Spain, Sweden, Switzerland, the United Kingdom, the United Nations, the United States and the World Bank, providing a diplomatic overlay for the implementation of the JAST and the Paris Declaration (URT 2006b).

The JAST has a monitoring framework that reflects five main objectives:

1. Strengthening national ownership and Government leadership of the development process;
2. Aligning Development Partner support to Government priorities, systems, structures and procedures;
3. Harmonizing Government and Development Partner processes;
4. Managing resources for achieving development results, in particular on Tanzania's National Strategy for Growth and Reduction of Poverty (MKUKUTA/MKUZA); and
5. Strengthening domestic and mutual accountability. (URT 2007a: 5)

These objectives closely reflect the principles of the Paris Declaration, but it is not clear to what extent the monitoring framework has been followed consistently in subsequent reports and evaluation studies.

One of the major Paris Declaration objectives is the achievement of reforms to improve the quality of public finance management (PFM), including tracking expenditure and auditing. The Tanzanian Ministry of Finance sets out a range of detailed targets and achievements from what is referred to as the PFMRP (Public Finance Management Reform Programme) (URT 2009f), the principal aims of which have been to maintain aggregate fiscal discipline and accountability, to allocate resources in accordance with Government priorities, and to ensure efficient delivery of service support. Parts of the PFMRP monitoring were subcontracted to international consultants, and a 2013 report by Oxford Policy Management (OPM) was funded by the Swedish aid agency (OPM 2013). This OPM report specifies shortcomings in the implementation of the PFMRP, but it also reports substantial progress in the achievement of targets. These targets are very relevant to the achievement of improved governance and the control of corruption. There is only very limited discussion of anti-corruption measures (OPM 2013: 24), but, as in other parts of the report, there are indications of positive progress being achieved in both implementation and achievement of targets.

The Tanzanian government's 2009 PFM performance report provides some telling information about the state of the systems in place at that time. The report makes it clear that there were distinct limitations in the quality of accessible information about the government's budget, in the identification of unreported expenditures, and in donor finance by-passing government systems.[14] Reports of financial outcomes were delayed and were not in the required formats. Although this raises concern about the standard of PFM, it is notable that these strictures appear in a document prepared and published by the Ministry of Finance.

A more recent PFM performance report, prepared by the consultancy Analysis for Economic Decisions (ADE) and funded by the EU, discusses achievements and limitations of PFM reform in a similar vein to the 2009 report (URT 2013c):

> This repeat PEFA assessment reveals significant progress in strengthening PFM systems, largely reflecting the impact of the Public Finance Management Reform Programme (PFMRP). Reforms are still on-going, so PFM systems should continue to strengthen. Two major problem areas remain that impact directly on the credibility of the budget. The first major problem area is weaknesses in non-salary internal control systems. ... The second major problem area is the fiscal risk to the budget posed by some public enterprises. (URT 2013c: i)

The overall conclusion of this 2013 report is represented by another quotation:

> Progress has definitely been made in PFM reform over the last few years and is continuing to be made. People may be disappointed that the number of improvements has not been higher in terms of PEFA ratings. However, PFM reform is a long process. (URT 2013c: xvii)

The inadequately reported expenditures mentioned as a problem in the 2009 report comprise 'well over 10 percent of expenditure' in the more recent, and more detailed, 2013 report (URT 2013c: iii), suggesting that a little more information has become available concerning these shortcomings.

---

[14] The remarks in this 2010 Tanzanian government report (URT 2010b), together with those in the 2005 report of the Independent Monitoring Group (URT 2005a), echo suggestions made in a 1998–9 Ugandan review (Tribe & Wanambi 2003). Disquiet is expressed that the Sector Wide approach lends itself to collusive attempts by sector specialists in, or funded by, donor institutions together with colleagues in recipient line ministries to bypass established recipient financial and planning procedures. This can lead to financial systems in Ministries of Finance being starved of financial information about the commitment and use of funds. This type of activity can account for the type of accounting and auditing problems referred to by both the 2005 and the 2010 reports.

Conclusions

Tanzania, Ghana and Uganda have received very significant amounts of ODA in recent years, with Tanzania being the largest 'beneficiary'. The ratio of ODA to GNI has been falling in all three countries, mainly because of the sustained high rates of economic growth that have been experienced. For these countries the high ratio of ODA to government expenditure has been particularly notable, with ODA funding a high proportion of non-recurrent or 'development' expenditure. In the case of Tanzania ODA still accounted for about 70 per cent of government expenditure in 2012, with Budget Support being an important part of this.[15]

There have been notable changes to the 'aid architecture' in the last two decades. One has been the rise of 'umbrella organizations', such as GAVI, the Global Fund and HIROs, which support medical/health programmes with funding from bilateral and multilateral ODA institutions, from major private foundations, traditional and 'new' NGOs, the pharmaceutical industry and from international private commercial bodies. This 'umbrella funding' has contributed funds equivalent to about 5 to 10 per cent of ODA, and is one example of what has been referred to as 'blending', where international funding of development programmes is assembled from a range of ODA institutions as well as the financial sector, with no single institution providing a dominant part of the funding. In this context the role of ODA may be partly of a 'catalytic' nature, with the ODA impact being direct (through ODA funding) and indirect (through a 'leveraging' function associated with the non-ODA funding).

A major question is that of whether ODA has had a positive impact on economic growth. Economists still cannot reach a consensus on this issue, although more recent robust international quantitative studies point towards the conclusion that ODA has a small but significant positive effect. There is still a dearth of detailed country studies that assess the impact of ODA on economic growth in the context of modern growth theory. However, there is some evidence that the role of ODA in sub-Saharan Africa has had a positive impact on growth through its leverage effect on economic reform and on its support of programmes designed to enhance governance and the policy environment. The research question has usually been in the form of 'does ODA have a positive effect on economic growth?' rather than the counterfactual question of 'what would the recipient countries' economic position have been in the absence of ODA?'

---

[15] While aid is important, it needs to be seen in perspective. The 2015 report of the AU/ECA on illicit financial flows estimated that in the last fifty years such flows were roughly equivalent to all of the official development assistance received by Africa over the same period.

Over the last two decades an increasing proportion of ODA has been committed to poverty reduction in a 'direct', rather than an 'indirect', fashion. 'Direct' commitments to poverty reduction are associated with social infrastructure programmes (e.g. health, education, water and sanitation), while 'indirect' commitments are associated with economic infrastructure (e.g. transportation and energy) and production (e.g. agricultural development and credit). 'Indirect' commitments should impact poverty reduction through the connection between economic growth and poverty reduction – with 'income poverty' being targeted in particular. 'Direct' commitments, such as those identified above, are more likely to impact broader definitions of poverty, such as those embodied in multidimensional indices, the HPI and the HDI. In recent years Tanzania has experienced some significant improvements in poverty reduction, although there appeared to be some 'flat-lining' in the early years of this millennium. In the cases of Ghana and Uganda there have been notable reductions in the levels of poverty as measured by the conventional indices. However conclusions relating to Ghana have to be qualified in that overall per capita income is significantly higher than for the other two countries and the household survey data that are used for calculating the relevant indicators are not available for any year later than 2006.

Budget Support (BS) was an increasing feature of ODA commitments, particularly after the international deliberations surrounding the Paris Declaration. Evaluations of ODA, and of BS in particular, have indicated significant success in achieving acceleration of development programmes through BS. The Tanzanian government has a preference for the BS form of ODA, but some donors have been less enthusiastic, particularly in respect of corruption and the paucity of robust financial tracking and accounting. The recent decision of the UK DfID to bring its BS provision to Tanzania to an end, in contradiction to the recommendations of a number of evaluations, may be a sign of impatience with the lack of substantial results from anti-corruption measures and public finance reform. Most evaluation studies have been very conscious of the inevitability of this 'slow speed', which has affected the reform of donor institution practices as much as those of recipient countries such as Tanzania.

This 'slow speed' of reform has also affected the implementation of the principles of the Paris Declaration (PD). The PD heralded significant changes to the relationship between donors and recipients – the 'development partners'. Evaluations tend to suggest that 'alignment' with the principles of the PD has been more difficult to achieve within the donor community than in recipients such as Tanzania, Ghana and Uganda. The high profile of the Tanzania Assistance Strategy (both the TAS and its successor JAST) is notable, as is the ready availability in the public domain of reports by the Tanzanian 'Development Partners Group' and of the Independent Monitoring Group. The literature refers to steady progress in Tanzania in achieving improvements to public finance management and to addressing the corruption issue, and it must be hoped that future responses from the donor community will be supportive of this steady progress.

12

Real Exchange Rate Changes and Export Performance in Tanzania and Ethiopia

David Potts and Kifle Wondemu

The importance of trade as an engine of growth is well established. In the last forty years the rate of growth of world trade has consistently exceeded the rate of growth of world GDP (WDI 2016). Empirical literature has also shown that the growth impact of exports is much stronger when the export basket is diversified (Naudé & Roussow 2008; Mengistu & Yokoyama 2009). This chapter assesses the influence of changes in the real exchange rate[1] (RER) in enhancing the supply and diversification of exports in Ethiopia and Tanzania.

The exchange rate has been a critical issue for the process of structural adjustment in many economies, including Tanzania and Ethiopia. It was the single most important issue in the disagreement between Tanzania and aid donors in the early 1980s.[2] This issue was also addressed in the later liberalization that took place in Ethiopia in the early 1990s. Both countries have experienced significant changes in both the nominal exchange rate (NER) and the RER. In both cases the NER has depreciated steadily over the period covered in this chapter. Both have also experienced rapid growth in GDP and exports. Exports as a percentage of GDP have increased in both countries, both economies have become more open and average tariff rates have been significantly reduced.[3] Overall the process of liberalization has been slower in Ethiopia and the Ethiopian economy remains less open and more protected than that of Tanzania. The proportion of import costs covered by export

---

[1] The real exchange rate (RER) is a measure of the price competitiveness of a country in external trade in relation to a given base year. An appreciation of the RER implies a fall in price competitiveness, while a depreciation of the RER implies greater competitiveness and therefore more incentive to export. Essentially, a depreciation of the RER implies that changes in the NER more than compensate for any difference between the internal rate of inflation of the country concerned and the average rate of inflation of trading partners, thereby ensuring that local production costs increase by less than the price imports and exports.

[2] Chapters 1–3 provide more background of the policy debates of the time.

[3] The simple average tariff rate in Ethiopia declined from 29.4 per cent in 1995 to 18.2 per cent in 2012. In Tanzania it declined from 15.5 per cent in 1993 to 13.0 per cent in 2014 (WDI 2016).

Table 12.1 Exports and Economic Indicators for Ethiopia and Tanzania

Country	Ethiopia		Tanzania	
Period	1990	2015	1990	2015
Annual average growth in real GDP	6.5%		5.2%	
Annual average growth in real exports	9.0%		7.3%	
Exports (% of GDP)	5.5%	9.8%	12.6%	20.8%
Exports (% of imports)	62.9%	35.9%	33.7%	72.3%
Openness (trade as % of GDP)	14.3%	37.2%	50.1%	49.5%
Nominal exchange rate (LCU:$US)	2.07	21.55	195.1	1991.4

Source: Derived from World Development Indicators 2015 and 2016

revenue has declined in Ethiopia, partly owing to a substantial increase of aid inflows, but it has increased in Tanzania (Table 12.1).

In both cases exports have grown faster than GDP, suggesting that it is exports that promote growth rather than the other way round. Trade boosts growth by enlarging market opportunities, permitting specialization according to comparative advantage and facilitating access to new technologies. Although the debate as to the direction of causation between exports and growth is contested, it is clear that exports are critical for growth, particularly for developing countries. However, the impact of exports on growth is influenced not only by export volume, but also by its composition. A horizontally diversified export basket generates faster and more sustainable growth than concentration on one or a few export products (Elbadawi, 1999). Reliance on the export of a limited range of primary commodities may have negative implications for growth if it results in short-run volatility in export revenue owing to commodity price fluctuations (Dawe 1996).

For a number of reasons, a vertically diversified export base may be more desirable for growth. First, exports of manufactured products are likely to grow faster when the global economy is expanding because of the higher income elasticity of demand for these products (Nouira et al. 2010). Second, owing to the higher price elasticity of demand and supply for such products, export earnings are less susceptible to the price variability associated with primary commodities. Third, dynamic productivity gains are higher in manufacturing than for non-manufacturing production. Therefore, on grounds of dynamic efficiency, a conscious effort by governments to alter the incentive structure to promote a shift towards non-traditional exports may be desirable.[4]

[4] See also Chapters 8 and 9 for a discussion of the issues surrounding industrialization in Tanzania.

Empirical studies have reported a significant relationship between export diversification and exchange rate changes (Nouira et al. 2010). Exchange rate adjustment can compensate to some extent for the financial loss imposed on exporters by duties on traded inputs. Balassa (1982, 1990) has argued that devaluation of the domestic currency is equivalent to a parallel imposition of import tariffs and export subsidies at equal rates. A move to freer trade and devaluation can be seen as replacing existing protective measures with a uniform rate of tariff and subsidy that will maintain the balance of trade unchanged. However, such a policy stance is based on the assumption that there are no other major market imperfections or, if there are, all sectors are equally affected.

Domestic institutional weaknesses and market imperfections in the goods and factor markets tend to inflate the costs of tradable sectors more than the non-tradable sectors because a higher proportion of the costs of the tradable sectors are influenced by government policies on indirect taxes and formal sector wage rates. Under such a situation, Rodrik (1986, 2008) has argued that deliberate undervaluation of the real exchange rate could be justified as a 'second-best' solution to partially alleviate the implied bias against the tradable sector. Such a policy measure neutralizes the incentive bias and shifts the internal terms of trade in favour of the tradable sector, thereby promoting structural change, enhancing exports and improving economic growth (Sachs & Warner 1995; Freund & Pierola 2008; Rodrik 2009). The Chinese growth experience can be cited as a case of rapid growth and structural change induced in part by an undervalued exchange rate (Rodrik 2009: 5).

Failure to make such adjustments undermines the profitability of export industries. This was a particularly serious issue in the 1980s when a number of countries, including Tanzania and Ethiopia, were reluctant to devalue their currencies sufficiently to compensate exporters for rising local costs owing to internal inflation. Initially, in response to external pressure, both Ethiopia and Tanzania devalued their currencies substantially in 1986 and 1992 respectively. These measures and subsequent further exchange rate changes, brought about through the economic reforms associated with structural adjustment, were expected to address the issue of real exchange rate overvaluation. However, the extent to which these measures were successful in improving export performance is open to question.

This chapter seeks to analyze the effectiveness of the trade and exchange rate policy measures implemented by Tanzania and Ethiopia in terms of offsetting the domestic incentive bias and improving the external competitiveness of the export sector. For our purpose, the RER is used as a proxy measure for the economy's external competitiveness, (Edwards 1989). First, we will assess the effectiveness of various internal and external macroeconomic developments in inducing changes in the RER over the reform periods. Next, we investigate the extent to which the *actual* RER diverged from a notional equilibrium level, and the extent to which the level and degree of misalignment in the RER have influenced the supply of traditional exports and the degree of horizontal and vertical export diversification.

Conceptual Framework

Traditional comparative advantage trade models attribute differences in resource endowment and technology as the key factors that determine the comparative advantage or trade pattern of a country. These models assume perfectly competitive markets and usually fail to take account of the role of trade and exchange rate policy in redefining comparative advantage and reshaping the trading pattern of a country. In fact, they predict that *any* policy induced trade pattern is sub-optimal. However, since many of the perfectly competitive assumptions that such models assume are not actually met, the policy conclusions drawn from these models are not necessarily the best for a country, particularly in the long run. Therefore, in situations where there are market failures, government policy interventions can be justified on efficiency grounds to achieve a more socially efficient production and trade pattern.

Among the macroeconomic policy instruments governments can use to influence the specialization pattern of a country, a proactive RER policy can be important. By manipulating the RER, the government is able to alter the overall incentive structure of the economy and subsequently the trajectory of the country's production or specialization pattern. Such a policy can be implemented both to increase the supply of traditional exports as well as to diversify production and exports into new areas.

In order to explore the link between the exchange rate and export supply and diversification, we used a modified Ricardian trade model with a continuum of goods as our theoretical framework (Blecker & Razmi 2010). In the traditional Ricardian trade model the technology of each country is described by the units of labour required to produce a given good. Goods may also differ in terms of their technological intensity. It is also clear that, although technology is important, for labour-intensive goods in particular, the wage rate prevailing in a country is a key variable that influences the goods that a country will export or import. Thus, in addition to the labour productivity and technological intensity of the good, the wage rate prevailing in a given country will influence the products each country will produce.

For any given wage rate, an improvement in technology at home will shift the cut-off point for the range of goods a country can produce and export competitively. A change in the wage ratio between two countries will have a similar impact on the specialization pattern. If we assume that goods and labour markets are competitive, one policy instrument that the government could use to alter wage ratios between the two countries is the RER.

Devaluation of the RER not only increases the profitability of the production of goods for which the country has a traditional comparative advantage, it can also shift the cut-off point for the range of goods that can be produced profitably in the home economy. This implies that, even in situations where opportunities for significant technological advances are limited, the RER could be manipulated to reshape the trajectory of the country's comparative advantage (Elbadawi & Helleiner 2008).

No clear consensus has yet emerged regarding the effectiveness of manipulating the RER in reshaping the comparative advantage of a country. Although there is agreement that avoiding RER overvaluation is necessary to maintain external competitiveness, there is no consensus on whether or not maintaining an undervalued currency is beneficial. Although the empirical evidence that misalignment owing to overvaluation has a negative effect on growth and exports is strong, evidence regarding the effect of undervaluation of the exchange rate on economic growth is mixed (Magud & Sosa 2010).

According to the Washington Consensus view, any real exchange rate misalignment implies a form of disequilibrium that could hamper growth (Haddad & Pancaro 2010). Overvaluation may be harmful to growth but undervaluation would produce unnecessary inflationary pressures and limit the resources available for domestic investment, hence curbing the growth of supply-side potential (ibid).

However, Rodrik (2009) has advanced a very different argument both about the reason why exchange rate misalignment matters for growth and also about the mechanisms by which this relationship works. He argued that, while overvaluation has a negative impact on growth, real undervaluation expands exports and can enhance growth by reducing the foreign currency value of the additional transactions costs that the tradable sectors incur disproportionately owing to domestic institutional weaknesses and market failures. He claimed that a proactive strategy that deliberately maintains an undervalued RER could provide a second-best policy instrument to compensate for the adverse effect of internal market failures on the tradable sector. Korinek and Servén (2010) have also claimed that undervaluation raises growth by generating additional learning-by-doing externalities in the tradable sector, effects that would not be obtained in the absence of such policy intervention. Levy-Yeyati and Sturzenegger (2007) have also argued that undervaluation is desirable for growth, claiming that it increases savings and capital accumulation.

This chapter investigates the extent to which Tanzania and Ethiopia maintained a competitive real exchange rate and whether periods of RER undervaluation in these countries were associated with increased export supply and diversification. We measure overvaluation and undervaluation of the real exchange rate by the degree of deviation between the observed RER and the estimated equilibrium RER (ERER). The ERER is the variable that we estimate. It represents the real exchange rate level that, for given sustainable values of relevant variables such as taxes, international prices and technology, result in simultaneous attainment of internal and external equilibrium.[5] The misalignment is an overvaluation if the observed RER is above the ERER and an under-valuation if the observed RER is below the ERER. The discussions in this chapter are mainly based on the findings of Wondemu and Potts (2016), and details of the theoretical and empirical models used for the estimation can be found in this source.[6]

The RER in Tanzania and Ethiopia

Estimates of the RER were derived for the period 1965 to 2014 and are shown in Figure 12.1. They show clearly the rapid real appreciation of the Tanzanian shilling in the crisis period of 1979–85. A similar but less dramatic appreciation occurred in Ethiopia from 1975 to 1985. Subse-quent dramatic real devaluation in Tanzania and less dramatic deval-uation in Ethiopia can also be seen, followed by a period of relative stability since the early 1990s.

The real exchange rate is a relative measure and the extent to which a currency is overvalued or undervalued can only be determined in rela-tion to a particular reference point, in this case the start year for the series (1965). According to Edwards (1989: 5), the equilibrium RER is considered to be the

> relative price of tradables to nontradables that, for given (equilib-rium or sustainable) values of other relevant variables such as trade taxes, international prices, capital and aid flows, and technology, results in the simultaneous attainment of internal and external equilibrium. Internal equilibrium means that the nontradable goods market clears in the current period and is expected to be in equilib-rium in the future.

Important factors determining this notional equilibrium are the terms of trade of the country, government expenditure, trade restrictions, the level of capital flows and technological progress (Chowdhury 2004).

---

[5] Internal equilibrium means that the non-tradable goods market clears in the current period and is expected to be in equilibrium in future periods (Edwards 1991). External equilibrium means that the current account balances (current and future) are compatible with long-run sustainable capital flows (Ibid.).
[6] There are slight differences in some figures owing to updating to include an additional year.

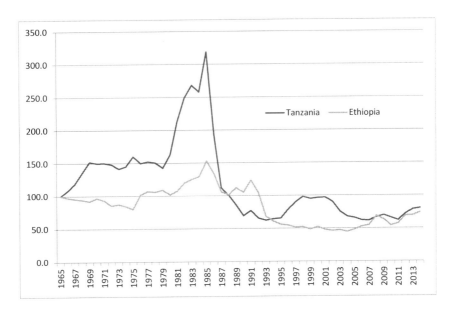

Source: Derived from http://bruegel.org/publications/datasets/real-effective-exchange-rates-for-178-countries-a-new-database/

Figure 12.1 Real Exchange Rate (RER) for Tanzania and Ethiopia (1965–2014, 1965 = 100)

Estimation of the Misalignment of the RER

In order to determine whether the actual RER is in line with its under-lying equilibrium level, it is necessary to estimate an equation for the equilibrium RER (ERER) to compare with the actual RER. The process of determining this equation and the definition of the variables used is described in Wondemu and Potts (2016: 11–13). The variables used in the equation included the ERER for the previous year, the level of open-ness of the economy, the terms of trade, total factor productivity and the ratios of government consumption expenditure to GDP and foreign exchange reserves to GDP.

In line with prior expectations, increases in the level of factor productivity had a significant impact on the evolution of the ERER. By increasing competitiveness and increasing the overall supply of goods and services, higher productivity saves or generates additional foreign exchange and tends to lead to appreciation of the RER. The terms of trade, the level of openness, the level of government consumption and reserve level were also significant explanatory variables. The results suggest that 1 per cent improvement in the terms of trade appreciates the ERER by 0.13 per cent.

The coefficient for the degree of openness was negative and significant. It suggests that, when the economy becomes more open, it requires a more depreciated equilibrium RER in order to maintain long-term competitiveness. It could also reflect the counteracting effects of increased export earnings, which lead to a fall in the real exchange rate and an import expansion, which normally leads to a rise in the real exchange rate.

The share of government consumption to GDP was also significant and had a negative sign. The result suggests that, for the trade balance to be sustainable, an increase in government consumption will either lead to or will require a real currency depreciation. It may also imply that government consumption is dominated by expenditure on tradable goods and services.

The coefficient for the ratio of reserves to GNP variable was significant and had a negative sign, suggesting that factors that increase the level of reserves, such as an increase in net capital and aid inflows, would require the economy to undergo a real currency depreciation. Since the terms of trade are included in the model, its coefficient should capture the impact of net capital inflows on the real exchange rate (RER) (Chudik & Mongardini 2007).

A growing body of empirical research reports an inverse link between aid flows and the RER, such that the RER depreciates following an increase in aid inflows. A number of explanations have been provided for this finding (Li & Rowe 2007). Most of them relate to the supply-side impacts of aid inflows. They suggest that aid inflows can induce a rapid supply-side response by more than the level necessary to offset the demand responses. Others argue that aid may be targeted at easing supply bottlenecks that could potentially offset the price increase of non-tradables owing to aid inflows (Hjertholm, Laursen & White 2000). However, Adam and Bevan (2003) argued that, if aid-financed public infrastructure investment spending induces a productivity gain in the non-tradable sectors, aid will depreciate the RER. It can also be argued that, if donors provide aid that allows the recipient to import donor country goods, and the value of these imports is greater than the original aid inflow, the real exchange rate could depreciate. Donors may also provide aid to support a change in an exchange rate regime, which could imply a strong devaluation of the nominal exchange rate. In general, it is likely that a number of these factors work together to produce the observed inverse relationship.

The coefficient of the lagged RER was positive and significant, signalling the importance of inertia in the evolution of the RER over time. Almost 50 per cent of the present movement of the RER is influenced by its past level. The ERER and its degree of misalignment were estimated on the basis of the so-called 'Fundamental Equilibrium Exchange Rate (FRER)' concept. A three-year moving average of the fundamental variables was used in the model. Each coefficient was deflated by assuming that, in steady state equilibrium, the level of the lagged RER is equal to the current RER. In addition, the constant term of the model was adjusted for each country by taking into account the country fixed effect.

From the predicted value of the model, which reflects the ERER, it appears that, although the observed RER showed some fluctuation over the periods covered, both countries were able to maintain a RER that was close to its equilibrium level (ERER). They seemed to be successful in managing the adverse impact of capital flows and terms of trade movements on the long-term competitiveness of their economies. If the RER policy is also supported by other effective export-promoting policies, an RER level that is close to the equilibrium level would be expected to be a key factor for the observed remarkable export growth. The magnitude of misalignment was also estimated as the difference between the observed RER and the ERER. Since the RER is measured in terms of the amount of foreign currency per unit of domestic currency, the misalignment is an overvaluation if the observed RER is above the ERER and an undervaluation if the observed RER is below the ERER.

Over the period 1980–2012, the RER in both countries exhibited both overvaluation and undervaluation, with the RER of Tanzania undervalued on average by 2.6 per cent, and the RER of Ethiopia on average 15 per cent overvalued. However, the level of overvaluation in Ethiopia during the post-reform period (post-1992) was lower (7 per cent). Similarly, when only the post-reform period is considered (post-1986), the RER in Tanzania was undervalued by an average of 4.3 per cent.

Our findings are consistent with previous empirical studies. For instance, Hobdari (2008) reported that in most recent years the REER of Tanzania has been undervalued by a significant margin, which reached as high as about 30 per cent. Tanzania, however, was able to maintain an undervalued currency for a long time by building up the reserve level. The reserve level showed a continuous increase throughout the reform period, and reached as high as 18 per cent of GDP. Although an undervalued currency is expected to expand the tradable sector, it comes at the price of a higher level of inflation owing to the impact of devaluation on the price of tradable goods. In contrast, Ethiopia seems to have contained inflation (pre-2008) by maintaining real overvaluation and accumulating large current account deficits.

The model was estimated for each country separately and by pooling the data. Among the variables, only relative total factor productivity, openness and reserves to GDP ratio are significant in explaining misalignment in Ethiopia. In Ethiopia, 77 per cent of the change in the level of misalignment can be attributed to factors that affect import demand and export supply, close to 13 per cent to movement in the terms of trade and 10 per cent to other factors. In the Tanzanian case, 69 per cent of the change in the level of misalignment is associated with movement in the terms of trade and 25 per cent with openness, with the balance explained by the remaining variables. The variables included in the model only account for 36 per cent of the movement in the ERER in the Ethiopian case but they account for 67 per cent of the movement in the case of Tanzania. This suggests that, in the case of Ethiopia, domestic supply and demand-related factors are important determinants of the ERER and its level of misalignment. For Tanzania, although domestic supply and demand factors are important, a substantial share of the movement in RER and its degree of misalignment is accounted for by changes in world market conditions. When pooled data are used to estimate the same model, the terms of trade and relative factor productivity reduce misalignment, but reserves increase it.

World Bank- and IMF-supported adjustment programmes put heavy emphasis on real exchange rate depreciation as a way to restore external balance and elicit a significant supply response. In both countries, the RER depreciated significantly after the reform programme, although in some years the trend was reversed. The results of the study suggest that Tanzania maintained an undervalued currency for most of the post-reform period while Ethiopia reduced the extent of currency over-valuation but still maintained a slightly overvalued currency. This chapter therefore considers the extent to which export supply is sensitive to movements in the RER and whether the apparent policy of deliberate undervaluation followed by Tanzania has been more effective in promoting vertical and horizontal export diversification than the Ethiopian policy.

Real Exchange Rate Misalignment and Export Diversification

One mechanism by which real exchange rate manipulation influences economic growth and structural transformation is through the effect of such policy measures on the relative prices of tradable and non-tradable goods. Since the prices of tradable goods are generally determined more competitively when compared to the prices of non-tradable goods, any domestic market or government failure would inflate the cost of production and disproportionately adversely affect the tradable sector. The tradable sector fully absorbs the cost increase but the non-tradable sector would pass it on to domestic consumers. As a result, domestic market failures not only undermine the competitiveness of the existing tradable production, but also stifle the emergence of potentially profitable tradable activities. Complete market liberalization or a significant reduction in tariff or protection will not fully nullify such bias unless such measures also completely eliminate all domestic market failures, which is unlikely to be the case. Therefore, deliberate undervaluation, which increases the relative prices of tradable goods, can be a second-best mechanism to partly alleviate the incentive bias imposed by domestic market failures. This increases the competitiveness of the existing tradable activities and encourages the emergence of other tradable activities and therefore export diversification of the country.

To examine the link between the RER and export diversification, we consider both vertical and horizontal diversification. Vertical diversification was measured in terms of the ratio of manufactured exports to total exports while the Hirschman diversification index was used to measure horizontal diversification (Elbadawi 1999; Munemo et al. 2007; Mengistu & Yokoyama 2009). To check the sensitivity of the result to measurement bias, the number of products exported was also used as an alternative measure of horizontal diversification (Herzer &d Nowak-Lehmann 2006). The information for the number of products exported by each country was drawn from the UNCTAD database.

The coefficient of the lagged diversification variable was positive and significant. The result shows that export diversification responds both to the level and the direction of the misalignment of the RER. The negative coefficient of the log RER variable implies that an appreciation of the RER tends to concentrate exports on a few products. The dummy for undervaluation, which was one if the observed RER was below its equilibrium or 0 otherwise, was positive and significant. This suggests that, while overvaluation undermines export diversification, undervaluation promotes it. This finding is consistent with previous studies (Elbadawi 1999; Rodrik 2008).

The variable representing the skill base (ratio of students enrolled in tertiary education) was positive and highly significant. It suggests that diversification is strongly associated with the level of human capital stock and corroborates the claim that improving human capital narrows down the productivity gap and promotes diversification (Cimoli et al. 2011). However, the ratio of factor productivity, serving as a proxy for technological capabilities, carried the expected sign but was not significant. The coefficient of lagged investment was not significant and also did not carry the expected sign. Although the constant term was not significant, the country-specific factor generated from the fixed effect model for Tanzania was positive while it was negative for Ethiopia. This suggests that there are relatively more favourable conditions for diversified exports in Tanzania than in Ethiopia. Moreover, there has been a significant horizontal export diversification towards other products and more sectors.

The result of the diversification model was estimated using the log number of goods exported. The model used per capita income as an additional explanatory variable. The result confirmed that the level and undervaluation of the real exchange rate significantly affects the number of export items the country export. The number of items each country exports was also significantly and positively associated with the average per capita income of the country.

The results suggest that the real exchange rate is a key policy variable that significantly influences the pace of horizontal diversification of the economy. While the currency should not be overvalued, real currency undervaluation can enhance horizontal export diversification. RER policy-induced horizontal diversification is likely to boost growth by generating significant knowledge spillover and a multiplier impact on the economy, even if most of the items are raw and semi-processed natural resource-based goods. Diversification into a completely new export sector generates positive externalities for the economy owing to contacts established with foreign firms and exposure to international competition (Herzer & Nowak-Lehmann 2006).

The result of the model for vertical diversification, which was measured in terms of the ratio of manufactured exports to total exports, shows that supply factors, as well as the level of incentive, are significant determinants of manufactured exports. As expected, elimination of currency overvaluation significantly increases the share of manufactured goods exports by making domestic sales less attractive. The undervaluation dummy is also significant and carries the expected sign. Although one cannot tell conclusively from the result whether depreciation of the RER promotes the production of manufactured goods, it confirms that, while overvaluation of the RER is harmful to industrial exports, undervaluation increases the share of manufactured exports. This observation is substantiated by comparison of the export structures of the two countries. In the period 1995–9, 89.8 per cent of Ethiopia's exports by value were agricultural products. By the period 2010–14 this proportion had declined slightly to 87.2 per cent. In the same period the contribution of agriculture to Tanzania's exports fell from 82.7 per cent to 47.6 per cent. There was virtually no change in the proportion of Ethiopian exports contributed by manufacturing (8.6 per cent to 8.7 per cent), while in Tanzania manufacturing exports increased from 15.6 per cent to 26.4 per cent of total exports (Potts 2017).

Although results show clearly that maintaining a RER that is close to its equilibrium as well as an undervalued currency will increase the share of manufacturing production exported, the overall impact of an undervalued RER on manufacturing sector production may be ambiguous. This is because the manufacturing sector imports a larger share of its inputs, in which case undervaluation will increase costs and thus reduce the competitiveness of domestic production unless it is accompanied by other offsetting measures. Although most manufactured export products in the two countries are resource based with low technological content, RER-induced diversification of manufactured exports is likely to generate strong spillover effects on the economy.

Real Exchange Rate and Export Supply

The results of the study suggest that real currency devaluation significantly increases exports. A deliberate policy of maintaining an undervalued real exchange rate boosts export supply. In addition to the level of incentives, the results showed that supply-side factors, represented by relative factor productivity and the lagged ratio of investment to GDP, were significant determinants of the supply of exports.

In particular, the volume of exports seems to be highly responsive to changes in factor productivity. Government expenditure policy is also significant, with the level of government consumption having a significant adverse effect on exports.

Similar conclusions also emerge when export supply is measured in terms of the share of exports to GDP. Appreciation of the RER reduces the share of exports to GDP, but undervaluation of the currency increases its share. The variables that capture supply-side factors as well as the macro policy environment were also significant and have the same sign. When considering the volume of exports of manufactured goods, supply-side and profitability factors still matter. The RER was significant at the conventional level and carried the expected sign. To isolate which factors are more important for the observed performance, the model was estimated in the first difference form for each country separately. In Ethiopia, an increase in export share was associated significantly with improved supply capability, undervaluation and depreciation of the RER. However, in Tanzania, real exchange rate depreciation was the most significant factor for strong export performance.

Product-level export supply models were also estimated to see if the results were sensitive to the level of aggregation. Coffee is a major export item for both countries, so a coffee supply model was estimated by pooling the data of the two countries. Tanzania has a more diversified export base than Ethiopia, so another export supply model was also estimated based only on Tanzanian data including cotton lint, raw tobacco, tea and cashewnut exports. The results suggested that a substantial share of export supply is determined by factors that affect the level of production. Again, in all product cases, an appreciation in the RER has a significant adverse impact on export supply. Appreciation of the RER had a stronger adverse impact on cashewnuts and unprocessed tobacco exports than on cotton. The ratio of exports to production for the three crops was also investigated in relation to the RER and undervaluation. The real exchange rate coefficient was significant for raw tobacco and cashewnuts, but not for cotton.

For coffee export supply, appreciation of the real exchange rate significantly reduces export volume.[7] However, although the undervaluation dummy had the expected sign, it was not significant. The estimated elasticity of supply with respect to the exchange rate was consistent with the findings of previous empirical studies. Balassa (1990), for instance, reported the elasticity of export supply to the real exchange

---

[7] A relevant factor in relation to coffee could be the proximity of other coffee-exporting countries and the possible option for coffee producers to sell their produce across the border. Lofchie (2014: 167) quotes Mshomba on the smuggling of arabica coffee from Kilimanjaro region into Kenya in the period 1977–86. More recently there have been reports of smuggling of robusta coffee from Kagera region into Uganda.

rate to be in the range 0.78 to 1.01. This result refutes the notion that changes in the real exchange rate would have less effect on the exports of perennial crops.

To identify in which of the two countries the adverse effect of RER appreciation is stronger, the model was re-estimated including an additional variable interacting the RER and a country dummy. The interaction term was significant, and suggests that appreciation of the RER had a more adverse impact on Ethiopia than on Tanzania. Compared to the other products, the elasticity of coffee export to production (0.51) is significantly less than 1 and the 95 per cent confidence interval of the estimates falls in the range of 0.23 to 0.78. This is consistent with the fact that a significant share of Ethiopian production of coffee is consumed domestically. The share of export to production in Tanzania is higher and also showed consistency over the years. Relatively low domestic consumption coupled with an undervalued real exchange rate seems to have been a key factor for Tanzania to maintain its export share. Real exchange rate undervaluation seems to have played a role at least in counteracting the substitution effect of food price increase on the production and export of export products. However, the stagnation of coffee production in Tanzania may suggest that the country has lost its comparative advantage in coffee. This conclusion is consistent with the evidence reported in Chapter 4 in relation to coffee production in the Kilimanjaro region.

The study also regressed the log volume indices of manufactured goods export on the real exchange rate, human capital base and relative factor productivity, share of investment and government consumption to GDP. The results indicated that incentives matter and appreciation of the RER discourages manufactured exports, but real undervaluation makes export sales more attractive. Based on the estimated country-specific effect, Tanzania has more favourable conditions for manufactured exports than Ethiopia. Relatively significant undervaluation could be one factor. This finding is consistent with some of the observations made above and in Chapter 9 in relation to the potential for export of manufactured goods in Tanzania.

When the undervaluation dummy was interacted with the country dummy and included as an additional variable in the model, the interaction term was highly significant. It implies that, *ceteris paribus*, real undervaluation of the currency in Ethiopia could have a significant impact on increasing manufactured exports. The significance of the interaction dummy may also suggest that there are relatively severe institutional weaknesses and market failures in Ethiopia. Controlling for incentives and supply, country-specific factors explain 20 per cent more manufactured exports from Tanzania than from Ethiopia.

The variable that represents the share of government consumption in GDP was also significant, and suggests that high government consumption/expansionary macro policies have an adverse impact on the volume of manufactured goods export. This may work through inflating the price of non-tradable goods or by increasing the cost to exporters, particularly if such consumption is financed by distortionary domestic taxes. However, spending on investment that expands productive capacity is a significant positive determinant of manufactured goods export. This suggests that more effective expenditure on productive public infrastructure such as roads, energy and water supply would have significant beneficial implications for the capacity to export manufactures. This conclusion is also in line with the findings in Chapters 8 and 9.

Conclusion

This chapter has assessed the influence of reform measures on the external competitiveness and export performance of Tanzania and Ethiopia. The analysis shows that, following economic reforms, both countries have attempted to maintain a real exchange rate that is fairly close to its equilibrium level.

From the empirical results it appears that exports in both countries are highly responsive to changes in the real exchange rate. Appreciation or overvaluation of the exchange rate has a negative effect on export performance. Maintaining a RER that is close to its equilibrium is necessary, but maintaining an undervalued currency can improve export performance. A major contributing factor to differences in export performance between the two countries is the difference in real exchange rate policy. Tanzania has maintained an undervalued real exchange rate for a long time, and this has increased the volume of exports.

A high rate of growth in exports is associated with periods of undervalued currency. Although this result is in contrast to the Washington Consensus view, which argues that any real exchange rate misalignment (either above or below its long-run value) is undesirable, it corroborates recent views that claim that undervaluation can be a desirable policy and serves as a second-best policy to nullify the additional transaction costs tradable sectors disproportionally suffer owing to institutional weaknesses and market imperfections. The result confirms that a deliberate policy of maintaining an undervalued real exchange rate is justifiable even on dynamic efficiency grounds since market imperfections, which tend to be more costly for the tradable than the non-tradable sector, are pervasive in developing countries. Under such situations, maintaining an equilibrium real exchange rate may not be sufficient to nullify the additional costs facing the tradable sector.

The export expansion achieved through undervaluation, however, is not costless for Tanzania. Tanzania managed to maintain an undervalued real exchange rate through accumulation of reserves and a relatively high rate of inflation. The rate of inflation was significantly higher for a long time in Tanzania than in Ethiopia, except in recent years. The net welfare effects of maintaining an undervalued real exchange rate through reserve accumulation therefore depend on the balance between the welfare losses that arise owing to higher inflation and lower tradable absorption (because undervaluation removes tradable goods from the economy) and the dynamic gains from higher growth that are derived from the positive externalities generated by expansion of the tradable sector.

Moreover, although undervaluation may serve as a second-best instrument to internalize the positive externalities the tradable sector generates, the materialization of such effects will depend on the responsiveness of private investment to the improved incentive structure, the capital-intensity of the tradable sector as well as on the willingness of consumers to substitute consumption inter-temporally. Similarly, if the import intensity of the tradable sector is very high, an undervalued real exchange rate could undermine growth by inflating the cost of imported inputs and reducing the profitability of production. A reduction in domestic saving and investment due to undervaluation-induced inflation could be the other channel by which undervaluation might undermine growth. Therefore, assessing the net welfare effect of RER undervaluation focusing particularly on its distributional impact could be a very fruitful area of research.

As the results suggest, macroeconomic stability also matters for exports. Excessive government expenditure in areas that do not contribute to the expansion of physical and social infrastructure has an adverse impact on exports. Identifying the channels by which such adverse effects are actually felt, such as whether it is through distortionary taxation or through its impact on the prices of non-tradables or a combination of both, could provide important policy inputs. The competitiveness of the domestic market structure as well as the supply and quality of infrastructural facilities and skill base of the economy are also important constraints that must be addressed to achieve a shift in export diversification.

13

Economic Leakage as a Constraint on Tourism's Effective Contribution to Local Economic Development in Tanzania

Faustin Kamuzora and Julia Jeyacheya

Introduction

The structure of the Tanzanian economy has changed significantly since independence, and particularly after economic liberalization in the 1980s and further reforms in the mid-1990s. The gradual move towards a free market economy was transformative for the tourism industry, which showed rapid growth year on year from 1995 onwards. International tourist arrivals in 1995 stood at 295,312, with a sharp increase to 627,325 by 1999. Following a period of decline, arrivals returned to a steady growth of about 10 per cent from 2006, with 644,124 arrivals rising to 1,140,156 in 2014 (Table 13.1. See below, p. 261). Contributions from tourism to employment, GDP and foreign exchange earnings have increased in a similar way over this period. In 2013 the total contributions of tourism to employment, GDP and foreign exchange earnings were 11 per cent, 13 per cent and 18 per cent respectively (WTTC 2015). By 2025, the country aims to attract 8 million international tourists and has recently been awarded a US$100 million loan from the World Bank group to implement a series of projects in four key natural resource areas (Tanzania Investment Centre 2017). Despite these impressive tourism facts and projected figures, the effective contribution of tourism to local socio-economic development can be questioned, as evidence suggests that there is unequal distribution of wealth derived from tourism and precarious employment opportunities (Kinyondo & Pelizzo 2015).

   This chapter begins with an overview of Tanzania's tourism industry from the latter years of the colonial period to the present day. Subsequently, socio-economic trends relating to tourism development in Tanzania since economic liberalization are discussed, followed by a review of the literature on economic leakage and its impact on Tanzania's economy. The chapter goes on to present best practice case studies where the contribution and distribution of tourism benefits are equitable, before ending with some policy-relevant implications.

A Brief History of Tourism Development in Tanzania

Tanzania, like much of East and Southern Africa, was a 'hunters' play-ground' in the late 1800s and early 1900s for the colonial rulers, and indeed the export of ivory and animal skins was a particularly lucrative business. Big game hunting was also an elite sport and attracted high-profile hunters, such as Frederick Selous, Winston Churchill and Theodore Roosevelt, whose motivation to hunt was for prestige and status or for 'scientific and educational purposes', rather than financial gain (MacKenzie 1997). The cumulative effect of this most exploitative commercial activity was a steep decline in the wildlife population, and particularly ivory-laden mega-fauna such as rhino and elephant, which resulted in a raft of shooting restrictions, beginning in 1891. Five successive regulations restricting hunting were implemented in 1889, 1900, 1903, 1905 and 1908 until, in 1911, a culmination of regulations finally resulted in implementation of the Hunting Act of 1911 (Baldus 2001). The Act placed species of wildlife and birdlife under different protective status and controlled licence numbers and fees; but animals deemed 'harmful' (predators, in other words) such as 'lions, leopards, wild dogs or crocodiles could be hunted freely and even for a reward' (ibid.: 3). Furthermore, it categorized the hunters according to their residential status and origin. With large tracts of land under conservation and legislation protecting some species only, hunting continued as a commercial activity and for conservation purposes (through culling, for example).

The conservation effort continued after independence in response to a 1960 United Nations (UN) Visiting Mission that had recommended the development and maintenance of extensive game reserves and national parks. This was noted in a speech, commonly known as the Arusha Manifesto, made in September 1961, when President Nyerere recognized the importance of the country's natural resources and the need for conservation by declaring that:

> The survival of our wildlife is a matter of grave concern to all of us in Africa. These wild creatures amid the wild places they inhabit are not only important as a resource of wonder and inspiration, but are an integral part of our natural resources and our future livelihood and well-being. In accepting the trusteeship of our wildlife we solemnly declare that we will do everything in our power to make sure that our children's grand-children will be able to enjoy this rich and precious inheritance. The conservation of wildlife and wild places calls for specialist knowledge, trained manpower, and money, and we look to other nations to co-operate with us in this important task; the success or failure of which not only affects the continent of Africa but the rest of the world as well. (Goldstein 2005: 481–515)

Interestingly, the same UN mission also recommended further development of tourist facilities so as to develop the industry into a major foreign exchange earner for the future. Unlike conservation, this

presented a dilemma for the socialist government and especially President Nyerere, who seemingly struggled with the concept of tourism,
deeming it a 'necessary evil' where 'tourists must be isolated from
the population' (Bryden 1973: 2). A similar view was taken by other
socialist nations, such as Cuba at the time, to 'protect' citizens from
this capitalist enterprise and community (the tourist) (Mazzei 2012).[1]

Some three decades later, in the 1990s, Tanzania was struggling to
meet the needs of the poorest and the rural populations as traditional
economic activities such as, for many, agriculture, failed to deliver
beyond subsistence level. Consequently, the potential of the tourism
industry to alleviate poverty through jobs and business creation
became a serious policy mandate. It was clear from historic data representing international visitor arrivals (see Table 13.1), that there was a
growing demand and that this brought much-needed foreign exchange
and investment. Accordingly, in 2002, President Mkapa called for 'a
heightened onslaught on poverty, using the weapon of tourism' (Nelson
2012: 360). In the same year, he delivered a keynote address at a Tourism
Investment Forum (Arusha) during which he recognized the impact of
foreign investment on local economies and urged for 'ways to invest in
ventures that will also fairly increase the share of tourism value-added
to Tanzania' (Mkapa 2002: 8). These 'ways to invest' are discussed later
in the chapter when economic leakage in tourism is reviewed.

Before moving on to the next section, it is important to mention
Zanzibar: a semi-autonomous state since 1964, it lies off the east
coast of Tanzania Mainland. Before tourism, Zanzibar was the world's
leading producer of cloves. Although this status was lost in the 1970s,
clove production and export is still significant to the island's economy
and, according to Sharpley and Ussi (2014: 91), 48.9 per cent of annual
exported goods can be attributed to this spice. Zanzibar's tourism
economy is younger than mainland Tanzania's, and was established in
the 1980s following an IMF structural adjustment programme and the
implementation of the Economic Recovery Programme (1987). A call
for foreign investment in tourist infrastructure (predominantly hotels)
followed, and this was answered by Italian investors already operating
in neighbouring Kenya. The total number of tourist arrivals recorded
in 1985 was 19,368. Within ten years, the figure reached 56,415 (1995),
and it continued to rise significantly throughout the 2000s, reaching
132,836 visitors in 2010 (Sharpley & Ussi 2014: 91).

The economic value of this export industry to Zanzibar in 2010 was

---

[1] This type of 'enclave' tourism product effectively stifles opportunities for
local communities to leverage tourism as an effective microeconomic development tool, as ownership, land rights and power (typically in the hands
of a few) prevent much reaching the targeted beneficiaries of tourism and
poverty-reduction policy.

Table 13.1 The Volume and Value of International Visitors to Tanzania, 1995–2014

Year	Number of Visitor Arrivals	Tourist Receipts (US$ million)
1995	295,312	259.44
1996	326,188	322.37
1997	359,096	392.39
1998	482,331	570.00
1999	627,325	733.28
2000	501,669	739.06
2001	525,000	725.00
2002	575,000	730.00
2003	576,000	731.00
2004	582,807	746.02
2005	612,754	823.05
2006	644,124	950.00
2007	719,031	1198.76
2008	770,376	1288.70
2009	714,367	1159.82
2010	782,699	1254.50
2011	867,994	1353.29
2012	1,077,058	1712.75
2013	1,095,884	1860.00
2014	1,140,156	2010.00

Source: Ministry of Natural Resources and Tourism, Tourism Division

enormous, contributing 80 per cent to total export earnings[2] and 25 per cent to GDP (from tourist expenditure) (ibid.: 90). The majority of this derives from the 3S of tourism (sun, sea and sand) or beach tourism, which is a popular 'add-on' at the end of a holiday itinerary that may include climbing Kilimanjaro and/or taking a safari in mainland Tanzania. Zanzibar's tourist offer is inextricably linked to that offered on mainland Tanzania as it provides a 'tropical island' destination for R&R (rest and relaxation) following a more strenuous holiday experience. However, despite the importance of tourism for the Zanzibar economy, the marine ecosystem is becoming seriously degraded and this threatens the sustainability of the industry (Lange & Jiddawi 2009: 521–3).

To conclude this section, it is clear that Tanzania's tourism industry today has become a pillar of the economy and an important, policy-led

[2] Note that Sharpley and Ussi's estimate of 48.9 per cent for cloves related to export *goods* whereas the figure of 80 per cent relates to total export earnings including services (i.e. tourism).

'weapon against poverty'. This is perhaps most clear in the renewed drive by the government to diversify the tourism product and expand the geographic range of the industry. Yet evidence suggests that local economic development is not raising communities sufficiently out of poverty, in spite of the impressive contributions made to the national GDP, exports and employment. This elicits many questions of tourism and its actual contribution (versus the projected contribution) to the socio-economic development of Tanzania. As a labour-intensive service industry, tourism relies on the natural (coasts, mountains, wildlife) and cultural resources to attract tourists; however, it also depends on capital-intensive development of infrastructure to support a growing market. Thus, the retention of the 'tourist dollar' within the Tanzanian economy and its equitable distribution to all host destinations and their citizens remains a critical barrier to poverty reduction programmes. Furthermore, the sustainability of the industry is critically dependent on protection of the natural environment.

Quantifying and Protecting Tanzania's Natural Resources

The focus on natural resources as the principal tourism product in Tanzania has ensured that those resources are protected by legislation and this is enforced through various means. As discussed, the conservation effort began during the colonial period and was continued after independence with support and guidance from international organizations and experts, and willingness from successive governments. These efforts have resulted in a total of 301,790 km^2, or 32 per cent of Tanzania's total land area (947,253 km^2) being placed under some form of protection, as well as 3 per cent (7,387 km^2) of the total marine area (243,130 km^2) (UNEP-WCMC 2016). These figures hide the true extent of conservation and types of protection that land and marine areas are afforded in Tanzania. Table 13.2 summarizes data derived from UNEP-WCMC (2016) to demonstrate this more robustly.

Table 13.2 represents just over 600 nationally designated protected areas in Tanzania in 2016. It does not include international designations, however, of which there are eleven (four UNESCO World Heritage Sites, three UNESCO-MAB Biosphere Reserves and four Ramsar Sites).

All of these areas form the core of a much larger protected ecosystem that has been set aside to preserve the country's rich natural heritage, and to provide secure breeding grounds where the diverse fauna and flora available can thrive safe from the ever-increasing threat of human encroachment (URT 2015b). As noted by World Bank (2015c), uncontrolled poaching is unfortunately reducing the numbers of elephants, giraffe and rhinos at an alarming rate. One of the major aims of conservation has been to reap the economic benefits emanating from international tourism; however, safari tourism comprises both photo and

Table 13.2 Number and Types of Nationally Designated Protected Land Areas in Tanzania,

Category	Number
Forest Reserve	496
Village Forest Reserve	35
Game Reserve	26
National Park	16
Wildlife Management Area	15
Nature Reserve	6
Conservation Area	4
Forest Reserve & Game Reserve	2
Marine Reserve	2
Marine Park	2
Locally Managed Marine Area	1
State Forest Reserve	1
Marine Sanctuary and Forest Reserve	1
Village Forest	1
Collaborative Fishery Management Area	1

(trophy) hunting options, with the latter being far more lucrative. The arguments for a ban on hunting in sub-Saharan Africa have been reignited recently, with Botswana enforcing an outright ban, but most other nations including Tanzania, did not. Tanzania is one of a few countries (including South Africa, Mozambique and Namibia) that reportedly 'have the most effective controls and the highest levels of transparency' (Maruping-Mzileni 2015). This contrasts with some views of what is actually happening on the ground, with Matinyi, Shutzer, Jones and Doherty (2015: 4) reporting that poaching 'has reached crisis levels' and elephant populations particularly have declined drastically, with figures of 80 per cent elephant decline in the Selous-Mikumi area over the past seven years and 44 per cent in Arusha National Park in the last five years to the time of writing.

Contribution of Tourism in Tanzania's Economy

As observed by Kamuzora (2006), Tanzania is among seven other developing countries where tourism is one of the highest export earners. The percentage of foreign exchange earned from tourism as a ratio of total foreign exchange in the small economy of Tanzania is quite high, averaging slightly over 22 per cent; however, it is not clear what proportion can be attributed to different sectors: wildlife tourism (photo and hunting), beach tourism (excluding Zanzibar) and the northern circuit including Kilimanjaro.

The growing dependence on one sector puts Tanzania's economy at risk, particularly with international tourism and tourists, a business that is sensitive to major external factors (domestic and international). Tanzania is certainly no stranger to this scenario. For example, in 1977, the break-up of the East African Community adversely affected tourist arrivals, as Tanzania had to close its border with Kenya. Furthermore, travel warnings issued by some source market governments affected bookings from those markets. A more recent example is the 2007 economic crisis. The impact of this reached Tanzania by 2009 where the value and volume of international tourists declined from 770,376 arrivals in 2008 to 714,367 the following year, while tourist receipts fell from US\$1288.70 million in 2008 to US\$1159.82 million in 2009 (Table 13.1). Interestingly, around the same time, UNCTAD (2010) reported that Tanzania's tourism industry was 'the country's top export earner, well above coffee and cotton, accounting for over 35 per cent of total goods and services exports'. So, despite the decrease in tourist arrivals and spending, earnings seemed less affected during this period.

Although tourist arrivals rose again in 2010, tourist spending did not, and it took three years for total tourist receipts to exceed the 2008 figure noted above. By 2014 tourism was buoyant again with steady increases in tourist arrivals and spending as well as an increase in direct travel to Tanzania, instead of via Kenya. This may be attributed, partly, to the 2013 terrorist attack at Westgate Mall in Nairobi and terrorist attacks along the coast in 2014, and at Garissa University the following year (FCO 2016), in neighbouring Kenya. It may also be attributed to increased consumer confidence in the established source markets, as well as rising numbers from emerging economies such as China. Tanzania aims to attract 10 million international tourists by 2025 (World Bank 2015c).

Economic Leakage and International Tourism

The tourism industry is highly complex and is dependent on many other industries, such as transport and the broader service sectors, including hospitality and retail. It is an export industry that relies on the customer buying a product in their country of origin but travelling to consume it in its country of origin. For most developing countries, foreign investment in infrastructure is critical to create an international destination; therefore there is much dependence on external organizations and businesses to generate the sales on the destination's behalf (UNCTAD 2010). This extends the supply chain, and for a package holiday, for example, this would begin in the tourist-generating country, where tour operators and travel agents sell the whole holiday, and end at the host destination with local food and beverage (F&B) suppliers. Typically, a package holiday includes full or part board and offers visitors ample on-site and in-house hospitality and activities, so less tourist spending takes place beyond the hotel or resort boundary. TUI, the largest global travel and tourism operator offering package as well as all-inclusive holidays, explains on its website that 'we control the end-to-end customer journey' by providing the marketing and sales, flights, cruises, inbound services, accommodation and integrated platforms and management[3] (TUI 2016).

The large cruise ship operators such as Carnival and Royal Caribbean use a similar business model where customer spending is maximized on-board (Hampton & Jeyacheya 2013). In both cases, there is great potential for import and export leakage from the host destination (UNEP-WCMC 2016).

Benavides (2001: 12) summarizes tourism economic leakage as:

> The process whereby part of foreign exchange earnings generated by tourism, rather than being retained by tourist-receiving countries, is either retained by tourist-generating countries or remitted back to them. It takes the form of profit, income and royalty remittances; payments for the import of equipment, materials, and capital and consumer goods catering for the needs of international tourists; the payment of foreign loans; various mechanisms for tax evasion; and overseas promotional expenditures...

This definition sums up what leakage is, but its actual impact on a destination can be difficult to measure as much tax, wages and profits are paid outside the area, thus the profit remaining in the destination is frequently low. According to UNEP-WCMC (2016), 'large-scale transfer of tourism revenues out of the host country' amount to 80 per cent of tourist expenditure on a holiday (including pre-trip spending and trip spend). The higher figure refers to the Caribbean, while a lower figure of 40 per cent is seen in India (ibid.). Interestingly, 80 per cent was also cited in a World Bank-funded report (2013) on Kenya's leisure and tourism industry. With reference to all-inclusive (AI) hotels and resorts in Mombasa – Kenya's principal coastal tourism destination – the report stated that funds were channeled to a tax-free offshore account (Ambrosie 2015: 103), leaving 20 per cent of tourism expenditure to cover the operating costs of the hotel or resort. UNCTAD (2010), on the other hand, provides figures for 'import-related leakage as between 40 and 50% of gross domestic earnings for small economies and 10 and 20% for the most advanced and diversified economies'.

The actual amount of leakage is difficult to analyze accurately. First, economic leakage is expressed in different ways (as a percentage of

---

[3] Ranger Safaris is their main 'destination management company' in Tanzania, for example.

gross domestic earnings or tourist expenditure, import-related leakage, for example), but often in simplistic terms. Second, the vertical integration of multi-national tour operators that are typically associated with international tourism in developing countries are highly complex, with tens or hundreds of subsidiary companies. According to Ambrosie (2015), who offers a great deal of knowledge in the operations of 'tightly integrated all-inclusive resorts' in the Caribbean and East Africa, such operators channel 80 per cent of the 'package price through a series of companies to peel the revenue of tax liabilities' (2015: 103), thus leaving a shortfall of 80 per cent. The additional activities, safaris and entertainment on offer to guests, are booked and paid for at the hotel, with the subsidiary companies providing the service. A cross-subsidy mechanism operates within the complex network of subsidiary companies allowing the hotel to recoup the losses (ibid.).

What is clear is that international tourism can offer economic benefits, most notably through employment and export/import earnings; but a country's dependence on foreign investment, multinational leisure and hospitality businesses and foreign tourists brings with it economic leakage. Furthermore, and in terms of employment opportunities, research has shown that local people are often employed in low-waged, low-skilled jobs that are increasingly precarious and offer little upward mobility (Lee, Hampton & Jeyacheya 2015, reporting on the Seychelles). This implies that the socio-economic benefits of certain forms of tourism are often based on misguided assumptions that are based on a narrow financial perspective, and over-inflated projections.

Economic Leakage and Tourism in Tanzania

This section focuses on several key challenges that face Tanzania's policy-makers in addressing and reversing economic leakage from tourism. The first challenge for Tanzania's tourism policy-makers is to increase economic linkage by strengthening the value chain, particularly at local and regional levels and among rural communities and those at the periphery. The current policy direction towards high-value, low-volume tourism has inherent links to the conservation efforts of successive governments for the country's natural and wildlife resources. This form of tourism, however, typically imports many goods and services to accommodate high-paying, high-value customers with matching expectations, thus excluding the local supply chain and diminishing tourism's contribution to the local value chain.

Figure 13.1 illustrates the tourism value chain in Tanzania, and is based on one of the author's research in 2006. It provides a comprehensive overview of the value chain of a holiday purchased by an international visitor and the value-added along that chain from pre-trip sales

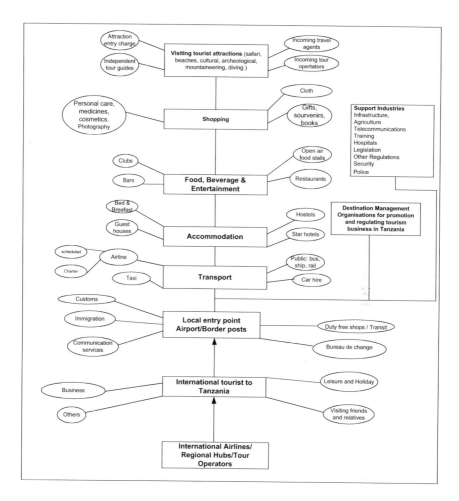

Source: Kamuzora (2006)

Figure 13.1 The Tourism Value Chain, Tanzania

to arriving at the destination to enjoy the holiday experience. At this point, there is the greatest opportunity to add value from each tourist by capturing as much expenditure as possible along the value chain.

Several clusters were identified by Kamuzora (2006) as strong contributors to the local value chain, including: local transport operators (road, air, sea particularly), local accommodation providers (guest houses, bed and breakfasts, hostels, hotels), local food stalls, as well as services and activities contributing to the night-time economy (restaurants, bars, clubs). The research found that local operators offering food and drink typically sourced their products from local farmers, markets and suppliers, thus strengthening the local and regional inter-sectoral linkages and adding value to the tourism chain. In addition, the direct income received from tourists buying additional services and products, such as utilities, insurance premiums, licences, and professional services (wildlife and hunting safaris, for example), together with tourism-related wages, all contribute to the 'tourism multiplier effect' in the destination and the surrounding regions.

The second challenge is to redress the balance between foreign and local ownership of tourism businesses and enterprises. Perhaps this is easier said than done; however, Kinyondo and Pelizzo highlight historic leakage caused by high foreign ownership (in 1990) where '60% of profits were repatriated' (2015: 10). They emphasize the continuing trend, more recently, by citing Salazar's research (2009), which reported 'the majority of the 210 tour operating companies were owned by foreign entrepreneurs' (ibid.). Research conducted by one of the authors (Kamuzora 2006) observed similar trends for three major tour operators in the country, where two are subsidiaries of international tour operators with headquarters in the source markets. Here, the marketing and financial activities take place including pre-trip tourist expenditure (transport, accommodation and agents' fees).[4] The local branches conduct the operational activities of transporting the tourist to destinations within Tanzania, thus excluding national and local operators. The cross-subsidisation and use of subsidiary companies mentioned earlier, is evidently, and perhaps not surprisingly, found in Tanzania. With a growing reliance on tourism, Tanzania, among other tourism dependent countries, is 'ranked in the top 25 out of 145 countries for tax losses as a proportion of their health budget through the shadow economy' (Ambrosie 2015: 229).

The final challenge is delivering a new tourism plan for southern Tanzania, currently underdeveloped in terms of infrastructure, education and thus human capacity, and with a declining wildlife population (Matinyi et al. 2015: 4). With a difficult operating environment, a report funded by USAID for the Tanzanian government states that 'existing and potential investors will require policy and regulatory support to enable them to remain competitive'. It goes on to state, however, that a 'lack of transparency on the use of revenue from fees and levies contributes to mistrust between investors and government' (ibid.: 35), and the range of taxes, fees and levies imposed on tour operators from national and local governments and associations amounts to 25 per cent (ibid.: 36). When considering the opaqueness of multi-national operators in addition to that of the government, there is a massive challenge ahead if economic leakage is to be effectively curbed.

Within the USAID (2015) report to the Tanzanian government, Matinyi et al. make reference to a tourist type coined 'beach extender'

---

[4] Murphy and Carmody (2015: Ch. 7) refer to the case of Zanzibar in their discussion of the importance of ICT in the intermediation of tourist arrivals and the associated costs and benefits.

who typically learns about natural and other attractions in the southern region while on a beach holiday in Zanzibar or mainland Tanzania. The beach and marine attractions in the southern region are also raised in this report as adding to the diversity of tourism opportunities available to investors and to local communities, providing the right training and financial support is offered.

However, there are lessons to be learnt from Zanzibar where enclave tourism has skewed and extended the supply chain for food-stuffs. According to Anderson (2011: 362), 'about 90% of the food stuffs consumed in local tourist hotels and restaurants in Zanzibar are imported', although there is greater expenditure by enclave tourists (all-inclusive) and other tourists in local restaurants, bars and enter-tainment than in other beach destinations, such as in the Caribbean. Contribution to the local day and night-time economy is important and should be promoted to increase local linkages, particularly in destina-tions where all-inclusive holidays are dominant. A balance between all-inclusive tourists and tourists on other travel arrangements (half board, transport only) is critical, as the former buy less from local businesses and contribute less to the local network of suppliers and producers (Anderson 2011: 375).

Community-Based Tourism (CBT)

Leading on from the final point in the section above, and to conclude this chapter, economic linkages from tourism activities can be strengthened in rural and marginalized regions if the business environment allows and is inclusive. Community-based tourism and community-based natural resource management are two approaches that have consider-able potential for contributing to a more sustainable and equitable form of tourism for the local host communities.

In Tanzania cultural CBT is usually an add-on to a safari or beach holiday, and is encouraged by the Tanzania Tourist Board (TTB) as it strengthens rather than weakens the local economy, and maintains rural populations. The idea for cultural CBT in Tanzania specifically originated from, and was sponsored by, The Netherlands Development Organization (SNV) in 1996. The approach was based on aspects of pro-poor tourism and involves villages and communities in actively participating, contributing to and benefiting directly from tourism, economically, socially and environmentally. Since 1996, 47 Cultural Tourism Enterprises (CTEs) have been established, including Friends of Usambara, which is based in Lushoto district, Tanga region.

Friends of Usambara Society (FoUS) was formed in 1996 following SNV's efforts in funding CBT. The overall goals of the society are to develop and promote sustainable tourism in the Usambara Mountains in the Tanga region and to contribute to the conservation of the area's

Table 13.3 Distribution of Tour Guide Fees among Stakeholders of Friends of Usambara Society

Tanzania Cultural Tourism Programme *Performance Reporting For First Quarter 2014*	
Number of Tourists	450
Village Development Fund (Tsh.)	1,720,000
Guide Fees (Tsh.)	6,976,000
Administration Fees (Tsh.)	325,000
Contact Person Fees (Warriors, Traditional Healer, Story Teller) (Tsh.)	265,000
Food (Traditional/Others)	1,150,000
Activities: Hiking, Biking, Cultural Tours, Boma Visit, Volunteering Fees etc. (TSh.)	590,000
Accommodation, Home Stay, Camping (Tsh.)	2,500,000
Handicrafts/Souvenirs	805,000
Voluntary Donations (for Education, Health, Water, Environment, Conservation, Orphanage)	3,420,000
Total	11,472,000

Source: FoUS (31 March 2014)

cultural and natural resources through sustainable tourism. Currently, the FoUS is one of the six local tour guide groups in Lushoto. The fees charged by members of FoUS for tour guide services (see Table 13.3) are distributed in three ways: (1) an allowance for tour guide(s), (2) a contribution to the communities and (3) a contribution to the village development fund (VDF). This fund is designed to provide financial assistance to local entrepreneurs to develop small enterprises near to main tourist attractions.

Table 13.3 provides a useful and transparent account of the proceeds generated from the tourism cultural programme for the first quarter of 2014. Although the data are basic they do differentiate tourist spending across various activities, services and products offered by the communities in Lushoto. This form of tourism is small and cannot be replicated in all destinations in Tanzania as it relies on small tourist numbers (not mass tourism), but its approach contributes to rural poverty-alleviation programmes. This is in clear contrast to the all-inclusive business model typified by multi-national tour operators, by retaining tourist expenditure locally.

Conclusion

This chapter has provided an overview of Tanzania's tourism industry since independence. It demonstrates how the tourism industry can and does contribute to the economy; however, it also highlights the shortfall in potential benefits when considering the nature of tourism. The business models associated with multinational and international operators selling 'all-inclusive' package holidays at the beach in Zanzibar or at an exclusive safari camp rely on products and services that *do* extend the supply chain significantly. This, coupled with the vertically integrated models typically associated with large tour operators, increases the opportunity for economic leakage. The greater the dependence on this form of tourism, the greater the potential loss to the economy, the environment, and ultimately the workforce.

The chapter also demonstrates how tourism can and does contribute to employment, and more particularly, to alleviating poverty in rural and marginalized areas. The role of conservation in the protection of wildlife has led to small-scale tourism enterprises being established among rural communities. This approach has proven that a mutually beneficial business model and a transparent accounting system can raise marginalized and rural communities out of poverty. However, reducing poverty through CBT initiatives is only possible if there is a willingness from all parties to establish an equitable arrangement for benefit-sharing.

The ever-increasing dependence on tourism to service the national economy and employment should be considered carefully by those implementing policies that explicitly or implicitly include tourism. Three specific policy implications end this chapter:

- Firstly, there is a need to plan for a mix of tourism products (and business models) in the selected regions for tourism development (southern circuit and coast, for example). The increasing reliance on foreign investment for large-scale 'mass tourism' infrastructure and high-value, low-volume products suggest economic leakage and extended supply chains will become the norm for many destinations. The planning stage should differentiate between destinations for all-inclusive tourism resort development, as in Zanzibar, and destinations for more sensitive tourism development (nature-based and community-based) to avoid total dependence on foreign investment and operators building and selling Tanzania's tourism products.
- Secondly, there is a need to implement a policy for greater transparency and accountability from all key stakeholders involved in the country's industry. The extent of economic leakage from international tourism activities is as complex as the industry, and provides too many opportunities to enhance profits (legally and illegally) at the expense of others. A strong administration and a robust

accounting system could significantly reduce the rate and extent of economic loss from tourism-related activities.

- Thirdly, there is a need to plan for a trained workforce with the necessary skills and knowledge to operate at higher levels of the industry, thereby increasing the number of nationals managing and directing large and medium tourism businesses, such as hotels and resorts. Equally, a trained workforce with the skills and knowledge to establish small businesses for day-time activities (attractions, restaurants for example) and the night-time economy (restaurants, bars, clubs) could help retain more of the tourist dollar at the destination, for longer.

14

Extractive Industry Revenues and their Expenditure in Local Government Authorities: The Case of the Gold Service Levy in Geita District Council in Tanzania*

Honest Prosper Ngowi and David Potts

Introduction

Mineral revenues have become increasingly important in Tanzania but questions have been asked about the extent to which they contribute to the development of the areas in which the minerals are located and to the wider economy. This chapter reviews some of the issues relating to the contribution of mineral wealth to the Tanzanian economy by investigating the case of the gold service levy in Geita District and its impact on the local community.

Local Government Authorities (LGAs) in Tanzania play a critical role in delivering governance and social and economic services directly to the people. Such services include infrastructure of all kinds, education, health, water, security and sanitation. According to the Local Government Act No. 9 of 1982 and the Policy on Local Government Reform of 1998, LGAs are supposed to identify and improve local revenue mobilization and to identify potential areas for investment to promote sustainable economic and social development activities in their respective jurisdictions.

Resource-rich LGAs usually expect local economies to benefit from the extraction of resources including oil, gas and mineral investments. Unfortunately, this has not always been the case. These LGAs have either been denied the fiscal space to collect revenues or do not always know how to take advantage of extractive activities to enhance sustainable economic development. Local investments in natural resources such as minerals and gas should in principle provide opportunities for LGAs to strengthen their revenues and to use the same for provision of public goods and services. It is in the context of the above that this chapter was prepared, partly based on a study by Ngowi (2015).

* Prosper Ngowi acknowledges the Christian Council of Tanzania (CCT) and the Inter-Faith Committee on Economic Justice and Dignity of Creation in Tanzania for funding the study on which much of this work is based.

Minerals and Development

Mineral wealth has been viewed as a mixed blessing in relation to development. While the income and foreign exchange generated contributes to the national balance of payments as well as to government revenue and to employment, the extent of positive impact depends critically on who gets the revenue and how it is used to strengthen both the local and national economy. Very often the mineral extraction process is managed by a large foreign company, and the share of the benefits that remains in the country depends on the agreements made. There is significant potential for corruption that may affect both the share that remains within the country and the share of the remainder that accrues to the local population.

Where a country derives a significant proportion of its foreign exchange revenue from minerals there may also be a potential negative effect on other export sectors, particularly agriculture, owing to the effect of increased export revenue on the level of the exchange rate. Sachs and Warner (2001) have pointed to a negative correlation between growth of per capita income and the share of the primary sector, and the possibility that resource abundance could crowd out other activities through the effect on the exchange rate. This does not yet appear to have been the case for Tanzania (see Chapter 12), but the effect on corruption is a significant issue. Gylfason (2001: 850) suggests that natural resource-abundant countries tend to have a higher incidence of corruption owing to the allocation of the rents accruing from mineral resources. This issue has arisen in Tanzania in relation to gold mining and it is relevant to the case presented in this chapter. Atkinson and Hamilton (2003: 1804) argue that 'there is stronger evidence that those governments in resource abundant countries that have consumed the proceeds of this abundance are those that, on average, have experienced a significant resource curse'. What matters is partly the proportion of the benefits from mineral resources that accrues to the host country, but also what those benefits are used for, in particular the extent to which the proceeds are invested rather than consumed.

The Extractive Sector in Tanzania

The growing importance of the mineral sector in Tanzania is highlighted by the proportion of total exports derived from ores and metals, mineral fuels, lubricants and related materials. This proportion rose from 2.8 per cent in 1997–2001 to 18.7 per cent in 2012–16, but it is still considerably lower than some of the other fast-growing countries of sub-Saharan Africa (Table 14.1).

This relatively low dependence on mineral exports may be helpful since it makes Tanzania less vulnerable to large changes in mineral

Table 14.1 Mineral Sector Exports as Percentage of Total Exports, 1995–2014

Period	1995–99	2000–04	2005–09	2010–14
Tanzania	2.4%	10.2%	15.4%	19.9%
Ghana	17.2%	17.4%	15.2%	35.8%
Mozambique	9.4%	63.0%	61.8%	66.8%
Rwanda	6.5%	67.8%	37.1%	50.6%
Zambia	72.2%	60.6%	74.6%	70.2%

Source: Derived from World Development Indicators 2016

export prices. The diversity of mineral resources may also be a positive factor in stabilizing revenues.

Lundstøl et al. (2013) point out that Tanzania has a considerable history of mineral exploration and production that goes back to the late nineteenth century during the German colonial era. This is mainly the case for gold, diamonds and gemstones such as tanzanite. Tanzania has about thirty different types of mineral deposits, many of which have very high economic potential. Following the Arusha Declaration of 1967, all major means of production, including mining, were nationalized. However, following the major reforms of the mid-1980s, mining as well as many other economic activities were liberalized and opened to both local and foreign investors. A total of six large-scale gold mining operations were opened between 1998 and 2005, comprising Geita, North Mara, Buzwagi, Bulyanhulu, Tulawaka and Golden Pride. This chapter concentrates on the specific case of gold mining in Geita and refers to both large and small operators.

Mineral Sector Revenue Management and Administration

Institutionally, the extractive sector in Tanzania is the responsibility of the Ministry of Energy and Minerals (MEM). Given Tanzania's high incidence of poverty, consistent budget deficits and poor quality and quantity of public goods and services, it is clear that the country has not fully unlocked the economic potential embedded in its vast mineral resource endowment. Ways of unlocking this economic potential could include optimization of levels of revenues from all these resources. *Inter alia*, this can be done by extracting revenues in the form of fees, charges, royalties and taxes from both small and large investors.

Various ministries and agencies manage revenue in the extractives sector. The MEM issues mining licences and, through the Tanzania Petroleum Development Corporation (TPDC), oversees the negotiation of Production Sharing Agreements (PSAs) for exploration of oil and gas. The Ministry of Finance is charged with fiscal policy issues in relation to tax administration through the Tanzania Revenue Authority (TRA).

Other public institutions dealing with various aspects of the mining sector include the Tanzania Mineral Audit Agency (TMAA) and the State Mining Corporation (STAMICO).

Extractive Industry Revenues

The issue of public revenue collection from various sources and the proper use of the same has received considerable attention in the recent past. In the African context, and in Tanzania in particular, this attention is partly owing to the increasing need for domestic sources to fund public goods and services such as health, education, water, infrastructure, and security, given increasing demand for such services.

Although this chapter focuses on the mining sector, the broader picture extends to tapping revenues from the pipelines of the newly discovered natural gas and oil in Tanzania. There seems to be a general consensus that, so far, Tanzania has not benefited sufficiently from mining sector revenues. As such it can be argued that the country should learn from past mistakes and experience elsewhere to ensure that both local communities and the national economy benefit more meaningfully from their extractive resources.

Curtis and Lisu (2008) found that, in the period 1997 to 2005, Tanzania exported gold worth more than US$2.54 billion, while the government only received around 10 per cent of this sum in tax and royalties over the nine-year period. They also argued (2008: 7) that 'the prioritisation of large-scale gold mining in the country has come at the expense of small-scale artisan miners, around 400,000 of whom have been put out of work'.

Curtis, Ngowi and Warris (2012) investigated the extent of revenue losses experienced by Tanzania through tax evasion, capital flight and tax incentives, and argued for a review of existing tax incentives and greater transparency for existing agreements and the presentation of tax information. One estimate suggests that, between 2000 and 2007, Tanzania lost around $425 million in non-paid royalties and taxes by mining companies (Purje et al. 2010: 26–7).

Lundstøl et al. (2013) examined the reasons for low government revenue from the mining sector in Tanzania and Zambia, and concluded that 'effective benefit-sharing in mining has been notoriously difficult to achieve'. They argued that 'profit-based corporate tax made a very modest contribution' to revenue.

In relation to the Tanzanian gold mining industry Lange (2011: 233) points out that 'investor-friendly contracts have resulted in extremely low government revenues from mining'. Cooksey (2011: 39) presents detailed evidence on the negotiations of mineral contracts, and raises the question whether the unsatisfactory outcomes were the result of lack of capacity or corruption. He concludes that 'the operational capacity and governance interpretations are not incompatible and that both have explanatory power'.

UNECA (2011) points to the importance of mineral-based linkages and related constraints in terms of skills, incentives and policies. It is argued that more attention needs to be paid to artisanal and small-scale mining. There are also capacity constraints in negotiating agreements and regional markets are not yet sufficiently developed to take advantage of potential linkages. The growing demand from India and China is an advantage in terms of markets and revenue, but there is a need to take proper account of social and environmental impacts and the lack of power of marginalized groups. More transparency is needed in revenue negotiations, and attention needs to be paid to the potential use of windfall taxes when there are substantial increases in mineral prices. The report takes the view that 'the allocation of mineral revenues to communities in mining areas should be designed to ensure lasting benefits beyond the life of the mine'.

Tanzania has not yet benefited from its considerable mineral wealth to the extent that might reasonably be expected. In 2017 President Magufuli announced plans to increase state control over the mining sector, including a ban on the export of mineral concentrates and metallic ores, both to ensure that processing of raw materials took place in Tanzania and that under-reporting of the mineral content of ores did not take place.

Specific concerns had been raised in an investigation of Acacia Mining, majority-owned by Barrick Gold Corporation of Canada. The concerns related to serious underreporting of the gold and copper content of mineral sand concentrates. Acacia Mining was also accused of human rights violations by security forces, leading to 22 deaths and 69 injuries (MAC: Mines and Communities 2017).

In July 2017 the Tanzania Parliament passed the Natural Wealth and Resources (Permanent Sovereignty) Bill 2017 and the Natural Wealth and Resources Contracts (Review and Re-Negotiation of Unconscionable Terms) Bill 2017. The stated aim was to improve transparency and increase the state's share of revenue. The legislation increased royalties on both uranium and gold, and allowed the government to cancel and renegotiate existing contracts for both mining and energy companies if the terms were deemed unfavourable. It also removed the right for companies operating in Tanzania to seek international arbitration.

However, the issue of the size of the revenue is not the only one. The issue of *how* and *by whom* the revenue is spent is also important since it relates to the long-term impact of this wealth on the livelihoods of the populations of mineral-rich areas. These issues are relevant to the case that is discussed in this chapter. Getting a fair share of the proceeds for the community is important, but how these proceeds are used is also important.

The Impact of Mining on Local Communities

The issue of the local share of mineral wealth relates not just to the revenues of governments and local authorities, which is the main subject of this chapter. It also relates to the incomes and rights of artisanal miners and farmers whose land may be acquired by mining companies. The process of formalizing contracts between foreign companies and national and local authorities may exclude those who have made a living from informal sector mining but do not have any formal property rights. Bush (2009) describes the dispossession of informal sector miners in Ghana as a result of contracts awarded to gold mining companies. Similar issues are described by Emel et a.l (2010) in relation to the dispossession of artisanal miners in North Mara, Tanzania. Fold et al. (2014) refer to both Tanzania and Ghana in arguing for formalized pathways for the marketing of the products of artisanal and small-scale mining.

Lange (2011: 247–8) notes irregularities in the compensation that should have accrued to villagers displaced by the Geita Gold Mine. Lange and Kolstad (2012) investigated the benefits streams from the mining sector in Tanzania in Geita Gold Mine (GGM) and Tanzanite One in Mererani. Both communities had experienced conflicts between small-scale miners and the foreign investors and problems with poor local governance and corruption in the process of management of the benefit stream. In the case of GGM, by focusing on a specific project to build a secondary boarding school for the district council, it was eventually possible to provide some tangible benefit to all the surrounding villages to overcome the previous problems with misuse of funds. The availability and use of funds derived from mineral levies in Geita is referred to in more detail below.

Expenditure from Extractives Revenue

Most debates on revenue in general and on mining sector revenues in particular have focused more on revenue collection than on the expenditure financed by those revenues. For example, Curtis and Lissu (2008) and Curtis, Ngowi and Warris (2012) refer mainly to shortfalls in the mining revenue collection side of the equation. While the relative silence of these works on the expenditure side is understandable, as one has to collect the revenue in order to spend, the issue of how the revenue is spent is also important. Extractives are non-renewable resources, and associated revenues need to be extremely well-managed and administered if they are to provide long-term benefits.

It is only by investing these finite natural resources in physical and human capital that this wealth can be conserved. The importance of prudent expenditure of extractive sector revenues cannot be overemphasized. Wise use of revenue includes investment in human capital, especially through education and health, as well as in development rather than recurrent expenditure. It is also important to take account of inter-generational considerations in using the revenues from the extractives sector. This means that while the current generation uses these revenues, it should use them in such a way that the future generations will also benefit. This includes using the revenues for investments in long-term infrastructure such as roads, health and education facilities.

It is vital to remember the interests of future generations in making spending decisions today. It would be a wise investment for Tanzania to borrow some of the principles embodied in Norway's 'Oil for Development' (OFD). OFD emphasizes the use of oil revenues to invest in development activities such as investment in infrastructure, education and health. The discovery in Tanzania of substantial commercial quantities of natural gas and possibly oil reinforces this need. Extraction of non-renewable resources does not make sense for future generations if those resources are sold too cheaply or if the revenues obtained are used to finance current consumption. Judgement on the expenditure of mining revenues can be made in relation to strategic development needs with a focus on investment in human capital and economic infrastructure for the future. The legal basis for determining the revenue available for local development in Tanzania is covered by the Local Government Finance Act (1982) and subsequent amendments.

The Local Government Finance Act (LGFA) 1982

The Local Government Finance Act (1982) is the main legal instrument that gives LGAs the legal power to collect revenues, not only from extractive companies but also from many other sources. The Act facilitates revenue mobilization from extractive operations for local authorities. It is:

> An Act to make provision for sources of revenue and the management of funds and resources of Local Government Authorities and for matters connected or incidental to securing the proper collection and sound management of finances in the local government system. (Local Government Finance Act, 1982)

Among other things, the Act grants LGAs the legal power to collect various types of revenues. It also allows LGAs to make their own by-laws that give them authority to collect revenues from various sources. The collection of the minerals service levy equal to 0.3 per cent of annual gross revenues is therefore enshrined in this law.

Selected parts of the LGFA 1982 are outlined in Figure 14.1, incorporating subsequent amendments since its enactment in 1982 up to 30 June 2000. This shows how the Act provides LGAs with legal

Sources of Funds for District Councils

Section **7** (1) of Part II of the Act, provides for a total of 27 sources of revenues, funds and resources of a district council. Those relevant to this study are the following:

(b) all moneys derived from any trade, industry, works, service or undertaking carried on or owned by the district council;

(e) all moneys derived from any rate imposed by the district council under or in pursuance of this Act or any other written law;

(aa) all monies derived from the service levy payable by corporate entities at the rate not exceeding 0.3 percent for the turn over net of the value added tax and the excise duty.

(2) Any other moneys lawfully derived by a district council from any other source not expressly specified in subsection (I) shall be and form part of the revenue, funds and resources of the district council.

PART III: Making and collection of rates

13. (1) Subject to this Act and to rules made by the Minister under this section, a local government authority may make by-laws imposing such rates to be paid by the inhabitants or such categories of inhabitants, for, on or in connection with such services, things, matters or acts as the authority may describe or specify in the by-laws in question.

14. Every district council and every urban authority shall, subject to this Act, make or levy such rates as will ensure the raising of income from rates which, in combination with income from other sources of revenue, will be sufficient to provide for such part of the estimated total expenditure to be incurred by it during the period in respect of which the rate is made or levied as is to be met out of money raised by rates including in that expenditure any additional amount as is, in the opinion of the authority, required to cover expenditure previously incurred or to meet contingencies or to defray any expenditure which may fall to be defrayed before the date on which the money to be received in respect of the next subsequent rate will become available; except that an authority which submits for the necessary approval a proposal to make or levy a rate which complies with the requirements contained in this section shall be deemed to have complied therewith.

PART III: Making and collection of rates

13 (2) The Minister shall, after consultation with the Minister responsible for finance, make rules, to be known as rating rules, prescribing limitations and imposing conditions upon which any local authority or category of local authorities may make legislation imposing rates under this section.

(5) The Minister may, by order in the Gazette, exempt any category of persons from payment of any rate chargeable under this Act.

Source: Extracted from Local Government Finance Act 1982

Figure 14.1 Selected Contents of Local Government Finance Act 1982

authority on various revenue issues including setting rates and collecting revenues from natural resources. In principle these revenues can then be used to finance development activities in the local area.

LGFA 1982 bestows huge legal power on LGAs to collect revenues from various sources, including from natural resources in general and gas and gold in particular. However, the Act has some potential barriers/ hindrances in the capacity of LGAs to collect revenue. It is seen from the above that a section of the Act gives the Minister responsible for finance power to give exemptions from paying some LGA revenues. If and when the Minister exercises this power and exempts companies from paying natural resources service levy therefore, the LGAs may be hindered from collecting such revenues.

LGFA 1982 does not hinder revenue mobilization from extractive operations. However, prior to the 2014/15 financial year, Mining Development Agreements (MDAs) entered between the government and mining companies conflicted with the Act. The MDAs conflicted with LGFA 1982 as they waived the requirement of charging 0.3 per cent of gross revenues as a service levy from mining companies to the relevant LGAs.

New Mining Fiscal Agreements

According to *The East African* newspaper[1] (11–17 October 2014, pp. 1 and 6), the Tanzanian government and big mining firms agreed on new rules for royalty payment, dropping value added tax (VAT) relief and changing the service levy from a fixed amount of $US 200,000 per year to 0.3 per cent of gross revenue per year. Anglo Gold Ashante and GGM (which became Acacia) were the first to sign the agreement that replaced the previous MDA. Royalty computation will be 4 per cent of gross value of minerals instead of 3 per cent of net profit. Royalty is set at 5 per cent for all gemstones. The service levy will cease to be a flat rate $US 200,000 and graduate to 0.3 per cent of turnover. Mining companies will also no longer enjoy a 15 per cent VAT tax waiver.

The October 2014 agreement on the new formula and rates stands to benefit the country in general and the LGAs that receive the service levy in particular. The move from a service levy based on a flat rate of $US 200,000 to 0.3 per cent of gross value stands to benefit LGAs if the gross value is big enough to give a 0.3 per cent value that is greater than $US 200,000. Assuming that the $US 1.8 million service levy cited by the Minister for Minerals and Energy is a representative figure, it means that LGAs that have been receiving $US 200,000 per year instead of the $US 1.8 million will get an extra $US 1.6 million per year. Not applying the law on 0.3 per cent service levy therefore has implied lost opportunity for the council and its people. By all standards, this amount 'lost' in the old fiscal regime could be a change-maker to the people of LGAs receiving the service levy in terms of economic infrastructure and social services such as education, health, water, sanitation and other public goods and services.

[1] 'Government seals new tax deal with miners, drops 15 percent waiver'.

According to the then Minister for Minerals and Energy (Professor Muhingo), as a result of the

October 2014 agreement, the district of Geita in Mwanza region will now receive $US 1.8

million as service levy per year instead of $US 200,000. *'This is a lot of money ... it is about Tsh 3*

billion. Geita will now have no reason to lack water or desks in classrooms. This money is not for

district councillors to spend on trips, it is for development' (Minister for Minerals and Energy)

Source: The East African, 11–17 October 2014, p. 1

Figure 14.2 Potential Benefits to Communities in Mining Areas from the Agreement

Issues on Remaining Mining Years

The extent to which the new fiscal agreement that will give LGAs 0.3 per cent of gross value as the service levy should be celebrated depends greatly on the number of mining years that remain. The LGAs will only benefit if there are 'many' mining years ahead, if there are substantial quantities of gold, and if prices are high. Short of these conditions, there will be no reason to celebrate the new mining fiscal agreement. Whereas the new agreement including execution of the 0.3 per cent mineral service levy is a welcome move, it may have come too late for some areas. Some gold mines have reserves that will last between ten and twenty years only, meaning the new agreement will be enjoyed for relatively few remaining mining years.

Findings from Geita District Council (GDC)

Geita District is located in the Geita Region of Tanzania. According to the 2012 census, the population of the district was 807,619. The district borders Shinyanga Region to the south-east, Mwanza Region to the north and east, Kagera Region to the north-west, Bukombe District to the south, and Chato District to the south-west. The district has a total land area of 5,325 km^2, a population of about 807,619 and is divided administratively into 35 wards.

Geita region is one of the most gold-rich regions in Tanzania, possessing substantial deposits, minimally exploited by large-scale and small-scale miners. The area under mining exploitation includes Geita district, where gold is within the greenstone belt. This belt has been the most productive in Tanzania with a continuous history of activities from 1932 to date. Intensive small-scale mining is done in Nyarugusu, Lwamgasa Nyakagwe, Nyamtondo, Iparamasa, Nyamalimbe, Kamena and Mgusu villages. Intensive large-scale mining is done in Mtakuja, Nyankanga and Nyakabale. There is one large-scale gold mine (Geita Gold Mine) and four small-scale mines (Moolman Mining Tanzania, Pamoja Mining, Nyarugusu Mining Company and Blue Leaf Mining Company).

Legal Basis for Revenue Collection in Geita District Council

Apart from the Local Government Finance Act of 1982 (section 290), revenue collection in Geita is guided by by-laws that were amended in 2014 and have to be read together with the Geita District Council By-laws (Fees and Levy) of 2008. GDC depends on many other sources of revenue apart from the revenues from gold. In Table 14.2 some revenue sources and rates stipulated in the by-law are outlined.

According to the study findings, GDC generated a substantial amount of revenue from the mining activities in the council from financial year 2010/11 to 2013/14. These are shown in Table 14.3.

With an average of 41.4 per cent of other sources of revenue and 29.2 per cent of total council revenue, the revenue from mining was a substantial source of revenue for the years under consideration. While this is good, it should raise concerns on likely overdependence on this source. It also implies that the other sources of revenues, although relatively well-diversified, are not bringing in substantial revenues. This calls for development and enhancement of revenues from these other sources, which can be partly done through investing goldrevenues.

According to the field findings, the council received revenue in the form of a service levy paid by companies that supply various goods and

Table 14.2 Current Rates of Fees and Levy for Various Sources

Sources of revenue	Old rates (Tsh.)	New rates from 2014 (Tsh.)
Fee for advertisements	500 per 100 square cm	20,000 per square metre
Livestock levy	1,000 per cow 500 per goat	5,000 per cow 1,500 per goat
Car parking fee at the main bus station	1,000 (big buses) 500 (minibuses)	3,000 (big buses) 2,500 (minibuses)
Fee for using council's properties	Council hall: 100,000 per day	150,000 per day
Butchery fee	25,000 per month	50,000 per month
Slaughter service fee	1,600 per cow 800 per goat	3,000 per cow 1,000 per goat
Fish transport fee	10 per kg	5% of buying price
Gold sand processing	0	7,500,000 per year
Fishing beach fee	0	10,000 per month

Source: Geita District Council By-laws, Revised May 2014

Table 14.3 Revenues Received by GDC from Mining Activities

Year	Revenue from (Tsh. '000)			Mining revenue as % of	
	Mining[i]	*Other sources*	*Total*	*other sources*[ii]	*total revenue*[iii]
2013/14	863,129	2,329,435	3,192,564	37.1%	27.0%
2012/13	666,458	1,425,403	2,091,861	46.8%	31.9%
2011/10	626,820	1,640,331	2,267,150	38.2%	27.6%
2010/11	612,967	1,408,447	2,021,413	43.5%	30.3%
				Average: 41.4%	Average: 29.2%

Source: Field findings, Geita DC, September 2014 and author's computations
Notes:
i   The source (GDC) did not specify the specific mining source of this revenue. It is assumed that this is from the 0.3 per cent service levy as required by the law
ii Computed by the author
iii Computed by the author

Table 14.4 Service Levy Revenue Received by Geita District Council

Year	*Service levy amount*	*Total revenue (Tsh. '000)*	*Service levy as % of total revenue*[i]
2010/11	318,567	2,021,414	15.8%
2011/12	302,010	2,267,150	13.3%
2012/13	351,458	2,091,861	16.8%
2013/14	380,263	3,192,564	11.9%
			Average: 14.5%

Source: Field findings, Geita, September 2014 and author's computation
Note:
i   Computed by the author

services to the mining companies in its jurisdiction. The amount of service levy received is presented in Table 14.4.

From Table 14.5, it is seen that mining revenues have contributed substantially to GDC's revenues. This is the case when compared to other sources of revenues as well as when compared to total revenue. In the financial year 2012/13, for example, mining revenues were 46.8 per cent of the council's other sources of revenue.

Whereas it is good that mining revenues are contributing substantially to the council's revenues, their dominance can also be a cause for concern, as minerals are depletable non-renewable extractives. Gold revenues are therefore likely to dry up upon exhaustion of the gold deposits or in the case of negative shocks that may lead to decline in the price of gold.

Assuming that mineral revenues to the council are paid based on the 0.3 per cent service levy, the amount paid will fluctuate with the volume of gold sold as well as price volatility in the world market. When gold is depleted, there will be no revenue to the council. It is important for GDC and other LGAs that are heavily dependent on mineral revenues to diversify their sources of own income away from such non-renewable resources. This is important for escaping unhealthy dependence from a few sources and thus ensuring continuous flow of streams of income upon the drying-up of mineral revenues. Diversification can be partly achieved by identifying and developing other sources of own revenues as well as by enhancing existing sources. Each of the diversified sources of revenue needs to be strengthened to sustain the LGA's income. However, it may not help to have a plethora of revenue sources if each of these contributes insignificantly to the council's revenues.

The average value of the service levy amounts to 14.5 per cent of total council revenue. While this is not very large it is an important source. It serves to demonstrate the extent to which companies servicing extractive industry companies can contribute to local economic development by widening the income base for LGAs' own sources of revenues.

Given the potential contribution to LGA revenues of the service levy from companies servicing extractive industry companies, there is a need to build the capacity and competitiveness of local enterprises so that they can become part of the supply chain of extractive industry companies and widen the LGAs' direct and indirect revenue bases through multiplier effects.

Spending of Revenues from Mining

LGAs including GDC have various options when it comes to using their revenues. According to the field findings the council has mainly used revenues from mining to facilitate projects in various wards from the financial year 2010/11 to 2013/14, as partly shown in Table 14.5.

Field findings show that there was more expenditure of mining revenues on recurrent than in development expenditure. This is indicated in Table 14.6. On average about 28 per cent of the mining revenues were used on projects, such as supporting education and projects in the wards in GDC. However, it could not be established how the rest of the mining revenue was used and the details of the ward projects that were supported were not given. Nevertheless, spending the mining revenues to invest in education is an investment in human capital for the future.

On average, 72 per cent of mining revenues were spent on recurrent expenditure. In the context of revenues extracted from non-renewable natural resources such as gold, spending more on recurrent than on development expenditure is bad economics because it is not increasing the capital stock to compensate for the loss of the natural resource.

Table 14.5 Geita District Council Allocation of Mining Revenue

Year	Allocated area	Amount spent (Tsh. '000)	Mining revenue (Tsh. '000)	Amount spent as % of mining revenue
2013/14	Building secondary schools/ supporting projects in wards	420,000	863,129	48.7%
2012/13	Supporting projects in wards	120,000	666,458	18.0%
2011/12	Supporting projects in wards	141,000	626,820	22.3%
2010/11	Supporting projects in wards	141,000	612,967	23.0%
				Average: 28%

Source: Field findings, Geita, September 2014 and author's computations

Table 14.6 Allocation of Mining Revenues: Recurrent and Development Expenditure

Year	Development Expenditure	Recurrent Expenditure
2014/15	49%	51%
2013/14	18%	82%
2012/13	22%	78%
2011/10	23%	77%
Average	28%	72%

Source: Field findings in Geita, September 2014 and author's computations

Although there were no details on what kind of development expenditure was done with the 28 per cent of the mining revenues, it is most likely that these were not spent on income-generating activities. Even if they were, they would be only a portion of the 28 per cent. Given the nature of revenues extracted from non-renewable extractives, it would make more sense to apportion some of these revenues to income-generating activities to ensure continuous streams of incomes when such revenues diminish with the depletion of the minerals, or in the case of reduction of mineral volumes and prices.

Conclusions

From the study it is concluded that Geita is mineral-rich but not necessarily economically rich. It has derived some revenue from the mining investments in forms of the service levy, but these are not necessarily making the council rich.

The council has used the funds from mining activities more for recurrent than development expenditure. This is a poor pattern of expenditure of revenues derived from non-renewable and depletable resources. The council has not invested the revenues from mineral resources into income generating activities let alone investing in future funds, revolving funds, endowment funds, municipal bonds or buying shares in publicly listed companies. This represents a missed opportunity for these (and arguably other) LGAs. However, the recent allocation of a significant proportion of funds (49 per cent) to the construction of a secondary school is a more appropriate use of these funds.

A number of policy implications can be derived from the findings of the study. In what follows, priority areas are outlined.

In order to ensure that LGAs get their fair share of revenues from extractive industry and use the same wisely, public expenditure tracking systems could be strengthened, including building the capacity of LGAs staff to ensure that a fair share of revenue is received and involvement of citizens in deciding how revenues are used. If recent legislation does lead to higher returns to the government from mineral revenues a case could also be made for an increase in the service levy.

Laws and guidelines need to be further developed to ensure that expenditures of revenues from extractive industry are directed more towards tangible long-term strategic development and income-generating activities, including the establishment of LGA investment funds rather than expenditure on short-term recurrent expenditures. LGAs could diversify their incomes away from extractive industry by, among other things, proportionately matching extractive industry revenues with revenues from non-extractives. Particular issues that are important are to ensure that the maximum possible revenue is derived for Tanzania from its mineral resources, and that this revenue is used equitably for the benefit of the national population as a whole and the district in which the mineral resource is located.

The study informing this chapter has identified some issues in relation to the generation and use of revenue based on non-renewable resources for a particular mineral-rich district. Conduct of similar studies in other LGAS could provide comparative case studies to provide a more general picture of the situation in Tanzania. The contribution of extractive industries to local employment, to local enterprise development and to linkages with the rest of the economy at local (LGAs) and national levels are important issues if the mineral wealth of Tanzania is to be harnessed for the future benefit of its citizens. More generally, there is a need to ensure that the negotiation of mineral contracts is more transparent, pays more attention to local interests and to sustainable development, and includes measures to capture a fair share of windfall gains associated with international price increases.

15

Conclusion
David Potts

Tanzania is changing continuously. Much has been learnt but the need for further research always remains. This book has raised a lot of questions, and I hope it has provided some answers, as well as restated some important lessons. This conclusion draws together some of the main issues and arguments, and provides some pointers towards future research.

There are around five times as many people in Tanzania as there were at independence, and their average income is about double the value at independence. At independence only just over 5 per cent of the population were living in the urban areas. By 2016 this had increased to over 32 per cent. Inequality has increased slightly, but the poorest 10 per cent have experienced similar percentage increases in income to the richest group. However, the second, third and fourth deciles have fared worse, suggesting some increase in relative poverty. The contribution of agriculture to GDP declined fairly steadily until 2007, but it has not changed much since then. Adult literacy has increased steadily until recently, and the gender gap has decreased significantly. Life expectancy has increased steadily, and is now 50 per cent greater than at independence.

Tanzania still retains some of the appearance of a parliamentary democracy and so far competitive elections have always taken place, albeit in a media context that favours the ruling party. However, there are increasing concerns about irregularities in the conduct of elections, intolerance of political dissent, suppression of the media and the treatment of minorities such as the LGBT community. The reputation of Tanzania as a reasonably fair, tolerant and open society is at risk if some of the current trends are allowed to continue.

Chapters 2 and 3 concur in many respects on the issues facing Tanzania, although they arrive at their conclusions by different approaches. Their key conclusions relate to the fairness of distributional outcomes, the closely related issue of corruption and the potential dangers of arbitrary measures taken by an authoritarian government. However, official justification of such measures to the public may be dressed up as measures to counter corruption. Is it too much to hope that the government could respond to public concerns about corruption without intimidation of political opponents?

At one time Tanzania would have been regarded as a land-surplus country. However, the combination of population growth and allocation of land to large-scale private ventures has given rise to land disputes, which has exacerbated tensions between pastoralists and agriculturalists. So far, the evidence presented in Chapter 4 suggests that there is healthy growth in the production levels of many of the major crops, so the agricultural sector is prospering in general, but who benefits from the improvement and is it sustainable?

Environmental degradation and deforestation are becoming more serious issues. There is therefore a need for a clear and transparent strategy on land use and land allocation that takes account of the interests of the majority and does not transfer too much of the most productive areas to large-scale commercial interests. Adequate consideration for the needs of pastoralist communities is also needed if conflicts with farming communities are to be avoided (Benjaminsen et al. 2009). Such conflicts can only be exacerbated by further allocation of agricultural land to large-scale farmers in areas where there are already conflicts over land.

While official statistics do indicate that the agricultural sector is growing steadily, evidence presented in Chapter 5 suggests that significant improvements in some of the areas studied may not always be reflected in the statistics, particularly where there is increased investment in fixed assets. However, the diversity of marketing channels and changes in power relations between small farmers and marketing organizations also suggest that some of the poorest farmers may become more and more marginalized, as implied in Chapter 6. Problems of land availability can be ameliorated by more intensive farming and better use of water through irrigation, but such schemes have their problems, as indicated in Chapter 7. Given the ongoing importance of agriculture to the majority of the population and increasing pressure on land resources, efforts to improve the productivity of small-scale farmers are a more equitable and efficient means of enhancing rural livelihoods than transfer of land to large-scale commercial interests.

Growth of the industrial sector has been rapid, and there is evidence that Tanzania can be competitive in some manufactured products (Chapters 8 and 9), but the proportion of the labour force employed in manufacturing is still relatively small. This has implications for the employment opportunities of the poorest groups in the urban areas, particularly young people (Chapter 10). Can Tanzania create more urban jobs through investment in the industrial products identified as competitive? Evidence in Chapter 12 relating to exchange rate policy suggests that Tanzania is in a better competitive position than Ethiopia to manufacture products for both import substitution and export, although it has only slightly lower levels of urban unemployment (Kibret 2014: 211; Banks 2016: 44).

The service sector is clearly growing in size, but does it provide rewarding and sustainable livelihoods for a younger generation who are increasingly educated but are often unable to find to find jobs that require the use of their education? What can Tanzania learn from other countries with growing urban populations? Vietnam has a similar distribution of population between urban and rural areas, but a much lower rate of urban unemployment (Socialist Republic of Vietnam 2016).

Tanzania has been a major recipient of aid (Chapter 11), but this prolongs dependency relationships that may be vulnerable to political disagreement, as the experience of the 1980s shows. The issues are not the same and there are more potential sources of funds, but does dependence on Western aid donors imply any more constraints on policy independence than reliance on investment from China? Western donors may be more judgemental about policy, but what are the long-term financial and physical resource constraints implied by investment from China, India or South Africa? Foreign investment may bring resource inflows and help to establish new commercial activities in the short run, but what are the longer-term implications of subsequent remittances? The issues raised in Chapter 14 and subsequent policy measures taken by the Tanzanian government point to the need for clarity in policy that ensures a fair return to both Tanzania and the investor.

The major policy issue of the 1980s was the overvalued exchange rate. Overvaluation is no longer a major source of concern but, as is argued in Chapter 12, Tanzania has maintained a policy of deliberate undervaluation. This policy enhances Tanzania's competitive position, particularly in manufacturing, but it increases the local price of imports that Tanzanians can buy. What is the cost of this policy to Tanzanians in terms of the imports their purchasing power? Are the benefits in terms of long-term economic growth greater than the short-term costs in reduced consumption of imports?

Tourism is increasingly important, particularly for Zanzibar (Chapter 13), and tourist numbers are increasing. This is an important source of foreign exchange, income and employment for the tourist areas, but what are the environmental, social and cultural implications of unrestricted growth of this sector? Much of the answer to this question depends on the type of society that people want, but how has this been articulated and have the lessons been heeded from the experience of unrestricted mass tourism in parts of Europe, South East Asia and the Caribbean?

Tanzania has substantial mineral wealth, which can be used in different ways (Chapter 14). It can be used to subsidize the short-term consumption of the rich or it can be invested in future physical and human capital. Measures have already been taken to try to ensure that Tanzania gains more from existing mineral resources and these funds can be reinvested in the country, but what proportion of the benefits should go to the communities affected by drilling and mining, and what measures need to be put in place to protect the livelihoods of the local population? There is plenty of evidence of environmental damage and deaths from accidents, but not enough evidence of concrete measures to ensure that such damage and deaths are drastically reduced.

There are many potential opportunities for Tanzania to have a bright and prosperous future, but there are also many problems to resolve, not least the political problem of restoring a greater degree of genuine democracy and participation. Tanzania is at a crossroads where the shortcomings of a political process that increasingly suppresses dissent may threaten the economic success of the last thirty years. Perhaps the most important question of all is whether the political system can provide a genuine opportunity for the people to choose their leaders and remove them if they do not deliver the kind of sustainable development that benefits the majority of both present and future generations rather than a fortunate present few. Julius Nyerere's original vision of a socialist Tanzania under a single-party democracy may have been flawed in terms of implementation, but many of the values were appropriate for a poor country with limited resources. Tanzania is not as poor now as it was then from an economic point of view, but some of those original values are becoming increasingly tarnished by corruption, intolerance and arbitrary decision-making. Is it too much to hope for a continued process of steady economic growth that is equitably distributed, sustainable and backed up by a political process that respects the right of all Tanzanians to democratic and accountable decision-making?

References

Abernethy, C. (1994) 'Sustainability of Irrigation Systems' *Zeitschrift fur Bewasserungswirtschaft* 29(2): 135–143

ActionAid (2004) *Turning off the Taps: Donor Conditionality and Water Privatisation in Dar es Salaam, Tanzania* London: ActionAid – available at www.actionaid.org.uk/policy-and-research/research-and-publications/

ActionAid (2011) *Real Aid 3: Ending Aid Dependency* London: ActionAid – available at www.actionaid.org.uk/policy-and-research/research-and-publications/

Adam, C. and Bevan, D. (2003) 'Aid and the Supply Side: Public Investment, Export Performance, and Dutch Disease in Low-Income Countries' *World Bank Economic Review* 20(2): 261–290

Adam, C., Collier, P. and Ndulu, B. (eds) (2017) *Tanzania: The Path to Prosperity* Oxford University Press

Adams, W., Watson, E. and Mutiso, S. (1997) 'Water, Rules and Gender: Water Rights in an Indigenous Irrigation System, Marakwet, Kenya' *Development and Change* 28(4): 707–730

Africa Progress Panel (2014) African Progress Report 2014. Geneva: Africa Progress Panel – available at http://africaprogresspanel.org/homepage/

African Development Bank (AfDB) (2006) *Tanzania Joint Assistance Strategy Review of the Harmonization Process in Five Countries* Tunis: African Development Bank – available at www.afdb.org

AfDB (2007) *Tanzania: Joint Assistance Strategy and Joint Programme Document – Cover Note* Tunis: African Development Bank – available at www.afdb.org

AfDB (2011) *The Middle of the Pyramid: Dynamics of the Middle Class in Africa* African Development Bank: Market Brief, 20 April

AgWater Solutions (2010) *Agricultural Water Management National Situation Analysis Brief* November 2010 International Water Management Institute – available at wm-solutions.iwmi.org/Data/Sites/3/Documents/PDF/Country_Docs/Tanzania/Situation%20analysis%20Brief%20Tanzania.pdf

Aman, H. (2005) 'Making Agriculture Impact on Poverty in Tanzania: The Case of Non-Traditional Export Crops' Paper presented to *Economic and Social Research Foundation (ESRF) Policy Dialogue for Accelerating Growth and Poverty Reduction in Tanzania* Dar-es-Salaam, 12 May

Ambrosie, L. (2015) *Sun & Sea Tourism: Fantasy and Finance of the All-Inclusive Industry* Cambridge Scholars Publishing

Amin, S. (1977) *Imperialism and Unequal Development* Monthly Review Press

Aminzade, R. (2013) *Race, Nation, and Citizenship in Post-Colonial Africa: The Case of Tanzania* Cambridge University Press

Amnesty International (2018) *The State of the World's Human Rights* 2017/18 – available at https://www.amnesty.org/download/Documents/POL1067002018ENGLISH.PDF

Anderson, W. (2011) 'Enclave Tourism and its Socio-Economic Impact in Emerging Destinations' *Anatolia* 22(3): 361–377

Arndt, C., Demery, L., McKay, A. and Tarp, F. (2015) *Growth and Poverty Reduction in Tanzania* UNU-WIDER Working Paper 2015/051.

Arndt, C., Jones, S. and Tarp, F. (2015) 'Assessing Foreign Aid's Long-Run Contribution to Growth in Development' *World Development* 69(5): 6–18

Arndt, C., Jones, S. and Tarp, F. (2016) 'What is the Aggregate Economic Rate of Return to Foreign Aid?' *World Bank Economic Review* 30(3): 446–474

Atkinson, A. and Lugo, M. (2010) *Growth, Poverty and Distribution in Tanzania* IGC Working Paper 10/0831

Atkinson, G. and Hamilton, K. (2003) 'Savings, Growth and the Resource Curse Hypothesis' *World Development* 31(11): 1793–1807

AU/ECA Conference of Ministers of Finance, Planning and Economic Development (2015) *Report of the High Level Panel on Illicit Financial Flows from Africa* AU/ECA

AU/ECA. (2015). Illicit Financial Flows: Report of the High Level Panel on Illicit Financial Flows from Africa. Report Commissioned by the AU/ECA Conference of Ministers of Finance, Planning and Economic Development. Addis Ababa: African Union/UN Economic Commission for Africa – available at https://www.uneca.org/sites/default/files/PublicationFiles/iff_main_report_26feb_en.pdf

Balassa, B. (1982) *Development Strategies in Semi-Industrial Economies* Baltimore, MD: Johns Hopkins University Press

Balassa, B. (1990) 'Incentive Policies and Export Performance in Sub-Saharan Africa' *World Development* 18(3): 383–391

Baldus, R. (2001) 'Wildlife Conservation in Tanganyika under German Colonial Rule' *Internationales Afrikaforum* 37(1): 73–78

Bank of Tanzania (BoT) (various) *Economic Bulletin* Bank of Tanzania: Dar es Salaam

Banks, N. (2015) *What Works for Young People's Development? A Case*

Study of BRAC's Empowerment and Livelihoods for Adolescent Girls programme in Uganda and Tanzania BWPI Working Paper No. 212, University of Manchester

Banks, N. (2016) 'Youth Poverty, Employment and Livelihoods: Social and Economic Implications of Living with Insecurity in Arusha, Tanzania' *Environment and Urbanization* 28(2): 437–454

Banks, N. (2017) 'Promoting Employment, Protecting Youth: BRAC's Empowerment and Livelihoods for Adolescents Programme in Uganda and Tanzania' in Lawson, D., Ado-Kofie L. and Hulme D. (eds.) *What Works for Africa's Poorest? Programmer and Policies for the Extreme Poor* Practical Action Publishing, pp. 89–104

Banks, N. and Sulaiman, M. (2012) *Problem or Promise? Harnessing Youth Potential in Uganda* Kampala: BRAC International

Baran, Paul (1957) *The Political Economy of Growth* Monthly Review Press

Barkan, J. (1983) 'Urban Bias, Peasants and Rural Politics in Kenya and Tanzania' Paper presented at the 1983 meeting of the American Political Science Association

Barkan, J. (2009) 'Rethinking Budget Support for Africa' in Joseph, R. and Gillies, A. (eds) *Smart Aid for African Development* Lynne Rienner, pp. 67–85

Barker, C., Bhagavan, M., Mitschke-Collande, P. and Wield, D. (1986) *African Industrialization: Technology and Change in Tanzania* Gower

Barker, J. (1971) 'The Paradox of Development: Reflections on a Study of Local–Central Relations in Senegal' in Lofchie, M. (ed.) *The State of the Nations: Constraints on Development in Independent Africa* University of California Press, pp. 47–63

Bates, R. (1981) *Markets and States in Tropical Africa: The Political Basis of Agricultural Policies* University of California Press

BBC (2001) 'Tanzania "Needs Costly Radar System"' *BBC News website* 21 December 2001 – available at www.bbc.co.uk/news

Beegle, K. et al. (2011) 'Migration and Economic Mobility in Tanzania: Evidence from a Tracking Survey' *Review of Economics and Statistics* 93(3): 1010–1033

Bellemare, M. (2010) 'Agricultural Extension and Imperfect Supervision in Contract Farming: Evidence from Madagascar' *Agricultural Economics* 41(6): 507–517

Benavides, D. (2001) 'The Sustainability of International Tourism in Developing Countries' *Seminar on Tourism Policy and Economic Growth* Berlin 6–7 March

Benjaminsen, T., Maganga, F. and Abdallah, J. (2009) 'The Kilosa Killings: Political Ecology of a Farmer–Herder Conflict in Tanzania' *Development and Change* 40(3): 423–445

Berg, E. (1964) 'Socialism and Economic Development in Tropical Africa' *Quarterly Journal of Economics* 78(4): 549–573

Berke, C. (2002) *Embedding SPs in the PRSP Process: A Framework for*

Discussion Desk-based Background Paper Commissioned by KfW for the Task Team 'Sector Programs' of the Strategic Partnership with Africa (SPA) – available at swap151 from www.swisstph.ch/

Betts, J. and Wood, B. (2013) 'The Paris Declaration Evaluation: Process and Methods' *Canadian Journal of Program Evaluation* 27(3): 69–102

Bigsten, A., Mutalemwa, D., Tsikata, Y. and Wangwe, S. (2001) 'Tanzania' in Devarajan, S., Dollar, D. and Holmgren, T. (eds) *Aid and Reform in Africa* Washington, DC: World Bank.

Birch-Thomsen, T. and Fog B. (1996) 'Changes Within Small-Scale Agriculture – A Case-Study from the Southwestern Tanzania' *Danish Journal of Geography* 96: 60–69

Birch-Thomsen, T. et al. (2001) 'A Livelihood Perspective on Natural Resource Management and Environmental Change in Semi-arid Tanzania' *Economic Geography* 77(2): 48–66

Blecker, R. and Ramzi, A. (2010) 'Export-led Growth, Real Exchange Rates and the Fallacy of Composition' in Setterfield, M. (ed.) *Handbook of Alternative Theories of Economic Growth* Edward Elgar

Boesen, J. and Mohele, A. (1979) *The 'Success Story' of Peasant Tobacco Production in Tanzania* Uppsala, Scandinavia Institute of African Studies

Borgerhoff-Mulder, M. (2009) 'Serial Monogamy as Polygyny or Polyandry?: Marriage in the Tanzanian Pimbwe' *Human Nature* 20(2): 130–150

Borgerhoff-Mulder, M. and Beheim, B. (2011) 'Understanding the Nature of Wealth and its Effects on Human Fitness' *Philosophical Transactions of the Royal Society B: Biological Sciences* 366(1563): 344–356

Boudreaux, K. (2012) *An Assessment of Concerns Related to Land Tenure in the SACGOT Region* USAID Tanzania

BRN (2013a) *Presentation to PER Annual Review Meeting, 4th October 2013*, Big Results Now –available at http://www.tzdpg.or.tz/fileadmin/documents/external/Aid_Effectiveness/PER_2012_-_2013/BRN_Overview_-_PER_Working_Group-4.pdf

BRN (2013b) *Agriculture Lab: National Key Result Area* Big Results Now available at http://api.ning.com/files/cvkfPcnbiYq9PR6DzTVz3saawb7m2rnU96h17TYM-RoW05h7IZJORgtTxjn8yCmEM7DihrdqETDEGZWk*7JEm8cMxRJrVAn*/20130407AgLabdetailedreport.pdf 5h7IZJORgtTxjn8yCmEM7DihrdqETDEGZWk*7JEm8cMxRJrVAn*/20130407AgLabdetailedreport.pdf

Brockington, D. (2001) 'Communal Property and Degradation Narratives: Debating the Sukuma immigration into Rukwa Region, Tanzania' *Cahiers d'Afrique* 20: 1–22

Brockington, D. (2001) 'Women's Income and Livelihood Strategies of Dispossessed Pastoralists: The Case of Mkomazi Game Reserve' *Human Ecology* 29(3): 307–338

Brockington, D. (2002) *Fortress Conservation: The Preservation of the Mkomazi Game Reserve, Tanzania* James Currey

Brockington, D. (2008) 'Corruption, Taxation, Democracy and Natural Resource Management in Tanzania' *Journal of Development Studies* 44(1): 103–126

Brockington, D. et al. (2016) *Economic Growth, Rural Assets and Prosperity: Exploring the Implications of a Twenty Year Record from Tanzania* – available at https://www.soas.ac.uk/cas/events/22feb 2016-economic-growth-rural-assets-and-prosperity-exploring-a -twenty-year-record-from-tanzania.html

Bruno, M. (1972) 'Domestic Resource Costs and Effective Protection: Clarification and Synthesis' *Journal of Political Economy* 80(1): 16–33

Bryceson, D. (2015) 'Youth in Tanzania's Urbanizing Mining Settlements: Prospecting a Mineralized Future' in Resnick, D. and Thurlow, J. (eds) *African Youth and the Persistence of Marganization: Employment, Politics and Prospects for Change* Routledge, pp. 85–108

Bryceson, D. and Jønsson, J. (2013) 'Pursuing an Artisanal Mining Career' in Bryceson et al. (eds) *Mining and Social Transformation in Africa: Mineralizing and Democratizing Trends in Artisanal Production* Routledge

Bryden, J. (1973) *Tourism and Development* Cambridge University Press

Burgess, T. (2005) 'Introduction to Youth and Citizenship in East Africa' *Africa Today* 51(3): vii–xxiv

Burton, A. (2010) 'Raw Youth, School-leavers and the Emergence of Structural Unemployment in Late Colonial Urban Tanganyika', in Burton, A. and Charton-Bigot, H. (eds) *Generations Past: Youth in East African History* Ohio University Press

Bush, R. (2009) 'Soon there will be no-one left to take the corpses to the morgue': Accumulation and Abjection in Ghana's Mining Communities' *Resources Policy* 34: 57–63

Byres, T. (1983) *Sharecropping and Sharecroppers* Routledge

Campling, L., Myamura, S., Pattenden, J. and Selwyn, B. (2016) 'Class Dynamics of Development: A Methodological Note' *Third World Quarterly* 37(10): 1745–1767

Carter, M. and Barrett, C. (2006) 'The Economics of Poverty Traps and Persistent Poverty: An Asset-based Approach' *Journal of Development Studies* 42(2): 178–199

Carter, M. and Lybbert, T. (2012) 'Consumption Versus Asset Smoothing: Testing the Implications of Poverty Trap Theory in Burkina Faso' *Journal of Development Economics* 99: 255–264

Chachage, C. (1999) 'Globalisation and Transitions in Tourism in Tanzania' *ICSTD Regional Trade and Environment Seminar for Governments and Civil Society* Harare, Zimbabwe 10–12 February

Chachage, C. and Mbunda, R. (2009) *The State of the then NAFCO, NARCO, and Absentee Landlord Farms/Ranches in Tanzania* Dar-es-Salaam: Land Rights Research and Resources Institute (HAKIARDHI)

Chang, Ha-Joon (2008) *Bad Samaritans: The Guilty Secrets of Rich*

Nations and the Threat to Global Prosperity Random House

Chang, Ha-Joon (2012) 'Industrial Policy: Can Africa Do It?' Paper presented at IEA/World Bank Roundtable on Industrial Policy in Africa, Pretoria, 3–4 July 2012 (revised version: 30 August 2012)

Chang, Ha-Joon (2013) 'Industrial Policy: Can Africa Do It?' in Stiglitz, J., Lin, J. and Patel, E. (eds) *The Industrial Policy Revolution II: Africa in the 21st Century* Macmillan

Chang, Ha-Joon (2014) *Taking Production Seriously: Why we Need a 'Productionist' Development Discourse* 20th Bradford Development Lecture – available at www.bradford.ac.uk/ssis/bcid/bdl/

Chowdhury, M. (2004) *Resources Boom and Macroeconomic Adjustment in Developing Countries* Ashgate

Christiansen, C., Utas, M. and Vigh H. (eds) (2006) *Navigating Youth, Generating Adulthood: Social Becoming in an African Context* Uppsala: The Nordic Africa Institute

Chudik, A. and Mongardini, J. (2007) *In Search of Equilibrium: Estimating Equilibrium Real Exchange Rates in Sub-Saharan African Countries* IMF Working Paper WP/07/90

Chuhan-Pole, P. and Angwafo, M. (2011). *Yes Africa Can: Success Stories from a Dynamic Continent* Washington, DC: The World Bank

Cimoli, M., Fleitas, S. and Porcile, G. (2011) *Real Exchange Rate and the Structure of Exports* Munich Personal RePEc Archive MPRA Paper No. 37846

Clarke, G. (2012) 'Manufacturing Firms in Africa: Some Stylized Facts about Wages and Productivity' Munich Personal RePec Archive – downloaded from http://mpra.ub.uni-muenchen.de/36122

Cleaver, F. and Toner, A. (2006) 'The Evolution of Community Water Governance in Uchira, Tanzania: The Implications for Equality of Access, Sustainability and Effectiveness' *Natural Resources Forum* 30(3): 207–218

Clemens, M., Radelet, S., Bhavnani, R. and Bazzi, S. (2012) 'Counting Chickens when they Hatch: Timing and the Effects of Aid on Growth' *The Economic Journal* 122(561): 590–617

Cliffe, L. and Saul, J. (1972) *Socialism in Tanzania, Vol. 1: Politics* East African Publishing House

Cliffe, L. and Saul, J. (1973) *Socialism in Tanzania, Vol. 2: Policies* East African Publishing House

Collier, P. (2000) 'Africa's Comparative Advantage' in Jalilian, H., Tribe, M. and Weiss, J. (eds) *Industrial Development and Policy in Africa* Edward Elgar, pp. 11–21

Continent Observer (2013) http://thecontinentobserver.com/energy/09/22/tanzania-projected-to-become-leading-iron-producer-in-africa, 22 September

Cooksey, B. (2011) *The Investment and Business Environment for Gold Exploration and Mining in Tanzania* Background Paper 3, Africa Power and Politics Programme Overseas Development Institute

Cooksey, B. (2013) *What Difference has CAADP Made to Tanzanian Agriculture?* Working Paper 074, Future Agricultures Consortium – available at www.future-agricultures.org

Coulson, A. (ed.) (1979) *African Socialism in Practice: The Tanzanian Experience* Nottingham: Spokesman with Review of African Political Economy

Coulson, A. (1982) *Tanzania: A Political Economy (first edition)* Oxford University Press

Coulson, A. (2012) 'Kilimo Kwanza: A New Start for Agriculture in Tanzania?' Talk given to the British Tanzania Society, London – available at http://www.bts.org.uk

Coulson, A. (2013) *Tanzania: A Political Economy (second edition)* (Oxford: Oxford University Press)

Coulson, A. (2014) 'The Agrarian Question: The Scholarship of David Mitrany Revisited' *Journal of Peasant Studies* 41(3): 405–419

Coulson, A. (2016) 'Cotton and Textiles Industries in Tanzania: The Failures of Liberalisation' *Review of African Political Economy* 43(1): 41–59

Crivello, G. (2011) 'Becoming somebody': Youth Transitions through Education and Migration in Peru' *Journal of Youth Studies* 14(4): 395–411

Curtis, M. and Lissu, T. (2008) *Golden Opportunity: How Tanzania is Failing to Benefit from Gold Mining* Interfaith Standing Committee on Economic Justice and the Integrity of Creation/Norwegian Church Aid – available at https://www.kirkensnodhjelp.no/contentassets/a11f250a5fc145dbb7bf932c8363c998/a-golden-opportunity-2nded.pdf

Curtis, M., Ngowi, H.P. and Warris, A. (2012) *The One Billion Dollar Question: How Can Tanzania Stop Losing So Much Tax Revenue?* Interfaith Standing Committee on Economic Justice and the Integrity of Creation/Norwegian Church Aid – available at http://curtisresearch.org/wp-content/uploads/ONE-BILLION-DOLLAR-QUESTION.Final-text.-June-2012.pdf

Da Corta, L. and Magongo, J. (2011) *Evolution of Gender and Policy Dynamics in Tanzania* Working Paper 203, Chronic Poverty Research Centre – available at http://www.chronicpoverty.org/uploads/publication_files/WP203%20Magongo-DaCorta.pdf

Da Silva, C. (2005) 'The Growing Role of Contract Farming in Agri-Food Systems Development: Drivers, Theory and Practice' *Agricultural Management, Marketing and Finance Service* Rome: FAO – available at http://www.fao.org/fileadmin/user_upload/ags/publications/AGSF_WD_9.pdf

Daily Mail (2014) 'Tory fury as increasing aid budget becomes law: Conservative MPs ordered to vote in favour of proposed Bill' *Daily Mail* 12 September 2014 – available at www.dailymail.co.uk

Daley, E. (2004) 'Land Tenure and Social Change in Tanzania: A Study of Kinyanambo Village, Mufindi District', SOAS PhD

Danielson, A. (2001) *Can HIPC Reduce Poverty in Tanzania?* UNU WIDER Discussion Paper No. 2001/106 World Institute for Development Economics Research

Dawe, D. (1996) 'A New Look at the Effects of Export Instability on Investment and Growth' *World Development* 24(12): 1905–1914

Dawson, N., Martin, A. and Sikor, T. (2016) 'Green Revolution in Sub-Saharan Africa: Implications of Imposed Innovation for the Wellbeing of Rural Smallholders' *World Development* 78: 204–218

Death, C., Hulme, D., Banks, N., Underhill, H., Arubayi, D. and Skidmore, P. (2015) *Is There a "Learning Crisis" in Africa? Education and Development Post-2015,* The Davies Papers: Africa Series No. 8, May

De Waal, A. (1989) *Famine that Kills: Darfur, Sudan, 1984–1985* Clarendon Press

De Weerdt, J. (2010) 'Moving out of Poverty in Tanzania: Evidence from Kagera' *Journal of Development Studies* 46(2): 331–349

Demombynes, G. and Hoogeveen, J. (2004) *Growth, Inequality and Simulated Poverty Paths for Tanzania, 1992–2002* World Bank Research Working Paper 3432, Washington, DC: The World Bank

Department of the Environment and Rural Affairs (DEFRA) (2016) *Food Statistics Pocketbook* London: DEFRA – available at https://www. gov.uk/government/uploads/system/uploads/attachment_data/ file/553390/foodpocketbook-2016report-rev-15sep16.pdf

Devarajan, S. (2013) 'Africa's Statistical Tragedy' *Review of Income and Wealth* 59: S9–S15.

Department for International Development (DfID) (2011a) *Bilateral Aid Review* London: DfID –available at www.dfid.gov.uk

DfID (2011b) *Bilateral Aid Review: Technical Report* London: DfID – available at www.dfid.gov.uk

DfID (2011c) *Multilateral Aid Review* London: DfID – available at www. dfid.gov.uk

DfID (2014) *Operational Plan 2011--2016 DFID Tanzania (Updated December 2014)* London: DfID

Dinh, Do Duc (2012) *Speech at the 17th REPOA Research Workshop* Dar es Salaam, March – available at http://www.repoa.or.tz/highlights/ videos/prof._do_duc_dinh_at_repoas_17th_annual_research_ workshop_-_1 and http://www.repoa.or.tz/highlights/videos/prof._ do_duc_dinh_at_repoas_17th_annual_research_workshop_-_2

Dinh, Do Duc (2013) *Growth with Equity – High Economic Growth and Rapid Poverty Reduction: The Case of Vietnam* Special Paper 12/4 REPOA, Dar es Salaam

Dinh, H. Palmade, V., Chandra, V. and Cossar, F. (2012) *Light Manufacturing in Africa: Targeted Policies to Enhance Private Investment and Create Jobs* Washington, DC: World Bank

Djurfeldt, G. et al. (2011) *African Smallholders: Food Crops, Markets and Policy* Wallingford: CABI d-portal.org (2014) Development Portal – available at http://d-portal. org/

Easterly, W. (2003) 'Can Foreign Aid Buy Growth?' *Journal of Economic Perspectives* 17(3): 23–48

Easterly, W. (2006) *The White Man's Burden: Why the West's Efforts to Aid the Rest have Done so Much Ill and so Little Good?* Penguin Books

Easterly, W., Levine, R. and Roodman, D. (2004) 'Aid, Policies, and Growth: Comment' *American Economic Review* 94(3): 774–780

Eaton, C. and Shepherd, A. (2001) 'Contract Farming: Partnerships for Growth' *FAO Agricultural Services Bulletin* 145 Rome: FAO, 132 – available at http://www.fao.org/docrep/014/y0937e/y0937e00.pdf

Economist Intelligence Unit (2017) *Country Report: Tanzania, April 2017* London: Economist Intelligence Unit

Edwards, S. (1989) 'Exchange Rate Misalignment in Developing Countries' *The World Bank Research Observer* 4(1): 3–21

Edwards, S. (2014) *Toxic Aid: Economic Collapse and Recovery in Tanzania* Oxford University Press

Elbadawi, I. (1999) *Can Africa Export Manufactures?: The Role of Endowment, Exchange Rates, and Transaction Costs* World Bank Policy Research Working Paper No. 2120

Elbadawi, I. and Helleiner, G. (2008), 'African Development in the Context of the New World Trade and Financial Regimes: The Role of the WTO and its Relationship to the World Bank and IMF' – available at https://www.africaportal.org/publications/african-development-in-the-context-of-new-world-trade-and-financial-regimes-the-role-of-the-wto-and-its-relationship-to-the-world-bank-and-the-imf/

Ellis, F. (1982) 'Agricultural Price Policy in Tanzania' *World Development* 10(4): 263–283

Ellis, F. and Mdoe N. (2003) 'Livelihoods and Rural Poverty Reduction in Tanzania' *World Development* 31(8): 1367–1384

Emel, J., Huber, M. and Makene, M. (2011) 'Extracting Sovereignty: Capital, Territory and Gold Mining in Tanzania' *Political Geography* 3: 70–79

Epstein, S., Suryananrayana, A. and Thimmegowda, T. (1998) *Village Voices: Forty Years of Rural Transformation in South India* Sage

ESRF (1997) *A Framework for a National Irrigation Policy and the Economic and Social Implications for Future Irrigation Development Programmes* Policy Dialogue Series No. 006, Economic and Social Research Foundation, Dar-es-Salaam, Tanzania

Evans, P. (2010) 'Constructing the 21st Century Developmental State: Potentials and Pitfalls' in Edigheji, O. (ed.) *Constructing a Democratic Developmental State in South Africa: Potentials and Challenges* HSRC Press – available at https://www.hsrcpress.ac.za/register?redirect=https%3A%2F%2Fwww.hsrcpress.ac.za%2Fbooks%2Fconstructing-a-democratic-developmental-state-in-south-africa

Fafchamps, M. and Quinn, S. (2012) 'Results of Sample Surveys of

Firms' in Dinh, H. and Clarke, G. (eds) *Performance of Manufacturing Firms in Africa: An Empirical Analysis*, Washington, DC: World Bank, pp. 139–211

Felipe, J. (ed.) (2015) *Development and Modern Industrial Policy in Practice* Edward Elgar

Ferreira, M. (1996) *Poverty and Inequality during Structural Adjustment in Rural Tanzania* Policy Research Working Paper No. 1641 Washington, DC: The World Bank, Policy Research Department

Filipski, M., Manning, D., Taylor, J., Diao, X. and Pradesha, A. (2013) *Evaluating the Local Economywide Impacts of Irrigation Projects, Feed the Future in Tanzania* IFPRI Discussion Paper 01247, Institute for Food Policy Research

Financial Times (2014) 'David Cameron's foreign aid pledge to cost extra £1bn' Financial Times 4t December 2014 – available at www.ft.com

Fold, N., Jonsson, J. and Yankson, P. (2014) 'Buying into Formalization? State Institutions and Interlocked Markets in African Small-scale Gold Mining' *Futures* 62: 128–139

Food and Agriculture Organisation (FAO): *FAOSTAT* (various years)

Foreign and Commonwealth Office (FCO) *Foreign Travel Advice Kenya* – available at https://www.gov.uk/foreign-travel-advice/kenya/terrorism

Fortmann, L. (1980) *Peasants, Officials and Participation in Rural Tanzania: Experience with Villagization and Decentralization* Cornell University, Rural Development Committee: Center for International Studies

Foster-Carter, A. (1985) *The Sociology of Development* Causeway

FoUS (2014) *Friends of Usambara: Performance Report Form – First Quarter* Lushoto

Freund, C. and Pierola, M. (2008) *Export Surges: The Power of a Competitive Currency* World Bank Policy Research Working Paper No. 4750

Garces-Restrepo, C., Vermillion, D. and Muñoz, G. (2007) *Irrigation Management Transfer: Worldwide Efforts and Results* FAO Water Reports No. 32 Rome: FAO

Gelb, A., Meyer, C. and Ramachandran, V. (2014) *Development as Diffusion: Manufacturing Productivity and Sub-Saharan Africa's Missing Middle* Centre for Global Development Working Paper 357, February – available at www.cgdev.org

Gereffi, G. (1994) 'Capitalism, Development, and Global Commodity Chains' in Sklair, L. (ed.) *Capitalism and Development* Routledge pp. 211–30

Gereffi, G. (2014) 'Global Value Chains in a Post-Washington Consensus World' *Review of International Political Economy* 21(1): 9–37

Global Financial Integrity (2014) *Hiding in Plain Sight* – available at http://www.gfintegrity.org/reports/

Global Partnership (2013) *Guide to the Monitoring Framework of the Global Partnership – Final Version July 2013* Geneva: Global Partner-

ship for Effective Development Cooperation – available at www.
effectivecooperation.org

Global Partnership (2016) *Nairobi Outcome Document* – available at
http://effectivecooperation.org/

Goldstein, G. (2005) 'The Legal System and Wildlife Conservation:
History and the Law's Effect on Indigenous People and Community
Conservation in Tanzania' *Georgetown International Environmental
Law Review* 17(3): 481–515

Gomanee, K., Girma, S. and Morrissey, O. (2005) 'Aid and Growth in
Sub-Saharan Africa: Accounting for Transmission Mechanisms'
Journal of International Development 17: 1055–1075

Goody, J. (1958) *The Developmental Cycle in Domestic Groups* Cambridge
University Press

Grant, M. and Furstenberg, F. Jr (2007) 'Changes in the transition to
adulthood in less developed countries', *European Journal of Population*
23: 415-428

Gray, H. (2012) 'Tanzania and Vietnam: A Comparative Political
Economy of Economic Transition', SOAS PhD – available at http://
eprints.soas.ac.uk/13610/1/Gray_3344_Redacted.pdf

Gray, H. (2013) 'Industrial Policy and the Political Settlement in
Tanzania: Aspects of Continuity and Change since Independence'
Review of African Political Economy 40(136): 185–201

Gray, H. (2015) 'The Political Economy of Grand Corruption in Tanzania'
African Affairs 114(456): 382–403

Gray, R. (1963) *The Sonjo of Tanzania: An Anthropological Study of an
Irrigation-Based Society* London: Oxford University Press for the
International African Institute

Greco, E. (2015) 'Landlords in the Making: Class Dynamics of the
Land Grab in Mbarali, Tanzania' *Review of African Political Economy*
42(144): 225–244

Green, R. (1980) *Developing State Trading in a Peripheral Economy:
Reflections on Tanzanian Experience and its Implications* Discussion
Paper 151 IDS Sussex

Green, R. (1983) 'Political Economic Adjustment and IMF Conditionality: Tanzania 1974–1981' in Williamson, J. (ed.) *IMF Conditionality*
Washington, DC: Institute for International Economics, pp. 347–280

Grenier, L., McKay, A. and Morrissey O. (2000) 'Ownership and Export
Performance in Tanzanian Enterprises' in Jalilian, H., Tribe, M. and
Weiss, J. (eds) *Industrial Development and Policy in Africa* Edward
Elgar

Griffin, K. (1970) 'Foreign Capital, Domestic Savings and Economic
Development' *Bulletin of the Oxford University Institute of Economics
& Statistics* (32)2: 99–112

Grogan, K. et al. (2013) 'Transition of Shifting Cultivation and its
Impact on People's Livelihoods in the Miombo Woodlands of Northern
Zambia and South-Western Tanzania' *Human Ecology* 41: 77–92

GSS (2010) Rebasing of Ghana's National Accounts to Reference Year 2006. Accra: Ghana Statistical Service. PDF available at www.stats-ghana.gov.gh.

GSS. 2018. Rebased GDP Presentation September 2018. Accra: Ghana Statistical Service. – PDF available at www.statsghana.gov.gh

Guardian (2006) 'Fraud Office inquiry into BAE Tanzania deal' Monday 13 November – available at theguardian.com

Guardian (2010) 'New bribery law puts overseas payments under scrutiny' Monday 12 April 2010 – available at theguardian.com

Guardian (2014) 'UK and international donors suspend Tanzania aid after corruption claims' Monday 13 October – available at theguardian.com

Guengant, J. and May J. (2013) 'African Demography' *Global Journal of Emerging Market Economies* 5(3): 215–267

Gupte, J., te Lintelo, D., and Barnett, I. (2014) *Understanding 'Urban Youth' and the Challenges they face in Urban Sub-Saharan Africa: Unemployment, Food Insecurity and Violent Crime* IDS Evidence Report 81, IDS

Guyer, J. (1981) 'Household and Community in African Studies' *African Studies Review* 24(2/3): 81–137

Gylfason, T. (2001) 'Natural Resources, Education, and Economic Development' *European Economic Review* 45(4–6): 847–859

Haddad, M. and Pancaro, C. (2010) *Can Real Exchange Rate Undervaluation Boost Exports and Growth in Developing Countries? Yes, But Not for Long* Economic Premise No. 20 Washington, DC: World Bank

Hakiardhi (2011) *Land Grabbing in a Post Investment Period and Popular Reaction in the Rufiji River Basin: A Research Report*

Hampton, M. and Jeyacheya, J. (2013) *Tourism and Inclusive Growth in Small Island Developing States* Commonwealth Secretariat, London

Hansen, K. (2005) 'Getting Stuck in the Compound: Some Odds against Social Adulthood in Lusaka, Zambia' *Africa Today* 51(4): 3–16

Hansen, K. (2015) 'Cities of Youth: Post-millennial Cases of Mobility and Sociality' in Resnick, D. and Thurlow, J. (eds) *African Youth and the Persistence of Marginalization: Employment, Politics and Prospects for Change* Routledge, pp. 67–84

Harrison, D. (ed.) (2002) 'The Background' in *Tourism and the Less Developed World: Issues and Case Studies* CABI Publishing, pp. 1–18

Harrison, E. and Mdee, A. (2017) 'Size Isn't Everything: Narratives of Scale and Viability in a Tanzanian Irrigation Scheme' *Journal of Modern African Studies* 55(2): 251–273

Havnevik, K. (1993) *Tanzania: The Limits to Development from Above* Motala and Dar es Salaam: Nordiska Afrikainstitutet and Mkuki wa Nyota Publishers, pp. 289–290

Helleiner, G. (1995) *Report of the Group of Independent Advisers on Development Cooperation Issues between Tanzania and Its Aid Donors* Copenhagen: Royal Danish Ministry of Foreign Affairs, reprinted in

Wangwe, S. (ed.) (2002) *NEPAD at Country Level: Changing Aid Relationships in Tanzania* Mkuki na Nyota

Helleiner, G. (2001) *Local Ownership and Donor Performance Monitoring: New Aid Relationships in Tanzania?* Department of Economics and Munk Centre for International Studies, University of Toronto – available at http://www.swisstph.ch/

Helvetas (2016*) Rural Livelihood Development Programme in Tanzania* – available at https://tanzania.helvetas.org/en/activities/projects_tanzania/rural_development_tanzania/

Herrmann, R. (2017) 'Large-Scale Agricultural Investments and Smallholder Welfare: A Comparison of Wage Labor and Outgrower Channels in Tanzania' *World Development* 90: 294–310

Herzer, D. and Nowak-Lehmann, D. (2006) 'What Does Export Diversification Do for Growth? An Econometric Analysis' *Applied Economics* 38: 1825–1838

Hess, S., van Beukering, P., Kayharara, G., Geofrey, V, and Haider, W. (2008) *Livelihoods in the Uluguru Mountains of Tanzania: Survey Report and Choice Model* PREM /Valuing the Ark project

Higgins, K. and da Corta, L. (2013) 'Understanding Structural Influences on Poverty Dynamics in Tanzania – Using a Relational Life History Q-Squared Approach' in Kessy, F., Mashindano, O., Shepherd, A. and Scott, L. (eds) *Translating Growth Into Poverty Reduction: Beyond the Numbers* Mkuki na Nyota, pp. 11–28

Hillbom, E. (2012) 'When Water is from God: Formation of Property Rights Governing Communal Irrigation Furrows in Meru, Tanzania, c. 1890–2011' *Journal of Eastern African Studies* 6(3): 423–443

Himanshu, Jha, P. and Rodgers, G. (2016) *The Changing Village in India: Insights from Longitudinal Research* Oxford University Press

Hindess, B. and Hirst, P. (1975) *Pre-Capitalist Modes of Production* Routledge

Hirji, K. (ed.) (2010) *Cheche: Reminiscences of a Radical Magazine* Mkuki na Nyota

Hjertholm, P., Laursen, J. and White, H. (2000) *Macroeconomic Issues in Foreign Aid* Department of Economics, University of Copenhagen: Discussion Paper No. 5

Hobdari, N. (2008) *Tanzania's Equilibrium Real Exchange Rate* IMF Working Paper WP/08/138

Hoffman, B. (2013) *Political Economy of Tanzania* – available at https://www.yumpu.com/en/document/view/33116756/political-economy-analysis-of-tanzania-democracy-and-society

Honwana, A. (2012) *The Time of Youth: Work, Social Change and Politics in Africa* Kumarian Press

Hoseah, E. (2008) *Corruption in Tanzania: The Case for Circumstantial Evidence* Cambria Press

House of Commons (2013a) *The 0.7% Aid Target* London: House of Common – available at www.parliament.uk

House of Commons (2013b) *Multilateral Aid Review: Fourth Report of Session 2013–14 (Volumes 1 and 2)* London: The Stationery Office – available at http://www.parliament.uk/business/committees/committees-a-z/commons-select/international-development-committee/inquiries/parliament-2010/multilateral-aid-review/

Human Rights Watch, Tanzania (2018) *Events of 2017* – available at https://www.hrw.org/world-report/2018/country-chapters/tanzaniaand-zanzibar

Hussain, A. and Tribe, K. (1981) *Marxism and the Agrarian Question, Volume 2* Macmillan

Hyden, G. (2005) 'Reaching the Poor: The Need for a New Donor Strategy' in Tribe, M., Thoburn, J. and Palmer-Jones, R. (eds) *Development Economies and Social Justice: Essays in Honour of Ian Livingstone* Ashgate, pp. 13–26

ICAI (Independent Commission for Aid Impact) (2012) *The Management of UK Budget Support Operations* London: ICAI

ICAI (2014) DfID's *Approach to Anti-Corruption and its Impact on the Poor* London: ICAI – available at www.icai.independent.gov.uk

Igbadun, H., Mahoo, H., Tarimo, A. and Salim, B. (2006) 'Crop Water Productivity of an Irrigated Maize Crop in Mkoji Sub-catchment of the Great Ruaha River Basin, Tanzania' *Agricultural Water Management* 85(2006): 141–150

Ilembo, B. (2015) 'Contract Farming and The Dynamics of Tobacco Value Chain in Tanzania' Mzumbe University PhD

Irish Aid/DfID (2010) *Joint Irish Aid and DFID Country Programme Evaluation: Tanzania 2004/05–2009-10* ITAD with Fiscus Ltd and Verulam Associates Ltd – Thornton, P., Dyer, K., Lawson, A., Olney, G., Olsen, H. and Pennarz, J., Dublin and London: Irish Aid and DfID

Isinika, A., Ashimogo, G. and Mlangwa, J. (2003) *Africa in Transition: Macro Study Tanzania* – available at http://www.keg.lu.se/en/sites/keg.lu.se.en/files/a8.pdf

Jacob, T. (2017) 'Competing Energy Narratives in Tanzania: Towards the Political Economy of Coal' *African Affairs* 116(463): 341–353

Jaffee, S. (1994) 'Contract Farming in the Shadow of Competitive Markets: The Experience of Kenyan Horticulture' in Little, P. and Watts, M. (eds) *Living Under Contract: Contract Farming and Agrarian Transformation in Sub-Saharan Africa* University of Wisconsin Press

Jalilian, H. and Weiss, J. (2000) 'De-industrialisation in Sub-Saharan Africa: Myth or Crisis' *Journal of African Economics* 9(1): 24–43

Jeffrey, C. (2012) 'Geographies of Children and Youth II', *Progress in Human Geography* 36(2): 245–253

Jeffrey, C. and McDowell, L. (2004) 'Youth in a Comparative Perspective: Global Change, Local Lives' *Youth and Society* 36(2): 131–142

Jenkins, B. (2012) *Mobilizing the Southern Agricultural Growth Corridor of Tanzania* Cambridge, MA: The CSR Initiative at the Harvard Kennedy School

Jerven, M. (2013a) *Poor Numbers: How we are Misled by African Development Statistics and what to do about it* Cornell Studies in Political Economy

Jerven, M. (2013b) 'Comparability of GDP Estimates in Sub-Saharan Africa: The Effect of Revisions in Sources and Methods Since Structural Adjustment' *Review of Income and Wealth* Series 59, October: S16–S36

Jerven, M. (2014) 'Measuring African Development: Past and Present. Introduction to the Special Issue' *Canadian Journal of Development Studies* 35(1): 1–8

JICA (Japan International Cooperation Agency) (2014) *Data Collection Survey on Promotion of Agro-industry and Industrial Human Resource Development in Tanzania*: FINAL REPORT: International Development Centre of Japan Inc. – available at http://open_jicareport.jica.go.jp/pdf/12181574.pdf

JICA/MoW (2013) *The Study on Water Resources Management and Development in Wami/Ruvu River Basin in the United Republic of Tanzania* Interim Report and Supporting Document, (JICA), Water Resources Division, Ministry of Water

Jones, G. and Chant, S. (2009) 'Globalising Initiatives for Gender Equality and Poverty Reduction: Exploring "Failure" with Reference to Education and Work among Urban Youth in The Gambia and Ghana' *Geoforum* 40: 184–196

Juarez, F., LeGrand, T., Lloyd, C., Singh, S. and Hertich, V. (2013) 'Youth Migration and Transitions to Adulthood in Developing Countries' *The ANNALS of the American Academy of Political and Social Science* 648: 6–15

Kaberuka, D. (2011) 'Development and Aid in Africa: What Have We Learned from the Past 50 Years?' in OECD DAC *Development Co-operation Report 2011* Paris: OECD DAC – available at www.oecd.org

Kabissa, J. (2014) *Cotton in Tanzania: Breaking the Jinx* Tanzania Education Publishers Ltd

Kadigi, R., Mdoe, N., Ashimogo, G. and Morardet, S. (2008) 'Water for Irrigation or Hydropower Generation? Complex Questions Regarding Water Allocation in Tanzania' *Agricultural Water Management* 95(2008): 984–992

Kahyarara, G. (2014) *Aid and Environment in Africa: The Case of Tanzania* UNU WIDER Working Paper 2014/077 Helsinki: United Nations University – available at www.wider.unu.edu/publications

Kamuzora, F. (2006) 'A Synthesis of Utilisation of Information and Communication Technologies in Tanzanian Tourism System: A Multimethodology Approach' Bradford, School of Informatics PhD

Kaplinsky, R. (1980) 'Capitalist Accumulation in the Periphery: The Case of Kenya Re-Examined' *Review of African Political Economy* 7(17): 83–105

Kaufman, D. and O'Connell, S. (1999) *The Macroeconomics of Delayed Exchange-rate Unification: Theory and Evidence from Tanzania*, Policy Research Working Paper Series 2060 Washington, DC: World Bank

Kay, G. (1975) *Development and Underdevelopment: A Marxist Analysis* Macmillan

Kelsall, T. (2012) 'Neo-Patrimonialism, Rent-Seeking and Development: Going with the Grain?' *New Political Economy* 17(5): 677–682

Kelsall, T. (2013) *Business, Politics, and the State in Africa: Challenging the Orthodoxies on Growth and Transformation* Zed Press

Keraita, B., Amoah, P., Drechsel, P. and Akple, M. (2010) 'Enhancing Adoption of Food Safety Measures in Urban Vegetable Production and Marketing Systems' *Acta Horticulturae* 1021: 391–399

Khan, M. (2000) *Rents, Rent-Seeking and Economic Development: Theory and Evidence in Asia* Cambridge University Press

Kharas, H. (2007) *Trends and Issues in Development Aid* Working Paper 1 Wolfensohn Center for Development Washington, DC: Brookings Institution – available at www.brookings.edu/wolfensohncenter

Kibret, F. (2014) 'Unemployment and Labor Market in Urban Ethiopia: Trends and Current Conditions' *Sociology and Anthropology* 2(6): 207–218

Kilama, B. (2013) 'The Diverging South: Comparing the Cashew Sectors of Tanzania and Vietnam' Leiden PhD – available at https://openaccess.leidenuniv.nl/bitstream/handle/1887/20600/fulltext.pdf?sequence=12

Killick, T. (2004) 'Monitoring Partnership-based Aid Relationships' *Development Policy Review* 22(2): 229–234

Kinyondo, A. and Pelizzo, R. (2015) 'Tourism, Development and Inequality: The Case of Tanzania' *Poverty and Public Policy* 7(1): 64–79

Klein, E (2014) 'Psychological Agency: Evidence from the Urban Fringe of Bamako' *World Development* 64: 642–653

Klugman, J., Neypati, B. and Stewart, F. (1999) *Conflict and Growth in Africa: Vol. 2: Kenya, Tanzania and Uganda* OECD: Development Studies Centre

Komakech, H., Van der Zaag, P., Marloes, L., Mul, T., Mwakalukwa, A. and Kemerink, J. (2012) 'Formalization of Water Allocation Systems and Impacts on Local Practices in the Hingilili Sub-catchment, Tanzania' *International Journal of River Basin Management* 10(3): 213-227

Koopman, J. and Faye, I. (2012) 'Land Grabs, Women's Farming, and Women's Activism in Africa' *Conference on Global Land Grabbing*, Cornell University – available athttp://www.cornell-landproject.org/download/landgrab2012papers/Koopman.pdf

Korinek, A. and Servén, L. (2010) *Undervaluation through Foreign Reserve Accumulation: Static Losses, Dynamic Gains* World Bank Policy Research Working Paper No. 5250

Krueger, A. (1966) 'Some Economic Costs of Exchange Control: The Turkish Case' _Journal of Political Economy_ October 74(5): 466–480

Krueger, A. and Bhagwati, J. (eds) (1974–1978) _Foreign Trade Regimes and Economic Development_ National Bureau of Economic Research

Lall, S. and Wangwe, S. (1998) 'Industrial Policy and Industrialisation in Sub-Saharan Africa' _Journal of African Economies_ 7(1): 70–107

Lam, D. (2006) _The Demography of Youth in Developing Countries and its Economic Implications_ World Bank Policy Research Working Paper No. 4022

Land Rights Research and Resources Institute (LRRRI) (2008) _The Agrofuel Industry in Tanzania: A Critical Enquiry into Challenges and Opportunities_

Lange, G-M. and Jiddawi, N. (2009) 'Economic Value of Marine Ecosystem Services in Zanzibar: Implications for Marine Conservation and Sustainable Development' _Ocean and Coastal Management_ 52: 521–532

Lange, S. (2011) 'Gold and Governance: Legal Injustices and Lost Opportunities in Tanzania' _African Affairs_ 110(439): 232–252

Lange, S. and Kolstad, I. (2012) 'Corporate Community Involvement and Local Institutions: Two Cases from the Mining industry in Tanzania' _Journal of African Business_ 13(2): 134–144

Larsson, R. (2001) 'Between Crisis and Opportunity: Livelihoods, Diversification and Inequality among the Meru of Tanzania' Lund University PhD

Lawrence, P. (2005) 'Explaining Sub-Saharan Africa's Manufacturing Performance' _Development and Change_ 36(6): 1121–1141

Lawrence, P. (2015) 'Is There an Africa problem?' in Weiss, J. and Tribe, M. (eds) _Routledge Handbook of Industry and Development_ Routledge pp. 350–81

Lee, D., Hampton, M. and Jeyacheya, J. (2015) 'The Political Economy of Precarious Work in the Tourist Industry in Small Island Developing States' _Review of International Political Economy_ 22 (1): 194–223

Legal and Human Rights Centre (2017) _Bi-Annual Tanzania Human Rights Report_ – available at http://www.humanrights.or.tz/assets/attachments/1509614852.pdf

Leliveld, A., Dietz, T., Wijnand, K., Kilama, B. and Foeken, D. (2013) _Agricultural Dynamic and Food Security Trends in Tanzania, Development Regimes in Africa (DRA)_ Project Research Report 2013-ASC-3 – available at http://www.institutions-africa.org/filestream/2014011 4-agricultural-dynamics-and-food-security-trends-in-tanzania

Lenin, V. (1899) 'The Development of Capitalism in Russia: The Process of the Formation of a Home Market for Large-scale Industry' _Collected Works_, Vol. 3 English Edition, Moscow: Progress Publishers, 1967

Lenin, V. (1917) 'Imperialism: The Highest Stage of Capitalism' _Collected Works_, Vol. 1 English Edition, Moscow: Progress Publishers, 1963

Lewis, W.A. (1953) *Report on Industrialisation and the Gold Coast* Accra: Government of the Gold Coast

Lewis, W.A. (1955) *The Theory of Economic Growth* Unwin

Levy-Yeyati, E. and Sturzenegger, F. (2007) *Fear of Appreciation* World Bank Policy Research Working Paper No. 4387

Li, Y. and Rowe, F. (2007) *Aid Inflows and the Real Effective Exchange Rate in Tanzania* World Bank Policy Research Working Paper No. 4456

Lin, J. (2012) *New Structural Economics: A Framework for Rethinking Development* – available at http://siteresources.worldbank.org/DEC/Resources/84797-1104785060319/598886-1104951889260/NSE-Book.pdf

Lin, J. (2016) *How to Jumpstart Industrialization and Structural Transformation in Africa* REPOA Annual Research Workshop, Dar es Salaam

Lintelo, D. (2012) 'Unspoken Assumptions: Youth, Participation and the African Policy Process', Paper prepared for the conference Young People, Farming and Food 19–21 March 2012, Accra, Ghana – available at http://dialogue2012.fanrpan.org/sites/default/files/publications/te_Lintelo_Unspoken_assumptions_revised.pdf

Lipton, M. (1977) *Why People Stay Poor: Urban Bias and World Development* Harvard University Press

Little, P. and Watts, M. (eds) (1994) *Living under Contract: Contract Farming and Agrarian Accumulation in Sub-Saharan Africa* University of Wisconsin Press

Locke, C. and te Lintelo, D. (2012) 'Young Zambians "waiting" for Opportunities and "working towards" Living Well: Lifecourse and Aspiration in Youth Transitions' *Journal of International Development* 24(6): 777–794

Lockwood, M. (1998) *Fertility and Household Labour in Tanzania: Demography, Economy, and Society in Rufiji District, c. 1870–1986* Oxford University Press

Lockwood, M. (2013) 'What Can Climate-Adaptation Policy in Sub-Saharan Africa Learn from Research on Governance and Politics?' *Development Policy Review* 31(6): 647–676

Lof, M., Mekasha, T. and Tarp, F. (2013) 'Aid and Income: Another Time-series Perspective' *World Development* 69: 19-30

Lofchie, M. (2014) *The Political Economy of Tanzania: Decline and Recovery* University of Pennsylvania Press

Loiske, V.-M. (1995) *The Village that Vanished: The Roots of Erosion in a Tanzanian Village* University of Stockholm

Lundahl, M. and Ndulu, B. (1987) 'Market-related Incentives and Food Production in Tanzania: Theory and Experience' in Hedlund, S. (ed.) *Incentives and Economic Systems* New York University Press

Lundstøl, O., Raballand, G. and Nyirongo, F. (2013) *Low Government Revenue from the Mining Sector in Zambia and Tanzania: Fiscal Design, Technical Capacity or Political Will?* ITCD Working Paper No. 9, IDS Brighton – available at http://www.ictd.ac/publication/2-working-papers/86-low-government-revenue-from-the-mini ng-sector-in-zambia-and-tanzania-fiscal-design-technical-capacity -or-political-will

Luttrell, W. (1986) *Post-Capitalist Industrialization: Planning Economic Independence in Tanzania* Praeger

MacDonald, J., Perry, J., Ahearn, M., Banker, D., Chambers, W., Dimitri, C., Key, N. and Nelson, K. (2004) *Contracts, Markets, and Prices: Organizing the Production and Use of Agricultural Commodities* Agricultural Economic Report AER87, US Department of Agriculture Economic Research Service – available at https://www.ers.usda.gov/ publications/pub-details/?pubid=41704

MacKenzie, J. (1997) 'The Empire of Nature: Hunting, Conservation and British Imperialism', Ch. 6 in *Exploration, Conquest and Game in East Africa* Manchester University Press, pp. 147–166

Maganga, F. (2003) 'Incorporating Customary Laws in Implementation of IWRM: Some Insights from Rufiji River Basin, Tanzania' *Physics and Chemistry of the Earth* 28: 995–1000

Magud, N. and Sosa, S. (2010) *When and Why Worry About Real Exchange Rate Appreciation? The Missing Link between Dutch Disease and Growth* IMF Working Paper WP/10/271

Magufuli, J. (2015) http://tz.one.un.org/media-centre/statements/ 186-the-speech-by-h-e-john-pombe-joseph-magufuli-officially-i naugurating-the-11th-parliament-of-the-united-republic-of-tan- zania, accessed 9/6/2017

Mahemba, C. and De Bruijn, E. (2003) 'Innovation Activities by Small and Medium-sized Manufacturing Enterprises in Tanzania' *Creativity and Innovation Management* 12(3): 162–173

Mains, D. (2007) 'Neoliberal Times: Progress, Boredom and Shame Among Young Men in Urban Ethiopia' *American Ethnologist* 34(4): 659–673

Malima, K. (1971) *Cotton, Agricultural and Economic Transformation in Tanzania* E.R.B. Paper 71.10 Economic Research Bureau, University of Dar es Salaam

Maruping-Mzileni, N. (2015) 'Hunting in Africa: To Ban or Not to Ban Is the Question' *The Conversation* 15 July – available at https:// theconversation.com/hunting-in-africa-to-ban-or-not-to-ban-is-the -question-44269

Marx, Karl (1867) *Das Kapital*, Volume 1

Marx, Karl (1894) *Das Kapital*, Volume 3 (edited by Frederick Engels)

Mashindano, O. et al. (2013) 'Growth Without Poverty Reduction in Tanzania – Reasons for the Mismatch Translating Growth into Poverty Reduction' in Kessy, F., Mashindano, O., Shepherd, A. and Scott, L. (eds) *Beyond the Numbers* Mkuki na Nyota pp. 121–42

Matchmaker Associates (2006) *Contract Farming: Status and Prospects for Tanzania* Final Report for the Ministry of Agriculture Food and Cooperatives Participatory Agricultural Development and Empow-

erment Project – available at http://www.fao.org/uploads/media/
Contract%20farming_Tanzania.pdf

Matfess, H. (2015) 'Rwanda and Ethiopia: Developmental Authoritarianism and the New Politics of African Strong Men' *African Studies Review* 58(2): 181–204

Matinyi, R., Shutzer, M., Jones, S. and Doherty, J. (2015) *A Strategy for Tourism Development in Southern Tanzania* USAID: Dalberg Global Development Advisors and Solimar International – available at: http://hat-tz.org/hattzorg/wp-content/uploads/2015/12/A-Strateg y-for-Tourism-Development-in-Southern-Tanzania_Final.pdf

Mazzei, J. (2012) 'Negotiating Domestic Socialism with Global Capitalism: So-called Tourist Apartheid in Cuba' *Communist and Post-Communist Studies* 45(1–2): 91–103

McGillivray, M., Feeny, S., Hermes, N. and Lensink, R. (2006) 'Controversies over the Impact of Development Aid: It Works; It Doesn't; It Can, But that Depends...' *Journal of International Development* 18(7): 1031–1050

McKnight Foundation (2006) *CCRP East African Regional Sweetpotato Project Annual Report* (April 2005 to March 2006) – available at http:// www.ccrp.org/sites/default/files/genetic_diversity_of_sweetpo- tato__year_4____assessment_of_genetic_diversity_farmer_partic- ipatory_breeding_and_sustainable_conservation_of_eastern_ african_sweetpotato_germplasm.pdf

McMillan, M. and Rodrik, D. (2011) *Globalisation, Structural Change and Productivity Growth* – available at drodrik.scholar.harvard.edu

McMillan, M., Rodrik, D. and Verduzco Gallo, I. (2014) 'Globalization, Structural Change, and Productivity Growth, with an Update on Africa' *World Development* 63: 11–32

Mdee, C. (2014) 'Can irrigated rice production improve agricultural livelihoods in Tanzania?' MSc, Bradford, Economics and Finance for Development

Mdee, A. (2017) 'Disaggregating Orders of Water Scarcity – The Politics of Nexus in the Wami-Ruvu River Basin, Tanzania' *Water Alternatives* 10(1): 100–115

Mdemu, M., Magayane, M., Lankford, B., Hatibu, N. and Kadigi, R. (2004) 'Conjoining Rainfall and Irrigation Seasonality to Enhance Productivity of Water in Rice Irrigated Farms in the Upper Ruaha River Basin, Tanzania' *Physics & Chemistry of the Earth* 29(11): 1119–1124

Meertens, H., Ndege, L. and Enserink, H. (1995) *Dynamics in Farming Systems: Changes in Time and Space in Sukumaland* KIT Publishers

Meinzen-Dick, R., et al. (2011) *Gender, Assets, and Agricultural Development Programs: A Conceptual Framework* CAPRi Working Paper No. 99

Mengistu, A. and Yokoyama, K. (2009), 'The Impacts of Vertical and Horizontal Export Diversification on Growth: An Empirical Study on

Factors Explaining the Gap between Sub-Saharan Africa and East Asia's Performances' *Ritsumeikan International Affairs* 7: 49–90

Merrey, D. and Cook S. (2012) 'Fostering Institutional Creativity at Multiple Levels: Towards Facilitated Institutional Bricolage' *Water Alternatives* 5(1): 1–19

Minde, I. and Mbiha, E. (1993) 'Production Technology and Constraints in a Sorghum and Millet Based Farming System' in Minde, I. and Rohrbach, D. (eds) *Sorghum and Millet Marketing and Utilization in Tanzania* Bulawayo: SADC/ICRISAT

Mines and Communities (2017) 'Tanzania: Barrick/Acacia blasted in Canada for multiple offences' – available at http://www.minesand-communities.org/article.php?a=13656

Ministry of Justice (2011) *Bribery Act 2010 – Guidance* London: Ministry of Justice – available at www.justice.gov.uk/downloads/legislation/

Minot, N. (2007) 'Contract Farming in Sub-Saharan Africa: Patterns, Impact and Policy Orientation' Case Study 6.3 in Andersen, P. and Cheng, F. (eds) *Food Policy for Developing Countries: The Role of Government in the Global Food System Volume 2*, Cornell University – available at https://cip.cornell.edu/DPubS/Repository/1.0/Dissemi-nate?view=body&id=pdf_1&handle=dns.gfs/1200428173

Minot, N. (2010) *Staple Food Prices in Tanzania International* Food Policy Research Institute, Washington, DC – available at https://core.ac.uk/download/pdf/6689793.pdf

Mitrany, D. (1951) *Marx against the Peasant: A Study in Social Dogmatism* Weidenfeld & Nicolson; 2nd edition, with new Introduction, Collier Books, 1961

Mkandawire, T. (2010) 'From Maladjusted States to Democratic Developmental States in Africa' in Edigheji, O. (ed.) *Constructing a Democratic Developmental State in South Africa: Potentials and Challenges* Cape Town: HSRC Press

Mkapa, B. (2002) 'Keynote Address by the President of the United Republic of Tanzania, His Excellency Benjamin William Mkapa' *Tanzania Tourism Investment Forum* Arusha International Conference Centre, 22 October 2002 – available at http://www.egov.go.tz/egov_uploads/documents/KEYNOTE_ADDRESS_BY_THE_PRESI-DENT_OF_THE_UNITED_REPUBLIC_OF_TANZANIA_sw.pdf

Mmari, D. (2015) 'The Challenge of Intermediary Coordination in Small-holder Sugarcane Production in Tanzania' *Journal of Modern African Studies* 53(1): 51–68

Monji, R. and Kuzilwa, J. (1984) 'The Need for A Closer Integration between Agro-Industries and Agricultural Producers' in Msam-bichaka, L. and Chandratheker, A. (eds) *Papers in Economic Policy in Tanzania* Economic Research Bureau, University of Dar es Salaam, pp. 85–95

Morgenstern, O. (1963) *On the Accuracy of Economic Observations* (2nd edn) Princeton, NJ: Princeton University Press

Morrisey, O. and Leyaro, V. (2016) 'Industrial Development in Tanzania: Reform, Performance and Issues' in Weiss, J. and Tribe, M. (eds) *Routledge Handbook of Industry and Development* Routledge

Moshi, H. (2001) 'The Impact of Reforms in Tanzania: The Case of Privatized Manufacturing Industries' in Szirmai, A. and Lapperre, P. (eds) *The Industrial Experience of Tanzania* Basingstoke: Palgrave, pp. 341–48

Mosley, P. (1980) 'Aid, Savings and Growth Revisited' *Oxford Bulletin of Economics and Statistics* 42(2): 79–95

Moyo, D. (2009) *Dead Aid: Why Aid is not Working and How There is a Better Way for Africa*, New York: Farrar, Straus and Giroux

Mpeta, D. (2015) 'Effects of Contract Farming on Production and Income of Sunflower Producers in Kongwa District in the Central Agricultural Zone of Tanzania' Mzumbe University PhD

Msanya, B., Kaaya, A., Araki, S., Otsuka, H. and Nyadzi, G., (2003) 'Pedological Characteristics, General Fertility and Classification of Some Benchmark Soils of Morogoro District, Tanzania', *African journal of Science and Technology* 4(2): 101–111

Mtei, E. (2009) *From Goatherd to Governor* Dar es Salaam: Mkuki na Nyota Publishers

Mueller, B. (2011) 'The Agrarian Question in Tanzania: Using New Evidence to Reconcile an Old Debate' *Review of African Political Economy* 38(127): 23–42

Munemo, J., Bandyopadhyay, S. and Basistha, A. (2007) *Foreign Aid and Export Performance: A Panel Data Analysis of Developing Countries* Federal Reserve Bank of St Louis Working Paper Series 2007-023A

Murphy, J. and Carmody, P. (2015) *Africa's Information Revolution: Technical Regimes and Production Networks in South Africa and Tanzania* Oxford: Wiley

Mushongah, J. and Scoones, I. (2012) 'Livelihood Change in Rural Zimbabwe over 20 Years' *Journal of Development Studies* 48(9): 1241–1257

Mussa, U. (2014) 'Industrial Development and its Role in Combating Unemployment in Tanzania: History, Current Situation and Future Prospects' *Paper presented at the VET Forum*, Arusha, 10–11 November 2014

Mutabazi, K., Wiggins, S. and Mdoe, N. (2013) *Commercialisation of African Smallholder Farming. The Case of Smallholder farmers in Central Tanzania* Future Agricultures Consortium, Working Paper 072 – available at www.future-agricultures.org

Mwakalila, S. and Noe, C. (2004) *The Use of Sustainable Irrigation for Poverty Alleviation in Tanzania: The Case of Smallholder Irrigation Schemes in Igurusi, Mbarali District* Research Report No. 04.1, Research on Poverty Alleviation (REPOA), Dar es Salaam: Mkuki na Nyota

Mwakikagile, G. (2009) *Nyerere and Africa: End of an Era* Pretoria: New Africa Press

Mwase, N. and Ndulu, B. (2008) 'Tanzania: Explaining four Decades of Episodic Growth' in Ndulu, B., Bates, R. and O'Connel, S. (eds) *The Political Economy of Economic Growth in Africa, 1960–2000*, Vol. 2, Cambridge University Press pp. 426–70

Nakano, Y., Tanaka, Y. and Otsuka, K. (2014) 'Can "Contract Farming" Increase Productivity of Small-Scale Cultivation in a Rain-fed Area in Tanzania?' – available at http://www.grips.ac.jp/r-center/wp-content/uploads/14-21.pdf

National Audit Office (NAO) (2008) *Department for International Development: Providing Budget Support to Developing Countries* London: NAO

National Bureau of Statistics (NBS) (2006) *Integrated Labour Force Survey 2006: Analytical Report* Dar es Salaam: National Bureau of Statistics

National Development Corporation (NDC) (2017) *Iron and Steel Metallurgical Complex* – available at http://ndc.go.tz/iron-and-steel-metallurgical-complex/

Naudé, W. and Rossouw, R. (2008) *Export Diversification and Specialization in South Africa: Extent and Impact* UNU WIDER Research Paper No. 2008/93, Helsinki

Ndulu, B. (1987) *Stabilization and Adjustment Policies and Programmes: Country Study 17: Tanzania* World Institute for Development Economics Research of the United Nations University

Ndulu, B. (2008) 'The Evolution of Global Development Paradigms and their Influence on African Economic Growth', in Ndulu, B., Bates, R. and O'Connel, S. (eds) *The Political Economy of Economic Growth in Africa, 1960–2000* Cambridge University Press, pp. 313–47

Ndulu, B. and Mwase, N. (2017) 'The Building Blocks towards Tanzania's Prosperity: Lessons from Looking Back, and the Way Forward' in Adam, C., Collier, P. and Ndulu, B. (eds) *Tanzania: The Path to Prosperity* Oxford University Press

Ndulu, B., O'Connel and Bates, R. (eds) (2008) *The Political Economy of Economic Growth in Africa, 1960–2000* Vol. 2 Cambridge University Press

Nellis, J. (2003) *Privatization in Africa: What Has Happened? What Is To Be Done?* Working Paper Number 25 Washington, DC: Center for Global Development

Nelson, F. (2012) 'Blessing or Curse? The Political Economy of Tourism Development in Tanzania' *Journal of Sustainable Tourism* 20(3): 359–375

Ngowi, H.P. (2015) *Pilot Study on Extractive Industry Revenue Expenditure in Kilwa, Tarime and Geita District Councils* Interfaith Standing Committee on Economic Justice and the Integrity of Creation: Dar es Salaam – available at http://www.policyforum-tz.org/sites/default/files/AnalyticalThinkPiecefinal.pdf

North, D. (1990) *Institutions, Institutional Change and Economic Performance* Cambridge University Press

Nouira, R., Plane, P. and Sekkat, K. (2010) *Exchange Rate Undervaluation to Foster Manufactured Exports: A Deliberate Strategy?* CERDI Working Papers No. 1148

Nurkse, R. (1953) *Problems of Capital Formation in Underdeveloped Countries* Oxford University Press

Nyerere, J. (1967) 'Socialism and Rural Development' reprinted in Cliffe et al. (eds) (1975) *Rural Cooperation in Tanzania* Dar es Salaam: Tanzania Publishing House

Nyoni, T. (1998) 'Foreign Aid and Economic Performance in Tanzania' *World Development* 26(7): 1235–1240

Organisation for Economic Cooperation and Development (OECD) (2014) *OECD Foreign Bribery Report: An Analysis of the Crime of Bribery of Foreign Public Officials* Paris: OECD – available at www.oecd-ilibrary. org/governance/

OECD Development Assistance Committee (DAC) (2005 and 2008) *The Paris Declaration on Aid Effectiveness – and The Accra Agenda for Action* Paris: OECD – available at: http://www.oecd.org/data-oecd/11/41/34428351.pdf

OECD DAC (2011) *Busan Partnership for Effective Development Co-operation* Paris: OECD –available at: http://www.oecd.org/dac/ aideffectiveness/49650173.pdf

OECD DAC (2014a) *Statistics* – available at http://www.oecd.org/dac/ stats/

OECD DAC (2014b) *DAC Glossary of Key Terms and Concepts* Paris: OECD – available at http://www.oecd.org/dac/dac-glossary.htm#ODF

OECD DAC (2015a) *The High Level Fora on Aid Effectiveness: A History* Paris: OECD – available at http://www.oecd.org/dac/effectiveness/ thehighlevelforaonaideffectivenessahistory.htm

OECD DAC (2015b) *Evaluation of Development Programmes* – available at www.oecd.org/development/evaluation/

ODI (2016) *Supporting the Preparation of Tanzania's Second Five Year Development Plan 2016/17 –2020/21 Final Report* – available at http:// set.odi.org/wp-content/uploads/2016/06/Supporting-Economi c-Transformation-in-Tanzania-Final-Report_May-2016.pdf

Östberg, W. (1995) *Land is Coming Up: The Burunge of Central Tanzania and their Environments* Stockholm Studies in Social Anthropology Stockholm University

Östberg, W. and Slegers, M. (2010) 'Losing Faith in the Land: Changing Environmental Perceptions in Burunge Country, Tanzania' *Journal of Eastern African Studies* 4(2): 247–265

Ostrom, E. (1990) *Governing the Commons: The Evolution of Institutions for Collective Action* Cambridge University Press

Ostrom, E. (2005) *Understanding Institutional Diversity* Princeton, NJ: Princeton University Press

Ouma, S., Boeckler, M. and Lindner, P. (2013) 'Extending the Margins of Marketization: Frontier Regions and the Making of Agro-export

Markets in Northern Ghana' *Geoforum* 48: 225–235

Oxford Policy Management (OPM) (2013) *Tanzania Public Finance Management Reform Programme Phase III Completion Report* prepared for SIDA Tanzania and Ministry of Finance of the Government of Tanzania – available at www.mof.go.tz/mofdocs/

Oya, C. (2007) 'Stories of Rural Accumulation in Africa: Trajectories and Transitions among Rural Capitalists in Senegal' *Journal of Agrarian Change* 7(4): 453–493

Oya, C. (2012) 'Contract Farming in Sub-Saharan Africa: A Survey of Approaches, Debates and Issues' *Journal of Agrarian Change* 12(1): 1–33

Paavola, J. (2008) 'Livelihoods, Vulnerability and Adaptation to Climate Change in Morogoro, Tanzania' *Environmental Science & Policy* 11(7): 642–654

Page, J. (2013) 'Should Africa Industrialise?' in Szirmai, A., Naude, W. and Alcorta, L. (eds) *Pathways to Industrialization in the Twenty-first Century: New Challenges and Emerging Paradigms* UNU-WIDER Studies in Development Economics Oxford University Press

Piketty, T. (2014) *Capital in the Twenty-First Century* Belknap Press/ Harvard University Press

Pitcher, A., Moran, M. and Johnston, M. (2009) 'Rethinking Patrimonialism and Neopatrimonialism in Africa' *African Studies Review* 52(1): 125–156

Poku, N. and Mdee, A. (2011) *Politics in Africa: A New Introduction* Zed Books

Policy Forum (2013) *Tanzania Governance Review 2012: Transparency with Impunity?* – available at http://www.policyforum-tz.org/ tanzania-governance-review-2012-transparency-impunity

Policy Forum (2015) *Tanzania Governance Review 2014: The Year of 'Escrow'* – available at http://www.policyforum-tz.org/ tanzania-governance-review-2014-year-escrow

Ponte, S. (2002) *Farmers and Markets in Tanzania* Oxford: James Currey

Potts, D. (2008) *Policy Reform and the Economic Development of Tanzania* BCID Research Paper No. 14 (University of Bradford: BCID) – available at http://core.kmi.open.ac.uk/download/pdf/5563.pdf

Potts, D. (2017) 'Development and Inequality in the African Lions' in Anand, P.B., Comim, F., Fennell, S. and Weiss, J. (eds) *Oxford Handbook of BRICS and Emerging Economies* New York: Oxford University Press

Potts, D., Ryan, P. and Toner, A. (eds) (2003) *Development Planning and Poverty Reduction* London: Palgrave Macmillan

Prebisch, R. (1963) *Towards a Dynamic Development Policy for Latin America* E/CN 12/680/Rev 1 New York: United Nations reprinted as 'Development Problems of the Peripheral Countries and the Terms of Trade' in Theberg, J. (ed.) (1968) *Economics of Trade and Development* Wiley

References

Purje, H., Ylönen, M. and Nokelainen, P. (eds) (2010) *Illegal Capital Flight from Developing Countries – "Development Assistance" from the Poor to the Rich* Report Series 101 KEPA The Service Centre for Development Cooperation

Radelet, S. (2010) *Emerging Africa: How 17 Countries Are Leading the Way* Washington, DC: Centre for Global Development

Raikes, P. (1986) 'Eating the Carrot and Wielding the Stick' in Boesen, J., Havnevik, K., Koponen, J. and Odgaard, R. (eds) *Tanzania: Crisis and Struggle for Survival* Uppsala: Scandinavian Institute of African Studies pp. 105–143

Rajabu, K. and Mahoo, H. (2008) 'Challenges of Optimal Implementation of Formal Water Rights Systems for Irrigation in the Great Ruaha Catchment in Tanzania' *Agricultural Water Management* 95(2008): 1067–1078

Rajan, R.G. and Subramanian, A. (2008) 'Aid and Growth: What Does the Cross-Country Evidence Really Show?' *Review of Economics and Statistics* 90(4): 643–665

Ralph, M. (2008) 'Killing Time' *Social Text* 97 26(4): 1–29

Ramirez, M. (2011*) Is Globalization Inevitable in the Marxian Paradigm?* Economics Department Working Paper No. 89 Yale University

Randall, S. and Coast, E. (2015) 'Poverty in African Households: The Limits of Survey and Census Representations' *Journal of Development Studies* 51(2): 162–177

Randall, S., Coast, E. and Leone, T. (2011) 'Cultural Constructions of the Concept of Household in Sample Surveys' *Population Studies* 65(2): 217–229

Rasmussen, T. (1986) 'The Green Revolution in the Southern Highlands', in Boesen, J. et al. (eds) *Tanzania: Crisis and Struggle for Survival* Uppsala: Scandinavian Institute of African Studies pp. 191–206

Reichert, W. (1980) *Probing the Problems of Parastatals: The Issues Facing Tanzania's National Milling Corporation* Working Paper No. 44 Washington, DC: The World Bank AGREP Division

Republic of Tanganyika (1962) *Development Plan for Tanganyika 1961/62–1963/64* Dar es Salaam: Government Printer

Resnick, D. and Thurlow, J. (2015) 'Conclusions: Moving beyond Conventional Wisdoms' in Resnick, D. and Thurlow, J. (eds) *African Youth and the Persistence of Marginalization: Employment, Politics and Prospects for Change* Abingdon and New York: Routledge, pp. 172–78

Rigg, J. and Vandergeest P. (2012) *Revisiting Rural Places: Pathways to Poverty and Prosperity in Southeast Asia* Singapore University Press and Hawaii University Press

Riggio, E. (2012) *Children in an Urban Tanzania, Dar es Salaam* Paper prepared for UNICEF Tanzania – available at http://ihi.eprints.org/532/

RLDC (Rural Livelihood Development Company) (2008) *Sunflower Sector, Market Development Strategy* Dodoma: RLDC

RLDC (2009) *Rice Sector Strategy: Improving Rice Profitability through increased Productivity and Better Marketing Focusing on Tanzania's Central Corridor* Dodoma: RLDC

RLDC (2010) *Annual Report 2010* Dodoma: RLDC

Rodrik, D. (1986) 'Disequilibrium Exchange Rates as Industrialization Policy' *Journal of Development Economics* 23(1): 89–106

Rodrik, D. (2008) 'The Real Exchange Rate and Economic Growth' *Brookings Papers on Economic Activity* 39(2): 1–76

Rodrik, D. (2009) 'Industrial Policy: Don't Ask Why, Ask How' *Middle East Development Journal* 1(1): 1–29

Rodrik, D. (2013) 'Unconditional Convergence in Manufacturing' *Quarterly Journal of Economics* 128(1): 165–204

Rodrik, D. (2014) *An African Growth Miracle?* Working Paper 20188 Cambridge MA: National Bureau of Economic Research – available at www.nber.org

Rodrik, D. (2015) *Premature De-industrialisation* – available at drodrik. scholar.harvard.edu

Romer, P. (1994) 'The Origins of Endogenous Growth' *Journal of Economic Perspectives* 8(1): 3–22

Rostow, W. (1960) *The Stages of Economic Growth: A Non-Communist Manifesto* Cambridge University Press

Rotberg, R. (2007) *Africa's Successes: Evaluating Accomplishment* Cambridge MA: Harvard University Program on Intrastate Conflict Report Series, Belfer Center for Science and International Affairs, John F. Kennedy School of Government – available at www.belfer-center.org/project/52/intrastate_conflict_program.html

Ruthenberg, H. (ed.) (1968) *Smallholder Farming and Smallholder Development in Tanzania* München: Weltforum Verlag

Rweyemamu, J. (1973) *Underdevelopment and Industrialization in Tanzania: A Study of Perverse Capitalist Industrial Development* Oxford University Press

Sachs, J. and Warner, A. (1995) *Economic Reform and the Process of Global Integration* World Bank Policy Research Working Paper No. 4750

Sachs, J. and Warner, A. (2001) 'The Curse of Natural Resources' *European Economic Review* 45: 827–838

Salazar, N. (2009) 'A Troubled Past, a Challenging Present, and a Promising Future: Tanzania's Tourism Development in Perspective' *Tourism Review International* 12: 1–14

Sandbrook, C. (2010) 'Putting Leakage in its Place: The Significance of Retained Tourism Revenue in the Local Context in Rural Uganda' *Journal of International Development* 22(1): 124–136

Selbervik, H. (1999) *Aid and Conditionality – The Role of the Bilateral Donor: A Case Study of the Norwegian–Tanzanian Aid Relationship* Report submitted to the Norwegian Ministry of Foreign Affairs by the Chr. Michelsen Institute, Oslo: NORAD – available at www.norad.no

Sender, J. and Smith, S. (1986) *The Development of Capitalism in Africa* Taylor and Francis

Severino, J-M. (2011) 'The Resurrection of Aid' Chapter 9 in *OECD–DAC Annual Report for 2011* Paris: OECD–DAC: 121–133 – available at www.oecd.org/dac/

Severino, J-M. and Ray, O. (2009) *The End of ODA: Death and Rebirth of a Global Public Policy* CGD Working Paper No. 167 Washington, DC: Center for Global Development – available at: www.cgdev.org

Severino, J-M. and Ray, O. (2010) *The End of ODA (II): The Birth of Hyper-collective Action* CGD Working Paper No. 218 Washington, DC: Center for Global Development – available at: www.cgdev.org

Shanin, T. (1983) *Late Marx and the Russian Road* Monthly Review Press

Sharpley, J. (1985) 'External versus Internal Factors in Tanzania's Macroeconomic Crisis: 1973–1983' *Eastern Africa Economic Review* n.s. 1(1): 71–86

Sharpley, R. and Ussi, M. (2014) 'Tourism and Governance in Small Island Developing States (SIDS): The Case of Zanzibar' *International Journal of Tourism Research* 16(1): 87–96

Shivji, I. (1970) 'The Silent Class Struggle' special issue of *Cheche* reprinted in Cliffe, L. and Saul, J. (eds) (1973) *Socialism in Tanzania Vol. 2: Policies* Nairobi: East African Publishing House

Shivji, I. (1976) *Class Struggles in Tanzania* Monthly Review Press

Shivji, I. (2006) *Let the People Speak: Tanzania Down the Road to Neo Liberalism* Council for the Development of Social Science Research in Africa

Singh, A. (1986) 'Tanzania and the IMF: The Analytics of Alternative Adjustment Programmes', *Development and Change* 17(3): 425–454

Skarstein, R. and Wangwe, S. (1986) *Industrial Development in Tanzania: Some Critical Issues* Dar es Salaam: Tanzania Publishing House

Snyder, K. (2005) *The Iraqw of Tanzania: Negotiating Rural Development* Boulder, CO: Westview Press

SNV (2012) *Edible Oil Subsector in Tanzania* Netherlands Development Organisation

Socialist Republic of Vietnam, Ministry of Labour-Invalids and Social Affairs (2016) *Urban Unemployment Rate below 4 percent in 2016* – available at http://www.molisa.gov.vn/en/Pages/Detail-news.aspx?IDNews=2566

Sokoni, C. (2001) 'The Influence of Agricultural Marketing Reforms on Highland Farming Systems in Tanzania: The Case of the Uporoto Highlands, Mbeya Region' University of Dar es Salaam PhD

Sommers, M. (2012) *Stuck: Rwandan Youth and the Struggle for Adulthood* Athens: University of Georgia Press

Stahl, M. (ed.) (2015) *Looking Back, Looking Ahead – Land Agriculture and Society in East Africa: A Festschrift for Kjell Havnevik* Nordiska Afrikainstutet – available at http://nai.diva-portal.org/smash/get/diva2:850493/FULLTEXT01.pdf

Stenning, D. (1958) 'Household Viability among the Pastoral Fulani' in Goody, J. (ed.) *The Developmental Cycle in Domestic Groups* Cambridge University Press

Stiglitz, J., Lin, J. and Patel, E. (2013) (eds) *The Industrial Policy Revolution II: Africa in the 21st Century* Macmillan

Szirmai, A. (2013) 'Manufacturing and Economic Development' in Szirmai, A., Naude, W. and Alcorta, A. (eds) *Pathways to Industrialization in the Twenty First Century* UNU-WIDER Studies in Development Economics Oxford University Press pp. 53–75

Szirmai, A., Naude, W. and Alcorta, A. (eds) (2013) *Pathways to Industrialization in the Twenty First Century* UNU-WIDER Studies in Development Economics Oxford University Press

Tagseth, M. (2008) 'The Expansion of Traditional Irrigation in Kilimanjaro, Tanzania' *International Journal of African Historical Studies* 41(3): 461–490

Tan, C. (2013) 'Problems vs. Polarities: The Importance of Understanding Stakeholder Nuances in Your Quest for Inclusive Growth' *REPOA Research Workshop*, keynote address, 3 April – available at http://www.repoa.or.tz/documents_storage/KN.pdf

Tanzania Bureau of Statistics (2011) *Tanzania National Household Budget Survey 2000–2001* Dar es Salaam

Tanzania Investment Centre (2017). *Tanzania Investors Guide* (Vol. 255) Dar-es-Salaam: Tanzania Investment Centre – available at http://www.tic.co.tz/images/uploads/INVESTMENT%20GUIDE.pdf

Tanzania Legal and Human Rights Centre (2017) *Bi-Annual Tanzania Human Rights Report 2017* – available at http://www.humanrights.or.tz/assets/attachments/1509614852.pdf

Tanzania National Business Council (TNBC) (2009) *Kilimo Kwanza: Towards Tanzania's Green Revolution* Dar es Salaam: TNBC

Tanzanian Affairs, A Budget Summary (July 1984) – available at http://www.tzaffairs.org/1984/07/a-budget-summary/

Tanzanian Affairs, Magufuli – The First Six Months (September 2016) – available at https://www.tzaffairs.org/category/issue-number/issue-115/

Temu, A. (1999) 'Empirical Evidence of Changes in the Coffee Market after Liberalization: A Case of Northern Tanzania' (Doctoral dissertation, University of Illinois, 1999)

The Tea Detective (n.d.) The Fall and Rise of Tanzania's Tea Industry – available at http://www.theteadetective.com/TeasOfTanzania.html

Therkildsen, O. (2011) *Policy Making and Implementation in Agriculture: Tanzania's Push for Irrigated Rice* DIIS Working Paper No. 2011:26 Copenhagen: Danish Institute for International Studies

Thomas, C. (1974) *Dependence and Transformation: The Economics of the Transition to Socialism* Monthly Review Press

Thurlow, J. (2015) 'Youth Employment Prospects in Africa' in Resnick,

D. and Thurlow, J. (eds) *African Youth and the Persistence of Marginalization: Employment, Politics and Prospects for Change* Abingdon and New York: Routledge pp. 23–46

Transparency International (TI) (2015) *Corruption Perceptions Index* Berlin: TI – available at www.transparency.org/research/cpi/overview

Tribe, M. (2013) *Aid and Development: Issues and Reflections* Discussion Paper 13-09 Department of Economics, University of Strathclyde May – available at http://www.strath.ac.uk/economics/departmentalresearch/discussionpapers/

Tribe, M. (2017) 'Quantifying Aid Allocation: A Critical Review of the DFID Needs-Effectiveness Index' *Global Policy* 8(1): 92–96

Tribe, M. and Wanambi, N. (2003) 'Development Expenditure Management in Uganda' in Potts, D., Ryan, P. and Toner, A. (eds) *Development Planning and Poverty Reduction* London: Palgrave Macmillan, pp. 148–163

Tripp, A. (2012) *Donor Assistance and Political Reform in Tanzania* UNU WIDER Working Paper No. 2012/37 Helsinki: United Nations University – available at www.wider.unu.edu/publications

TUI Group (2016) *Strategy and Equity Story: Our Vertical Integrated Business Model* – available at: http://preview.tui-group.dievision.de/en-en/investors/tui-group-at-a-glance/strategy-and-equity-story

Umali-Deininger, D. (1997) 'Public and Private Agricultural Extension: Partners or Rivals?' *World Bank Research Observer* 12(2): 203–224

United Nations Conference on Trade and Development (UNCTAD) (2010) 'The Contribution of Tourism to Trade and Development', *UNCTAD Second Session* Geneva 3–7 May 2010 – available at: http://unctad.org/en/Docs/cid8_en.pdf

United Nations Development Programme (UNDP) (2012a) *Tanzania Economic Growth – Challenges and Opportunities* UNDP with United Republic of Tanzania, Dar-es-Salaam

UNDP (2012b) *World Urbanization Prospects: The 2011 Revision* New York: United Nations Department of Economic and Social Affairs

UNDP (2015) *Human Development Reports* New York: UNDP – available at www.hdr.undp.org/en/reports

United Nations Economic Commission for Africa (UNECA) (2011) *Minerals and Africa's Development: The International Study Group Report on Africa's Mineral Regimes* Addis Ababa: UNECA

UNECA (2016) *Transformative Industrial Policy for Africa* Addis Ababa: UNECA – available at https://www.uneca.org/sites/default/files/PublicationFiles/tipa-full_report_en_web.pdf

United Nations Environment Programme (UNEP-WCMC) (2016) *Global Statistics from the World Database on Protected Areas (WDPA)* Cambridge, UK: UNEP-WCMC – available at: https://www.protectedplanet.net/country/TZA#ref1

United Nations Industrial Development Organisation (UNIDO) (2013)

Industrial Development Report 2013 Vienna: UNIDO

United Republic of Tanganyika and Zanzibar (URTZ) (1964) *Tanganyika Five Year Plan for Economic and Social Development 1st July, 1964–30th June, 1969* Dar es Salaam: Government Printer

United Republic of Tanzania (URT) (1967) *A Mid-Term Appraisal of the Achievements under the Five Year Plan July, 1964–June 1969* Dar es Salaam: Ministry of Economic Affairs and Development Planning

URT (1968a) *An Act to establish the National Milling Corporation and to Provide for its Constitution and Functions* – available at http://bunge. parliament.go.tz/PAMS/docs/19-1968.pdf

URT (1968b) *Background to the Budget: An Economic Survey 1968/9* Dar es Salaam: Ministry of Economic Affairs and Development Planning

URT (1969) *Tanzania Second Five Year Plan for Economic and Social Development 1st July 1969–30th June, 1974* Dar es Salaam: Government Printer

URT (1981) *National Economic Survival Programme* Dar es Salaam: Ministry of Planning and Financial Affairs

URT (1982a) *Structural Adjustment Programme for Tanzania* Dar es Salaam: Ministry of Planning and Economic Affairs

URT (1982b) *The National Agricultural Policy (Final Report)* Dar es Salaam: Ministry of Agriculture, Task Force on National Agricultural Policy

URT (1996) *Sustainable Industries Development Policy 1996–2020* Dar es Salaam: Ministry of Industries and Trade – available at http://www. tanzania.go.tz/egov_uploads/documents/Sustainable-Industrie s-Development-Policy_sw.pdf

URT (2004) *Tanzania Assistance Strategy Annual Implementation Report 2003/04* Dar es Salaam: Ministry of Finance – available at www.mof. go.tz/mofdocs/external/tas.doc

URT (2005a) *Enhancing Aid Relationships in Tanzania: Report of the Independent Monitoring Group to the Government of Tanzania and the Development Partners Group – 2005* Dar es Salaam: Ministry of Finance and the Economic and Social Research Foundation – available at www.mof.go.tz/

URT (2005b) *National Strategy for Growth and Reduction of Poverty (Mkukuta)* Dar es Salaam: Vice-President's Office – available at http://www.povertymonitoring.go.tz/Mkukuta/MKUKUTA_ MAIN_ENGLISH.pdf

URT (2006a) *Joint Assistance Strategy for Tanzania* Dar es Salaam: Ministry of Finance – available at www.mof.go.tz/mofdocs

URT (2006b) *Memorandum of Understanding on the Joint Assistance Strategy for Tanzania (JAST) between the Government of the United Republic of Tanzania and Development Partners* Dar es Salaam: Government of the United Republic of Tanzania – available at www. tzdpg.or.tz/fileadmin/documents/dpg_internal/

URT (2006c) *Morogoro Regional Socio-Economic Profile* Morogoro Regional Office

URT (2007a) *Joint Assistance Strategy for Tanzania (JAST): Action Plan and Monitoring Framework Working Document* Dar es Salaam: Ministry of Finance – available at www.tzdpg.or.tz/fileadmin/ documents/dpg_internal/dpg_main/for_new_dpg_members/JAST_ Action_Plan_and_Monitoring_Framework_working_document -__2007_01.doc

URT (2007b) *Household Budget Survey 2007 Main Report* Dar es Salaam: National Bureau of Statistics

URT (2007c) *Uluguru Landscape Management Framework (ULMF), Conservation and Management of the Eastern Arc Mountains & Forests Project* Dar es Salaam: Forestry and Beekeeping Division, Ministry of Natural Resources & Tourism

URT (2008) *Agriculture Sector Review and Public Expenditure Review 2008/09, Ministry of Agriculture, Food Security and Cooperation Final Report,* Dar es Salaam

URT (2009a) *Agriculture Sample Census Survey 2007/08* Dar es Salaam: National Bureau of Statistics

URT (2009b) *Ten Pillars of Kilimo Kwanza (Implementation Framework)* – available at http://www.tzonline.org/pdf/tenpillarsofkilimokwanza.pdf

URT (2009c) *The National Irrigation Policy (draft)* Dar es Salaam: Ministry of Water and Irrigation

URT (2009d) *Sheria ya Usimamizi za Rasilimali za Maji* No 11 ya Mwaka 2009 Ministry of Water and Irrigation (produced with support of WWF/EU)

URT (2009e) *Management Plan for the Uluguru Nature Reserve, Five years Plan, 2009/10–2013/14* Dar es Salaam: Forestry and Beekeeping Division, Ministry and Natural Resources and Tourism

URT (2009f) *PFMRP Annual Progress Report 2008–2009* Dar es Salaam: Ministry of Finance and Economic Affairs – available from www. mof.go.tz

URT (2010a) *National Strategy for Growth and Reduction of Poverty II (NSGRP II)* Dar es Salaam: Ministry of Finance – available at www. mof.go.tz

URT (2010b) *2009 Public Financial Management Performance Report on Mainland Tanzania* Dar es Salaam: Ministry of Finance – available at www.mof.go.tz/mofdocs/PFMRP/PEFA/

URT (2011) *The Tanzania Five Year Development Plan 2011/2012– 2015/2016: Unleashing Tanzania's Latent Growth Potentials* Dar es Salaam: Planning Commission – available at http://www.tralac.org/ files/2012/12/5Year_development-plan.pdf

URT (2012) *Micro, Small and Medium Enterprises in Tanzania: A Baseline Survey* Dar es Salaam: Ministry of Trade and Industry and Financial Sector Deepening Trust

URT (2013a) *Agriculture Sector Development Programme II – Basket Fund, Draft Programme Document, Volume 1 main report; Volume 2 annexes* Dar es Salaam

URT (2013b) *National Census 2012* Dar-es-Salaam

URT (2013c) *Public Expenditure and Financial Accountability (PEFA) Assessment Mainland Tanzania (Central Government) – September 2013* Dar es Salaam: Ministry of Finance and Economic Affairs – available at www.mof.go.tz/mofdocs/PFMRP/PEFA/

URT (2013d) *The Economic Survey 2012* Dar es Salaam: Ministry of Finance and Economic Affairs

URT (2014a) *Press Release on Highlights of the Revised GDP Estimates for Tanzania Mainland* Dar es Salaam: National Bureau of Statistics – available at http://www.nbs.go.tz/nbs/

URT (2014b) Hotuba ya Waziri wa Kilimo, Chakula na Ushirika Mheshimiwa Mhandisi Christopher Kajoro Chiza (MB) kuhusu Makadirio ya Mapato na Matumizi ya Fedha ya Wizara ya Kilimo, Chakula na Ushirika kwa Mwaka 2014/2015

URT (2015a) *Tanzania Human Development Report 2014: Economic Transformation for Human Development* Dar es Salaam: Economic and Social Research Foundation

URT (2015b) 'Tanzania Tourist Attractions' Ministry of Natural Resources and Tourism – available at http://www.mnrt.go.tz/attractions

URT (2015c) Hotuba ya Waziri wa Kilimo, Chakula na Ushirika Mheshimiwa Stephen Masato Wasira (MB) kuhusu Makadirio ya Mapato na Matumizi ya Fedha ya Wizara ya Kilimo, Chakula na Ushirika kwa Mwaka 2015/2016

URT (2016a) *Second Five Year Development Plan, 2016/17–2020/21: 'Nurturing Industrialization for Economic Transformation and Human Development'* Dar es Salaam: Ministry of Finance and Planning – available at http://www.mof.go.tz/mofdocs/msemaji/Five%20 2016_17_2020_21.pdf

URT (2016b) *Statistical Abstract 2015* Dar es Salaam: National Bureau of Statistics

URT with NEPAD and FAO (2005) 'Crop and Livestock Private Sector Development' *NEPAD–CAADP Bankable Investment Profile*, Volume IV of VII, Addis Ababa: African Union, Comprehensive African Agricultural Development Plan

USAID (1984) *Rapid Mini Appraisal of Irrigation Development Options and Investment Strategies for Tanzania/USAID* Water Management Synthesis Project WMS Report 23 Washington, DC

Valentine, G. (2003) 'Boundary Crossings: Transitions from Childhood to Adulthood' *Children's Geographies* 1(1): 37–52

Van Arkadie, B. and Do Dinh, Duc (2004) *Economic Reform in Tanzania and Vietnam: A Comparative Commentary* William Davidson Institute Working Paper No. 706 – available at https://deepblue.lib.umich.edu/bitstream/handle/2027.42/40092/wp706.pdf;sequence=3

Van Arkadie, B. and Mallon, R. (2003) *Vietnam: A Transition Tiger?* Asia Pacific Press

Van Dijk, R., de Bruijn, M., Cardoso, C. and Butter, I. (2011) 'Introduction: Ideologies of Youth', *Africa Development* XXXVI (3&4): 1–17

Van Eeden, A., Mehta, L. and van Koppen, B. (2016) 'Whose Waters? Large-scale Agricultural Development and Water Grabbing in the Wami-Ruvu River Basin' *Tanzania Water Alternatives* 9(3): 608–626

Van Koppen, B., Giordano, M. and Butterworth, J. (2007) *Community Based Water Law and Water Resource Management Reform in Developing Countries* Wallingford: CABI

Viergever, R. (2011) 'Aid Alignment for Global Health Research' *Health Research Policy Systems* 9(12) – available at http://www.health-policy-systems.com/content/pdf/1478-4505-9-12.pdf

Wade, R. (2004) *Governing the Market: Economic Theory and the Role of Government in East Asian Industrialization* Princeton and Oxford: Princeton University Press

Wade, R. (2012) 'Return of Industrial Policy?' *International Review of Applied Economics* 6(2): 223–239

Wangwe, S. (1997) *The Management of Foreign Aid in Tanzania* ESRF Discussion Paper No. 15 Dar es Salaam: Economic and Social Research Foundation

Wangwe, S. (2001) 'Economic Reforms, Industrialization and Technological Capabilities in Tanzanian Industry' in Szirmai, A. and Lapperre, P. (eds) *The Industrial Experience of Tanzania* Basingstoke: Palgrave, pp. 349–66

Wangwe, S. (ed.) (2002) *NEPAD at Country Level: Changing Aid Relationships in Tanzania* Dar es Salaam: Mkuki na Nyota

Wangwe, S. and Ndulu, B. (1997) *Managing Tanzania's Economy in Transition to Sustained Development* ESRF Discussion Paper No. 14 Dar es Salaam: Economic and Social Research Foundation

Wangwe, S., Mmari, D., Aikaeli, J., Rutatina, N., Mboghoina, T. and Kinyondo, A. (2014) *The Performance of the Manufacturing Sector in Tanzania*, WIDER Working Paper 2014/085

Warren, B. (1980) *Imperialism, Pioneer of Capitalism* London: New Left Books

Watts, M. (1994) 'Life under Contract: Contract Farming, Agrarian Restructuring and Flexible Accumulation' in Little, P. and Watts, M. (eds) *Living under Contract: Contract Farming and Agrarian Accumulation in Sub-Saharan Africa* University of Wisconsin Press, pp. 21–77

Weiss, J. (1988) *Industry in Developing Countries* London: Croom Helm

Weiss, J. (2011) *The Economics of Industrial Development* Routledge

Weiss, J. and Jalilian, H. (2016) 'Manufacturing as an Engine of Growth' in Weiss, J. and Tribe, M. (eds) *Routledge Handbook of Industry and Development* Routledge, pp. 26–37

Whitfield, L. (ed.) (2009) *The Politics of Aid: African Strategies for Dealing with Donors* Oxford University Press

Whitfield, L. and Fraser, A. (2009) 'Introduction: Aid and Sovereignty' in Whitfield, L. (ed.) (2009) *The Politics of Aid: African Strategies for Dealing with Donors* Oxford University Press, pp. 1–26

Whitfield, L. and Buur, L. (2014) 'The Politics of Industrial Policy: Ruling Elites and their Alliances' *Third World Quarterly* 35(1): 126–144

Wiggins, S. (2013) *Agriculture and Growth in Low Income Countries: Overview of Debates and Links to Current Projects in the DFID ESRC Growth Research Programme* London: Overseas Development Institute

Wondemu, K. and Potts, D. (2016) *The Impact of the Real Exchange Rate Changes on Export Performance in Tanzania and Ethiopia* African Development Bank Working Paper No. 240 World Institute for Development Economics Research Helsinki: UNU-WIDER

Wood, A. and Berge, K. (1997) 'Exporting Manufactures: Human Resources, Natural Resources and Trade Policy' *Journal of Development Studies* 34: 35–59

Wood, B. and Betts, J. (2013) 'Results of the Paris Declaration Evaluation' *Canadian Journal of Program Evaluation* 27(3): 103–128

Wood, B., Betts, J., Etta, F., Gayfer, J., Kabell, D., Ngwira, N., Sagasti, F. and Samaranayake, F. (2011) *The Evaluation of the Paris Declaration – Phase 2: Final Report* Copenhagen: Danish Institute for International Studies – available at www.oecd.org/dac/evaluationnetwork/pde

Woodhouse, P., Veldwisch, G., Venot, J., Brockington, D., Komakech, H., and Manjichi, A. (2016) 'African Farmer-led Irrigation Development: Re-framing Agricultural Policy and Investment?' *Journal of Peasant Studies* 44:1, 213–33, DOI: 10.1080/03066150.2016.1219719

World Bank (1961) *The Economic Development of Tanganyika* Baltimore, MD: Johns Hopkins University Press

World Bank (1981) *Accelerated Development in Sub-Saharan Africa: An Agenda for Action (The Berg Report)* Washington, DC: The World Bank

World Bank (1999) *Tanzania: Social Sector Review* Washington, DC: The World Bank

World Bank (2000) *Agriculture in Tanzania Since 1986: Follower or Leader of Growth?* Washington, DC: The World Bank

World Bank (2001) *Tanzania at the Turn of the Century: From Reforms to Sustained Growth and Poverty Reduction* Washington DC: The World Bank

World Bank (2002a) *Poverty Reduction Strategy Papers Sourcebook* Washington, DC: The World Bank – available at http://go.worldbank.org/3I8LYLXO80

World Bank (2002b) *Tanzania at the Turn of the Century: Background Papers and Statistics* Washington, DC: The World Bank

World Bank (2007) *World Development Report 2007: Development and the Next Generation* Washington, DC: The World Bank

World Bank (2011) *Country Assistance Strategy for the United Republic of Tanzania for the Period FY 2012–2015* Washington, DC: International Development Association, International Finance Corporation and

Multilateral Investment Guarantee Agency – available at www-wds.worldbank.org/external/

World Bank (2012) *Tanzania Economic Update: From Growth to Shared Prosperity* Washington, DC: The World Bank – available at http://www-wds.worldbank.org/external/default/WDSContentServer/WDSP/IB/2012/10/24/000386194_20121024053815/Rendered/PDF/733460WP0P133400Box371944B00PUBLIC0.pdf

World Bank (2013) *Standing Out from the Herd: An Economic Assessment of Tourism in Kenya* Washington DC – available at http://documents.worldbank.org/curated/en/573241507036299777/pdf/AUS16758-WP-REVISED-P156577-OUO-9-Tourism-report-FINAL.pdf

World Bank (2014a) *Poverty Reduction Strategy Papers* Washington, DC: The World Bank – available at http://go.worldbank.org/CSTQBOF730

World Bank (2014b) *Tanzania Overview – Economic Performance and Outlook* Washington, DC: The World Bank – available at http://www.worldbank.org/en/country/tanzania/overview

World Bank (2015a) *Tanzania Mainland Poverty Assessment* Washington, DC: The World Bank

World Bank (2015b) *Corruption and Economic Development* Washington, DC: The World Bank – available at www1.worldbank.org/public-sector/anticorrupt/corruptn/cor02.htm

World Bank (2015c) *The Elephant in the Room: Unlocking the Potential of the Tourism Industry for Tanzanians* Washington, DC: The World Bank – available at http://documents.worldbank.org/curated/en/716911468305677763/Tanzania-economic-update-the-elephant-in-the-room-unlocking-the-potential-of-the-tourism-industry-for-Tanzanians

World Bank (2016) *World Development Indicators 2016* Washington, DC: The World Bank

World Bank (2017) *United Republic of Tanzania Systematic Country Diagnostic: 'To the Next Level of Development'* Report No. 110894-TZ Washington, DC: The World Bank – available at http://documents.worldbank.org/curated/en/510681488823616126/Tanzania-Systematic-country-diagnostic

World Tourism Organisation (WTO) (2001) *Sustainable Development of Ecotourism: A Compilation of Good Practices* Madrid: WTO

World Travel and Tourism Council (WTTC) (2015) *Travel and Tourism – Economic Impact: Tanzania* London: WTTC

World Wildlife Fund et al. (2007) *Equitable Payments for Watershed Services: Phase 1, Making the Business Case: Final Report* on *Social and Livelihoods Assessment for the Villages around East Usambara and Uluguru Mountains* A Joint WWF, CARE, IIED with PREM project – available at http://www.easternarc.or.tz/groups/webcontent/documents/pdf/UluguruandEastUsambaravillagelivelih.pdf

Worth, N. (2009) 'Understanding Youth Transition as "Becoming": Identity, Time and Futurity' *Geoforum* 40(6): 1050–1060

Wuyts, M. and Gray, H. (2017) *Situating Social Policy in Economic Trans-formation: A Conceptual Framework* Tanzania Human Development Report Background Paper No. 4

You, L., Ringler, C., Wood-Sichra, U., Robertson, R., Wood, S., Zhu, T, Nelson, G., Guo, Z. and Sun, Y. (2011) 'What is the Irrigation Potential for Africa? A Combined Biophysical and Socioeconomic Approach' *Food Policy* 36(6): 770–782

Young, A. (2012) 'The African Growth Miracle' *Journal of Political Economy* 120(4): 696–739

References to figures are indicated in *italics*, references to tables in **bold**. References to footnotes consist of the page number followed by the letter 'n' followed by the number of the note.

Printed in the United States
By Bookmasters